FROMMER'S

EasyGuide

TO

MONTRÉAL AND QUÉBEC CITY

By

Leslie Brokaw, Erin Trahan, and Matthew Barber

EasyGuides are • Quick To Read • Light To Carry • For Expert Advice • In All Price Ranges

FrommerMedia LLC

Published by
FROMMERMEDIA LLC

ISBN 978-1-62887-018-3 (paper), 978-1-62887-048-0 (ebk)

Editorial Director: Pauline Frommer
Editor: Lorraine Festa
Production Editor: Jana M. Stefanciosa
Cartographer: Roberta Stockwell
Cover Design: Howard Grossman

For information on our other products or services, see www.frommers.com.

FrommerMedia LLC also publishes its books in a variety of electronic formats. Some content that appears in print may not be available in electronic formats.

Manufactured in the United States of America

5 4 3 2 1

CONTENTS

1 THE BEST OF MONTRÉAL & QUÉBEC CITY 1

2 SUGGESTED ITINERARIES 8

3 MONTRÉAL & QUÉBEC CITY IN CONTEXT 17

4 SETTLING INTO MONTRÉAL 30
- Essentials 30
- Getting Around 37

5 WHERE TO STAY IN MONTRÉAL 42
- Downtown/Centre-Ville 43
- Vieux-Montréal 48
- Plateau Mont-Royal 51

6 WHERE TO EAT IN MONTRÉAL 53
- Centre-Ville/Downtown 55
- Vieux-Montréal 59
- Plateau Mont-Royal 65
- Mile End & Beyond 69
- Gay Village 73
- Little Burgundy 74

7 EXPLORING MONTRÉAL 75
- Downtown 78
- Vieux-Montréal 82
- Mont Royal & Plateau Mont-Royal 87
- Olympic Park 89
- Organized Tours 91
- Outdoor Activities 93
- Especially for Kids 97

8 FESTIVALS & NIGHTLIFE IN MONTRÉAL 99

9 MONTRÉAL WALKING TOURS 110

10 DAY TRIPS FROM MONTRÉAL 128

11 SETTLING INTO QUÉBEC CITY 136
- Essentials 136
- Getting Around 140

12 WHERE TO STAY IN QUÉBEC CITY 144
- Haute-Ville 145
- Basse-Ville/Vieux-Port 150
- Parliament Hill 151
- St-Roch 152
- Just Outside the City 153

13 WHERE TO EAT IN QUÉBEC CITY 155
- Haute-Ville 157
- Basse-Ville/Vieux-Port 161
- Parliament Hill 163
- St-Roch 164

14 EXPLORING QUÉBEC CITY 166
- Basse-Ville 167
- Haute-Ville 172
- Parliament Hill 176
- St-Roch: Shopping 177
- Shopping Complexes 178
- Organized Tours 179
- Outdoor Activities 180
- Especially for Kids 183

15 FESTIVALS & NIGHTLIFE IN QUÉBEC CITY 185

16 QUÉBEC CITY WALKING TOURS 191

17 DAY TRIPS FROM QUÉBEC CITY 205

18 PLANNING YOUR TRIP 212

ABOUT THE AUTHORS

Leslie Brokaw has been a travel writer since 2006, contributing to 10 Frommer's guides to Montréal, Québec City, and New England. Her first books were coauthored with her stepfather, long-time Frommer's contributor Herbert Livesey.

Erin Trahan is a Boston-based writer and editor. In addition to co-authoring recent editions of Frommer's guides to Québec, she edits and publishes "The Independent," a magazine about independent film, online at www.independent-magazine.org. She also writes about movies for WBUR, Boston's NPR news station. Learn more at www.erintrahan.com.

Matthew Barber is a freelance writer who has contributed to two previous Frommer's guides. He is a correspondent for the food section of the "Boston Globe" and writes about home cooking and vegetable gardening at the website www.crispybits.com. He lives in Boston with wife, Leslie Brokaw, and their son and dog.

ABOUT THE FROMMER TRAVEL GUIDES

For most of the past 50 years, Frommer's has been the leading series of travel guides in North America, accounting for as many as 24% of all guidebooks sold. I think I know why.

Though we hope our books are entertaining, we nevertheless deal with travel in a serious fashion. Our guidebooks have never looked on such journeys as a mere recreation, but as a far more important human function, a time of learning and introspection, an essential part of a civilized life. We stress the culture, lifestyle, history and beliefs of the destinations we cover, and urge our readers to seek out people and new ideas as the chief rewards of travel.

We have never shied from controversy. We have, from the beginning, encouraged our authors to be intensely judgmental, critical—both pro and con—in their comments, and wholly independent. Our only clients are our readers, and we have triggered the ire of countless prominent sorts, from a tourist newspaper we called "practically worthless" (it unsuccessfully sued us) to the many rip-offs we've condemned.

And because we believe that travel should be available to everyone regardless of their incomes, we have always been cost-conscious at every level of expenditure. Though we have broadened our recommendations beyond the budget category, we insist that every lodging we include be sensibly priced. We use every form of media to assist our readers, and are particularly proud of our feisty daily website, the award-winning Frommers.com.

I have high hopes for the future of Frommer's. May these guidebooks, in all the years ahead, continue to reflect the joy of travel and the freedom that travel represents. May they always pursue a cost-conscious path, so that people of all incomes can enjoy the rewards of travel. And may they create, for both the traveler and the persons among whom we travel, a community of friends, where all human beings live in harmony and peace.

Arthur Frommer

THE BEST OF MONTRÉAL & QUÉBEC CITY

1

If the province of Québec had a tagline, it could be: "Any excuse for a party." An enormous *joie de vivre* pervades the way that Montréal and Québec City go about their business. The calendars of both cities are packed with festivals and events that bring out both locals and guests from around the world year-round.

Montréal is a modern city with pizzazz at every turn. Downtown skyscrapers come in unexpected shapes and non-corporate colors. There's a beautifully preserved historic district, Vieux-Montréal (Old Montréal), and a subway system (Métro) that's modern and swift. And the city's creative inhabitants provide zest to the ever-changing neighborhoods of Plateau Mont-Royal and Mile End, large neighborhoods of artists' lofts, boutiques, cafes, and miles of restaurants—many of which are unabashedly clever and stylish.

Québec City, more traditional and more French, is replacing its former conservatism with sophistication and playfulness. With an impressive location above the St. Lawrence River and carefully tended 18th- and 19th-century houses in its historic *quartier,* this city is almost impossibly romantic—and unlike any other in North America.

MONTRÉAL'S best AUTHENTIC EXPERIENCES

- **Enjoy an Afternoon or Evening of Jazz:** In downtown, Vieux-Montréal, and the Plateau, jazz is a favorite pastime of locals and visitors—especially in July, during the renowned Festival International de Jazz. See p. 102.
- **Savor Gourmet Meals at Affordable Prices:** Experience all of French cuisine's interpretations—traditional, *haute,* bistro, Québécois—the way the locals do: by ordering the table d'hôte specials. You'll get to indulge in two or three or more courses for a fixed price that is only slightly more than the cost of a single main course. Most restaurants offer the option. See p. 58.
- **Explore Vieux-Montréal:** The city's oldest quarter has an overwhelmingly European flavor. Place Jacques-Cartier is a popular outdoor square, and in every direction from there you'll find museums, bistros, and boutiques worth savoring. A revitalized waterfront just adjacent also inspires strolling or biking. A walking tour of the neighborhood is on p. 110.

Romantic Québec City

Every narrow street, leafy plaza, sidewalk cafe, horse-drawn calèche, pitched roof, and church spire breathes recollections of France's provincial towns. But to get the full Québec City treatment, amble those streets in the evening and find a bench on Terrasse Dufferin, the promenade alongside the Château Frontenac. The river below will be the color of liquid mercury in the moon's glow, and on a clear night, you'll see a sky of stars. Faint music from the *boîtes* in Lower Town is a possibility. Romance is a certainty.

QUÉBEC CITY'S best AUTHENTIC EXPERIENCES

- **Linger at an Outdoor Cafe:** Tables are set out at Place d'Armes in Upper Town, in the Quartier du Petit-Champlain in Lower Town, and along the Grande-Allée. It's a quality-of-life invention the French and their Québécois brethren have perfected. See chapter 13.
- **Soak Up Lower Town:** Once all but abandoned to the grubby edges of the shipping industry, the riverside neighborhood of Basse-Ville/Vieux-Port has been reborn. Antiques shops, bistros, and chic boutique hotels now fill rehabilitated 18th- and 19th-century buildings. See p. 200 for a walking tour.
- **Get Serious About *Terroir*:** After a few centuries in the making, it's safe to say that the best Québécois cuisine reflects the seasons and prioritizes ingredients within reach. Duck, deer, and mackerel are on many menus for that reason, as are Québec-made cheeses, microbrews, and dishes with maple syrup. The practice of going-local isn't limited to traditional recipes, either. Nearly every recommended restaurant embraces Québec's *terroir* and if a menu doesn't broadcast its origins, it's probably being modest. Just ask. Chances are there's at least one local star.

MONTRÉAL'S best RESTAURANTS

- **Europea,** 1227 rue de la Montagne (✆ **514/398-9229**): For the full treatment, order the 10-course *menu degustation.* You'll see why chef Jérôme Ferrer, whose roots are in France and Spain, is a designated "Grand Chef" of the esteemed Relais & Châteaux community of restaurants and hotels. See p. 55.
- **Brasserie T,** 1425 rue Jeanne-Mance (✆ **514/282-0808**): At a more moderate price point, Brasserie T is the little sister of chef/owner Normand Laprise's **Toqué!**, another top choice (see p. 60). But Brasserie T has a few extras in its favor: it's open for both lunch and dinner, and it has a fun patio overlooking the Quartier des Spectacles plaza (complete with dancing waters in warm months). See p. 56.

QUÉBEC CITY'S best RESTAURANTS

- **Le Saint-Amour,** 48 rue Sainte-Ursule (✆ **418/694-0667**): The epicurean cuisine draws in the stars (Sir Paul McCartney, to be precise), and Sir Paul left a vegetarian legacy at this otherwise thoroughly Québécois (meaning meat-centric) restaurant. Whatever your tastes, dining here is unforgettable. See p. 157.
- **Panache,** 10 rue St-Antoine (✆ **418/692-1022**): Romance all the way, from the fireplace and velvet couches to the wrought-iron staircase leading to hideaway attic corners. French-Canadian cuisine with a kick, inside the knockout **Auberge St-Antoine.** For a cheaper option, look for Panache's new mobile food truck in the warm months. See p. 162.

MONTRÉAL'S best HOTELS

- **Hôtel Gault,** 449 rue Ste-Hélène (✆ **866/904-1616** or 514/904-1616): Other hotels have more amenities, but for an experience that is uniquely Montréal, the sleek and minimalist Gault, with exposed brick walls, enveloping beds, and slightly tucked away location provides a romantic getaway option. See p. 49.
- **Le Saint-Sulpice Hôtel Montréal,** 414 rue St-Sulpice (✆ **877/785-7423** or 514/288-1000): First-class service just short of full luxury in the heart of Vieux-Montréal. All rooms here are suites, so they're big in addition to modern and chic. The hotel also has a fine in-house restaurant with a beautiful hidden terrace. Thorough, professional, and affordable. See p. 50.

QUÉBEC CITY'S best HOTELS

- **Auberge St-Antoine,** 8 rue St-Antoine (✆ **888/692-2211** or 418/692-2211): Sure, there's the hotel Château Frontenac, looming on the cliffs above, the very symbol of the city. But for a more intimate visit, stay in Basse-Ville (Lower Town). This romantic luxury hotel has grown into one of Québec's most desirable lodgings, with an arresting lounge and a top restaurant (**Panache;** see Québec City's Best Restaurants, above) to boot. See p. 162.
- **Hôtel Le Germain-Dominion,** 126 rue St-Pierre (✆ **888/833-5253** or 418/692-2224): An anchor in the successful redevelopment of the once-dreary Vieux-Port, the Dominion has bedding so cozily enveloping that you may not want to go out. Do, though—for the fireplace, croissants, and café au lait in the lobby, if nothing else. See p. 150.

MONTRÉAL'S best HISTORICAL LANDMARKS

- **Pointe-à-Callière (Montréal Museum of Archaeology and History),** 350 Place Royale (✆ **514/872-9150**): A first visit to Montréal might best begin here. This strikingly modernistic structure at the edge of Vieux-Montréal marks the spot where the first European settlement put down roots in the city. It stands atop extensive excavations that unearthed not only remains of the French newcomers, but also of the native bands that preceded them. On the self-guided tour, you wind your way through the subterranean complex. See p. 85.

- **Musée du Château Ramezay,** 280 rue Notre-Dame est (✆ **514/861-3708**): This house, in Vieux-Montréal, was built in 1705. It became the local headquarters to the American Continental Army in 1775 when revolutionary forces took control of the city from the British, and Benjamin Franklin even stayed here when he was trying to get the Québécois to side with the Americans in revolt against the British. See p. 85.

QUÉBEC CITY'S best HISTORICAL LANDMARKS

- **Château Frontenac,** 1 rue des Carrières (✆ **866/540-4460**): About 36 tonnes (or 80,000 lbs.) worth of stunning copper cover the rooftops and spires of this landmark hotel. Its signature silhouette was erected at the end of the 19th century and inspired other grand buildings, such as Gare du Palais (Québec City's train station) to follow its architectural lead. See p. 172.
- **Basilique Cathédrale Notre-Dame de Québec,** 20 rue Buade (✆ **418/694-0665**): The staying power of this vast Catholic institution is evident in both the basilica's structure (dating back as early as 1647 and rebuilt several times since) and its spirit. The basilica is home to the Notre-Dame de Québec parish, which celebrates its 350th anniversary in 2014. See p. 172.

MONTRÉAL'S best MUSEUMS

- **Musée des Beaux-Arts,** 1380 rue Sherbrooke ouest (✆ **514/285-2000**): Canada's first museum devoted exclusively to the visual arts opened in 1912 and is now the most glorious in the province. A 2011 expansion opened an important pavilion devoted to Québécois and Canadian Art. The permanent collection is always free to view, and temporary exhibits on scheduled for 2014 include shows on Scottish painter Peter Doig, Fabergé eggs, and German Expressionism. See p. 79.
- **Musée McCord,** 690 rue Sherbrooke ouest (✆ **514/398-7100**): Exhibits here are compact, but there are always a half dozen or so, making for a satisfying trip. Permanent shows explore the history of Montréal and the role of clothing to establish identity among members of First Nations. Temporary exhibits have focused topics as varied as actress Grace Kelly, toys, and the costumes of Cirque du Soleil. See p. 80.

QUÉBEC CITY'S best MUSEUMS

- **Musée de la Civilisation,** 85 rue Dalhousie (✆ **866/710-8031** or 418/643-2158): Here is that rarity among museums: a collection of cleverly mounted temporary and permanent exhibitions that both children and adults find engrossing, without talking down or metaphysical maunderings. Make time for "People of Québec . . . Then and Now," a permanent exhibit that is a sprawling examination of Québec history. See p. 167.

- **Musée National des Beaux-Arts du Québec,** Parc des Champs-de-Bataille (✆ **866/220-2150** or 418/643-2150): Known simply as Musée du Québec, this museum highlights modern art (Jean-Paul Riopelle especially) and has a large, important collection of Inuit art, much produced in the 1980s and 1990s. See p. 176.

MONTRÉAL'S best FREE THINGS TO DO

- **Walk up Mont Royal, the Mountain That Gives the City its Name:** If you take the most direct (and steepest) route, it only takes an hour to walk up and back down Mont Royal, going from the downtown entrance to the chalet at the top. Most people, though, set a more leisurely pace, strolling the broad pedestrian-only chemin Olmsted and stopping by the lake, cemetery, and sculptures at the top of the park. See p. 124 for a suggested walking tour.
- **Hover Around the Edges of Festivals:** Montréal's calendar boasts over 100 festivals over the course of the year (see p. 100 for some highlights). Most, including the internationally famous jazz festival and the Just for Laughs comedy festival (both held in summer), feature tons of free performances right on the city streets and plazas.

QUÉBEC CITY'S best FREE THINGS TO DO

- **Ooh Over Pyrotechnics:** Bassin Louise (✆ **888-523-3389**): In August, crowds gather along the Vieux-Québec port to see which nation will shock and awe with the biggest, loudest, or most creative fireworks displays in this 6-night-long, international competition known as **Les Grand Feux Loto-Québec.** See p. 38.
- **Chill in Place-Royale:** One of the most beautiful and historic public plazas, Place-Royale is where you linger, gaze at the surrounding stone homes and jaunty roofs, and feel the European charm promised by all the travel guides. See p. 95.

MONTRÉAL'S best OF OUTDOORS

- **Bike the City:** Montréalers' enthusiasm for bicycling has provided the impetus for the ongoing development of bicycle paths that wind through downtown areas and out to the countryside. Rentals are available from shops (for day trips) and the BIXI network (for short trips)—BIXI has put thousands of bikes onto the streets for inexpensive, frequent, limited-distance borrowing. See p. 38.
- **Traverse the Lachine Canal:** First constructed in the early 1800s to detour around the rapids of the same name, the canal was reopened for recreational use in 1997 after much renovation. It connects Vieux-Port with Atwater Market. You can explore the canal and its surroundings on foot, on a rented bicycle, or by guided boat tour. See p. 95.

QUÉBEC CITY'S best OF OUTDOORS

- **Take a Walking Tour:** Combine immersion in Québec's rich history with a good stretch of the legs among the battlements and along the storied city's cobblestoned streets. Follow the walking tours in chapter 16 or go on a group tour. See p. 179.
- **Drive to Montmorency Falls:** Eleven km (6¾ miles) north of the city is the impressive Montmorency Falls—higher than Niagara Falls, although far narrower. It's a spectacular cascade in all four seasons. There is an easy path to the base of the falls, and both stairs and a cable car to the top. A footbridge crosses the water where it flows over the cliff, for those with nerves of steel. See p. 208.

MONTRÉAL'S best FOR FAMILIES

- **Visit the Biodôme de Montréal:** Perhaps the most engaging attraction in the city for younger children. The Biodôme houses replications of four ecosystems: a Laurentian forest; the St. Lawrence marine system; a polar environment; and, most appealingly, a tropical rainforest. See p. 89.
- **Spend a Day at the Centre des Sciences de Montréal:** Running the length of a central pier in Vieux-Port, this ambitious science center, geared especially toward ages 9 to 14, has permanent interactive displays as well as special exhibits on everything from sharks and dinosaurs to the archeological adventures of Indiana Jones and an extremely candid look at sex. It's also home to a popular IMAX theater. See p. 84.

QUÉBEC CITY'S best FOR FAMILIES

- **Watch the Changing of the Guard: La Citadelle** is the fortress built by the British to repel an American invasion that never came. It's still an active military post, and the ceremonial Changing of the Guard is colorful and doesn't take too much time. See p. 173.
- **Celebrate Summer (or Winter, Spring, or Fall): Festival d'Eté** (Summer Festival), **Carnaval de Québec**, or any number of festivals hosted throughout the calendar year, cater especially to families. Free activities abound and special guests like Bonhomme (an enormous snow figure) pop in for a skate, or to help reach that tippy-top spot of the snow sculpture. See chapter 15.

MONTRÉAL'S best NON-TOURIST DESTINATIONS

- **Shopping the Marché Jean-Talon:** We're not saying there won't be out of towners here, at one of Montréal's pre-eminent fruit, vegetable, and foods markets, but there will be fewer than at **Marché Atwater,** simply by virtue of Jean-Talon's location at the northern end of Mile End, beyond where most visitors wander. Consider a visit

> **A Note About English and French in this Book**
>
> Like the Québécois themselves, this guidebook goes back and forth between using the French names and the English names for areas and attractions. Most often, we use French. Québec's state-mandated language is French, and most signs, brochures, and maps in the region appear in French. However, we use the English name or translation as well, if that makes the meaning clearer. *Bon voyage!*

to spice shop Olives & Épices, what "Food & Wine" magazine named one of the best shops in Montréal, citing its *ras el hanout,* "which contains 24 ingredients, including saffron and three kinds of dried roses." See p. 89.

- **Spending a Summer Evening at Théâtre de Verdure:** At this open-air theater nestled in the Plateau Mont-Royal's Parc La Fontaine, everything is free: music, dance, and theater, often with well-known artists and performers. Many in the audience pack picnics. So why so few tourists? Probably because all the promotional material is in French. Details at **www.espacelafontaine.com** and p. 94.

QUÉBEC CITY'S best NON-TOURIST DESTINATIONS

- **Hanging Out in St-Roch:** For locals, this neighborhood has been up and coming for at least a decade. But that doesn't mean the tourists have caught on. Along rue St-Joseph you'll find coffee shops, *boulangeries,* secondhand stores, high-end clothing by Québécois designers, and an eclectic mix of nightlife from experimental bistros to ethnic cuisine. See p. 177 and p. 190.
- **Strolling Rue St-Jean Outside the Gate:** Some of the city's finest food purveyors are just outside the St-Jean Gate, in a neighborhood called Faubourg St-Jean. The truly ambitious explorers can walk another 1.5km (9⁄10 mile) to get to avenue Cartier and turn left. You'll find yourself in the heart of the non-touristy Montcalm neighborhood, flush with eateries, clothing boutiques, and city-dwellers. See p. 175 and p. 178.

SUGGESTED ITINERARIES

2

While some suggestions are best for warm weather, most of the recommendations here are appropriate for all seasons—just remember to bundle up in wintertime. Public transportation in Montréal is excellent, and Québec City is compact, so unless noted, you won't need a car for these tours.

THE BEST OF MONTRÉAL IN 1 DAY: HISTORIC MONTRÉAL

This exploration of historic Montréal allows time for random exploring, shopping, or lingering in sidewalk cafes. If you're staying only 1 night, book a room in one of Vieux-Montréal's boutique hotels. Visitors find themselves drawn to the plazas and narrow cobblestone streets of this 18th- and 19th-century neighborhood, so you might as well be based there. ***Start:*** *Vieux-Montréal, at Place d'Armes.*

---

1 Place d'Armes ★★★

Begin your day in this outdoor plaza, the heart of **Vieux-Montréal** ★★★, at the site of the city's oldest building, the **Vieux Séminaire de St-Sulpice** (p. 113), erected by priests who arrived in 1657. Next to it is the **Basilique Notre-Dame** ★★★ (p. 83), an 1824 church with a stunning interior of intricately gilded rare woods. Its acoustics are so perfect that the late, famed opera star Luciano Pavarotti performed here several times.

Consider taking the walking tour on p. 110, which takes you past every historic structure in Vieux-Montréal and eventually to our next stop. Or, to go to Pointe-à-Callière directly, walk down the slope from the basilica.

2 Pointe-à-Callière ★★★

The **Pointe-à-Callière (Museum of Archaeology and History)** is our favorite museum for a full immersion into Québec history. Its below-ground tunnels have remnants of Amerindian camps and early French settlements. See p. 85.

3 Olive et Gourmando ☕ ★★★

This funky cafe is a city highlight. Eat in, or take out if the weather's nice for a picnic lunch by the river. The Cuban sandwich is a popular choice. 351 rue St-Paul ouest. ✆ 514/350-1083. See p. 64.

Unless you're a very ambitious walker, take a cab, the Métro to Guy-Concordia, or a BIXI rental bike to get to:

4 Musée des Beaux-Arts ★★★

This is the city's glorious fine-arts museum. Permanent exhibits are free, and temporary shows are dazzling. See p. 79.

5 Rue Crescent ★

From the museum, walk south on rue Crescent. If you're in a shopping mood, Ste-Catherine, 2 blocks down, is the nexus for department stores and mid-priced shopping (turn left and head east). Rue Crescent itself is downtown's primary nightlife district, albeit a touristy one. If it's warm, grab a seat on a terrace for great people-watching.

6 Sir Winston Churchill Pub ★

Epicenter of the rue Crescent scene for ages, this pub is filled with chatty 20- to 40-somethings. It's a good spot to nurse a pint while taking in the passing parade. 1459 rue Crescent. ✆ 514/288-3814. See p. 105.

For dinner options downtown or further afield, consult the listings in chapter 6.

THE BEST OF MONTRÉAL IN 2 DAYS: IMMERSION INTO A RICH FRENCH HERITAGE

With the absolute essentials of historic Old Montréal and downtown Anglophone cultural institutions under your belt on Day 1, take a journey into French Montréal on your second day in Montréal. Residents here spend time outdoors all times of the year, and this itinerary nudges you in the same direction. ***Start:*** *Viau Métro station.*

---

1 Jardin Botanique ★★★

These lush, romantic, year-round botanical gardens comprise 75 hectares (185 acres) of plants and flowers with 10 exhibition greenhouses. Summertime's popular **Mosaïcultures internationals** program presents spectacular, otherworldly topiary creatures. See p. 90.

Take the Métro to Sherbrooke and walk 1 block west to rue St-Denis, turning left (north).

2 Rue St-Denis ★★

Rue St-Denis is the thumping central artery of Francophone Montréal, thick with cafes, bistros, offbeat shops, and lively nightspots. As you head north into the lower precincts of Plateau Mont-Royal, there are no must-see sights, so wander at will and surrender to the heart of French Montréal's color and vitality.

See chapter 6 for eating options in the Plateau. Take the Métro to Place des Arts for evening options.

3 Quartier des Spectacles ★★

What to do tonight? The Quartier des Spectacles is a district just south and west of the Plateau that includes the **Place des Arts** plaza. Ballet, opera, symphony orchestras—they are all here. Even if you don't speak French, consider getting tickets for a French-language show for a fully immersive experience. Regular priced and same-day discount tickets are available at the high-tech ticketing center at **La Vitrine,** at 2 Ste-Catherine est (✆ **866/924-5538** or 514/285-4545).

Last- minute bargains are also posted online at www.lavitrine.com; these deals are highlighted by a distinctive red dot.

Whether you get tickets or not, this area is still a good spot for finding a meal or strolling. If there's a festival going on, chances are more than good that parts of it will be spilling over, for free, right here.

THE BEST OF MONTRÉAL IN 3 DAYS: THE GREAT OUTDOORS

If you've followed the above itineraries on Days 1 and 2, you've already visited Montréal's primary must-see sights. Today, take in the great parks and waterways of the city. ***Start:*** *Peel Métro station (if you're in the mood for a hike) or a taxi ride to Lac des Castors at the top of Parc du Mont-Royal.*

1 Parc du Mont-Royal ★★

The hill that rises behind downtown is the small mountain, Mont Royal, that gave the city its name. Its rounded crest became a public park somewhat according to plans by architect Frederick Law Olmsted. Throngs of people come for its woods, paths, and meadows in all four seasons. You can join them with a stroll up from Peel station (see p. 124 for a walking tour) or a taxi ride to Lac des Castors (Beaver Lake).

Make your way either by bus and Métro, or by taxi, to the southern end of the city.

2 Vieux-Port ★★★

The Old Port at the edge of Vieux-Montréal has been transformed into a broad, vibrant park. Principal among the attractions is the **Centre des Sciences de Montréal** (p. 84), on quai (pier) King Edward. It contains interactive exhibits that enthrall most everyone's inner geek.

In the warm months, **Les Sautes-Moutons** (✆ **514/284-9607**) depart from the park's east end, near the old clock tower. Also known as Lachine Rapids Tours, the company provides wave-jumper powerboats with which to take on the St. Lawrence River's roiling Lachine Rapids. Other companies provide more sedate river cruises. See p. 92.

You can also rent **bicycles** and **in-line skates** by the hour or day from here, and then head out to the peaceful **Lachine Canal,** a nearly flat 11km (6.8-mile) bicycle path that's open year-round. See p. 95.

3 Le Jardin Nelson ☕ ★★

Vieux-Montréal has plenty of good restaurants—one of the most popular is Le Jardin Nelson, on the main square, Place Jacques-Cartier. It's open in the warm months and has a back terrace where jazz musicians perform during the day and evening. The menu offers a roster of main-course and dessert crepes. 407 Place Jacques-Cartier. ✆ 514/861-5731. See p. 105.

A ROMANTIC DAY IN MONTRÉAL

Romance is in the eyes of the beholder, which makes this a tricky tour to propose. Sitting hand in hand on a quiet park bench might be all you need for a moment to be luminous—while your best friend might dream of dropping C$300 on a luxurious

DON'T BE shy, GIVE BIXI A TRY

I love the BIXI concept—take a bike, ride it around, drop it anywhere—but I had to wonder: Are those gray-and-red cruisers really for anyone, even little ole non-Montréaler me? The answer: *Mais oui!* A visit to www.bixi.com showed the BIXI bike stations closest to my hotel. At the station, I planned my route and drop-off point using the large posted map (and I took note of the bike lanes that are everywhere). I put my bag into BIXI's iron-clad front rack and bungee, which could secure a barrel of daredevils plunging down Niagara Falls. One swipe of a credit card, and off I careened—I was in Montréal, on a bike! Without a helmet!

I'm comfortable with urban biking, but I'll admit to wobbling my first few BIXI kilometers. By design, the bikes are unisex and supersturdy, and I am neither. As I watched one neighborhood roll into the next, I realized my feet could barely reach the pedals. Seat height is adjustable, so I took a break and lowered it, *pas de problème*.

In BIXI's early days I had trouble finding open spots at stations when it came time for drop offs. Then I discovered that if there are no vacancies, you automatically get 15 extra minutes to find another location. As BIXI has expanded its presence, I haven't had that issue as often, and when the sun is shining down the Main, there's really no better way to get from croissant to bagel. (For more on BIXI, see p. 95.)

—Erin Trahan

dinner in a sky-high restaurant. Options here range from the modest to the opulent. This day starts in Plateau Mont-Royal then moves to Vieux-Montréal and stays there. ***Start:*** *Mont-Royal Métro station.*

1 Stroll Parc La Fontaine ★

Start at the park's northern end, along rue Rachel est. This park in Plateau Mont-Royal is one of the city's most popular. Half is landscaped in the formal French manner, half in the more casual English style. A central lake is used for ice-skating in winter (you can rent skates), while in summer, you can walk the paths and cuddle up lakeside. See p. 94. (Alternately, if you haven't been yet, head to **Jardin Botanique,** the city's lush, year-round botanical gardens. See "The Best of Montréal in 2 Days," above.)

Travel back to Vieux-Montréal, where the rest of this itinerary takes place. To get there, hop a BIXI bike or take the Métro to Place d'Armes.

2 Take the Waters at Scandinave Les Bains ★

Do like the Swedish do. This center in Vieux-Montréal offers Euro-style relaxation through water. Visitors (in bathing suits) have the run of the complex. There's a warm bath the size of a small swimming pool, with jets and a waterfall, and a steam room thick with the scent of eucalyptus oil. See p. 86.

3 Sweets for your Sweet ★

Perhaps cupcakes from the cute bakery **Les Glaceurs** in Vieux-Montréal (453 rue St-Sulpice)? Or maybe treats by local chocolatier **Les Chocolats de Chloé,** which spices up offerings with cardamom, buckwheat honey, and Espelette pepper? (The chocolates are sold in their shop at 546 rue Duluth est in the Plateau and at the Vieux-Montréal restaurant **Olive et Gourmando;** see p 64.)

4 Check into Auberge du Vieux-Port ★★

Exposed brick and stone walls, massive beams, and polished hardwood floors define the hideaway bedrooms. Rates include a "welcome cocktail," which can be enjoyed from an intimate roof top terrace. See p. 48.

5 A Dinner Cruise on Le Bateau-Mouche

This glass-enclosed vessel is reminiscent of those on the Seine in Paris. It's a floating restaurant and terrasse, and the 7 to 10pm dinner is a chichi affair. The staff is outfitted in black-tie and women will be comfortable in cocktail dresses. If you coordinate your trip with the fireworks festival, the pyrotechnics will explode right above you. See p. 92.

THE BEST OF QUÉBEC CITY IN 1 DAY: STEP BACK INTO THE 17TH AND 18TH CENTURIES

With an ancient wall surrounding the oldest part of the city, Québec City sustains the look of a provincial European village that keeps watch over the powerful St. Lawrence River. For a short visit, book a hotel in the Old City, either within the walls of the Haute-Ville (Upper Town) or in the quieter Basse-Ville (Lower Town). ***Start:*** *Château Frontenac.*

1 Château Frontenac ★★★

As soon as you're done unpacking, head to **Château Frontenac** (p. 172)—its peaked copper roofs are visible from everywhere. It's posh bar and pretty cafe are great for a splurge. The long promenade alongside the hotel, the **Terrasse Dufferin,** offers panoramic views of the St. Lawrence River and of the city's **Basse-Ville (Lower Town).** In winter, an old-fashioned toboggan run is set up on the steep staircase at the south end.

Head down to Basse-Ville either by the *funiculaire,* the glass-encased outdoor elevator, or the staircase called L'escalier du Casse-Cou. They're right next to each other. Both routes end at the top of rue du Petit-Champlain, a touristy pedestrian street of shops and restaurants. Save that for later, and instead walk ahead on rue Sous-le-Fort and make the first left turn to reach:

2 Place-Royale ★★★

This small but picturesque square was the site of the first European colony in Canada and is surrounded by restored 17th- and 18th-century houses. The **church** on one side was built in 1688. A visit to the **Musée de la Place Royale** is an option here. See p. 171.

Past the Musée de la Place Royale, at the end of rue Notre-Dame, turn around to view a ***trompe l'oeil* mural** depicting citizens of the early city. Continue past the mural and turn right to walk toward the river. Turn left on rue Dalhousie and walk to:

3 Musée de la Civilisation ★★★

A city highlight. This ambitious museum, filled with fascinating exhibits, can easily fill 2 or 3 hours. Don't miss the permanent exhibit, "People of Québec . . . Then and Now," which explores the province's roots as a fur-trading colony and gives visitors a rich sense of Québec's daily life over the generations. See p. 167.

Leaving the museum, turn left on rue Dalhousie, left on rue St-Paul, and walk to rue du Sainte-au-Matelot.

4 A Bounty of Bistros

Within a block of the corner of rues St-Paul and du Sault-au-Matelot are some of the city's best bistros and casual eateries. Almost any of them will do for a snack or a meal, but our top choice is L'Échaudé ★, 73 rue du Sault-au-Matelot (✆ 418/692-1299). It offers classic French dishes and puts out sidewalk tables in summer. See p. 162.

5 Rue St-Paul & Antiquing

The northern end of the short street rue St-Paul is great for browsing for antiques and collectibles.

Turn right at rue St-Thomas and cross rue St-André.

6 Marché du Vieux-Port ★★

This large market is open year-round, and offers produce and other agricultural products for sale. See p. 172.

THE BEST OF QUÉBEC CITY IN 2 DAYS: MILITARY HISTORY THAT RESOUNDS TODAY

During repeated conflicts with the British in the 18th century, the residents of New France moved to the top of the cliffs of Cap Diamant. Over the years, they created fortifications with battlements and artillery emplacements that eventually encircled the city. Most of the defensive walls remain, although many have been restored repeatedly. For your second day in Québec City, these historic mementos are the centerpiece of your tour. ***Start:*** *Terrasse Dufferin.*

1 Promenade des Gouverneurs ★

Walk south to the end of Terrasse Dufferin. At the end, go up the staircase to the **Promenade des Gouverneurs.** This path was renovated in 2007 and skirts the sheer cliff wall, climbing up and up past Québec's military **Citadelle,** a fort built by the British army between 1820 and 1850 that remains an active military garrison. The promenade/staircase ends at the grassy **Parc des Champs-de-Bataille,** about 15 minutes away.

From here, walk around the rim of the fortress.

2 La Citadelle ★★

The Citadelle has a low profile, dug into the land, instead of rising above it. A ceremonial changing of the guard takes place daily at 10am in summer (June 24 to the first Mon of Sept) and can be viewed from here. See p. 173.

Walk down the hill toward the road. Grande-Allée passes through the city walls at porte (gate) St-Louis, our next destination.

3 Porte St-Louis & the Walls

After Grande-Allée passes through **porte St-Louis,** it becomes rue St-Louis, a main road through Old Town. The long greenway on the inside of the walls here is **Parc l'Esplanade.** Stroll along it and down a steep hill to another main gate in the wall, **porte St-Jean** (a 20th-century re-creation). Nearby is the **Parc de l'Artillerie,** where you can view an officer's mess and quarters and an old iron foundry. See p. 181.

Walk west on rue St-Jean through the gate. This is Place d'Youville, a plaza with hotels, a concert hall, and restaurants. Many of the city's festivals, in both summer and winter, set up outdoor stages here.

4 Ristorante il Teatro

A good bet for lunch or dinner, with sidewalk seating in warm weather. Pasta and risotto are specialties. The restaurant is part of Le Capitole, a hotel-theater complex. 972 rue St-Jean. ✆ 418/694-9996.

Walk back through the gate to browse along:

5 Rue St-Jean

One of the liveliest of Vieux-Québec's streets, rue St-Jean is lined with an ever-updated variety of shops, pubs, and restaurants. Some of the shopping possibilities here are listed in chapter 14.

At the end of rue St-Jean, bear right up Côte de la Fabrique. At the end is:

6 Basilique Cathédrale Notre-Dame de Québec ★★★

What with bombardments, fires, and repeated rebuilding, this home of the oldest Christian parish north of Mexico is nothing if not perseverant. Parts of it, including the bell tower, survive from the original 1647 building, but most of what remains is from a 1771 reconstruction. Step inside to see the blindingly bright gold leaf. See p. 172.

Leaving the church, walk left along rue du Buade and turn right onto the narrow pedestrian alley rue du Trésor. Artists set up here and sell etchings, drawings, and watercolors. Directly on the street at no. 8, go inside for:

7 Québec Expérience ★

This 3-D show re-creates in vivid detail some of the grim realities of being a settler. Guns and cannons explode at audiences, a simulated bridge crashes down, and walls of water simulate storms at sea. Kids love it. See p. 174.

Rue du Trésor ends at the central plaza of Upper Town, Place d'Armes. Château Frontenac is directly across the plaza.

8 Outdoor Cafe Dining

If it's warm, snag an outdoor table at any of the restaurants on rue Ste-Anne. One favorite is Le Pain Béni, the restaurant at the Auberge Place d'Armes (p. 160). You can try Québécois classics with modern twists, or more simple pastas.

THE BEST OF QUÉBEC CITY IN 3 DAYS: FRESH ARTS & FRESH AIR

While the romance of the capital is largely contained within Vieux-Québec's Lower and Upper Towns, there is much to experience outside the Old City. On your third day, try to make time for at least one or two of the following attractions, toward the western end of Parc des Champs-de-Bataille (Battlefields Park). ***Start:*** *Musée des Beaux-Arts.*

1 Musée National des Beaux-Arts du Québec ★★★

Inside **Parc des Champs-de-Bataille (Battlefields Park,** which contains the Plains of Abraham) is the capital's most important art museum. It focuses on Inuit sculpture and the works of Québec-born artisans. The original 1933 museum is connected to a newer structure by a glass-roofed pavilion that has a reception area, museum shop, and cafe. See p. 176.

Walk outside into:

2 Parc des Champs-de-Bataille ★★★

Get some fresh air with a stroll through the 108 hectares (267 acres) that comprise Canada's first national urban park and the city's playground. Within its rolling hills are two Martello towers, cylindrical stone defensive structures built between 1808 and 1812, as well as cycling paths and picnic grounds. See p. 180.

Head back to the main street, Grand-Allée, and cross over to the perpendicular street:

3 Avenue Cartier

Just a few blocks from the museum, avenue Cartier is part of the laid-back residential Montcalm district. There are intriguing shops and restaurants here.

4 Café Krieghoff ★★★

This cheerful cafe has an outdoor terrace a few steps up from the sidewalk. On weekend mornings, it's packed with artsy locals of all ages, whose tables are piled high with bowls of café au lait and huge plates of egg dishes, sweet pastries, or classics like steak *frites.*1089 av. Cartier. ✆ 418/522-3711.

5 Grande-Allée

Walk back to Grande-Allée and turn left to get back to the Old City. There's a gentle downhill slope. After about 3 blocks, the shoulder-to-shoulder rows of cafes and clubs begin. One great way to end the day is with a stop at **L'Astral,** the restaurant and sometimes-bar atop Loews le Concorde Hotel, at the corner of Cours du Général-De Montcalm. The room spins slowly and lets you look back at all the places you've been. See p. 189.

ROMANTIC QUÉBEC CITY

We'll acknowledge for a second time that romance is rather personal (see "Romantic Montréal," above) but this endearing city has so many charms, we wanted to provide a few ideas for how to unlock them. ***Start:*** *Château Frontenac.*

---

1 Let a Horse be Your Guide

Hiring a **horse-drawn carriage** (or *calèche*) may sound like a romantic cliché, but how many times have you actually done it? There's no better place, or perhaps time, to try. **Calèches Québec** will customize a tour to suit your needs or you can opt for one of three city tours, which can start in front of Château Frontenac. The 40-minute "La Découverte" is C$90 (four passenger maximum) and winds along Upper Town's historic streets and through Parc des Champs de Bataille. "Le Grand Tour" will take you as far as the **Gare du Palais,** a train station with architectural majesty that rivals its inspiration: Frontenac. This 2-hour trip costs C$270.

If your trip ends at Château Frontenac, take rue Fort (pass Place d'Armes on your left), turn left on rue de Buade, and then right on Côte de la Fabrique, where at no. 2 you can:

2 Embrace the French Language

There's a reason so many English-speakers associate the French language with romance—it truly slides off the tongue. Québec is deeply proud of its Francophone past, present, and future. Better acquaint yourself with all three at **Musée de l'Amérique Francophone** ★★. While you're at it, why not memorize a few phrases to take home. How about: *Tu es ma joie de vivre.* (You are the joy of my life.) Too sappy? *Attache ta tuque* means Get, ready, let's go! (Or more literally, Put on your winter hat.) See p. 174.

From here, turn left on rue de Buade, grab your partner's hand, and keep going down the steep grade of the curved Côte de la Montagne, where you'll find stairs to:

3 Amble Down rue de Petit-Champlain

You can't leave town without a stroll down the old-world, amiable rue de Petit-Champlain, especially after dark, when the shops are lit from within. You'll find a few of them listed in chapter 14.

Take a moment to bask in the enchanting backdrop, and then do what most travelers do, plan your next meal. If you want, you can:

4 Celebrate a Milestone & Join the Party

Whether you are falling in love, marking an anniversary, or simply thrilled at your first-ever horse-drawn carriage ride, it doesn't matter—you name the milestone, and then make like the Québécois, and celebrate! This city loves its festivals and there's likely a citywide party underway somewhere that you can throw yourself into (see ch. 15 for a list).

5 Romantic Table for Two, Please

To top off a romantic day, consider a meal at the legendary **Le Saint-Amour** restaurant ★★★ at 48 rue Sainte-Ursule in Upper Town (✆ **418/694-0667**). Or, venture totally off the tourist grid to the St-Roch neighborhood. For a classy, contemporary bistro experience book a table for two at **Le Clocher Penché Bistrot** ★★★, 203 rue St-Joseph est (✆ **418/640-0597**). And if a perfect bottle of wine and tapas is more your style, head for **Le Cercle** ★★★, 226½ rue St-Joseph est (✆ **418/948-8648**). See p. 157, 165, or 165.

MONTRÉAL & QUÉBEC CITY IN CONTEXT

3

Montréal and Québec City, the twin cities of the province of Québec, have a stronger European flavor than Canada's other municipalities. French is the first language of most residents, and a strong affiliation with France continues to be a central facet of the region's personality.

The defining dialectics of Canadian life are culture and language, both thorny issues that have long threatened to tear the country apart. Many Québécois have long believed that making Québec a separate, independent state is the only way to maintain their rich French culture in the face of the Anglophone ocean that surrounds them. Québec's role within the Canadian federation has been the most debated and volatile topic of conversation in Canadian politics.

There are reasons for the festering intransigence, of course—about 250 years' worth. After France lost power in Québec to the British in the 18th century, a kind of linguistic exclusionism developed, with wealthy Scottish and English bankers and merchants denying French-Canadians access to upper levels of business and government. This bias continued well into the 20th century.

Many in Québec stayed committed to the French language and culture after British rule was imposed. Even with later waves of other immigrant populations pouring into the cities, there was still a bedrock loyalty held by many to the province's Gallic roots. France may have relinquished control of Québec to Great Britain in 1763, but France's influence, after its 150 years of rule, remained powerful—and still does. Many Québécois continue to look across the Atlantic for inspiration in fashion, food, and the arts. Culturally and linguistically, it is that tenacious French connection that gives the province its special character.

Two other important cultural phenomena have emerged over the past decade and a half. The first is an institutional acceptance of homosexuality. By changing the definition of "spouse" in 39 laws and regulations in 1999, Québec's government eliminated all legal distinctions between same-sex and heterosexual couples and became Canada's first province to recognize the legal status of same-sex civil unions. Gay marriage became legal in all of Canada's provinces and territories in 2005. Montréal, in particular, has transformed into one of North America's most welcoming cities for gay people.

The second phenomenon is an influx of even more immigrants into the province's melting pot. "Québec is at a turning point," declared a 2008 report about the province's angst over the so-called reasonable accommodation of minority religious practices, particularly those of Muslims and Orthodox Jews. "The identity inherited from the French-Canadian past is perfectly legitimate and it must survive," the report said, "but it can no longer occupy alone the Québec identity space." Together with aboriginal people from 11 First Nation tribes who live in the province, immigrants help make the region as vibrant and alive as any on the continent.

THE TWIN CITIES TODAY

The centuries-old walls that protected Québec City over the centuries are still in place, and the streets and lanes within their embrace have changed little, preserving for posterity the heart of New France.

Not so in Montréal. It was "wet" when the U.S. was "dry" during U.S. Prohibition from 1920 to 1933. Bootleggers, hard drinkers, and prostitutes flocked to this large city situated so conveniently close to the American border, mixing with rowdy people from the port, much to the distress of many of Montréal's citizenry. For 50 years, the city's image was decidedly racy, but in the 1950s, a cleanup began alongside a boom in high-rise construction, and restoration began in the old port area, which had become a derelict ghost town. In 1967, Montréal welcomed international audiences to Expo 67, the World's Fair.

Today, much of what makes Montréal special is either very old or very new. The city's great gleaming skyscrapers and towering hotels, the superb Métro system, and the highly practical underground city date mostly from the nearly 50 years since the Expo. The renaissance of much of the oldest part of the city, Vieux-Montréal, blossomed in the 1990s.

To understand the province's politics, you need to back up about 50 years. A phenomenon later labeled the Quiet Revolution began bubbling in the 1960s. The movement focused on transforming the largely rural, agricultural province into an urbanized, industrial entity with a pronounced secular outlook. French-Canadians, long denied access to the upper echelons of desirable corporate careers, started to insist on equal opportunity with the powerful Anglophone minority.

In 1968, Pierre Trudeau, a bilingual Québécois, became Canada's prime minister, a post he held for 18 years. More flamboyant, eccentric, and brilliant than any of his predecessors, he devoted much time to trying to placate voters on both sides of the French-English issue.

Also in 1968, the Parti Québécois was founded by René Lévesque, and a separatist movement began in earnest. Inevitably, there was a radical fringe, and it signaled its intentions by bombing Anglophone businesses. The FLQ (Front de Libération du Québec, or Québec Liberation Front), as it was known, was behind most of the terrorist attacks. Most Québécois separatists, of course, were not violent, but the bombings fueled passions and contributed to a sense that big changes were coming.

Secession remained a dream for many Québécois. In 1995, a referendum on sovereignty lost by a mere 1 percent of the vote. During the 1990s, an unsettled mood prevailed in the province. Large businesses left town, anxious that if the province actually did secede, they would find themselves based outside of Canada proper. Economic opportunities were limited.

By 2000, things began to change. The Canadian dollar began to strengthen against the U.S. dollar. Unemployment, long in double digits, shrank to less than 6 percent, the lowest percentage in more than 20 years. Crime in Montréal, which was already one of the continent's safest cities, hit a 20-year low. The presence of skilled workers made Canada a favored destination for Hollywood film and TV production. The rash of FOR RENT and FOR SALE signs that disfigured Montréal in the 1990s was replaced by a welcome shortage of retail and office space.

In 2002, the 28 towns and cities on the island of Montréal merged into one megacity with a population of 1.8 million.

Today, the quest for separatism seems to be fading. Conversations with ordinary Québécois suggest they're weary of the argument. In March 2007, the separatist Parti Québécois placed a distant third in elections with just 28 percent of the vote. The moment marked, many think, the beginning of the end of the campaign for independence.

As significantly, the proportion of foreign-born Québec citizens continues to grow. After the arrival of 1.1 million immigrants to the country between 2001 and 2006, foreign-born nationals made up 20 percent of Canada's population, with Montréal, Toronto, Vancouver, and Calgary their prime destinations. The province of Québec welcomed over 50,000 permanent residents in 2010, with over 46,000 of them settling in Montréal, and another 2,600 in Québec City. Visitors to Montréal may notice large pockets of neighborhoods where the primary languages spoken are Mandarin and Cantonese.

LOOKING BACK: MONTRÉAL & QUÉBEC CITY HISTORY

First Immigrants

The first settlers of the region were the Iroquois, who spent time in what's now called Québec long before the Europeans arrived. The Vikings landed in Canada more than 1,000 years ago, probably followed by Irish and Basque fishermen. English explorer John Cabot stepped ashore briefly on the east coast in 1497, but it was the French who managed the first meaningful European toehold.

When Jacques Cartier sailed up the St. Lawrence in 1535, he recognized at once the tremendous strategic potential of Québec City's Cap Diamant (Cape Diamond), the high bluff overlooking the river. But he was exploring, not empire building, and after stopping briefly on land, he continued on his trip.

Montréal, at the time, was home to a fortified Iroquois village called Hochelaga, composed of 50 longhouses. Cartier was on a sea route to China but was halted by the fierce rapids just west of what is now the Island of Montréal. (In a demonstration of mingled optimism and frustration, he dubbed the rapids "La Chine," assuming that China was just beyond them. Today, they're still known as the Lachine.) He visited the Indian settlement in what's now Old Montréal before moving on.

Samuel de Champlain arrived 73 years later, in 1608, motivated by the burgeoning fur trade, obsessed with finding a route to China, and determined to settle Québec. He was perhaps emboldened after the Virginia Company founded its fledgling colony of Jamestown, hundreds of miles to the south, just a year before.

Called Kebec, Champlain's first settlement grew to become Québec City's Basse-Ville, or Lower Town, and spread across the flat riverbank beneath the cliffs of Cap Diamant. In 2008, Québec City hosted major celebrations of the 400th anniversary of this founding.

Champlain would make frequent trips back to France to reassure anxious investors that the project, which he said would eventually "equal the states of greatest kings," was going apace. In truth, the first years were bleak. Food was scarce, and scurvy ravaged many of the settlers. Demanding winters were far colder than in France. And almost from the beginning, there were hostilities, first between the French and the Iroquois, then between the French and the British (and later, the Americans). At issue was control of the lucrative trade of the fur of beavers, raccoons, and bears, and the hides of deer, as the pelts were being shipped off to Paris fashion houses. The commercial battle lasted nearly a century.

To better defend themselves the settlers in Québec City built a fortress at the top of the cliffs. Gradually, the center of urban life moved to inside the fortress walls.

The French and British struggle for dominance in the new continent focused on their explorations, and in this regard, France outdid England. Far-ranging French fur trappers, navigators, soldiers, and missionaries opened up not only Canada, but also most of what eventually became the United States, moving all the way south to the future New Orleans. At least 35 of the subsequent 50 U.S. states were mapped or settled by Frenchmen, and they left behind thousands of city names to prove it, including Detroit, St. Louis, Duluth, and Des Moines.

Paul de Chomedey, Sieur de Maisonneuve, arrived at what is now the island of Montréal in 1642 to establish a colony and to plant a crucifix atop the rise he called Mont Royal. He and his band of settlers came ashore and founded Ville-Marie, dedicated to the Virgin Mary, at the spot now marked by Place-Royale in the old part of the city. They built a fort, a chapel, stores, and houses. Pointe-à-Callière, the terrific Montréal Museum of Archaeology and History, is built on the site where the original colony was established.

Life was not easy. The Iroquois in Montréal had no intention of giving up land to the Europeans. Fierce battles raged for years. Today, at Place d'Armes, there's a statue of de Maisonneuve marking the spot where the settlers defeated the Iroquois in bloody hand-to-hand fighting.

Still, the settlement prospered. Until the 1800s, Montréal was contained in the area known today as Vieux-Montréal. Its ancient walls no longer stand, but its colorful past is preserved in the streets, houses, and churches of the Old City.

England Conquers New France

In the 1750s, the struggle between Britain and France had escalated. The latest episode was known as the French and Indian War (an extension of Europe's Seven Years' War), and strategic Québec became a valued prize. The French appointed Louis Joseph, Marquis de Montcalm, to command their forces in the town. The British sent an expedition of 4,500 men in a fleet under the command of a 32-year-old general, James Wolfe. The British troops surprised the French by coming up and over the cliffs of Cap Diamant, and the ensuing skirmish for Québec, fought on September 13, 1759, became one of the most important battles in North American history: It resulted in a continent that would be under British influence for more than a century.

Fought on Québec City's Plains of Abraham, today a beautiful and much-used city park, the battle lasted just 18 to 25 minutes, depending on whose account you read. It resulted in more than a thousand deaths and serious injuries, and both generals died as a result of wounds received. Wolfe lived just long enough to hear that the British had won. Montcalm died a few hours later. Today, a memorial to both men overlooks Terrasse Dufferin in Québec City and uniquely commemorates both victor and vanquished of the same battle. The inscription—in neither French nor English, but Latin—is translated as, simply, "Courage was fatal to them."

The capture of Québec determined the war's course, and the Treaty of Paris in 1763 ceded all of French Canada to England. In a sense, this victory was a bane to Britain: If France had held Canada, the British government might have been more judicious in its treatment of the American colonists. As it was, the British decided to make the colonists pay the costs of the French and Indian War, on the principle that it was their home being defended. Britain slapped so many taxes on all imports that the infuriated U.S. colonists openly rebelled against the crown.

George Washington felt sure that French-Canadians would want to join the American revolt against the British crown, or at least be supportive, but he was mistaken on both counts. The Québécois detested their British conquerors, but they were also devout Catholics and saw their contentious American neighbors as godless republicans. Only a handful supported the Americans, and three of Washington's most competent commanders came to grief in attacks against Québec and were forced to retreat.

Thirty-eight years later, during the War of 1812, the U.S. army marched up the banks of the Richelieu River where it flows from Lake Champlain in what's now northern Vermont to the St. Lawrence in Québec. Once again, the French-Canadians stuck by the British and drove back the Americans. The war ended essentially in a draw, but it had at least one encouraging result: Britain and the young United States agreed to demilitarize the Great Lakes and to extend their mutual border along the 49th parallel to the Rockies.

The Rise of French Separatism in Québec

In 1867, the British North America Act created the federation of the provinces of Québec, Ontario, Nova Scotia, and New Brunswick. It was a kind of independence for the region from Britain, but was unsettling for many French-Canadians, who wanted full autonomy. In 1883, *"Je me souviens"*—a defiant, proud "I remember"—became the province's official motto. From 1900 to 1910, 325,000 French-Canadians emigrated to the United States, many settling in the northeast states.

In 1968, the Parti Québécois was founded by René Lévesque, and the separatist movement began in earnest. One attempt to smooth ruffled Francophones was made in 1969, when federal legislation stipulated that all services across Canada were henceforth to be offered in both English and French, in effect declaring the nation bilingual.

That didn't assuage militant Québécois, however. They undertook to guarantee the primacy of French in their own province. To prevent dilution by newcomers, the children of immigrants were required to enroll in French-language schools, even if English or a third language was spoken in the home.

Nevertheless, immigrants made Montréal their own. Ruth Reichl, the editor of the now defunct "Gourmet" magazine, wrote in the March 2006 special issue about the city that when she lived there in the 1960s, "[I]t was strangely segregated. The Anglophones I trailed through the staid streets were a proper lot, more English than the English, with their umbrellas and briefcases. . . . The Jewish community I found in another part of town was an entirely different experience. The people were boisterous, and their streets were rich with the scent of garlic, cloves, and allspice emanating from the mountains of pickles and deliciously rich smoked meat that I spied each time a restaurant door swung open. The French-Canadians had their own territory, too, and they stuck to themselves, speaking their own robust and expressive language. . . . What

MARCH OF THE LANGUAGE police

When the separatist Parti Québécois took power in the province in 1976, it wasted no time in attempting to make Québec unilingual. Bill 101 made French the provincial government's sole official language and sharply restricted the use of other languages in education and commerce. While the party's fortunes have fallen and risen and fallen, the primacy of Française has remained.

In the early days, agents of L'Office de la Langue Française, the French Language Police, fanned out across the territory, scouring the landscape for linguistic insults to the state and her people. MERRY CHRISTMAS signs were removed from storefronts, and department stores had to come up with a new name for Harris Tweed. About 20 percent of the population spoke English as a primary language, and they instantly felt like second-class citizens. Francophones responded that it was about time they knew what second-class citizenship felt like.

Affected, too, was the food world. By fiat and threat of punishment, hamburgers became *hambourgeois* and hot dogs were rechristened *chiens chaud.* And Schwartz's Montréal Hebrew Delicatessen, one of the city's fixtures since 1928? It became Chez Schwartz Charcuterie Hébraïque de Montréal.

struck me most, as a New Yorker accustomed to the hodgepodge piling up of one culture on another, was the barriers between them. They kept themselves strictly separate, each cleaving to their own language, rituals, and food."

In 1977, Bill 101 passed, all but banning the use of English on public signage. The bill funded the establishment of enforcement units, a virtual language police who let no nit go unpicked. The resulting backlash provoked the flight of an estimated 400,000 Anglophones to other parts of Canada.

In 1987, Canadian Prime Minister Brian Mulroney met with the 10 provincial premiers at a retreat at Québec's Meech Lake to cobble together a collection of constitutional reforms. The Meech Lake Accord, as it came to be known, addressed a variety of issues, but most important to the Québécois was that it recognized Québec as a "distinct society" within the federation.

Manitoba and Newfoundland, however, failed to ratify the accord by the June 23, 1990, deadline and as a result, support for the secessionist cause burgeoned in Québec. An election firmly placed the Parti Québécois in control of the provincial government again. A 1995 referendum on succession from the Canadian union was only narrowly defeated. The issue continued to divide families and dominate political discourse.

The year 2007 may have marked the beginning of the end the issue. In provincial elections, Parti Québécois placed third, with just 28 percent of the vote. The election was perceived by many as the first step in closing the door on the campaign for independence. The party has been headed by Pauline Marois since 2007, and she is the current Premier of Québec.

Today, Montréal may well be the most bilingual city in the world. Most residents speak at least a little of both French and English. And Québécois, it must be said, are exceedingly gracious hosts. Most Montréalers switch effortlessly from one language to the other as the situation dictates. Telephone operators go from French to English the instant they hear an English word, as do most store clerks, waiters, and hotel staff.

This is less the case in country villages and in Québec City, but for visitors, there is virtually no problem that can't be solved with a few French words, some expressive gestures, and a little goodwill.

Political Power for the First Nations

The French colonialists eventually came to realize that it was only through trade, alliances, and treaties—rather than force—that relations between native peoples and themselves could develop. From early on, formal alliances were part of the texture of their uneasy relationship.

Describing and characterizing the long history of the treatment of native peoples is difficult. Assimilation of natives into European identity, for instance, was once perceived as a positive goal but has since been repudiated by natives, who are collectively known today as First Nations. The 1876 Indian Act established federal Canadian authority over the rights and lands of "Indians" and set in place an assimilation process. Indians who wanted full rights as Canadians had to relinquish their legal Indian status and renounce their Indian identity. Participation in traditional dances, for instance, became punishable by imprisonment.

Those laws changed slowly. It was only in 1985 that the law was modified so that an Indian woman who married a non-Indian would not automatically lose her Indian status. In 2007, the United Nations General Assembly adopted the Declaration on the Rights of Indigenous Peoples, recognizing the right of aboriginals to self-determination.

The interests of native peoples are today represented by the Assembly of the First Nations, which was established in 1985. Economic interests are represented in part by Société Touristique des Autochtones du Québec (STAQ), the aboriginal tourism corporation (www.tourismeautochtone.com).

ART & ARCHITECTURE

Classic European art and architectural influences meet with an urbane, design-heavy aesthetic in Montréal and Québec City. Here are some art highlights.

Frederick Law Olmsted & Parc du Mont-Royal

American landscape architect Frederick Law Olmsted (1822–1903), well known for creating New York City's Central Park, also designed the park that surrounds the "mountain" in the center of Montréal. Parc du Mont-Royal, as it is known, opened in 1876. Olmsted's vision was to make the landscape seem more mountainous by using exaggerated vegetation—shade trees at the bottom of a path that climbs its side, for instance—to create the illusion at the lower elevations of being in a valley. Unfortunately, Montréal suffered a depression in the mid-1870s, and many of the architect's plans were abandoned. The path was built, but not according to the original plan, and the vegetation ideas were abandoned. Still, Parc du Mont-Royal is an urban oasis used year-round. For a walking tour of the park, see p. 124.

Bruce Price & Château Frontenac

It is an American architect, Bruce Price (1845–1903), who is responsible for the most iconic building in the entire province of Québec: Château Frontenac, Québec City's visual center.

"The Château" opened as a hotel in 1893; with its castlelike architecture, soaring turrets, and romantic French-Renaissance mystery, it achieved the goal of becoming the most talked-about accommodation in North America. It continued to operate as a hotel and today this high-end property managed by the Fairmont chain.

The Château was one of many similar-styled hotels commissioned by the Canadian Pacific Railway in the late 19th century during constructing Canada's first transcontinental railway. Company bigwigs believed the luxury accommodations would encourage travelers with money to travel by train. As part of the same Canadian Pacific Railway project, Price also designed Montréal's Windsor Station; the Dalhousie Station in Montréal; the facade of Royal Victoria College in Montréal; and the Gare du Palais train station in Québec City, whose turrets echo those of the Château Frontenac.

Architecture professor Claude Bergeron of Québec City's Univérsité Laval noted that as the leading practitioner of the château style, Price "is sometimes credited with having made it a national Canadian style."

Avant-Garde Vision

In 1967, Montréal hosted the World's Fair, which it called Expo 67. The event was hugely successful—62 nations participated, more than 50 million people visited, and Montréal became a star overnight. With its avant-garde vision on display, it was viewed as a prototype for a 20th-century city.

One of the most exhilarating buildings developed for the event was Habitat 67, a 158-unit housing complex on the St. Lawrence River. Designed by Montréal architect Moshe Safdie (b. 1938), it still is arresting: it looks like a collection of modular concrete blocks all piled together. The vision was to show what community housing could look like. The complex is still full of residents, although it's not open to the public for touring. You can view it from the western end of Vieux-Port on online online at Safdie's website, www.msafdie.com.

Palais des Congrès (Convention Center), at the northern edge of Vieux-Montréal, is an unlikely design triumph, too. Built between 2000 and 2002 as part of a renovation and extension of the center, the building's transparent glass exterior walls are a crazy quilt of pink, yellow, blue, green, red, and purple rectangles. You get the full effect when you step into the inside hallway—when the sun streams in, it's like being inside a kaleidoscope. It's the vision of Montréal architect Mario Saia.

Design Montréal

Montréal is one of North America's most stylish cities. In 2006, UNESCO (the United Nations Educational, Scientific, and Cultural Organization) designated Montréal a "UNESCO City of Design" for "its ability to inspire synergy between public and private players." Montréal joined Buenos Aires and Berlin, other honorees, as a high-style city worth watching.

Much of what constitutes cutting-edge design is creative reuse of older buildings and materials. The city encourages and promotes the creativity in its design competitions; completed new works are listed online at **mtlunescodesign.com/en**. Two festivals of note: the Montréal Fashion & Design Festival (usually held in summer), and Montréal Fashion Week (the 2013 edition was held in September, right before New York Fashion Week). Details are at **www.sensationmode.com**.

The city's aesthetic was well summed up by one fashionista in the "Montréal Gazette:" "I'm all about the black, the white, and beige. Fall is about comfort—not that American style of sloppy comfort, but casual style."

geography 101: MOUNTAINS AND MOLEHILLS

Montréal is an island that's part of the Hochelaga Archipelago. The island is situated in the St. Lawrence River near the confluence with the Ottawa River.

At Montréal's center is a 232m (761-ft.) hill, which natives like to think of as a mountain. Called Mont Royal, it's the geographic landmark from which the city takes its name.

Real mountains, however, do rise nearby. The Laurentides, also called the Laurentians, comprise the world's oldest range and are the playground of the Québécois. Their highest peak, Mont-Tremblant, is 968m (3,176 ft.). Also, the Appalachians' northern foothills separate Québec from the U.S., adding to the beauty of the bucolic Cantons-de-l'Est region on the opposite side of the St. Lawrence. This area was once known as the Eastern Townships and is where many Montréalers have country homes.

Inuit Art

The region's most compelling artwork is indigenous. In Montréal, the Musée McCord has a First Nations room that displays objects from Canada's native population, including meticulous beadwork, baby carriers, and fishing implements. The city's annual First Peoples Festival (www.nativelynx.qc.ca; ✆ **514/278-4040**), held in summer, highlights Amerindian and Inuit cultures by way of film, video, visual arts, music, and dance.

In Québec City, the Musée National des Beaux-Arts du Québec is home to an important Inuit art collection assembled over many years by Raymond Brousseau. Also in Québec City, a permanent exhibition at the Musée de la Civilisation, "Nous, les Premières Nations" ("We, the First Nations"), provides a fascinating look at the history and culture of the Abenakis, Algonquins, Atikamekw, Crees, Hurons-Wendat, Inuit, Malecites, Micmacs, Innu, Mohawks, and Naskapis—the 11 First Nation tribes whose members inhabit Québec today.

Those External Staircases

Stroll through Montréal's Plateau Mont-Royal and Mile End neighborhoods, and one of the first things you'll notice are the exterior staircases on the two- and three-story houses. Many are made of wrought iron, and most have shapely, sensual curves. Two theories exist above their provenance: Some say they were first designed to accommodate immigrant families who wanted their own front doors, even for second-floor apartments while other suggest it was the landlords, who put the stairs outside to cut down on common interior space that wouldn't count toward rental space.

The Catholic Church, ever a force in the city, was originally all for the stairs because they allowed neighbors to keep an eye on each other. After the aesthetic tide turned, however, brick archways called loggia were built to hide the stairways. But the archway walls created ready-made nooks for teens to linger in, and the church helped push through legislation banning new exterior staircases entirely. That ban was lifted in the 1980s so that citywide efforts to maintain and renovate properties could keep the unique features intact.

MONTRÉAL & QUÉBEC CITY IN POPULAR CULTURE

BOOKS & THEATER The late Jewish Anglophone Mordecai Richler (1931–2001) inveighed against the excesses of Québec's separatists and language zealots in a barrage of books and critical essays in newspapers and magazines. Richler wrote from the perspective of a minority within a minority and set most of his books in the working-class Jewish neighborhood of St. Urbain of the 1940s and 1950s, with protagonists who are poor, streetwise, and intolerant of the prejudices of other Jews, French-Canadians, and WASPs from the city's English-side Westmount neighborhood. His most famous book is "The Apprenticeship of Duddy Kravitz" (Pocket Books, 1959), which in 1974 was made into a movie of the same name starring Richard Dreyfuss. In 2010, a film version of his "Barney's Version" starred Dustin Hoffman and Paul Giamatti.

Playwright Michel Tremblay (b. 1942), an important dramatist, grew up in Montréal's Plateau Mont-Royal neighborhood and uses that setting for much of his work. His "Les Belles-Sœurs" ("The Sisters-in-Law"), written in 1965, introduced the lives of working-class Francophone Québécois to the world.

MUSIC In 2008, the Putumayo World Music record label released a compilation CD called "Québec" in honor of Québec City's 400th anniversary. It's a collection of 11 songs that reflect the province's rich musical diversity, and it provides a terrific introduction to Québécois music. Highlights include the upbeat, angelic-voiced Chloé Sainte-Marie (b. 1962; "Brûlots"); the pop band DobaCaracol ("Etrange"), which fuses a reggae groove with African rhythms and French-language pop; and the Celtic folk of La Bottine Souriante ("La Brunette Est Là"), the preeminent representatives of traditional Québécois music, which has its roots in French, English, Scottish, and Irish folk traditions.

Montréal has a strong showing of innovative musicians who hail from its clubs. Singer-songwriter Leonard Cohen (b. 1934) is the best known internationally. He grew up in the Westmount neighborhood and attended McGill University. He was inducted into the U.S. Rock and Roll Hall of Fame in 2008. He also wrote two novels set in Montréal: 1963's "The Favorite Game" (Vintage, 2003) and 1966's "Beautiful Losers" (Vintage, 1993).

Rufus Wainwright (b. 1973), a popular singer-songwriter (and son of folk great, and Montréal native, Kate McGarrigle [1946–2010]) grew up in Montréal and got his start at city clubs. Alternative rock bands Arcade Fire and Wolf Parade are both from the city. (The band Of Montréal, however, is a U.S. band from Athens, Georgia.)

FILM & TELEVISION Many U.S. films are made beyond the northern border for financial reasons, even when their American locales are important parts of the stories. Québécois films—made in the province, in French, for Québec audiences—can be difficult to track down outside the region. The Cinémathèque Québécoise (www.cinematheque.qc.ca; ✆ **514/842-9763**) is a great resource for fun and research. It's located at 335 boul. de Maisonneuve est in Montréal.

Recent notable features made by Québécois filmmakers include "Rebelle" ("War Witch") by Kim Nguyen, "Monsieur Lazhar" by Philippe Falardeau, and "Incendies" by Denis Villeneuve—all three competed in the U.S. Academy Awards as Canada's representative in the Best Foreign Language Film category. To seek out additional recent Canadian films, many of which are made in Québec, look for winners of Canada's national Genie Awards (**www.genieawards.ca**) or winners of Quebec's provincial Jutra Awards (**www.lesjutra.ca**).

Alanis Obomsawin (b. 1932) is an important documentarian. A member of the Abenaki Nation who was raised on the Odanak Reserve near Montréal, she began making movies for the National Film Board of Canada (www.nfb.ca) 40 years ago and has produced more than 30 documentaries about the hard edges of the lives of aboriginal people. In 2008, "the first lady of First Nations film"—as the commissioner of the National Film Board called her—received the Governor General's Performing Arts Award for Lifetime Artistic Achievement. She has documented police raids of reservation lands, homelessness among natives living in cities, and a wrenching incident in 1990 that pitted native peoples against the government over lands that were slated to be turned into a golf course. That last event, detailed in "Kanehsatake: 270 Years of Resistance," took place an hour west of Montréal and included a months-long armed standoff between Mohawks and authorities.

In 2007, the CBC television show "Little Mosque on the Prairie" began offering a peek into the religious and cultural issues faced by Canada's large immigrant population. It remains a popular program and had its final episode in 2012.

EATING & DRINKING

A generation ago, most Montréal and Québec City restaurants served only French food. A few *temples de cuisine* delivered haute standards of gastronomy, while numerous accomplished bistros served up humbler ingredients in less grand settings and folksy places offered the hearty fare that employed the ingredients long available in New France—game such as caribou, maple syrup, and root vegetables.

The 1990s recession put many restaurateurs out of business and forced others to reexamine their operation. In Montréal, especially, immigrants brought the cooking styles of the world to the city. Today, the city's food scene is wildly adventurous, and is a reason that many people travel from around the world to visit and indulge.

Restaurants are colloquially called "restos," and they range from moderately priced bistros, cafes, and ethnic joints to swank luxury epicurean shrines.

Menu Basics

Always look for **table d'hôte** meals. These are fixed-price menus, and with them, three- or four-course meals can be had for little more than the price of an a la carte main course. (See the sidebar on p. 58 in chapter 6 for details.)

Many higher-end establishments offer **tasting menus,** with an array of small dishes for a sampling of the chef's skills. Gaining popularity are **surprise menus,** also called "chef's whim," where you don't know what you're getting until it's in front of you. Fine restaurants often offer wine pairings with meals, as well, where the sommelier selects a glass (or half glass, if you ask) for each course.

Local Food Highlights

Be sure to try regional specialties. A Québécois favorite is *poutine:* French fries doused with gravy and cheese curds. It's ubiquitous in winter.

Game is popular, including venison, quail, goose, caribou, and wapiti (North American deer). Many menus feature emu and lamb raised north of Québec City in Charlevoix. Mussels and salmon are also standard.

Québec cheeses deserve attention, and many can be sampled only in Canada because they are often unpasteurized, made of *lait cru* (raw milk), and therefore subject to strict export rules. Better restaurants will offer them as a final course. Of the more than 500 varieties available, you might look for Mimolette Jeune (firm, fragrant, orange), Valbert St-Isidor (similar to Swiss in texture), St-Basil de Port Neuf (buttery), Cru des Erables (soft, ripe), Oka (semisoft, made of cow's milk in a monastery), and Le Chèvre Noire (a sharp goat variety covered in black wax). Québec cheeses pick up armfuls of prizes each year in the American Cheese Society competition, North America's largest.

Cheeses with the *fromages de pays* label are made in Québec with whole milk and no modified milk ingredients. The label represents solidarity among artisanal producers and is supported by Solidarité Rurale du Québec, a group devoted to revitalizing rural communities. It's also supported by Slow Food Québec, which promotes sustainable agriculture and local production. Information is available at www.fromageduquebec.qc.ca.

Beer & Wine

Alcohol is heavily taxed, and imported varieties even more so than domestic versions, so if you're looking to save a little, buy Canadian. That's not difficult when it comes to beer, for there are many regional breweries, from Montréal powerhouse Molson to micro, that produce delicious products. Among the best local options are Belle Gueule and Boréal. The sign BIERES EN FUT means "beers on draft." The Montréal beer festival, the Mondial de la bière (www.festivalmondialbiere.qc.ca), is a giddy event where typically over 100 breweries present their wares. The 21st edition will be held in June 2014 at the Palais des congrès.

Wine is another matter. It is not produced in significant quantities in Canada due to a climate generally inhospitable to the essential grapes. But you might try bottles from the vineyards of the Cantons-de-l'Est region (just east of Montréal). Sample, too, the sweet "ice wines" and "ice ciders" made from grapes and apples after the first frost; many decent ones come from vineyards and orchards just an hour from Montréal.

One popular winery is Vignoble de L'Orpailleur (www.orpailleur.ca). *L'orpailleur* refers to someone who mines for gold in streams—the idea being that trying to make good wine in Québec's cold climate requires a similar leap of faith in the ability to defy the odds.

WHEN TO GO

High season in the province of Québec is summer, from June 24 (Jean-Baptiste Day) through early September (Labour Day). Festivals listed in chapters 8 and 15 give you a peek at some of the back-to-back options for partying. In Québec City, the period from Christmas to New Year's and February weekends during the big winter Carnaval are especially busy, too. Celebrating the holidays *a la française* is a particular treat in Québec City, where the streets are almost certainly banked with snow and nearly every ancient building sports wreaths, decorated fir trees, and glittering white lights. Just north of Montréal, the Laurentian Mountains do big ski business in the cold months (typically late Nov to late Mar). Hotels are most likely to be full and charge their highest rates in these periods.

Low season is during March and April, when fewer events are scheduled and winter sports start to be iffy. The late-fall months of October and November are also slow due to their all-but-empty social calendars. But autumn is still a lovely time to visit: a walk in the cities' parks are a refreshing tonic, the trees still have their fall color, and the roads are less crowded for day trips into the countryside from either city.

Bracing for Montréal's Winter Chill

City dwellers that live through Montréal's winter more than half the year know a thing or two about dressing for the cold. Wearing layers is essential and practicality trumps fashion. In Montréal, a dark wool or down coat can serve both gods, but sporty ski clothes are seem to work here and elsewhere in the province. Consider packing a hat, scarf, thermal socks, and waterproof boots with traction. Don't be surprised if umbrellas pop open on snowy days, but mind the wind, especially between tall buildings downtown. Long underwear is probably only needed for outdoor activities but a second pair of shoes, if the preferred ones get soaked, can save a vacation.

Weather

Temperatures are usually a few degrees lower in Québec City than in Montréal. Spring, short but sweet, arrives around the middle of May. Summer (mid-June through mid-Sept) tends to be humid in Montréal, Québec City, and other communities along the St. Lawrence River, and drier at the inland resorts of the Laurentides and the Cantons-de-l'Est. Intense, but usually brief, heat waves mark July and early August, but temperatures rarely remain oppressive in the evenings.

Autumn (Sept–Oct) is as short and changeable as spring, with warm days and cool nights. It's during this season that Canadian maple trees blaze red and orange.

Winter brings dependable snows for skiing in the Laurentides, Cantons-de-l'Est, and, north of Québec City, Charlevoix. Snow and slush are present in the city from November to March. For many, Montréal's underground city is a climate-controlled blessing during this time.

For the current weather forecast, check **weather.gc.ca**.

Average Monthly Temperatures (°F/°C)

MONTRÉAL	JAN	FEB	MAR	APR	MAY	JUNE	JULY	AUG	SEPT	OCT	NOV	DEC
High (°F)	21	24	35	51	65	73	79	76	66	54	41	27
High (°C)	–6	–4	1	10	18	22	26	24	18	12	5	–2
Low (°F)	7	10	21	35	47	56	61	59	50	39	29	13
Low (°C)	–13	–12	–6	1	8	13	16	15	10	3	–1	–10
QUÉBEC CITY	**JAN**	**FEB**	**MAR**	**APR**	**MAY**	**JUNE**	**JULY**	**AUG**	**SEPT**	**OCT**	**NOV**	**DEC**
High (°F)	18	21	32	46	62	71	76	74	63	50	37	23
High (°C)	–8	–6	0	7	16	21	24	23	17	10	2	–5
Low (°F)	2	5	16	31	43	53	58	56	46	36	25	9
Low (°C)	–16	–15	–8	0	6	11	12	13	7	2	–3	–12

Holidays

Canada's important public holidays are New Year's Day (Jan 1); Good Friday and Easter Monday (Mar or Apr); Victoria Day (the Mon preceding May 25); St-Jean-Baptiste Day, Québec's own "national" day (June 24); Canada Day (July 1); Labour Day (first Mon in Sept); Canadian Thanksgiving Day (second Mon in Oct); and Christmas (Dec 25).

SETTLING INTO MONTRÉAL

4

Montréal is the most eclectic of Canada's cities: The island metropolis hosts international gigs such as the Jazz Fest, delights culinary crowds with innovative French-Canadian cuisine, and struts a Euro-heritage along its newly revitalized historic streets. Impressively bilingual in English and French, Montréal's global mix is a diverse microplanet of French, Scottish, Chinese, Haitian, Arabic, Eastern European, Italian, Portuguese, Filipino, and Greek immigrants. All this is wrapped up in a vibrant arts and culture scene and energized by an exuberant university community.

It's easy to make like a local and hop on a public BIXI bike to zip around the city. Maybe you'll wind your way up Mont Royal, the central landmark that Montréal gets its name from, and then fly downhill to the Old Port for a stroll along the canal. Microbrasseries beckon for sampling Québec's famous local ales, and cafes invite leisurely people watching. Restaurants in the postcard neighborhood of Vieux-Montréal offer authentic old-world ambience and sophisticated European flair.

ESSENTIALS

Arriving

Served by highways, transcontinental trains and buses, and several airports, Montréal is easily accessible from within Canada, the U.S., or overseas.

BY PLANE

Most of the world's major airlines fly into the **Aéroport International Pierre-Elliott-Trudeau de Montréal** (airport code YUL; www.admtl.com; ✆ **800/465-1213** or 514/394-7377), more commonly known as Montréal-Trudeau Airport.

Tip: Save time and hassle by arranging your flights so that your Customs entry takes place at your final Canadian destination. For instance, if you are flying from the U.S. and have to make one or more stops en route to Canada, try to make the transfer in the U.S. Otherwise, when you land in Canada you'll have to collect your bags, pass through Customs, and then check your bags again before continuing on to your final destination.

Montréal-Trudeau is 21 km (13 miles) from downtown Montréal. The airport is served by **Express Bus 747,** which debuted in 2010. It operates 24 hours a day, 7 days a week, and runs between the airport and the Berri-UQAM Métro station (the city's main bus terminal). Its 11 designated stops are mostly along downtown's boulevard René-Lévesque. A trip takes 45 to 60 minutes, depending on traffic, and buses leave every 20 to 30 minutes. One-way tickets are sold at the airport for C$9 from machines at the international arrivals level. You can also pay with cash on the bus (coins only, exact change). In the city, tickets are available at Métro stations and at the Hilton hotel downtown. The ticket is good for 24 hours on subways and buses. The schedule of stops is at **www.stm.info/info/747.htm**.

A taxi trip to downtown Montréal costs a flat fare of C$40, plus tip (C$4–$C6). Call ✆ **514/394-7377** for more information.

Roughly two dozen hotels offer airport shuttles; for a complete list check the airport's website under "Access and Parking."

BY BUS

Montréal's central bus station, called **Gare d'autocars de Montréal** (✆ **514/842-2281**), is at 1717 rue Berri; it replaced the city's old bus station in 2011. The station has a restaurant, a boutique, information booth, storage lockers, and Wi-Fi access. Connected to the terminal is **Berri-UQAM Station,** the junction of several Métro lines. (UQAM—pronounced "*Oo*-kahm"—stands for Université de Québec à Montréal.) Alternatively, **taxis** usually line up outside the terminal building.

BY CAR

All international drivers must carry a **valid driver's license** from their country of residence. A U.S. license is sufficient as long as you are a visitor and actually are a U.S. resident. A U.K. license is sufficient, as well.

In Canada, highway distances and speed limits are given in kilometers (km). The speed limit on the autoroutes is 100kmph (62 mph). Buckle up; there's a stiff penalty for neglecting to wear your seatbelt.

From Toronto to Montréal, the drive is about 5 hours. Most of your route is along the 401 highway (Macdonald-Cartier Hwy.), which you'll take until you reach "the 20" (Autoroute du Souvenir) at the Ontario-Québec border. From there it's about an hour to downtown Montréal.

From Québec City to Montréal, there are two options: Autoroute 40, which runs along the St. Lawrence's north shore, and Autoroute 20, on the south side (although not hugging the water at all). The trip takes about 3 hours.

Driving north to Montréal from the U.S., the entire journey is on expressways. From New York City, all but about the last 64km (40 miles) of the 603km (375-mile) trip are within New York State on Interstate 87. I-87 links up with Canada's Autoroute 15 at the border, which goes straight to Montréal.

Fill Up Before Crossing Over

Gasoline in Canada is expensive by U.S. standards. Gas is sold by the liter, and 3.78 liters equals 1 gallon. Recent prices of about C$1.40 per liter are equivalent to about US$5.12 per gallon. If you're driving from the U.S., fill up before crossing the border.

From Boston, I-93 goes up through New Hampshire's White Mountains and merges into I-91 to cross the tip of Vermont. At the border, I-91 becomes Autoroute 55. Signs lead to Autoroute 10 west, which goes into Montréal. Boston to Montréal is 518km (322 miles).

Heads up: Radar detectors are prohibited in the province of Québec. They can be confiscated, even if they're not being used.

See "Montréal by Car," later in this chapter for other rules of the road.

In 2008, Québec became the first province to mandate that residents have **radial snow tires** on their cars in winter. Visitors and their cars are exempt, but the law does give an indication of how harsh winter driving can be. Consider using snow tires when traveling in the region from December through March. Members of the American Automobile Association (AAA) are covered by the Canadian Automobile Association (CAA) while driving in Canada. See "Fast Facts: Montréal & Québec City," in chapter 18.

BY TRAIN

If you're coming from Toronto, you'll board the train at Union Station, which is downtown and accessible by subway. Montréal is a major terminus on Canada's **VIA Rail** network (www.viarail.ca; ✆ **888/842-7245** or 514/989-2626). Montréal's station, **Gare Centrale,** is centrally located downtown at 895 rue de la Gauchetière ouest (✆ **514/989-2626**). The station is connected to the Métro subway system at **Bonaventure Station.** (Gare Windsor, which you might see on some maps, is the city's former train station. The castlelike building is now used for offices.)

VIA Rail trains are comfortable—all major routes have Wi-Fi, and some trains are equipped with dining and sleeping cars.

The U.S. train system, **Amtrak** (www.amtrak.com; ✆ **800/872-7245**), has one train per day to Montréal from New York City's Penn Station that makes intermediate stops. Called the *Adirondack,* it's very slow, but its scenic route passes along the Hudson River's eastern shore and west of Lake Champlain. It takes about 11 hours from New York if all goes well, although delays aren't unusual.

The train ride between Montréal and Québec City takes about 3 hours.

BY BOAT

Both Montréal and Québec City are stops for cruise ships that travel along the St. Lawrence River (in French, Fleuve St-Laurent). The Port of Montréal, where ships dock, is part of the lively Vieux-Port (Old Port) neighborhood and walking distance from restaurants and shops.

Visitor Information

The main tourist center for visitors in downtown Montréal is the large **Infotouriste Centre,** at 1255 rue Peel (✆ **877/266-5687** or 514/873-2015; Métro: Peel). It's open daily, and the bilingual staff can provide suggestions for accommodations, dining, car rentals, and attractions.

In Vieux-Montréal, there's a teeny **Tourist Welcome Office** at 174 rue Notre-Dame est, at the corner of Place Jacques-Cartier (Métro: Champ-de-Mars), with brochures, maps, and a helpful staff. It's open daily from April 1 to November 15, and closed otherwise except for big events such as Nuit Blanche in February.

The city of Montréal maintains a terrific website at **www.tourisme-montreal.org**, which also includes an "insider" blog packed with great tips and up-to-the-minute suggestions.

City Layout

BASIC LAYOUT At the southern end of the city is Vieux-Port (along the St. Lawrence River) and Vieux-Montréal, or Old Montréal. Just north of Vieux-Montréal are Quartier International, where the convention center is located, and then Quartier des Spectacles, where Places des Arts (a complex of fine arts music halls) is located. Downtown is west of there, and the Plateau Mont-Royal is north.

The north-south artery boulevard St-Laurent (also known as The Main) serves as the line of demarcation between east and west Montréal. Most of the areas featured in this book lie west of boulevard St-Laurent.

MONTRÉAL: WHERE THE SUN RISES IN THE SOUTH

For the duration of your visit to Montréal, you'll need to accept local directional conventions, strange as they may seem. The boomerang- or croissant-shaped island city borders the St. Lawrence River, and as far as locals are concerned, the river is south, with the U.S. not far off on the other side. Never mind that the river, in fact, runs almost north and south at this section. For this reason, it has been observed that Montréal is the only city in the world where the sun rises in the south. Don't fight it: Face the river. That's south. Turn around. That's north. All is clear?

Note that directions given throughout the Montréal chapters conform to this local directional tradition. However, the maps in this book also have the true compass on them. When examining a map of the city, note that prominent thoroughfares, such as rue Ste-Catherine and boulevard René-Lévesque, are said to run either "east" or "west." The dividing line is boulevard St-Laurent, which runs "north" and "south."

In earlier days, Montréal was split geographically along cultural lines. English speakers lived mainly west of boulevard St-Laurent, while French speakers were concentrated to the east. Things still do sound more French as you walk east, as street names and Métro stations change from Peel and Atwater to Papineau and Beaudry.

In addition to the maps in this book, neighborhood street plans are available at www.tourisme-montreal.org and from the information centers listed above.

FINDING AN ADDRESS Boulevard St-Laurent is the dividing point between east and west (*est* and *ouest*) in Montréal. Pay attention: *Numbers go in both directions.* Make sure you know your east from your west and confirm the cross street for all addresses. For east-west streets, the numbers start at St-Laurent and then go east or west. That means, for instance, that the restaurants Chez l'Épicier, at 311 rue St-Paul est, and Marché de la Villette, at 324 rue St-Paul ouest, are 1km (about a half mile, or 13 short blocks) from each other—not directly across the street. Similarly, 500 rue Sherbrooke est is quite a hike from the same address in the west. Take note—or bring change for *l'autobus* or taxi.

There's no equivalent division for north and south (*nord* and *sud*)—the numbers start at the river and climb from there, just as the topography does.

In general, most addresses on the south side of the street are even and those on the north side are odd.

Neighborhoods in Brief

Downtown (also known, in French, as Centerville) This area contains the Montréal skyline's most dramatic elements and includes most of the city's large luxury and chain hotels, prominent museums, corporate headquarters, main transportation hubs, and department stores.

The principal east-west streets include boulevard René-Lévesque, rue Ste-Catherine, boulevard de Maisonneuve, and rue Sherbrooke. The north-south arteries include rue McGill and boulevard St-Laurent (aka the Main), which serves as the line of demarcation between east and west Montréal. The district is loosely bounded by rue

Sherbrooke to the north, boulevard René-Lévesque to the south, boulevard St-Laurent to the east, and rue Drummond to the west.

Within this neighborhood is the area called "the Golden Square Mile," an Anglophone district once characterized by dozens of mansions erected by the wealthy Scottish and English merchants and industrialists who dominated the city's political life well into the 20th century. Many of those stately homes were torn down when skyscrapers began to rise here after World War II, but some remain.

Rue Crescent, at the western side of downtown, is one of Montréal's major dining and nightlife streets. While the northern end of the street houses luxury boutiques in Victorian brownstones, its southern end holds dozens of restaurants, bars, and clubs of all styles. The street's party atmosphere spills over onto neighboring streets. In warm weather, the area's 20- and 30-something denizens take over sidewalk cafes and balcony terraces.

At downtown's northern edge is the urban campus of prestigious McGill University, an English-language school.

Vieux-Montréal & Vieux-Port The city was born here in 1642, down by the river at Pointe-à-Callière. Today, especially in summer, many people converge around Place Jacques-Cartier, where cafe tables line narrow terraces. This is where street performers, strolling locals, and tourists congregate.

The main thoroughfares are rue St-Jacques, rue Notre-Dame, and rue St-Paul. The waterfront road that hugs the promenade bordering the St. Lawrence River is rue de la Commune.

The neighborhood is larger than it might seem at first. It's bounded on the north by rue St-Antoine, and its southern boundary is the Vieux-Port (Old Port), now dominated by a well-used waterfront promenade that provides welcome breathing room for cyclists, in-line skaters, and picnickers. To the east, Vieux-Montréal is bordered by rue Berri, and to the west, by rue McGill.

Several small but intriguing museums are housed in historic buildings here, and the district's architectural heritage has been substantially preserved. Restored 18th- and 19th-century structures have been adapted for use as shops, boutique hotels, galleries, cafes, bars, offices, and apartments. In the evening, many of the finer buildings are beautifully illuminated. In the summer, sections of rue St-Paul turn into pedestrian-only lanes. The neighborhood even has an official website: www.vieux.montreal.qc.ca.

About a 20-minute walk west of Vieux-Montréal is a neighborhood called Little Burgundy. You'll pass through it if you head to the Atwater Market. It's a small stretch along rue Notre Dame ouest that is slowly but surely becoming a hipster haven for its vintage shops, antique and quirky item boutiques, bars, and—especially—its eateries. This strip is mentioned in the restaurant and nightlife chapters.

Plateau Mont-Royal & Mile End "The Plateau" is where many Montréalers feel most at home—away from downtown's chattering pace and the more touristed Vieux-Montréal. It's where locals dine, shop, play, and live.

Bounded roughly by rue Sherbrooke to the south, boulevard St-Joseph to the north, avenue Papineau to the east, and rue St-Urbain to the west, the Plateau has a vibrant ethnic atmosphere that fluctuates and shifts with each new immigration surge.

Rue St-Denis runs the length of the district from south to north and is the thumping central artery of Francophone Montréal, as central to French-speaking Montréal as boulevard St-Germain is to Paris. It is thick with cafes, bistros, offbeat shops, and lively nightspots, and is a great walking street for taking in the pulse of Francophone life. There are no museums or important galleries on St-Denis, nor is the architecture notable, which relieves visitors of the chore of obligatory sightseeing. Do as the locals do: pause over bowls of café au lait at any of the numerous terraces that line the avenue.

Boulevard St-Laurent, running parallel to rue St-Denis, has a more polyglot flavor. Known as "the Main," St-Laurent was the boulevard first encountered by foreigners tumbling off ships at the waterfront. They simply shouldered their belongings and walked north, peeling off into adjoining streets when they heard familiar tongues or smelled the drifting aromas of food reminiscent of the old country. Without its gumbo of languages and cultures, St-Laurent would be something of an urban eyesore. It's not pretty in the conventional sense. But its ground-floor windows are filled with glistening golden chickens, collages of shoes and pastries and aluminum cookware, curtains of sausages, and the daringly far-fetched garments of designers on the forward edge of Montréal's active fashion industry.

Other major streets are avenue du Mont-Royal and avenue Laurier.

Many warehouses and former tenements in the Plateau have been converted to house this panoply of shops, bars, and high- and low-cost eateries, their often-garish signs drawing eyes away from the still-dilapidated upper stories.

Adjoining Plateau Mont-Royal at its northwest corner, Mile End is a blossoming neighborhood contained by boulevard St-Joseph on the south, rue Bernard in the north, rue St-Laurent on the east, and avenue du Parc on the west. It's outside of the usual tourist orbit but has a growing number of retail attractions, including designer boutiques, shops specializing in household goods, and some great restaurants.

Mile End has many pockets of ethnic mini neighborhoods, including Italian, Hassidic, Portuguese, and Greek. The area some still call Greektown, for instance, runs along avenue du Parc and is thick with restaurants and taverns.

Parc Du Mont-Royal Not many cities have a mountain at their core. Reality insists that Montréal doesn't either, as what it calls a "mountain" would be seen as a very large hill by many other people. Still, Montréal is named for this outcrop—its "Royal Mountain."

No matter; the park here is a soothing urban pleasure. With trails for hiking and cross-country skiing, the park is well used by Montréalers, who refer to it simply and affectionately as "the Mountain." Buses travel through the park, and if you're in moderately good shape you can walk to the top in 1 to 3 hours from downtown, depending on the route taken. See p. 124 for a suggested walking tour.

On its northern slope are two cemeteries, one that used to be Anglophone and Protestant, the other Francophone and Catholic—reminders of the city's historic linguistic and religious division.

OTHER AREAS OF THE CITY

These neighborhoods, islands, and *quartiers* are mentioned less frequently in this book, but each has a special character and an appeal for pockets of visitors.

Olympic Park A 20-minute drive east of downtown on rue Sherbrooke is Olympic Park, named for Stade Olympique (Olympic Stadium), the stadium Montréal built for the 1976 Olympic Games. The stadium itself is not likely to be particularly appealing to most visitors, but within walking distance from the stadium are the city's lovely Jardin Botanique (Botanical Garden) and three attractions of special interest to children: Biodôme de Montréal, Insectarium de Montréal, and the new Rio Tinto Alcan Planétarium.

Quartier International When Route 720 was constructed in the early 1970s, it left behind a desolate swath of empty space, smack-dab between downtown and Vieux-Montréal. It has blossomed in the decades since into a business center, with new parks, office buildings (notably agencies or businesses with an international focus, hence the name "International Quarter"), and the Palais des Congrès (Convention Center). The convention center, in fact, is a design triumph, as unlikely as that seems. Transparent glass exterior walls are a crazy quilt of pink, yellow, blue, green, red, and purple rectangles. You can step into the inside hallway for the full effect—when the sun streams in, it's like being inside a huge kaleidoscope. The walls are the vision of Montréal architect Mario Saia.

A small plaza opposite the convention center's west side is named for Jean-Paul Riopelle (1923–2002), a prominent Québec artist. One of his sculptures stands here (and more can be seen at the Musée des Beaux-Arts). The well-regarded restaurant Toqué! is on this square.

The Quartier is bounded, more or less, by rue St-Jacques on the south, avenue

Viger on the north, rue St-Urbain on the east, and rue University on the west.

Quartier Des Spectacles This 1-square kilometer spot is known as the city's cultural heart. It's here that you'll find venues for opera, music concerts, many of the city's indoor and outdoor festivals, comedy shows, digital art displays, and more. There are, in fact, 80 cultural venues here, including Place des Arts and the Musée d'Art Contemporain de Montréal. It has its own website, at www.quartierdesspectacles.com. The Quartier is bounded by boulevard René-Lévesque, rue Sherbrooke, City Councillors, and rue St-Hubert.

The Village Also known as the Gay Village (really), Montréal's gay and lesbian enclave is one of North America's largest. It's a compact, but vibrant district filled with dance clubs, cafes, clothing stores, and antiques shops. It runs along rue Ste-Catherine est from rue St-Hubert to rue Papineau and onto side streets. A rainbow, the symbol of the gay community, marks the Beaudry Métro station, which is on rue Ste-Catherine in the heart of the neighborhood.

In recent years, the city has made the length of rue Ste-Catherine in the Village pedestrian-only for the entire summer. Bars and restaurants build ad-hoc terraces into the street, and a summer-resort atmosphere pervades.

Parc Jean-Drapeau: Ile Ste-Helene & Ile Notre-Dame Connected by two bridges, these two small islands make up Parc Jean-Drapeau (www.parcjeandrapeau.com), which is almost entirely car-free and accessible by Métro.

St. Helen's Island was altered extensively to become the site of Expo 67, Montréal's very successful World's Fair in 1967. In the 4 years before the Expo, construction crews doubled its surface area with landfill, and then went on to create Ile Notre-Dame beside it. When the World's Fair was over, the city preserved the site and a few of its exhibition buildings.

Today, people flock to the park to use the popular summertime Aquatic Complex, the La Ronde amusement park, and the Casino de Montréal.

Latin Quarter The southern end of rue St-Denis runs near the concrete campus of the Université du Québec à Montréal (UQAM). This is the Latin Quarter (in French, Quartier Latin), and decidedly student-oriented, rife with the visual messiness that characterizes student and bohemian quarters. Loud indie rock pours out of cheap bars, and young adults in jeans and leather swap philosophical insights and telephone numbers.

The Underground City During Montréal's long winters, life slows above-ground on the streets of downtown as people escape into *la ville souterraine*, an extensive subterranean universe (though it is used year-round). Here, in a controlled climate that recalls an eternal spring, it's possible to arrive at the railroad station, check into a hotel, shop for days, and go out for dinner—all without stepping outdoors.

The city calls it the "underground pedestrian network," but most locals still use the colloquial name "underground city." It got its start when major downtown developments—including as Place Ville-Marie (the city's first skyscraper), Place Bonaventure, Complexe Desjardins, Palais des Congrès, and Place des Arts—put their below-street-level areas to profitable use, leasing space for shops and other enterprises. Over time—in fits and starts, and with no master plan—these spaces became connected with Métro stations, and then with each other through underground tunnels. It slowly became possible to travel much of downtown through a maze of corridors, tunnels, and plazas. Today, some 1,000 retailers and eateries are in or connected to the network.

The term "underground city" is not 100 percent accurate because of how some complexes funnel people through their spaces. In Place Bonaventure, for instance, passengers can exit the Métro and find themselves peering out a window several floors above the street.

Natural light is let in wherever possible, which drastically reduces the feeling of

JULY 1: citywide MOVING DAY

Montréal is an island of renters, and close to 100,000 people move from old apartments to new ones every July 1—on that date, and only that date. That's the day all rental leases are required to start, a date chosen in part so that it doesn't fall within the school year. The date also, not coincidentally, coincides with Canada's National Day, ensuring that separatist-minded Francophone Québécois won't have time to celebrate that national holiday.

All but certain to be miserably hot and humid, July 1 is a trial that can, nevertheless, be hilarious to observe. See families struggle to get bedroom sets and large appliances down narrow outdoor staircases! Watch sidewalks become obstacle courses of baby cribs, bicycles, and overflowing cardboard boxes! Listen to the cacophony of horns as streets become clogged with every serviceable van, truck, and SUV! Later in the day, hundreds of people arrive at their new digs and discover gifts of junk no longer desired by their predecessors—busted furniture, pantries of old food, pitiful plants. Unless you're interested in observing the mayhem or taking advantage of the best trash picking of the year, you'll want to avoid strolls or drives in residential areas on that day.

claustrophobia that some malls evoke. However, the underground city covers a vast area without the convenience of a logical street grid, so it can be confusing. There are plenty of signs, but it's wise to make careful note of landmarks at key corners along your route if you want to return to where you started. Expect to get lost, but consider it part of the fun of exploring.

GETTING AROUND

By Foot

Montréal is a terrific walking city. All the neighborhoods listed in this book are compact enough to be easily experienced by foot. Other transportation—Métro, bus, bike, taxi, car—will generally only be necessary when traveling from one neighborhood to another.

One thing to keep in mind when walking is to cross only at street corners and only when you have a green light or a walk sign. City police are known to issue tickets to jaywalkers in an attempt to cut down on the number of accidents involving pedestrians.

Travelers in wheelchairs or using strollers will find the city generally accommodating. Sidewalks have curb cuts for easy passage onto the streets. See p. 213 for more information about navigating the city by wheelchair.

By Métro

For speed and economy, nothing beats Montréal's **Métro system,** operated by the **STM (Société de transport de Montréal).** The stations are marked on the street by blue-and-white signs that show a circle enclosing a down-pointing arrow. The Métro is relatively clean, and quiet trains whisk passengers through a decent network. It runs from about 5:30am to 12:30am, Sunday through Friday, and until about 1am on Saturday night (technically Sun morning). Information is available online at www.stm.info or by phone at ✆ **514/786-4636.**

Fares are set by the ride, not by distance. A single ride, on either the bus or Métro, costs C$3. You can purchase tickets for cash only from a booth attendant at a Métro station, where you can buy a set of 10 tickets for C$24.50. Automatic vending machines take credit cards. There is also the added option of buying a two-trips ticket for C$5.50. Tickets serve as proof of payment, so hold onto them for the duration of your trip. Transit police make periodic checks at transfer points or upon exiting and the fine for not having a ticket can run as high as C$500.

One-day and three-day passes are a good deal if you plan to use the Métro more than twice a day. You get unlimited access to the Métro and bus network for 1 day for C$9 or 3 consecutive days for C$18. The front of the card has scratch-off sections like a lottery card—you scratch out the month and day (or 3 consecutive days) on which you're using the card. They're available at select stations; find the list at www.stm.info.

You'll see locals using the plastic OPUS smart card, on which fares can be loaded on automated machines. The transit authority is pushing the use of the new cards, which create less trash and whose purchase can be automated. Blank OPUS cards must first be purchased for C$6 before any value is loaded onto them, so unless you're a frequent traveler to the city, the paper tickets and 1- or 3-day passes are your best bets.

To pay, either slip your paper ticket into the slot in the turnstile and take it as it comes out, or show your pass to the booth attendant. A single paper ticket acts as its own transfer ticket; there are 2 hours from the time a ticket is first validated to transfer, and you insert the ticket into the machine of the next bus or Métro train.

The system is not immune to transit strikes, and convenient as it is, there can be substantial distances between stations. Accessibility is sometimes difficult for people with mobility restrictions or parents with strollers.

Smartphone users can download the STM app for iPhone and Android from the App Store and Google Play. You can access daily bus and subway schedules, view first and last departure times, and save routes, among other options.

By Bus

Bus fares are the same as fares for Métro trains, and Métro tickets are good on buses, too. Exact change is required if you want to pay on the bus. Although they run throughout the city and give tourists the advantage of traveling aboveground, buses don't run as frequently or as swiftly as the Métro (see "Montréal by Métro," above).

By Bike

Montréal has an exceptionally great system of bike paths, and bicycling is common not just for recreation, but for transportation, as well.

Since 2009, a self-service bicycle rental program called BIXI (www.bixi.com; ✆ **877/820-2453**) has become a big presence in the city. A combination of the words *bicyclette* and *taxi,* BIXI is similar to programs in Paris, Barcelona, and Toronto, where users pick up bikes from designated stands throughout the city and drop them off at any other stand, for a small fee. Some 5,000 bikes are in operation and available at 400 stations in Montréal's central boroughs. While 1-year and 30-day subscriptions are available, visitors can buy a 24-hour access pass for C$5. During those 24 hours, you can borrow bikes as many times as you want, and for each trip, the first 45 minutes are free. Trips longer than 45 minutes incur additional charges, which are added onto the initial C$5 fee. Depending on your needs, zipping on and off BIXI bikes throughout the day can be both an economical and a fun way to get around. Take note that BIXI only operates from April through November before shutting down during the harsh winter months. See p. 11 for a personal take on BIXI.

If you're looking for a bike for a full day or longer, it will be cheaper to rent a bike from a shop (you'll also need to rent helmets and locks, as BIXI doesn't provide these). One of the most centrally located is **Ça Roule/Montréal on Wheels** (www.caroulemontreal.com; © **877/866-0633** or 514/866-0633), at 27 rue de la Commune est, the waterfront road in Vieux-Port.

A huge network of bicycle paths runs throughout the city, with whole sections of roads turned into bike lanes during the warm months. The nonprofit biking organization **Vélo Québec** (www.velo.qc.ca; © **800/567-8356** or 514/521-8356) has the most up-to-date information on the state of bike paths and offers guided tours throughout the province (*vélo* means "bicycle" in French).

Passengers can take bicycles on the Métro from 10am to 3pm and after 7pm on weekdays, and all day weekends and holidays. This rule is suspended on special-event days, when trains are too crowded. Board the first car of the train, which can hold a maximum of four bikes (if there are already four bikes on that car, you have to wait for the next train). Details are online at **www.stm.info/en/info/advice/bicycles**.

Several taxi companies participate in the **Taxi+Vélo** program. You call, tell them you have a bike to transport, and a cab with a bike rack arrives. Up to three bikes can be carried for an extra fee of C$3 each. Participating companies are at www.velo.qc.ca (search for *taxi+vélo*); **Taxi Diamond** (© **514/273-6331**) is one choice.

By Taxi

Cabs come in a variety of colors and styles, so their principal distinguishing feature is the plastic sign on the roof. At night, the sign is illuminated when the cab is available. The initial charge is C$3.30. Each additional kilometer (½ mile) adds C$1.70, and each minute of waiting adds C63¢. A short ride from one point to another downtown usually costs under C$8. Tip about 10 to 15 percent.

Members of hotel and restaurant staffs can call cabs, many of which are dispatched by radio. They line up outside most large hotels or can be hailed on the street.

Montréal taxi drivers range in temperament from unstoppably loquacious to sullen and cranky—just like any other city. Similarly, some know the city well; others have sketchy geographical knowledge and poor language skills. It's a good idea to have your destination written down—with the cross street—to show your driver. Also keep in mind that not all drivers accept credit cards.

By Car

Montréal is an easy city to navigate by car, although traffic during morning and late-afternoon rush hour can be horrendous. As well, seemingly endless construction in the downtown corridor can be a nightmare. If you'll be doing much driving, pick up the pocket-sized atlas published by JDM Géo and MapArt (www.mapartmaps.com), sold for about C$10 at gas stations throughout Canada. The map offers good detail, especially in the areas outside the primary tourist orbit.

If you've got a smartphone that you've enabled with an international data plan before your arrival, you can easily use your device's GPS navigation function, although this uses a lot of data roaming and can be prohibitively expensive. There are apps that can be downloaded to your mobile device such as **NavFree GPS Canada** which can be used in offline mode to view pre-loaded maps much as you would a traditional paper map.

It can be difficult to park for free on downtown Montréal's heavily trafficked streets, but there are plenty of metered spaces. Traditional meters are set well back from the curb so they won't be buried by plowed snow in winter. Computerized Pay and Go stations are in use in many neighborhoods, too. Look for the black metal kiosks, columns about 1.8m (6 ft.) tall with a white "P" in a blue circle. Press the "English" button, enter the letter from the space where you are parked, and then pay with cash or a credit card, following the onscreen instructions. Depending on which part of town you're in, parking costs C$3 to C$4 per hour, and meters are in effect every day until 9pm. Be sure to check for signs noting parking restrictions, usually showing a red circle with a diagonal slash. The words LIVRAISON SEULEMENT mean "delivery only."

Most downtown shopping complexes have underground parking lots, as do the big downtown hotels. Some hotels offer in and out privileges, letting you take your car in and out of the garage without a fee—useful if you plan to do some sightseeing by car.

The limited-access expressways in Québec are called autoroutes, with distances given in kilometers (km) and speed limits given in kilometers per hour (kmph). Because French is the province's official language, most highway signs are only in French, though Montréal's autoroutes and bridges often bear dual-language signs. In Québec, the highway speed limit is 100 kmph (62 mph), and toll roads are rare.

One traffic signal function often confuses newcomers: Should you wish to make a turn and you know that the street runs in the correct direction, you may be surprised to initially see a green arrow pointing straight ahead instead of a green light permitting the turn. The arrow gives pedestrians time to cross the intersection. After a moment, the light will turn from an arrow to a regular green light and you can proceed with your turn.

A blinking green light means that oncoming traffic still has a red light, making it safe to make a left turn. Turning right on a red light is prohibited on the island of Montréal, except where specifically allowed by an additional green arrow. Off the island, it is legal to turn right after stopping at red lights, except where there's a sign specifically prohibiting that move.

Drivers using cellphones are required to have hands-free devices. Radar detectors are illegal in Québec. Even if it's off, you can be fined for having one in sight.

While most visitors arriving by plane or train will want to rely on public transportation and cabs, a **rental car** can come in handy for trips outside of town or if you plan to drive to Québec City. Terms, cars, and prices for car rentals are similar to those in the rest of North America and Europe, and all the major companies operate in Québec. A charge is usually levied when you return a car at a location other than the one from which it was rented.

Québec is the first Canadian province to mandate that residents have radial snow tires on their cars in winter. The law, which went into effect in 2008, runs from mid-December until March 15. Rental-car agencies are required to provide snow tires on car rentals during that period, and many charge an extra, nonnegotiable fee.

The minimum driving age is 16 in Québec, but some car-rental companies will not rent to people under 25. Others charge higher rates for drivers under the age of 21. Renters under 25 may be asked for a major credit card in the same name as their driver's license.

[Fast FACTS] MONTRÉAL

Below are useful facts and phone numbers while you're traveling in the city. For more information about the province overall, see chapter 18.

ATMs/Banks ATMs *(guichet automatique)* and banks are easy to find in all parts of the city. In Canada, some debit cards require a four-digit pin and if your card has a longer one it might be declined. Alerting your bank or credit card companies in advance of travel can prevent them from freezing your account.

Also, as in other countries, it's common to be charged fees when withdrawing from ATMs.

Business Hours Most stores in the province are open from 9 or 10am until 5 or 6pm Monday through Wednesday, 9 or 10am to 9pm on Thursday and Friday, 9 or 10am to 5 or 6pm on Saturday, and Sunday from noon to 5pm.

Doctors & Hospitals Hospitals with emergency rooms include **Hôpital Général de Montréal,** 1650 rue Cedar (✆ **514/934-1934**), and **Hôpital Royal Victoria,** 687 av. des Pins ouest (✆ **514/934-1934**). **Hôpital de Montréal pour Enfants,** 2300 rue Tupper (✆ **514/412-4400**), is a children's hospital. All three are associated with McGill University.

Embassies & Consulates See p. 214 in Chapter 18.

Emergencies Dial 911 for police, fire, or ambulance assistance.

Internet Access Many public spaces such as cafes have free Wi-Fi. Hotel lobbies are often free Wi-Fi hotspots, but many charge a daily access rate.

Mail & Postage English-language services are offered at about one out of four post offices in the city, including 157 rue St-Antoine ouest in Vieux-Montréal and 800 René-Lévesque ouest in downtown. See p. 216 in Chapter 18 for postage rates.

Newspapers & Magazines "The Globe and Mail" (www.theglobeandmail.com) is Canada's national English-language paper, and the "Montréal Gazette" (www.montrealgazette.com) is the city's primary English-language paper.

Pharmacies A pharmacy is called a *pharmacie;* a drugstore is a *droguerie.* A large chain in Montréal is **Pharmaprix**. Its branch at 5122 Chemin De La Cote-Des-Neiges (www.pharmaprix.ca; ✆ **514/738-8464**) is open 24 hours a day, 7 days a week.

Safety Montréal is an extremely safe city. See p. 218 for more.

WHERE TO STAY IN MONTRÉAL

5

Montréal's boutique hotels are the superstars for travelers' accommodations. In Vieux-Montréal, historical buildings have been transformed into chic modern getaways—it's hard to top the ambience of old stone walls while you cozy up in crisp white sheets. Decor ranges from Asian minimalist to country luxury. A good room in one of these smaller hotels could provide the best memory of your trip.

On the flipside, familiar hotel chains, many of which were built for Expo 67, may have time against them, but their central location downtown is key, particularly for festival-goers. Recent renovations at several addresses have put some back in the stylish category, often with the added bonus of a pool. For some travelers, they will hold more appeal.

The tourist authorities in the province of Québec have their own rating system (zero to five stars) for establishments that host travelers. A shield bearing the assigned rating is posted near the entrance to most hotels. The Québec system is based on quantitative measures such as the range of services and amenities.

The stars you see in this book are based on our own rating system, developed by Frommer's, which is more subjective than the state's. We take into account price-to-value ratios, quality of service, ambience, and helpfulness of staff.

All rooms have private bathrooms unless otherwise noted. Most Montréal hotels are entirely nonsmoking.

Because the region is so cold for so many months of the year, tourism here is cyclical. That means that prices drop—often steeply—for many properties much of the September-through-April period. Hotel rates are highest during the region's busiest times, from May to October, reaching a peak during Grand Prix in June, and remaining highest in July and August. Rates also inflate during the winter carnivals in January and February. (Festivals and dates are listed on p. 100.) For those periods, reserve well in advance.

Most goods and services in Canada have a federal tax of 5 percent (the TPS). On top of that, the province of Québec adds a tax that comes out to 7.88 percent (the TVQ). An additional accommodations tax of 3.5 percent is in effect on hotel bills in Montréal. Prices listed in this book do not include taxes.

best HOTEL BETS

- **Best Hotels for a Romantic Getaway:** The sunny atrium, cozy lobby, and luxurious amenities at **Hôtel Nelligan**—not to mention the cobblestoned streets and passing horse-drawn carriages outside—make this

WHERE TO FIND HOTEL bargains

The city-run Tourisme Montréal offers **"Sweet Deals"** on hotels year round. From June 1 to October 15 book 2 nights and get 50 percent off a third night; the rest of the year you get your second night for half price. Many of the hotels listed in this book are included. When you book a Sweet Deal package you also get a booklet of coupons that include discounts at museums, cruises, and spas. For more information, visit www.tourisme-montreal.org/Offers for details.

Deals for some city's smaller hotels are available through the **Association des Petits Hôtels de Montréal** (www.petitshotelsmontreal.com/en). Of course, you might also find discounts of up to 20 percent for rooms on websites such as Hotels.com or Expedia.com.

Old Montréal spot a choice retreat for couples. See p. 49. **Auberge du Vieux-Port,** around the corner and owned by the same hotel group, is smaller and cozier still. See p. 48.

- **Best Value:** The decor at **Auberge Bonaparte** is quintessential Old Montréal, and morning meals are large and served in the elegant Bonaparte restaurant. See p. 49. If you want to be closer to the arts district of Quartier des Spectacles, consider **Hôtel Le Dauphin Montréal-Downtown,** which offers sparkly competence. See p. 47. And if you want to be based in the Plateau, **Hôtel de l'Institut,** run by students at the city's premier hospitality school, is always in tip-top shape and has an excellent in-house restaurant to boot. See p. 52.
- **Best High-End Design Hotel: Hôtel Gault** leaves its raw concrete uncovered and incorporates candy-colored furniture. See p. 49.
- **Best Bets for Families:** Downtown, rooms in the converted warehouse **Le Square Phillips Hôtel & Suites** provide ample space and everything needed for a home away from home, including en-suite kitchens. A pool and rooftop terrace are nice bonuses. See p. 47. In Vieux-Montréal at **Le Saint-Sulpice Hôtel Montréal,** every unit is a suite, and every nearby street has some sort of attraction targeted to kids (p. 50). (There's even a cupcake cafe just across the street.)
- **Best Uniquely Québec B&B–like Hotel:** In a 1723 structure in Vieux-Montréal, **Auberge Les Passants du Sans Soucy** is more upscale and stylish than most of its peers, and it's near the Old City's top restaurants. See p. 50.

DOWNTOWN/CENTRE-VILLE

Montréal's central business area is home to big hotel chains, but you can also find a sprinkling of boutique hotels. This area holds a lot of appeal for business travelers or folks attending any of the festivals that take place around the Quartier des Spectacles. Shoppers, too, will appreciate this area since you're in the heart of retail heaven. The downside, however, is that most of the newest bars and restaurants are in Vieux-Montréal or the Plateau, so staying here might require a few taxi rides.

Good global chain outposts are **Sofitel Montréal Golden Mile** (1155 rue Sherbrooke ouest; www.sofitel.com; ✆ **800/763-4835** or 514/285-9000); **Le Centre Sheraton Montréal Hôtel** (1201 boulevard René-Lévesque ouest; www.sheraton.com/lecentre; ✆ **888/627-7102** or 514/878-2000); **Hilton Montréal Bonaventure**

Downtown Montréal Hotels

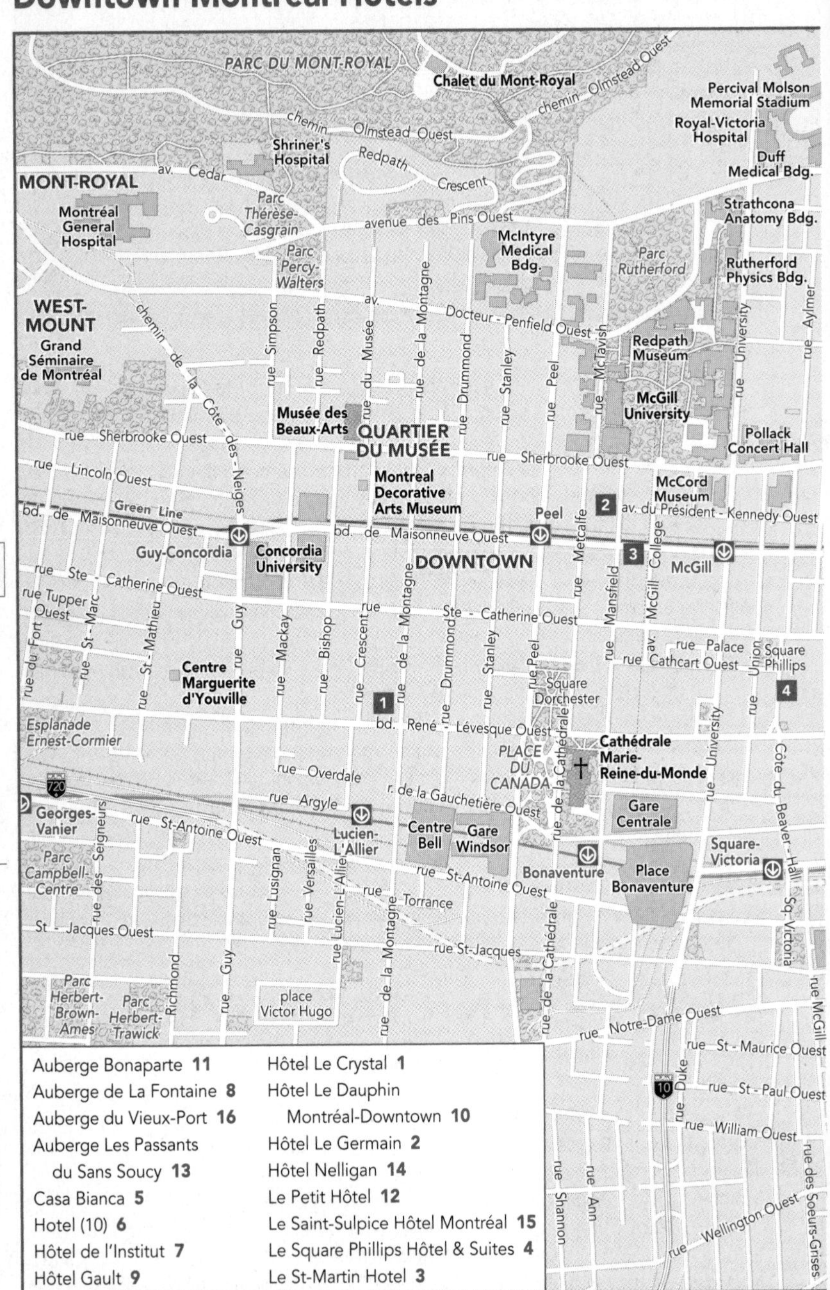

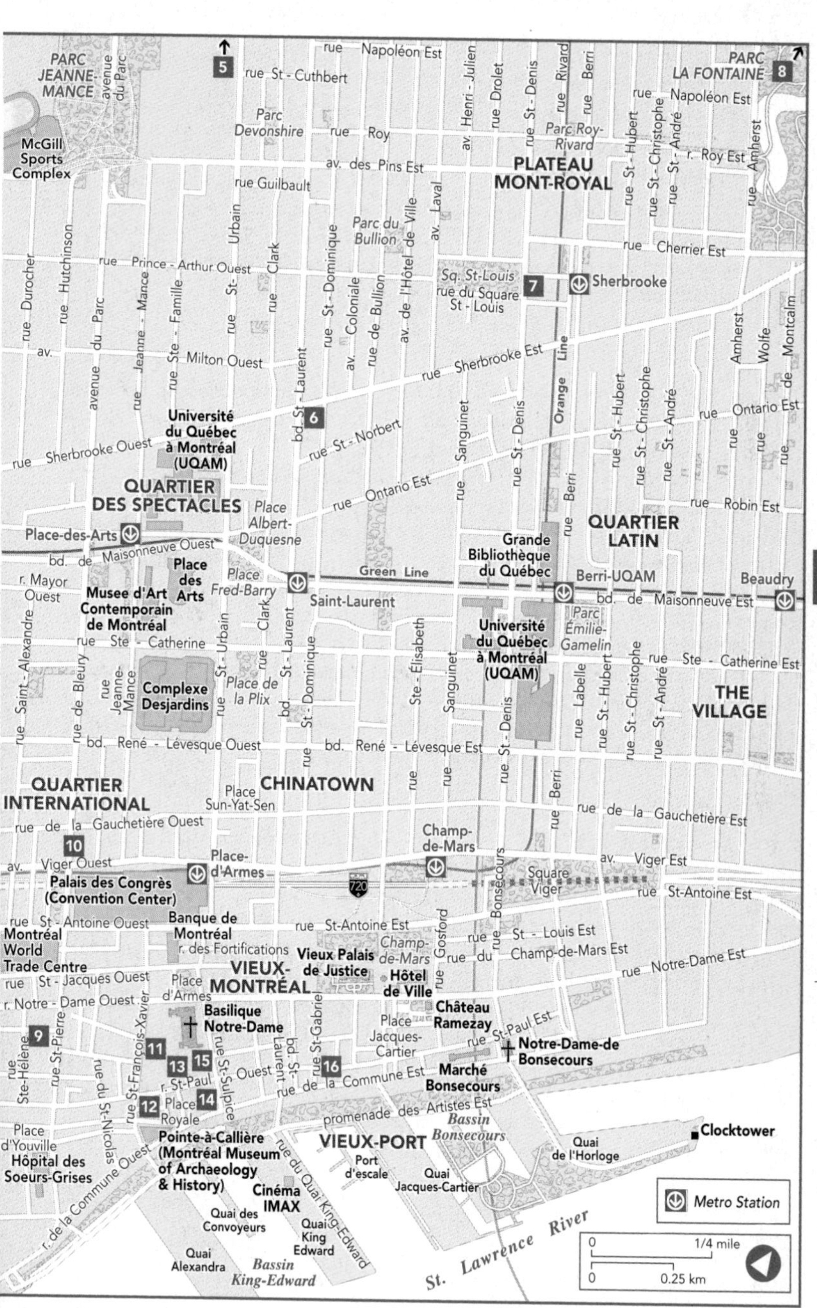

PARC JEANNE-MANCE
McGill Sports Complex
rue Napoléon Est
rue St-Cuthbert
Parc Devonshire
rue Roy
av. des Pins Est
rue Guilbault
PLATEAU MONT-ROYAL
Parc Roy-Rivard
PARC LA FONTAINE
r. Roy Est
rue Cherrier Est
Parc du Bullion
rue Prince-Arthur Ouest
Sq. St-Louis
rue du Square St-Louis
Sherbrooke
av. Milton Ouest
rue Sherbrooke Est
rue Sherbrooke Ouest
rue St-Norbert
rue Ontario Est
rue Robin Est
Université du Québec à Montréal (UQAM)
QUARTIER DES SPECTACLES
Place Albert-Duquesne
Place-des-Arts
bd. de Maisonneuve Ouest
Place des Arts
Place Fred-Barry
Musee d'Art Contemporain de Montréal
r. Mayor Ouest
Green Line
Orange Line
Saint-Laurent
Grande Bibliothèque du Québec
QUARTIER LATIN
Berri-UQAM
Beaudry
bd. de Maisonneuve Est
Parc Émilie-Gamelin
rue Ste-Catherine
rue Ste-Catherine Est
Complexe Desjardins
Place de la Plix
THE VILLAGE
bd. René-Lévesque Ouest
bd. René-Lévesque Est
QUARTIER INTERNATIONAL
Place Sun-Yat-Sen
CHINATOWN
rue de la Gauchetière Ouest
rue de la Gauchetière Est
Champ-de-Mars
av. Viger Ouest
av. Viger Est
Place-d'Armes
Palais des Congrès (Convention Center)
Square Viger
rue St-Antoine Est
rue St-Antoine Ouest
Banque de Montréal
r. des Fortifications
Montréal World Trade Centre
Vieux Palais de Justice
Champ-de-Mars
rue St-Louis Est
rue du Champ-de-Mars Est
rue Notre-Dame Est
rue St-Jacques Ouest
Place d'Armes
VIEUX-MONTRÉAL
Hôtel de Ville
r. Notre-Dame Ouest
Basilique Notre-Dame
Château Ramezay
Place Jacques-Cartier
rue St-Paul Est
Notre-Dame-de Bonsecours
r. St-Paul Ouest
rue de la Commune Est
Marché Bonsecours
Place Royale
promenade des Artistes Est
Bassin Bonsecours
Place d'Youville
Pointe-à-Callière (Montréal Museum of Archaeology & History)
VIEUX-PORT
Port d'escale
Quai de l'Horloge
Clocktower
Hôpital des Soeurs-Grises
Quai Jacques-Cartier
Cinéma IMAX
Quai des Convoyeurs
Quai King Edward
rue du Quai King-Edward
r. de la Commune Ouest
Quai Alexandra
Bassin King-Edward
St. Lawrence River
Metro Station
0 1/4 mile
0 0.25 km

Hotel Rates in Montréal

Following is an explanation of the hotel rates as we define them in this book:

Expensive	C$200 and up
Moderate	C$100–C$200
Inexpensive	Under C$100

As with Quebéc City's hotels, the prices listed in this book are by no means written in stone, and should be used more as a guideline for comparing properties.

Rates provided in this book are typical of Montréal's high season in summer (typically June–Aug), though rates may be even higher when there are popular tourist events going on, such as the Grand Prix weekend in June and the Festival International de Jazz in late June and early July. Rates can be much lower when tourism is slow (Jan–Mar and Apr).

(900 de la Gauchetière ouest; www.hiltonmontreal.com; ✆ **800/HILTONS** or 514/878-2332); and **Hilton Garden Inn** (380 rue Sherbrooke ouest; www.hiltongardenmontreal.com; ✆ **877/STAY-HGI** or 514/840-0010).

You can also find your fill of dependable high-end chain properties too: **Ritz-Carlton Montréal** (1228 rue Sherbrooke ouest; www.ritzmontreal.com; ✆ **800/363-0366** or 514/985-0464), which recently underwent a C$150-million renovation; **Fairmont the Queen Elizabeth** (900 boul. René-Lévesque ouest; www.fairmont.com/queen-elizabeth-montreal; ✆ **800/257-7544** or 506/863-6310), with 982 rooms; **Hyatt Regency** (1255 rue Jeanne-Mance; www.fairmont.com/queen-elizabeth-montreal; ✆ **877/571-6584** or 514/982-1234), which won gold in the province's tourism awards a few years ago; and the ever-chic **Loews Hôtel Vogue** (1425 rue de la Montagne; www.loewshotels.com; ✆ **800/465-6654** or 514/285-5555).

The hotels listed below offer either exceptional value for budget-minded travelers or an atmosphere that is unique to Montréal.

Expensive

Hôtel Le Crystal ★★ The Crystal was a big deal when it opened in 2008: a boutique hotel in a neighborhood not known for them (most are in Vieux-Montréal). Today, it's still a most welcome property for the area. Its location close to the Centre Bell arena (home to the beloved Canadiens hockey team and venue for big touring musical events) ensures that the swanky Crystal gets its share of visitors who are taking in (or performing at) these shows. A top-floor pool (indoor, ringed by glass windows) and outdoor all-season Jacuzzi and well-maintained wooden terrace are a big part of the Crystal's appeal. All the rooms are suites and the smallest, called the "Urban Suite," is certainly ample for most guests: 495 square feet, with separate living and sleeping areas and a kitchenette with an espresso machine. Enveloping sheets and luxurious mattresses are part of the mix, of course. The concierge was quick to offer advice and tips. The raucousness of rue Crescent and the endless shopping of rue Ste-Catherine are steps away, too.

1100 rue de la Montagne (at boul. René-Lévesque). www.hotellecrystal.com. ✆ **877/861-5550** or 514/861-5550. 131 units. From C$209 suite. Children 17 and under stay free in parent's room. Packages available. Valet parking C$32. Métro: Lucien L'Allier. Pets accepted (C$75 cleaning fee). **Amenities:** Restaurant; wine bar; concierge; exercise room; Jacuzzi; pool; room service; spa service; free Wi-Fi.

Hôtel Le Germain ★★ Stylish design, comfortable beds, large bathrooms with quality amenities, and a location on a quiet street just steps from main thoroughfares—those are four big pluses in this trim hotel's favor. As at its sister boutique hotel, the equally desirable **Hôtel Le Germain-Dominion** in Québec City (p. 47), this Germain creates a cozy-chic atmosphere, from the lobby (elegant and cool) to the hallways (with side tables with bowls of apples for the taking) to the rooms themselves (white bedding with accents in fuchsia and lime green). The hotel draws a mix of business people, vacationers, and families of students at McGill University, which is just up the street. The ample "deluxe continental" breakfast buffet, included in the room rate, usually includes egg dishes, cold cuts, cheeses, chocolate croissants, *crêpes,* fruit, yogurt, cappuccinos, and Montréal bagels.

2050 rue Mansfield (at av. du President-Kennedy). www.hotelgermain.com. ✆ **877/333-2050** or 514/849-2050. 101 units. From C$210. Rates include breakfast. Packages available. Valet parking C$27. Métro: Peel. Pets accepted (C$35 per day). **Amenities:** Restaurant; bar; concierge; exercise room; room service; free Wi-Fi.

Moderate

Hôtel Le Dauphin Montréal-Downtown ★★ The modest little Dauphin tries so hard and succeeds so well. It attracts both business people on a budget—it's right next door to the convention center—and families. The modest breakfast room where the free continental breakfast is served has a kind of genial hostel feeling. All rooms are the same size, but with different bed configurations. A few have 2 beds, about a quarter have kings, and the rest have queens. There are 4 junior suites. Rooms are simple, but still modern (think Ikea), and kept in tip-top shape; they received fresh paint and granite countertops in 2013. The location is generally quiet except nights when there are big festivals at the convention center, and it's about a 15-minute walk to Vieux-Montréal in one direction and the Quartier des Spectacles in the other. Because so many guests are single travelers, listed prices are for one guest, with a second guest for an additional C$10 per night. The hotel is entirely non-smoking and has a charging station for electric cars.

1025 rue de Bleury (near av. Viger). www.hoteldauphin.ca. ✆ **888/784-3888** or 514/788-3888. 72 units. C$120–C$180 single; C$10 for a second person. Rates include breakfast. Packages available. Parking C$20 at convention center. Métro: Place d'Armes. **Amenities:** Exercise room; free Wi-Fi.

Le Square Phillips Hôtel & Suites ★★ One of the great downtown hotel options for families, especially on weekends when business travelers have cleared out and the prices are often lower. Rooms here are big with high ceilings, thanks to the building's previous life as a warehouse, and some have dramatic columns and arches, also remnants from its previous incarnation. Even the smallest of rooms are decent-sized studios, with the bed separated from the living area. There's an indoor rooftop pool and a laundry room, and every unit has a full kitchen including a large fridge and stove. The staff has been getting raves from customers for years for their helpfulness, particularly for visiting families. The warehouse walls are also handy for muffling the noise: rooms here are close to a lot of action (both the busy shopping street rue Ste-Catherine and the Quartier des Spectacles arts district are around the corner), but seem to be totally insulated from it. Exactly what you want on a holiday.

1193 Square Phillips (south of rue Ste-Catherine ouest). www.squarephillips.com. ✆ **866/393-1193** or 514/393-1193. 160 units. Studios from C$140; suites from C$160. Rates include breakfast. Packages available. Valet parking C$22. Métro: McGill. **Amenities:** Babysitting; concierge; exercise room; laundry room; heated indoor pool; free Wi-Fi.

One More Reason to Work Out

If you're staying at a hotel that doesn't have a fitness center or whose exercise room is modest, keep **Club Sportif MAA** in mind (www.clubsportifmaa.com; ✆ **514/845-2233**). Located centrally downtown at 2070 rue Peel, between rue Sherbrooke and boulevard de Maisonneuve, the luxury facility has a 743-sq.-m (8,000-sq.-ft.) state-of-the-art gym with cardio and strength-training equipment, a lap pool, and a full schedule of classes—everything from spinning to Pilates to yoga. Day passes are available for C$25 and include most classes and use of the pool.

Le St-Martin Hotel ★ New in 2010, the St-Martin has a bit of a nightclubby feel to it, with its neon pink and cobalt blue accent lighting, chic in-house restaurant, and outdoor lap pool, which has a small, cute bridge that crosses it, and profuse greenery in warm months. The restaurant (**L'Aromate**), spills out to a sidewalk terrace for al fresco dining, and has a mezzanine in the lobby, too. Some rooms have unique glass corner windows, while others have modern-design standalone bathtubs or electric fireplaces. Given its young age, all the furniture and public areas are especially fresh and updated. Highrises on this block are tall, so rooms don't have much of a view, but that won't matter for most guests.

980 boul. de Maisonneuve ouest (at rue Mansfield). www.lestmartinmontreal.com. ✆ **877/843-3003** or 514/843-3000. 123 units. From C$195 double. Packages available. Valet parking C$29. Métro: Peel. **Amenities:** Restaurant; bar; fitness lounge; heated pool; room service; free Wi-Fi.

VIEUX-MONTRÉAL

Abutting the St. Lawrence River, Old Montréal was once the epicenter of all activity in the city. As Montréal grew, a "new" downtown emerged slightly to the north, and by the 1980s Vieux-Montréal had fallen to disrepair. Beginning in the 1990s, though, local business owners began a concerted effort to revitalize the neighborhood. Today, Vieux-Montréal is thriving and vibrant. Bars and avant-garde fashion boutiques have followed the hotelier's lead into the area, making it one of the city's hottest areas for both tourists and locals. Couples love it for its romantic appeal and foodies flock here for it great restaurants. Be prepared for lots of tourists, especially in summer.

Expensive

Auberge du Vieux-Port ★★ The stately Auberge du Vieux-Port offers a level of luxury that many try to copy, but few get right. Many rooms have expansive views of Vieux-Port and the St. Lawrence River, and the rooftop terrace provides an unobstructed panorama of both the waterfront and the old city—the perfect backdrop to enjoy a meal or sip a cocktail while drinking in the view. As with many upscale hotels in the Old City, here the owners celebrate the building's centuries-old history by incorporating the original brick, stone, and exposed beams into the architecture, while providing tasteful contemporary touches, as evidenced by the sleek and modern bathrooms in all rooms. Beds are enveloping and sexy. ***Tip:*** the rooftop terrace is a perfect spot to enjoy a drink while watching the Montréal Fireworks Competition, which runs from late June through July. The owners also offer a selection of studio, 1-, and

2-bedroom loft style apartments not far from the hotel, ideal for families and long-term stays.

97 rue de la Commune est (near rue St-Gabriel). www.aubergeduvieuxport.com. ✆ **888/660-7678** or 514/876-0081. 45 units. C$219–C$285 double. Rates include full breakfast and a "welcome cocktail." Valet parking C$28. Métro: Place-d'Armes or Champs-de-Mars. **Amenities:** Bar; babysitting; concierge; exercise room at sister hotel; room service; free Wi-Fi.

Hôtel Gault ★★ The Gault sets itself apart from its counterparts in many ways. For starters, although it's located in an ornate building from 1871, the interior design is sleek and minimalist. The blond wood and smooth concrete walls and floors of the lobby are counterbalanced by colorful contemporary furniture and photography by local artists. At just 30 rooms, attention to detail and style is customized by room, all of which are spacious. Some feature exposed brick walls adorned with several pieces of art; others feel more modern and feature taupe curtains and painted gray walls with gorgeous wood entryways. Colorful area rugs offset the cool feeling of the concrete floors and polished steel architect lamps. Rooms on the top floor all have balconies, providing a gorgeous view. The lobby has plenty of seating for guests' and the library behind the check-in desk area features books and design magazines—underscoring the management's commitment to detail.

449 rue Ste-Hélène (near rue Notre-Dame). www.hotelgault.com. ✆ **866/904-1616** or 514/904-1616. 30 units. C$179–C$249 double; C$209–C$569 suite. Rates include full breakfast. Packages available. Valet parking $32. Métro: Square Victoria. Pets accepted (C$50 per day). **Amenities:** Cafe; bar; babysitting; concierge; exercise room; room service; spa; free Wi-Fi.

Hôtel Nelligan ★★ Named after local 19th-century poet Émile Nelligan, this is the perfect compromise between the spaciousness of an upscale chain hotel and the chic decor and personalized service of a boutique property. Located in a series of converted 19th-century warehouses, the romantic 105-room Nelligan incorporates vintage style while maintaining the comforts and amenities of the 21st century. Amid all the brick and grey stonewalls, dark wood, and leather furnishings, the rooms are comfortable and welcoming. The common spaces create a communal feel that will make you want to stay all day—certainly doable considering the many private corners for reading or enjoying a cocktail from the either the atrium bar or rooftop terrace. A breathtaking central atrium adorned with contemporary art provides a glimpse toward the glass ceiling several stories up, and many rooms have a window overlooking it. But be warned: chatter from the downstairs **Verses Bar,** which serves drinks and food into the evening, can create unwanted background noise in some rooms.

106 rue St-Paul ouest (at rue St-Sulpice). www.hotelnelligan.com. ✆ **888/507-4084** or 438/899-9614. 105 units. From C$240 double. Packages available. Valet parking C$32. Métro: Place d'Armes. **Amenities:** 2 restaurants; bar; babysitting; concierge; exercise room; room service; free Wi-Fi.

Moderate

Auberge Bonaparte ★★ Auberge Bonaparte is one of the best deals in the city. The accommodations, quality of service, and amenities are comparable to its higher-priced competitors, yet you'll pay significantly less. A chandelier and oak-paneled walls greet you in the lobby, and rooms show off hardwood floors. Rooms at the lowest price point are on the small side but are comfortable and perfectly adequate. Square footage increases as you move up in price. Some rooms feature gorgeous exposed brick walls, and all of them have custom-built chairs and benches. Rooms on the courtyard side have a view of the Basilique Notre-Dame, which can also be seen from a rooftop terrace accessible to all guests. In 2013, the **Bonaparte** restaurant got a new bar and more dining space; this graceful restaurant is where your complimentary breakfast is served. In the evenings, the restaurant is usually packed, dishing out excellent renditions of French classics.

447 rue St-François-Xavier (just north of rue St-Paul). www.bonaparte.com. ✆ **514/844-1448.** 30 units. C$150–C$240 double; C$355 suite. Rates include full breakfast. Parking C$15 per day. Métro: Place d'Armes. **Amenities:** Restaurant; babysitting; concierge; access to nearby health club; room service; free Wi-Fi.

Auberge Les Passants du Sans Soucy ★★ Located smack dab in the center of Vieux-Montréal, this cozy inn feels like you've stepped into the world of Masterpiece Theater. Originally built in 1684, the building burned down, was rebuilt in 1723, and served as a fur warehouse for much of its existence. Many rooms feature original mortar and stonewalls and hand-hewn wooden beams that still bear the original carpenter's marks. With just nine rooms, service is very personalized—to the point where the hotel's owner will make you your choice of omelet for breakfast in the kitchen adjacent to the cozy dining area, which features stained glass artwork. Rooms are appealing and feel like a country cottage, with lace curtains and antique furniture design. The lobby doubles as an art gallery for local artists, so be sure to check out what's on display when you visit. ***Tip:*** Sans Soucy has legions of regulars who come back year after year, so book well in advance.

171 rue St-Paul ouest (at rue St-François-Xavier). www.lesanssoucy.com. ✆ **514/842-2634.** 9 units. C$165–C$195 double; C$230 suite. Rates include full breakfast. Parking C$16.50 per day. Métro: Place d'Armes. **Amenities:** Dry cleaning service; free Wi-Fi.

Le Petit Hôtel ★ Opened in 2009, Le Petit Hôtel has emerged as a chic newcomer to Old Montréal's hospitality landscape. The design caters to a younger, trendy demographic. The entire building feels like a showroom: the halls feature monochromatic artwork, but rather than spiffing up individual rooms with artwork, the units themselves become the art. Stonewalls are generally left unadorned, making way for the black furniture, white bedspreads, and neon orange chairs that create appealing contrast of colors. In the lobby, an orange ruffled crepe paper lamp dominates the room, and on the far back wall is a black and white sketched collage that's vaguely psychedelic. Rooms vary in size from tiny to extra large, so take your pick to suit your needs. There's a breakfast area as well as a coffee bar right at the front desk.

168 rue St-Paul ouest (at rue St-François-Xavier). www.petithotelmontreal.com. ✆ **877/530-0360** or 514/940-036024 units. C$209–C$299 double. Rates include continental breakfast. Packages available. Valet parking C$28. Métro: Place d'Armes. **Amenities:** Cafe; concierge; access to exercise rooms at sister hotels Hôtel Nelligan and Place d'Armes; free Wi-Fi.

Le Saint-Sulpice Hôtel Montréal ★★★ The Saint-Sulpice stands out from nearly all other boutique hotels in city in that each of its 108 units is a suite with fully equipped kitchen. Even the smallest units are spacious and feel like decked-out efficiency apartments. The middle and upper tier of room options feature separate bedrooms and larger floor plans. Rooms have a modern chic aesthetic—predominantly

A Room *Without* a View

Some of the more popular areas for hotels, including rue St-Paul in Vieux-Montréal, have bars and nightlife close by—great for partying, maybe not so good for sleeping. Bars are open until 3am in Montréal, so light sleepers should request rooms that face the back of the hotel or an inside courtyard.

The (Green) Keys to the City

The Hotel Association of Canada (HAC) oversees the **Green Key Eco-Rating Program** (in French, *Clé Verte*), which awards a rating of one to five green keys to hotels that minimize waste and reduce their carbon footprint. While HAC does not verify the audits on a national scale, the Corporation de l'industrie touristique du Québec (www.citq.info) does so within the province of Québec. Recipients often display a Green Key/Clé Verte plaque in a prominent location alongside other commendations. To locate Green Key hotels, visit **www.greenkeyglobal.com**.

shades of charcoal, sand, and mahogany, offset by touches of red. The main lobby area continues this color scheme. The suites are well suited for travelers who need extra space, and are ideal for families. All have a pullout sofa, and several have two bedrooms. In the lobby is a well-stocked bar, and there's an outdoor terrace where you can enjoy a meal prepared by the **Sinclair Restaurant,** which serves contemporary French cuisine in the full dining room on the bottom floor. Customer service is of the highest order here, from the valets who open the doors to the thoughtful cleaning crew who often fold stray articles of clothing you've left laying about.

414 rue St-Sulpice (near rue St-Paul ouest). www.lesaintsulpice.com. ✆ **877/785-7423** or 514/288-1000. 108 units. From C$179 suite. Rates include continental breakfast. Parking C$28 per day plus taxes. Pets accepted (C$50 per stay). Métro: Place d'Armes. **Amenities:** Restaurant; concierge; access to nearby health clubs and spa; room service; free Wi-Fi.

PLATEAU MONT-ROYAL

Staying in this working-class area, with its arty bohemian feel, gives you the chance to bypass the tourist-heavy locations and spend some time where real Montréalers live, work, and play. But because it's residential community there's not a huge selection of hotels, virtually nothing on par with the design or grandeur of downtown or Vieux-Montréal.

Expensive

Hotel (10) ★ Here's a hotel with dual personalities: On weekdays it hosts business clients and some families, but on the weekends, clubbers pack the expansive terrace of its **Brooke** bar and transform the corner location into a Montréal nightlife hotspot. It's a great option for tourists who want to stay where they play. The structure began life in 1914 as the first poured-concrete building in North America and was a boutique hotel named for its architect, Joseph-Arthur Godin, until the Opus group purchased it in 2007. A late 2012 transformation softened the all-nighter ambience with improved lighting and more neutral décor, but sound still reverberates through the bedrooms' concrete ceilings. For a quieter room, ask for one facing rue Clark.

10 rue Sherbrooke ouest (near rue St-Laurent). www.hotel10montreal.com. ✆ **855/390-6787** or 514/843-6000. 136 units. C$209–C$429 double; C$349–C$599 suite. Children 12 and under stay free in parent's room. Packages available. Valet parking C$28 (indoor garage). Pets accepted (C$50 per stay). Métro: St-Laurent. Car service to downtown (free). **Amenities:** Restaurant; bar; concierge; health club; room service; free Wi-Fi.

Moderate

Auberge de La Fontaine ★★ There are four things in particular to like about this easygoing hotel: it's across the street from a pretty part of Parc de La Fontaine, it's along some central bike path arteries (a feature used by many guests), it's within walking distance to Plateau dining and shops, and it has a friendly, hostel-like atmosphere even though the rooms are private. Guests can raid the kitchen for a free afternoon snack or buy beer or wine from the front desk and head to the third floor terrace, which overlooks the park. Families are often and warmly accommodated. The breakfast buffet (pastries, cereals, yogurt, fresh fruit, local cheeses, and cold cuts), always included, is one reason guests return to this *auberge* time and time again.

1301 rue Rachel est (at rue Chambord). www.aubergedelafontaine.com. 21 units. ✆ **800/597-0597** or 514/597-0166. May–Oct from C$157 double, from C$205 suite; Nov–Apr from C$122 double, from C$159 suite. Rates include breakfast. Packages available. 3 free parking spots; free street parking. Métro: Mont Royal. **Amenities:** Concierge; kitchen; free Wi-Fi.

Casa Bianca ★★ As the name suggests, this elegant B&B is a white house, as well as an architectural landmark. It's on the corner of a tree-lined residential street in Montréal's hip Plateau neighborhood, adjacent to Parc Jeanne-Mance, and close to shops on boulevard St-Laurent and avenue Mont-Royal. If the weather is cooperating, the organic breakfast is served on a breezy patio. Yoga instruction can be planned in advance. Rooms are spacious with antique touches; and many have claw-foot bathtubs that add to the homey feel. A growing reputation has attracted celebrity guests.

4351 av. de L'Esplanade (at rue Marie-Anne). www.casabianca.ca. ✆ **866/775-4431** or 514/312-3837. 5 units. C$119–C$269 double; from C$199 suite. Rates include breakfast. Packages available. Self-parking C$10. Métro: Mont Royal. Pets not accepted. **Amenities:** free Wi-Fi.

Hôtel de l'Institut ★★★ For visitors who've "done" Old Montréal and want access to the Plateau's buzz of everyday Montréal life, there is no better option. Primely located and well priced, this elegant hotel is expertly run by students who are learning the Province's signature style of hospitality. Rooms are up to date, tidy, and spacious. There's a work desk if needed, but better to throw open the curtains and catch a sunset from the 8th floor, ideally on a Mont Royal–facing terrace. Each stay includes breakfast in the student-run **Restaurant de l'Institut** (p. 66), a fine choice for any meal, even amidst the plethora of neighborhood spots. During the school year there's also dining at Salle Paul-Émile-Lévesque on the second floor. Parking is conveniently located below the hotel.

3535 rue Saint-Denis (near rue Sherbrooke). www.ithq.qc.ca/en/hotel. ✆ **855/229-8189** or 514/282-5120. 42 units. From C$129 double, from C$229 suite. Rates include breakfast. Packages available. Children 12 and under stay free in parent's room. Self parking C$19. Métro: Sherbrooke. **Amenities:** Babysitting; concierge; 2 restaurants (one seasonal); shop; free Wi-Fi.

WHERE TO EAT IN MONTRÉAL

6

Foie gras, *tartare,* and charcuterie plates are just a few of the rich, savory items that highlight Montréal's hedonistic, culinary scene. Add a penchant for quality, local produce (known as *terroir*) such as duck, award-winning cheeses, and iconic maple syrup, and you could happily spend your entire visit grazing in all the corners of the city.

While white-linen restaurants remain a classic Québec culinary art, the heart of Montréal's new food culture is found in its bustling, come-as-you-are yet decidedly upscale bistros. Foodies may want to consider a trip around the annual **Montréal en Lumière** culinary festival in February (see p. 101) or the new **Taste of Montréal** restaurant week (**www.mtlatable.com**), which takes place in November.

Like many big cities, the food-truck phenom has hit the streets of Montréal, with about a dozen trucks rotating in and out of pre-determined spots from late June to early October. Check Tourisme Montréal's Guide to Street Food (**www.tourisme-montreal.org/blog/guide-to-food-trucks-and-street-food-in-montreal**) for details; on Twitter, check #foodtruckmtl.

best EATING BETS

- **Best Classic French Bistro:** Plateau Mont-Royal's most Parisian spot, **L'Express** (p. 66), is where you come to see what the Francophone part of this city is all about. From the black-and-white-checkered floor to the grand, high ceilings to the classic cuisine, this is where Old France meets New France. Another good bet is **Leméac** (p. 70) in the chichi Outremont neighborhood.
- **Best Guilty Treat:** *Poutine* is a plate of French fries *(frites)* drenched with gravy afloat with cheese curds; it's the bedrock of Québec comfort food and the national hangover remedy. **La Banquise,** near Parc La Fontaine's northwest corner, offers upwards of 30 variations and is open 24 hours a day, 7 days a week. See p. 69.
- **Best Smoked Meat:** There are other contenders, but **Chez Schwartz Charcuterie Hébraïque de Montréal,** known simply as Schwartz's, serves up the definitive version of regional brisket. A takeout-only counter next door is a practical option if the line for sit-down spots snakes its way down the street. See p. 69.
- **Best Vegan:** A standard-bearer since 1997, Plateau Mont-Royal's **Aux Vivres** packs in vegans, vegetarians, and the meat eaters who love them. See p. 71.

- **Best Bagel:** Even native New Yorkers give it up for Montréal's bagels, which are sweeter and chewier than those produced south of the border. (The secret, they say, is dipping the dough in honey water.) Both **St-Viateur Bagel & Café** (p. 72) and **Fairmount Bagel** (p. 72) are the places to assess the comparison. See p. 70 for more on Montréal's beloved bagels.
- **Best Breakfast:** The city has six outposts of **Eggspectation,** and they all do brisk business serving funky, creative breakfasts with loads of egg options. The menu is extensive, prices are fair, and portions are huge. See p. 58. For a more elevated experience, **Lawrence,** in Mile End, serves up wonderfully rich British-style brunch. See p. 70.
- **Best Restaurants for a Special Event:** Chef Normand Laprise keeps Vieux-Montréal's **Toqué!** (p. 60) in sparkling shape. This dazzlingly postmodern venue is now a deserving member of the gold-standard organization Relais & Châteaux. Downtown, **Europea** (p. 55) offers a spectacular tasting menu in an elegant, old-world surrounding.

RESTAURANTS BY CUISINE

BAKERY

Fairmount Bagel ★★★ ($, p. 72)
Nocochi ★ ($, p. 59)
Olive et Gourmando ★★★ ($, p. 64)
St-Viateur Bagel ★★ ($, p. 72)

BISTRO

Lawrence ★★★ ($$$, p. 70)
Leméac ★★ ($$$, p. 70)
L'Express ★ ($$, p. 66)
Marché de la Villette ★ ($, p. 64)
Modavie ★ ($$, p. 63)

BRASSERIE

Brasserie T ★★★ ($$, p. 56)
Holder ★ ($$, p. 63)
Méchant Boeuf ★ ($$, p. 63)

BREAKFAST/BRUNCH

Café Cherrier ★ ($$, p. 66)
Eggspectation ★★★ ($, p. 58)

CONTEMPORARY FRENCH

Beaver Hall ★★ ($$, p. 56)
Europea ★★★ ($$$, p. 55)
Le Local ★ ($$$, p. 60)
Restaurant de l'Institut ★ ($$$, p. 66)
Toqué! ★★★ ($$$, p. 60)

CONTEMPORARY QUÉBÉCOIS

Au Pied de Cochon ★ ($$$, p. 65)
Chez l'Épicier ★ ($$$, p. 59)
Hôtel Herman ★★ ($$, p. 71)
Le Club Chasse et Pêche ★★★ ($$$, p. 60)

DELI

Schwartz's ★ ($, p. 69)

DESSERT

Bilboquet ★★ ($, p. 71)
Juliette et Chocolat ★ ($, p. 69)

DINER

Beauty's Luncheonette ★★ ($, p. 68)
Deville Dinerbar ★ ($$, p. 56)
Wilensky Light Lunch ★★ ($, p. 73)

ITALIAN

Graziella ★★★ ($$$, p. 59)
Hostaria ★ ($$$, p. 69)

LIGHT FARE

Green Panther ★★ ($, p. 72)
Java U ★ ($, p. 59)
La Banquise ★ ($, p. 69)
Nocochi ★ ($, p. 59)
Olive et Gourmando ★★★ ($, p. 64)

KEY TO ABBREVIATIONS:
$$$** = Expensive **$$** = Moderate **$ = Inexpensive

St-Viateur Bagel ★★ ($, p. 72)
Titanic ★ ($, p. 64)

PIZZA

Magpie Pizzeria ★ ($, p. 72)

PORTUGUESE

Ferreira Café ★★★ ($$$, p. 55)

SEAFOOD

Ferreira Café ★★★ ($$$, p. 55)
Joe Beef ★★ ($$$, p. 74)
Le Garde Manger ★★ ($$$, p. 60)

SOUTH AMERICAN

Mezcla ★★★ ($$$, p. 73)

STEAKHOUSE

Joe Beef ★★ ($$$, p. 74)
Moishes ★★ ($$$, p. 66)
Vieux-Port Steakhouse ★ ($$, p. 64)

TAPAS

Le Filet ★★ ($$$, p. 65)

TRADITIONAL FRENCH

Julien ★★ ($$, p. 58)

VEGETARIAN/VEGAN

Aux Vivres ★★ ($, p. 71)

CENTRE-VILLE/DOWNTOWN

In addition to the restaurants listed below, we recommend the excellent wine bar **Pullman** (p. 105) in downtown.

Expensive

Europea ★★★ CONTEMPORARY FRENCH Montréal has a handful of celebrity chefs, and Europea's Jérôme Ferrer is justifiably one of them: his elegant, white tablecloth venue is one of the special spots in the city. For the full treatment, order the extravagant *menu dégustation,* which starts with a lobster cream "cappuccino" with truffle puree and goes on to include maple bark stewed foie gras, swiss chard ravioli, cornish hen with root vegetable fondant, and *l'arbre à sucreries de Sainte Culpabilité,* translated as "candy tree from Guilty land." There are two (relatively) moderate ways to experience Ferrer's touch: come at lunch, when a 3-course meal goes for C$49.50 (and a la carte mains priced at C$26–C$29), or try his **Beaver Hall** restaurant (p. 56), which is also downtown. Europea is a member of the prestigious Relais & Châteaux.

1227 rue de la Montagne (near rue Ste-Catherine). www.europea.ca. ✆ **514/398-9229.** Reservations recommended. Main courses C$43–C$49; table d'hôte C$70; 10-course *menu dégustation* C$100. Tues–Fri noon–2pm; daily 6–10pm. Métro: Peel.

Ferreira Café ★★★ SEAFOOD/PORTUGUESE Ferreria exude a warm, festive, Mediterranean grace, and you can't go wrong with its take on Portuguese classics, including oysters (*huîtres à la portugaise;* 3 for C$13), salted cod (*gratin de morue sale;* C$32), and bouillabaisse (C$37). A smaller, late-night menu for C$24 is available from 10pm Monday through Saturday. For lighter and less expensive fare, Ferreira's sister venue, **Café Vasco de Gama,** on the same block, at 1472 rue Peel, offers big breakfasts, a variety of salads, and delectable desserts indoors and at sidewalk tables in warm months. It's open daily into the

The Price You'll Pay

Here's what you can expect to pay for your main course at a Montréal restaurant:

Expensive	C$20 and up
Moderate	C$10–C$20
Inexpensive	Under C$10

early evening. The owners also operate the innovative **F bar,** a restaurant in a glass box on the sidewalk of the Quartier des Spectacles, next to and similar to **Brasserie T,** below.

1446 rue Peel (near boul. de Maisonnueve). www.ferreiracafe.com. ✆ **514/848-0988.** Main courses C$30–C$46. Mon–Fri 11:45am–3pm; Sun–Wed 5:30–11pm; Thurs–Sat 5:30pm–midnight. Confirm Sun hours in winter. Métro: Peel.

Moderate

Beaver Hall ★★ CONTEMPORARY FRENCH With the same chef as the esteemed **Europea** (p. 55), this "Bistro Gourmand par Europea" offers similarly spectacular food, but with a less over-the-top service experience (and at a more relaxed price). Great mains include homemade cavatelli with pesto and a panko-crusted poached egg, fish and chips, and a *tourte au bison,* or bison meat pie. Desserts include *macarons* from Europea and maple French toast. Big picture windows look down the street towards Basilique-Cathédrale Marie-Reine-du-Monde, a cathedral that is a copy of Rome's St. Peter's Basilica (see our Downtown Walking Tour, p. 119). The location north of the Convention Center and Vieux-Montréal and east of downtown is not likely next to anything you'd be visiting, but it's an easy 15-minute walk from the heart of both downtown and Vieux-Montréal.

1073 Cote du Beaver Hall (at rue Belmont). www.beaverhall.ca. ✆ **514/866-1331.** Main courses C$17–C$31; table d'hôte C$36. Mon 11:30am–3pm; Tues–Wed 11:30am–10pm; Thurs–Fri 11:30am–10:30pm; Sat 5–10:30pm. Métro: Square Victoria.

Brasserie T ★★★ BRASSERIE This new restaurant from chef Normand Laprise of the city's top restaurant, **Toqué!** (p. 60), is fun, flirty, adventurous, and romantic; it wows us at every turn. Its location, in a unique all-glass box perched on a sidewalk in the city's newly renovated fine-arts neighborhood, the Quartier des Spectacles, is right in front of the Musée d'Art Contemporain de Montréal. The food is spectacular: We love the garlic sea snails, pan-seared foie gras with candied fennel, strawberries, and popcorn, the *saucisse de Montréal* (sausage) with quinoa salad, and shrimp roll on a perfectly grilled hot dog bun. You can make a creative meal out of just the appetizers, charcuteries, and *tartares.* At night in warm months, a pool of water alongside the restaurant and the length of a city block has a "dancing waters" lightshow. The *al fresco* dining area is extremely popular, so make reservations.

1425 rue Jeanne-Mance (near rue Ste-Catherine). www.brasserie-t.com. ✆ **514/282-0808.** Main courses C$18–C$25. Sun–Wed 11:30am–10:30pm; Thurs–Sat 11:30am–11:30pm. Métro: Place-des-Arts.

Deville Dinerbar ★ DINER This splashy downtown restaurant is packed with local businesspeople at lunchtime and a partying crowd at night—and kids love it, too. It claims to take its cue from American diners, but that goes only as far as its use of booths for some of the seating and its enormous portions; you'd be hard pressed to find an American diner with a marble bar, sparkly chandeliers, and reputation for killer fish tacos. Choices include salads, sandwiches, burgers, pastas, and specialties such as lamb shanks, diver scallops, and chicken schnitzel and spaetzle. If you have the stomach for it, try the so-called "R-rated shakes" such as The Beaux Dimanches: a concoction of Montréal-made Sortilège maple whiskey, coconut cream, and vanilla ice cream.

1425 Stanley St. (at rue Ste-Catherine). www.devilledinerbar.com. ✆ **514/281-6556.** Main courses C$20–C$45. Sun–Thurs 11am–11pm; Fri–Sat 11am–midnight. Métro: Peel.

Downtown Restaurants

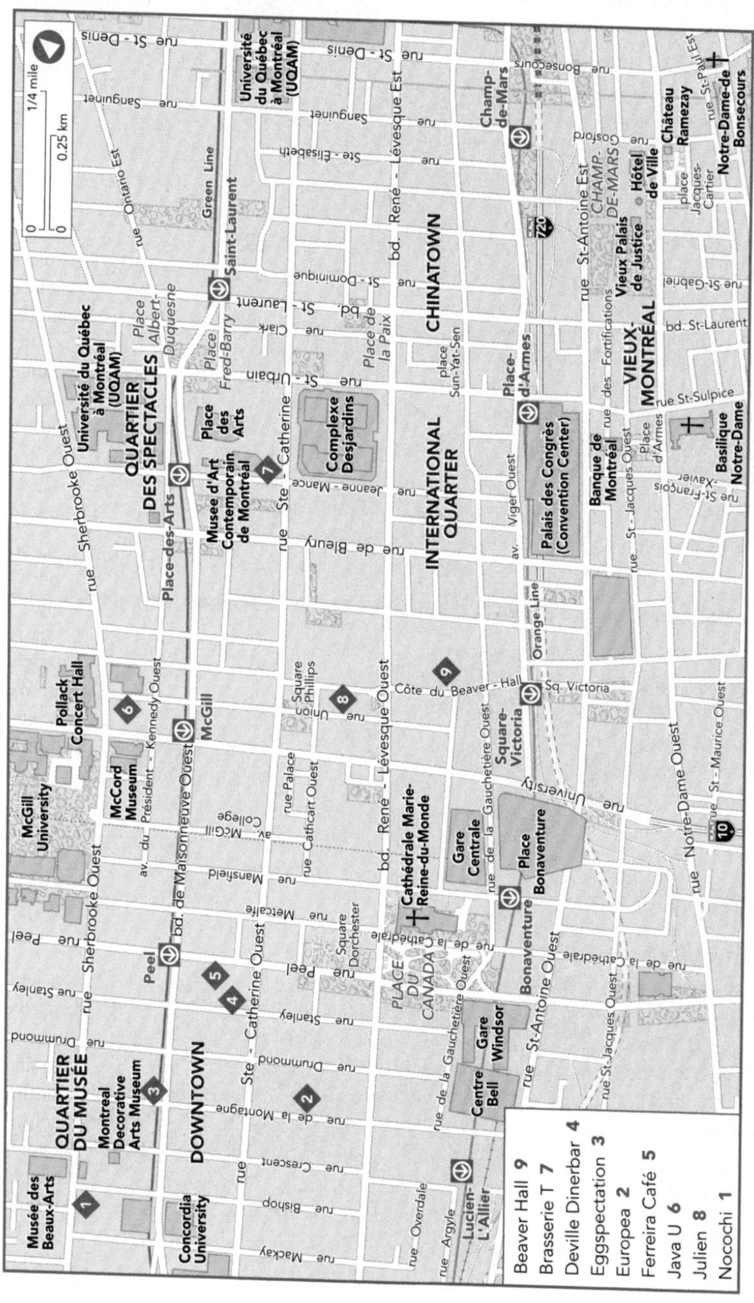

TABLE D'HÔTE & MORE RESTAURANT basics

Our number-one tip when eating in Québec: *always* look for **table d'hôte meals.** These are fixed-price menus with three or four courses, and they usually cost just a little more than a single main course. You'll find them at restaurants of all price ranges, and they present the best dining value. To sample some of the city's top restaurants for a bargain, check if they have table d'hôte menus at lunch, when the menus are even cheaper.

A few **French dining terms** that are important to know: the midday meal is called ***dîner*** (which is lunch, not dinner) and the evening meal is *souper* (supper). An ***entrée*** is an appetizer, and a ***plat principal*** is a main course.

Prices listed are for supper unless otherwise indicated and do not include the cost of wine, tip, or the 5 percent federal tax *and* 9.975 percent provincial tax that are tacked on the restaurant bill. Lunch prices are usually lower. Montréalers consider 15 percent of the check (before taxes) to be a fair tip, increased only for exceptional food and service. In all, count on taxes and tip to add another 30 percent to the bill.

Except in a handful of luxury restaurants, **dress codes** are nonexistent. But Montréalers are a fashionable lot and manage to look smart, even in casual clothes. Save the T-shirts and sneakers for another city.

Insider websites featuring reviews and observations about the Montréal dining scene include **www.endlessbanquet.blogspot.com,** the Twitter feed of "Montréal Gazette" restaurant critic Lesley Chesterman at **twitter.com/lesley chestrman**, and **www.midnightpoutine.ca/food**.

Julien ★★ TRADITIONAL FRENCH This is truly a traditional Parisian-style bistro: beef tartar, sausage and ratatouille, and "Julien's duck confit" are among the classics on the menu. There's not much new here, but that's part of the appeal; year in and year out Julien remains a favorite for locals and an appealing option for tourists thanks to decent prices (slightly lower still at lunch), friendly service, and a heated terrace with outside tables much of the year.

1191 av. Union (at boul. René-Lévesque). www.restaurantjulien.com. ✆ **514/871-1581.** Main courses C$20–C$27; table d'hôte C$26–C$33. Mon–Fri 11:30am–3pm and 5–10pm; Sat 5:30–10pm. Métro: McGill.

Inexpensive

Eggspectation ★★★ BREAKFAST/BRUNCH Don't be put off by the goofy name, the 15-page menu, or the fact that this is a small chain (there are six outposts in Montréal alone). This breakfast-centric restaurant delivers. Food is fresh and comes out fast, even when there are crowds. There are 10 versions of eggs benedict alone ("Montréal Style" comes with smoked meat) as well as non-breakfast foods such as burgers and club sandwiches. In addition to this location, other central outposts include 190 Ste-Catherine oust at the Complexe Desjardins shopping mall in downtown and 12 rue Notre Dame est in Vieux-Montréal.

1313 de Maisonneuve ouest (at rue de la Montagne). www.eggspectations.com. ✆ **514/842-3447.** Most items cost less than C$12. Daily 6am–5pm. Métro: Peel.

Java U ★ LIGHT FARE This cheery Java U is part of a local cafe chain that got its start in 1996 at Concordia University. College students and families make up most of the clientele at this particular outlet, which is a buttoned-up venue with friendly, laid-back staff. Options include quiches, salads, sandwich wraps, croissants, ice cream from local purveyor Bilboquet, and St-Ambroise beer, brewed at Montréal's own Brasserie McAuslan. Coffee options include espresso "con panna," which is espresso with whipped cream.

626 rue Sherbrooke (at av. Union). www.java-u.com. ✆ **514/286-1991.** Most items cost less than C$9. Mon–Fri 7am–8pm; Sat–Sun 8am–7pm. Métro: McGill.

Nocochi ★ BAKERY/LIGHT FARE For a breakfast *crêpe* or omelet, or a afternoon sweet treat (*macarons* are a specialty) or a glass of wine, try this bright little cafe and patisserie just 1 block west of the Musée des Beaux-Arts. The airy room is a balm after taking in the mountains of art at the museum or browsing the upscale antique shops and boutiques nearby.

2156 rue Mackay (at rue Sherbrooke). www.nocochi.com. ✆ **514/989-7514.** Most plates under C$10. Mon–Wed 8am–7pm; Thur–Sat 8am–8pm; Sun 9am–8pm. Métro: Guy-Concordia.

VIEUX-MONTRÉAL (OLD MONTRÉAL)

In addition to the restaurants listed below, food is also available in **Le Jardin Nelson** (p. 105), which has live jazz and a terrace, and is popular with families and kid-free folks alike.

Expensive

Chez l'Épicier ★ CONTEMPORARY QUÉBÉCOIS Chef Laurent Godbout's inspiring haute cuisine menu provides a perfect example of modern gastronomy in Montréal. The ever-changing menu offers local ingredients prepared with a playful, global feel. Case in point: soybean risotto with vegetables, soy broth, and Parmesan foam. It's a delight. The Magret duck with port juniper sauce is another must-try. But truly, it's hard to find fault with any part of the menu. The many windows provide a light, airy feeling throughout, with stone and exposed brick walls punctuated by a long, robin's egg blue wall with chalkboards displaying the evening's specials. You'll feel welcomed and comfortable from the moment you sit down. One minor complaint: for such a high-end restaurant, the abundance of food items for sale comes across as tacky (this includes bags of nachos and other items lining the windows adjacent to the street.)

311 rue St-Paul est (at rue St-Claude). www.chezlepicier.com. ✆ **514/878-2232.** Main courses C$18–C$38; 7-course tasting menu C$85. Daily 5:30–10pm. Métro: Champ-de-Mars.

Graziella ★★★ ITALIAN Graziella's open kitchen plan lets diners watch chef-owner Graziella Battista and her staff prepare modern Italian dishes served in understated yet beautiful presentations, like little works of art. Blonde wood and soft, creamy tones create a calming backdrop, and the high ceilings and votive candles on the tables add to the spa-like atmosphere. It's a special-occasion restaurant that you can still feel comfortable in. Here, a competent, friendly staff provides the highest level of service. Everything on the menu is outstanding, but be sure to try the gravlax appetizer, rolled to look like a flower blossom, and the succulent, falling-off-the-bone *osso buco*. Reservations are recommended.

116 rue McGill (3 blocks east of rue Notre-Dame ouest). www.restaurantgraziella.ca. ✆ **514/876-0116.** Main courses C$26–C$42. Tues–Fri noon–2:30pm; Tues–Sat 6–10pm. Métro: Square-Victoria.

Le Club Chasse et Pêche ★★★ CONTEMPORARY QUÉBÉCOIS In English, the name means Hunting and Fishing Club, paying homage to the sportsmen's club that once occupied the building. The short, but well-executed menu keeps this theme going: sea fare such as grilled octopus or hamachi *tartare* share the menu with the likes of smoked bison and roasted duck. Think of it as modern-day surf and turf. Like many restaurants in Montréal, chef Claude Pelletier's menu changes frequently. Despite that, some customer favorites are always on the menu, including braised piglet risotto with fois gras shavings. (If you try only one thing here, let it be this!) The nondescript entrance is easily missed, marked only by a small sign with a crest on it. The stone and brick dining room is dark and masculine, with leather chairs and waterfowl-themed light fixtures. You can almost imagine yourself hunting in a forest at dusk. Reservations are recommended. For a more casual experience, check out sister restaurant **Le Filet** (p. 65) in the Plateau neighborhood.

423 rue St-Claude (btw. rue St-Paul and rue Notre-Dame). www.leclubchasseetpeche.com. ✆ **514/861-1112.** Main courses C$33–C$39. Year-round Tues–Sat 6–10:30pm. In summer in good weather, the restaurant serves lunch in the garden of the nearby Musée du Château Ramezay, p. 85; call to confirm. Métro: Champ-de-Mars.

Le Garde Manger ★★ SEAFOOD At this supper club, everything is a little different. For starters, the staff greet you in English, not French. There is no signage other than a dimly lit neon pink square out front. The interior decor is half hunting lodge, half antique shop. Chef-owner Chuck Hughes, star of the Canadian Food Network show "Chuck's Day Off," features an ever-changing menu of creative, playful seafood. The lobster *poutine* is legendary, and on a recent visit, devilled eggs with bacon-wrapped oysters were a hit, as was the pork liver sausage paired with octopus and cheese grits. Meatier choices may include braised short ribs (always on the menu) and seared fois gras paired with some kind of meat (recently: a perfectly seared pork chop) over a maple-soaked waffle. Just don't be surprised if you arrive to find an almost entirely new menu! Expect a packed house, loud music blaring overhead, and a cool crowd in skinny jeans and trucker caps. Reservations recommended.

408 rue St-François-Xavier (north of rue St-Paul). www.crownsalts.com/gardemanger. ✆ **514/678-5044.** Main courses C$28–C$36. Tues–Sun 6–11:30pm. Bar Tues–Sun 6pm–3am. Métro: Place d'Armes.

Le Local ★ CONTEMPORARY FRENCH Located in a brick building that was a foundry many lifetimes ago, the interior at Le Local is industrial-chic: polished cement floors and exposed beam-and-brick ceilings and walls hint of the building's former life, while contemporary touches such as black leather furniture, colorful throw pillows, and gorgeous chestnut tables provide a clubby feel. It's a hotspot among local trendsetters, and the place is packed even on weeknights. An attractive, fashionably dressed staff provides competent service. The open kitchen cranks out French bistro classics such as beef and salmon *tartare* and duck leg confit, along with creative French inspired-dishes such as seared halibut with olive spaetzle and a creamy artichoke mousseline. For those looking for a bargain, grab a seat at the bar (if you can get one) and opt for the bar menu, which features cheaper fare.

740 rue William (at rue Prince). www.resto-lelocal.com. ✆ **514/397-7737.** Main courses C$23–C$32; bar menu C$5–C$7. Mon–Tues 11:30am–11:30pm; Wed–Fri 11:30am–midnight; Sat 5:30pm–midnight; Sun 5:30–11:30pm. Métro: Square-Victoria.

Toqué! ★★★ CONTEMPORARY FRENCH When chef Normand Laprise opened this 5-diamond gem in 1993, the city's culinary reputation was virtually

Vieux-Montréal Restaurants

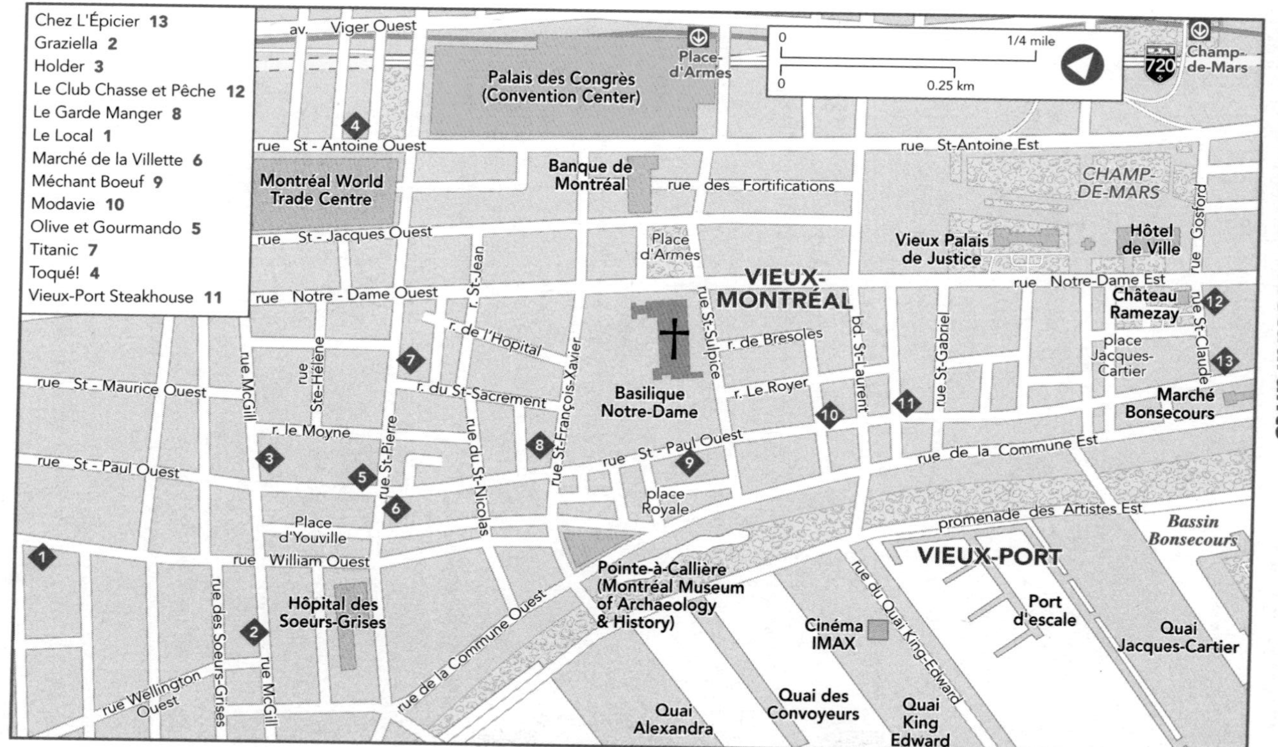

vegging out IN MEATY MONTRÉAL

Québec cuisine is traditionally very meat-centric, but vegetarian foods have made inroads onto menus as both perfunctory options and centerpiece main events. Whether you are totally meat-adverse or simply looking for lighter fare after days of indulgence, here are some places to keep in mind:

- **Aux Vivres** (p. 71): Aux Vivres, on the Plateau, continues to serve some of the best veggie-friendly cuisine in town. Chapati flatbread wraps are made-to-order and stuffed with flavors from every corner of the globe.
- **La Banquise** (p. 69): Not only is the Plateau's Banquise known citywide for its *poutine,* but it's open 24 hours a day, every day—that is, whenever the urge strikes to indulge in any of two dozen varieties of French fries with gravy and cheese curds. The menu includes a 100 percent vegetarian *poutine* option as well as omelets, grilled cheese, and salads for non-meat eaters. At the northwest corner of Parc La Fontaine.
- **The Green Panther** (p. 72). Another good bet on the Plateau, with the option for smallish portions (you can order a half pita) and a full menu of power drinks such as a wheat grass–"boosted" smoothie.
- **Le Commensal.** Food here is buffet-style, and you pay by the weight of your plate (about C$10 for an ample portion). While most of the dishes are vegetarian or vegan, the restaurant has begun including fish and chicken (as "garnishes") for its semi-vegetarian customers. The second-floor downtown location overlooks rue Ste-Catherine (1204 av. McGill College; www.commensal.com; ✆ **514/871-1480**). Open daily for lunch and dinner.
- **Le Taj.** There are 12 vegetarian main courses (C$10–C$14) at this great Indian restaurant in downtown but if you come at lunch take a look at the C$16 buffet (C$8 for kids 10 and under), which includes samosas, lentil curry, and vegetable dishes. The decor is just fancy enough to feel special without being intimidating. (2077 rue Stanley; www.restaurantletaj.com; ✆ **514/845-9015**). It's open for lunch Sunday through Friday and daily for dinner.
- **Gandhi.** Another good Indian option, in Vieux-Montréal right on rue St-Paul. It's bright, airy, and fast. There are duck, lamb, and chicken dishes on the menu but also over a dozen vegetarian options, including classics such as the chickpea dish *chana masala* and *matter panir,* a homemade cheese with green peas. (230 rue St-Paul ouest; www.restaurantgandhi.com; ✆ **514/845-5866**). It's open for lunch on weekdays and dinner daily.

non-existent. Toque! changed all that, and 20 years later it's still the top of the heap. The decor is both refined and whimsical: a playful sunflower sculpture greets you out front, and inside you'll marvel at the glass-paneled wine cellar that extends from below-ground to create a visual centerpiece with wine bottles suspended in midair. The menu is heavily influenced by local ingredients and changes regularly, but you're likely to find some perennial favorites such as roast Magret duck with chamomile sauce, along with newer favorites including cavatelli with lobster, wild chantarelles, and asparagus. Adventurous eaters should try the seven-course tasting menu; it's pricey (C$110), but changes nightly and serves up the best the kitchen has to offer. For a more casual option, visit **Brasserie T** (p. 56), also owned by Laprise. Reservations, not always necessary in this city, are recommended here.

900 Place Jean-Paul-Riopelle (at rue St-Antoine). www.restaurant-toque.com. ✆ **514/499-2084.** Main courses C$42–C$52; tasting menu C$110. Tues–Fri 11:30am–2pm; Tues–Sat 5:30–10:30pm. Métro: Square-Victoria.

Moderate

Holder ★ BRASSERIE This large, high-ceilinged space offers a chic atmosphere with copper walls, tall columns, and expansive windows overlooking busy rue McGill. Chalkboards dotted throughout feature the day's specials, along with wine and beer selections. Holder offers good value for what you get: the expansive menu of primarily French classics will satisfy nearly every appetite. Standout items include *fois gras au torchon* and gravlax appetizers, and classic beef *tartare* in both appetizer and main course sizes. Holder's take on steak frites featuring grilled hanger steak is dependably good, as is the lobster ravioli, served with truffle oil and beurre blanc. The weekend brunch offers more modestly priced items that are just as good, but more along the lines of breakfast food. Reservations are recommended on weekends.

407 rue McGill (corner of rue St. Paul). www.restaurantholder.com. ✆ **514/849-0333.** Main courses C$17–C$23; table d'hôte weekdays C$20. Mon–Fri 11:30am–11pm; Sat–Sun 10am–3pm; Sat 5:30–11pm; Sun 5:30–10pm. Métro: Square-Victoria.

Méchant Boeuf ★ BRASSERIE Come here for a lively and energetic dining experience, that's also great for a group. Here, a young, stylish crowd piles in during happy hour and doesn't seem to leave. There's a DJ set up front and center playing techno and electro-pop loudly overhead. The menu has a large selection of appetizers such as fried calamari, chicken wings, and crab cakes, all served in large enough portions to share. The real focus, though, is beef, with an array of well-crafted burgers that will satisfy even the most discriminate burger aficionado, and AAA-grade cuts of beef such as New York strip and bone-in filet mignon will leave any carnivore feeling satiated. A well-stocked raw bar offers fresh-shucked oysters along with creative options including spicy-citrusy shrimp ceviche. A late-night bar menu is on the offing for those who wander in after 11pm. Reservations recommended on weekends.

124 rue St-Paul ouest (near rue St-Sulpice). www.mechantboeuf.com. ✆ **514/788-4020.** Main courses C$16–C$58. Sun–Tues 5–11pm (bar until 1am); Wed–Sat 5pm–1am (bar until 3am). Métro: Champs-de-Mars.

Modavie ★ BISTRO Featuring a unique combination of French bistro classics and Italian-influenced pasta dishes, Modavie hits all the right notes. It's a place where the atmosphere is loud but convivial, and everyone seems to be in a good mood. The service is attentive without being overbearing—you'll leave feeling well taken care of. There is live jazz every evening in the upstairs lounge (no cover), making this a comfortable place for singles as well as couples and groups. On the menu, steak frites are always excellent, and an entire section of the menu is dedicated to lamb. The lamb *mille-feuilles* features succulent braised lamb shank and mushrooms tucked between layers of flaky puff pastry—so delicious you may just want to order it again for dessert.

1 rue St. Paul ouest (corner of rue St.Laurent) www.modavie.com. ✆ **514/287-9582.** Main courses C$20–C$38; table d'hôte lunch C$15, dinner C$29. Sun–Thurs 11:30am–10:30pm; Fri–Sat 11:30am–11pm. Metro: Place d'Armes.

Vieux-Port Steakhouse ★ STEAKHOUSE Bring a huge appetite to this massive (we're talking seating for 1,200) steakhouse and tuck into one of their hearty options that includes T-Bone, filet mignon, and New York–cut sirloin, among others. Other choices include a tangy Santa Fe grilled chicken and herbed rack of lamb. A lunchtime table d'hôte (C$14–C$19) includes soup or salad plus a wide selection of mains (an optional dessert is C$2 more). In summer you may want to opt for a table on the 300-seat outdoor terrace. The place runs like a well-oiled machine: a veritable army of servers, cooks, runners, and other staff are always on the go. Thanks to its size, you probably won't have to wait for a table, either.

39 rue St-Paul est (at rue St-Gabriel). www.vieuxportsteakhouse.com. ✆ **514/866-3175.** Main courses C$15–C$41; table d'hôte lunch C$14-C$19, dinner C$18–C$41. Mon–Thurs 11:30am–11pm; Fri–Sat 11:30am–midnight; Sun 10am–11pm. Métro: Place d'Armes.

Inexpensive

Marché de la Villette ★ BISTRO This rustic-looking deli was originally a boucherie (butchery) and charcuterie, evidenced by the old-fashioned lettering on the window. These days, it's known to locals as one of the best spots for a weekday lunch. The decor is kitschy: every inch of wall is covered with something, be it plastic ivy, jars of condiments for sale, or fake plastic hams hanging from the ceiling. But don't let that deter you. This is a place for stick-to-your-ribs fare, including homemade pâtés, a variety of quiches, and a delicious, addictive *cassoulet de maison.* Locals swear by their *soupe à l'oignon gratinée* (French onion soup) and there are also lighter options including salads and crêpes.

324 rue St-Paul ouest (at rue St-Pierre). www.marche-villette.com. ✆ **514/807-8084.** Most items under C$15; table d'hote C$15. Daily 9am–6pm. Métro: Square-Victoria.

Olive et Gourmando ★★★ BAKERY/LIGHT FARE This place started as a bakery, but soon expanded to include a dining room and quickly became the go-to lunch spot in Vieux-Montréal. The wide-ranging menu is a hit with everyone from grown-ups to toddlers. You're greeted by a gorgeous display of baked goods, ranging from croissants and muffins to biscotti, and a warm, nature-inflected decor. A branch and twig chandelier adds a quirky touch of earthiness to the dark red room. Check the chalkboard menu to see what's available. Must-try options include the Cuban sandwich, a Cajun chicken sandwich with guacamole, mangoes, and fresh tomato, and a deliriously good truffle mac 'n cheese with caramelized onions.

351 rue St-Paul ouest (at rue St-Pierre). www.oliveetgourmando.com. ✆ **514/350-1083.** Most items under C$15. Cash only. Tues–Sat 8am–6pm. Métro: Square-Victoria.

Titanic ★ LIGHT FARE The ambience at this lunchtime spot could best be described as *frayed chic.* Feeling a bit like you're entering a 1920s speakeasy, you descend a flight of stairs into a basement with a labyrinth of pipes overhead, chipped exposed brick walls, and worn wooden floors. The bare-bones room is counterbalanced by pops of artistic bric-a-brac and black and white photography that ties it all together. The decor sets the scene nicely: These are arguably the best sandwiches in town. Everything is made from scratch, including the baguettes. Don't miss the pork Milanese sandwich: thin pork cutlets breaded and fried to a crisp and served on a ciabatta bun with coleslaw and veggies. It sells out daily, so come early. There are also a variety of other meat and vegetarian options, plus hot and cold entrees.

445 rue St-Pierre (1 block south of rue Notre-Dame). www.titanicmontreal.com. ✆ **514/849-0894.** Most sandwiches cost C$10. Cash only. Mon–Fri 8am–5pm. Métro: Square-Victoria/Place d'Armes.

QUÉBEC'S BEST comfort FOODS

While you're in Montréal, indulge in at least a couple of Québec staples. Though you'll find them dolled up on some menus, these are generally thought of as the region's basic comfort foods:

- ***Poutine:*** French fries doused with gravy and cheese curds. Poutine's profile has risen outside of the province in recent years, with "The New Yorker" magazine positing that the "national joke" may be becoming the national dish.
- ***Tarte au sucre:*** Maple-sugar pie, like pecan pie without the pecans. A French-Canadian classic.
- **Bagels:** Here, the rings of bread are crispy on the outside, chewy on the inside, and have a touch of sweetness. See the sidebar, "The Great Bagel Debate," on p. 70 for more on this Montréal obsession.
- **Smoked meat:** A maddeningly tasty sandwich component particular to Montréal. Its taste is similar to pastrami and corned beef.
- ***Cretons:*** A pâté of minced pork, allspice, and parsley.
- ***Tourtière:*** A meat pie of spiced ground pork, often served with tomato chutney.
- ***Queues de Castor:*** A deep-fried pastry the size of a man's footprint served with your choice of sweet or savory toppings. The name means "beaver tails."

PLATEAU MONT-ROYAL

Expensive

Au Pied de Cochon ★ CONTEMPORARY QUÉBÉCOIS Celebrity chef Martin Picard led Montréal's meat "new wave" by opening Au Pied de Cochon (translation: the pig's foot) in 2001, and its patrons and personnel today bank on a seemingly indelible reputation. The foie gras, served at least seven different ways, one as *poutine,* still merits high praise. And sure enough, it's fun to open Duck in a Can right at the table. But in all the bustle and frenzy you may receive your entrée a split second after your salad and be asked if you want dessert a minute after that. Tables of four or greater seemed to have more time and space to have a few drinks and laughs. An elaborate raw bar is on view near the entrance of this low-key, upscale, always packed restaurant, and includes oysters, lobster, and local catch. Picard's newest expansion includes a seasonal *cabane à sucre* (sugar shack) and an award-winning cookbook with its recipes. Reservations are recommended.

536 rue Duluth est (near rue St-Hubert). www.restaurantaupieddecochon.ca. ✆ **514/281-1114.** Main courses C$14–C$51. Tues–Sun 5pm–midnight. Métro: Sherbrooke.

Le Filet ★★ TAPAS Seafood's profile gets bumped up another few notches on Montréal's map with Le Filet, which opened in late 2011. Let the menu's categories of Raw, Warm Tide, Amphibians, and Earthly add an air of intrigue since there really is no wrong choice. Oysters are creatively garnished with yuzu marmalade or jalapeno and maple cracker. The macadamia cod has a sprinkling of chorizo flakes. Plates are small and meant to be shared (order at least 2 per person) and the pasta is homemade. Fans of **Le Club Chasse et Pêche** restaurant (p. 60), take note: the same team is in charge here and thus there are also game meat options. Seats on the terrace have a view of Parc Jeanne-Mance. Reservations are recommended.

219 av. du Mont-Royal ouest (near av. du Parc). www.lefilet.ca. ✆ **514/360-6060.** Main courses C$12–C$28. Tues–Sat 5:30pm–midnight. Métro: Mont Royal.

Moishes ★★ STEAKHOUSE Montréal has a handful of culinary institutions and for steak lovers it's Moishes. Long-time patrons may favor the classic bone-in rib steak while the younger crowd opts for marinated shish kabab or organic salmon. With an ever-evolving menu and cozy, but sophisticated atmosphere, it's common to find three generations at one table celebrating a special occasion (the prices alone make it one). But there is a way to have your shrimp cocktail and martini, too: after 9pm there's a C$25 three-course menu. The restaurant's rich history reaches back more than 75 years, when Moishe Lighter worked his way up from busboy to mignon mogul. Moishes' sons, co-owners Lenny and Larry, carry on the tradition and are often on hand to suggest pairings from the restaurant's reputable wine list. Reservations are recommended.

3961 boul. St-Laurent (north of rue Napolean). www.moishes.ca. ✆ **514/845-3509.** Main courses C$28–C$54. Mon–Fri 5:30–11pm; Sat–Sun 5–11pm. Métro: Sherbrooke.

Restaurant de l'Institut ★ CONTEMPORARY FRENCH Apart from the name, you'd never know that this restaurant is run largely by students from the Institut de Tourisme et d'Hôtellerie du Québec. The menu reflects of-the-moment experimentation by beginner chefs and is presented by warm and eager wait staff in training. For value, try the C$19 three-course lunch (served weekdays) or the C$25 and C$35 three-course dinners (Tues–Wed evenings). Floor-to-ceiling windows and louvered wooden blinds add elegance to the comfortable dining room. Upstairs is a training hotel at a remarkably good value (see p. 52).

3535 rue St-Denis (1 block north of rue Sherbrooke). www.ithq.qc.ca. ✆ **514/282-5161.** Main courses C$22–C$28; table d'hôte lunch C$19; table d'hôte dinner Tues–Wed. Mon–Fri 7–9:30am and noon–1:30pm; Sat–Sun 7:30–10:30am; Tues–Sat 6–9:30pm. Métro: Sherbrooke.

Moderate

Café Cherrier ★ BREAKFAST/BRUNCH It's not about the food, exactly, at this amiable cafe—though it is quite tasty. Through rain, sleet, or shine, students, older couples, and families gather under the wrap-around awning to sip coffee and people watch. In summer, there are bowls of gazpacho and crisp pours of white wine. In winter, there's grilled steak and Cabernet at the indoor counter. A group of actors could be crammed into a corner, talking shop, or it could just as easily be politicians or bankers. Brunch is especially busy though some tables stay full long after dark. For a charming bistro atmosphere, especially in fair weather, it's a keeper.

3635 rue St-Denis (2 blocks north of Sherbrooke). www.cafecherrier.ca. ✆ **514/843-4308.** Main courses C$14–C$26; table d'hôte lunch C$17–C$24; table d'hôte dinner C$18–C$29. Mon–Fri 7:30am–11pm; Sat–Sun 8:30am–11pm. Métro: Sherbrooke.

L'Express ★ BISTRO Beloved by Montréalers and visitors alike for its old-timey Parisian style, there's almost always a wait for tables at L'Express. Main courses include the usual bistro fare, from pot-au-feu to duck confit, and the maple syrup pie is outstanding. (It's possible that the globe lights, glossy maroon walls, and checkered floor make the food taste even more French.) A 50-person service team runs a smooth ship, though at busier times, like brunch, the kitchen may grind to a halt. Try for a

Plateau Mont-Royal & Mile End Restaurants

QUICK EATS & picnic FOODS

If you're planning a picnic, bike ride, or simply a meal in, pick up supplies in Vieux-Montréal along rue St-Paul. On the street's west end is **Olive et Gourmando** (p. 64) at no. 351 and, just across the street, **Marché de la Villette** (p. 64) at no. 324. Both sell fresh breads, fine cheeses, sandwiches, salads, and pâtés.

Or, make a short excursion by bicycle or Métro (the Lionel-Groulx stop) to **Marché Atwater** (Atwater Market), the farmers market at 138 av. Atwater. It's open daily. The long interior shed is bordered by stalls stocked with gleaming produce and flowers. The two-story center section is devoted to vintners, butchers, bakeries, and cheese stores. In the marché, **Boulangerie Première Moisson** (**© 514/932-0328**) is filled with the tantalizing aromas of breads and pastries—oh, the pastries!—and has a seating area at which to nibble baguettes or sip a bowl of café au lait. Nearby, **Fromagerie du Marché Atwater** (**© 514/932-4653**) lays out more than 750 local and international cheeses—with hundreds from Québec alone—as well as pâtés and charcuterie. **Crudessence** (www.crudessence.com/en/marche-atwater), in the small food court pop up tent at the front of the market, offers vegetarian sandwiches, wraps, salads, and an "Om Burger." *Note:* Marché Atwater is on the Lachine Canal, where you can stroll and find a picnic table.

Locals rely on **Marché Jean-Talon** in Mile End (just north of the Plateau) as a point of sale for regional farms' seasonal harvests—from strawberries and asparagus in late spring to squash of all shapes and colors in fall. Several shops, some permanent and some seasonal, sell smoked seafood, cured meat, fresh flowers, and local wine and cheese. There's also a counter (**La Boite aux Huitres;** www.laboiteauxhuitres.ca; **© 514/277-7575**) that shucks oysters while you wait, C$30 per dozen.

reservation or drop in to see if there's an opening at the bar. One more thing: it's easy to miss. Look for the name spelled out in tile on the sidewalk out front.

3927 rue St-Denis (just north of rue Roy). www.restaurantlexpress.ca. **© 514/845-5333.** Main courses C$12–C$26. Mon–Fri 8am–2am; Sat 10am–2am; Sun 10am–1am. Métro: Sherbrooke.

Inexpensive

Beauty's Luncheonette ★★ LIGHT FARE At this iconic diner, you'd be right to deduce that a long line means good food, as it has since 1942. On Saturdays and Sundays the breakfast line often wraps around the corner and down the street. If you're lucky, Beauty himself (a bowling nickname for the 90-year-old owner, Hymie Sckolnick) will see that you have strong coffee and a banquette seat as quickly as possible. The bagels are local, from **St-Viateur Bagel** (see p. 72), and the orange juice is fresh-squeezed. Loyalists debate which of the two signature dishes is more quintessentially Montréal: the Mish-Mash omelet with hot dog, salami, fried onion, and green pepper, or Beauty's Special, a bagel sandwich with lox, cream cheese, sliced tomato, and onion—Beauty calls it their "Big Mac." If you want a delicious, home-cooked slice of Montréal, get in line!

93 av. du Mont-Royal ouest (corner of rue St-Urbain). www.beautys.ca. **© 514/849-8883.** Most items cost less than C$12. Mon–Fri 7am–3pm; Sat-Sun 8am–4pm. Métro: Mont Royal.

Chez Schwartz Charcuterie Hébraïque de Montréal ★ DELI Tell friends you've recently visited Montréal and one will inevitably ask if you made it to the famous Schwartz's deli. Smoked meat sandwiches here are hand-sliced and come piled high on fresh rye; the plates have a side of fries, sour pickle, and cole slaw. There's a "fat" choice to make and most folks opt for medium or medium-fat. It's one of many city landmarks created by a Jewish immigrant, in this case by Reuben Schwartz in 1928, making it Canada's oldest deli. Tables are communal and space is at a premium so come prepared to rub elbows with strangers. Take-out is an option, as is a midnight snack—Schwartz's is open till 12:30am during the week, and later on the weekend.

3895 boul. St-Laurent (just north of rue Roy). www.schwartzsdeli.com. ✆ **514/842-4813.** Sandwiches and meat plates C$7–C$18. No credit cards. Daily 8–10:30am takeout only; Sun–Thurs 10:30am–12:30am; Fri 10:30am–1:30am; Sat 10:30am–2:30am. Métro: Sherbrooke.

Juliette et Chocolat ★ DESSERT This chocolate-centric cafe has been steadily expanding its locations over the years, probably because it fills the broad need of coffee house, luncheonette, and purveyor of exceptional chocolate desserts. You can also order wine or beer, and savory options, too, such as buckwheat *crêpes* and a salad with dark chocolate vinaigrette. Chocolate comes in all forms: as hot and cold beverages, in crepes, in dense brownies (11 kinds!), as sauce over ice cream, in fondue. Take-home goodies like chocolate shaped into fried-egg or avocado forms add to the fun. Additional locations in Outremont at 377 rue Laurier ouest (✆ **514/510-5651**) and in the Latin Quarter at 1615 St-Denis (✆ **514/287-3555**).

3600 boul. St-Laurent (corner of rue Prince Arthur ouest). www.julietteetchocolat.com. ✆ **438/380-1090.** Reservations available for parties of six or more before 9pm. Most items under C$15. Sun–Thurs 11am–11pm; Fri–Sat 11am–midnight. Métro: Sherbrooke.

La Banquise ★ LIGHT FARE The classic French-Canadian *poutine* is served here in a dizzying 30-plus ways, all day, every day. Twists on the classic comfort food include La Dan Dan (with pepperoni, bacon, and onions) and La Kamikaze (merguez sausages, hot peppers, and Tabasco). And yes, vegetarian is now on the menu. Despite *poutine*'s reputation for being a post-2am binge food, La Banquise is incredibly kid-friendly and located on the north end of the Plateau's Parc La Fontaine, where the whole family can stretch their legs after a meal or snack. In addition to *poutine* and breakfast items, salads, burgers, hot dogs, pogos (meat on a stick), and cold beer round out the menu. If you've worked your way through the menu and need a new challenge, step into the hot debate about the dish's origin . . . although you may need to argue *en Français.*

994 rue Rachel est (near rue Boyer). www.restolabanquise.com. ✆ **514/525-2415.** Poutine plates C$7–C$15; most other items less than C$14. Cash only. Daily 24 hr. Métro: Mont Royal.

MILE END & BEYOND

Expensive

Hostaria ★ ITALIAN Not only has Hostaria garnered attention for its simple, but formidable Italian cuisine, developed from inherited recipes, but there's not a bad seat in the house. In this intimate restaurant, established in 2009, tables are draped in white tablecloths, even at lunch, and most overlook a quiet side street in Little Italy. Dishes are arranged as expected—antipasti, primi, secondi, and so on, and portions are modest. That's OK because flavors plumb rich and earthy depths, especially so in the

THE GREAT bagel DEBATE

Ketchup or pickle potato chips? Atlantic or Pacific oysters? Canadians loves to debate and defend their homegrown cuisine and Montréal's bagels often top that list. While locals may lock horns over **Fairmount Bagel** (p. 72) versus **St-Viateur Bagel** (p. 72), and tourists pilgrimage to both to determine their favorite, the debate often boils down to just how much better Montréal's bagels are than "all the rest." As one blogger puts it, the Montréal-style bagel has to be made by hand, "while those NY bagels can be (and are) made by soulless, and probably quite aggressive, machines."

This city's thin O-shapes are made crispy and slightly sweet by being proofed in honey water and then baked in wood-fire ovens. Sure, the taste is out of this world, but what makes the Montréal bagel truly special is that they are only of this world, here in Montréal. The baking process is a marvel in itself and on view 24/7; and in the case of Fairmount, it's a process that hasn't changed since 1919. Though the shops are probably open right now while you are reading this (Fairmount, anyway, is open 24 hrs), in our humble opinion, the case for the Montréal bagel is closed.

marinated vegetable antipasti, homemade pasta, and perfectly seasoned Petite-Nation Bison rib eye. Wine is a showpiece here, literally encased in a glass walk-in, and staff will guide you to a bottle that fits your budget. Sitting in a swivel chair along the lengthy marble-top bar is an ideal spot from which to taste test. It's out of the way for the average tourist, which may be exactly why you seek it out. The location is three subway stops north of Mile End in the Rosemont-La-Petite-Patrie neighborhood, near the Jean-Talon Market. Reservations are recommended.

236 Rue Saint Zotique est (at rue Alma). http://hostaria.ca. ✆ **514/273-5776.** Antipasti and primi C$9–C$26; main courses C$24–C$43. Wed 6pm–midnight; Thurs–Fri noon–midnight; Sun 6pm–midnight. Métro: Beaubien.

Lawrence ★★★ BISTRO When clotted cream gets top billing, you know a place is serious about their brunch. Lawrence serves one of the best biscuit-like pancake marvels we have ever had: the stuff of dreams, soaked in Canadian maple syrup and topped with local strawberries. Blatant about its British affections (hello, plaid couch), Lawrence takes masterful turns with pub standards like bubble and squeak or classic English breakfast for brunch. Lunch and dinner lean more contemporary Québécois: oysters, charcuterie, grilled mackerel, and lamb's liver, for example. Whatever the provenance, the food is excellent. Service is friendly even if you're not one of the regulars, who all seem to be 30-somethings who biked over in vintage dresses and bowling shirts. Reservations recommended.

5201 blvd. St. Laurent (at av. Fairmount est). www.lawrencerestaurant.com. ✆ **514/503-1070.** Brunch main courses C$12–C$17. Dinner main courses C$26–C$30. Wed–Fri 11:30am–3pm and 5:30–11pm; Sat 10am–3pm and 5:30–11pm; Sun 10am–3pm. Métro: Laurier.

Leméac ★★ BISTRO For dinner or weekend brunch, this classic bistro is competent, elegant, yet refreshingly at ease. Tucked on the western end of the upscale avenue-Laurier, it's a neighborhood go-to as well as a destination for those who want beef *tartare* or *moules frites* and want it done right. Service is gracious and unassuming. The kitchen often prepares as many as 12 different desserts (moist chocolate and banana cake with house-made popcorn ice cream, for example). The colorful split fieldstone floor and cherry wood ceiling add subtle flair to the ambience. With a lovely terrace for al fresco dining and an intense wine list, it's a **Café Cherrier** (p. 66) for the well-heeled foodie. Planning a late night? After 10pm there's a C$27 appetizer-plus-main menu.

1045 av. Laurier ouest (corner of av. Durocher). www.restaurantlemeac.com. ✆ **514/270-0999.** Main courses C$23–C$46; late-night menu C$27; weekend brunch C$11–C$18. Mon–Fri noon–midnight; Sat–Sun 10am–midnight. Métro: Laurier.

Moderate

Hôtel Herman ★★ CONTEMPORARY QUÉBÉCOIS Hôtel Herman re-defines hip, both in atmosphere and food quality. First the interior: pine plank floors, industrial fixtures, and exposed brick could add up to retro-chic blah, yet the U-shaped, beaming white bar anchors the establishment and transforms the place to impeccably cool. And the food: on paper it's spare, *terroir* (meaning locally sourced), and predictably Québécois ("Duck from the Goulu farm, sweet onions, black chanterelles"), but one bite in and, *wow,* a new genre emerges. Plates range from small to mid-size and you'll want to order at least two per person. The restaurant is intense about cocktails, too, down to the glassware. The one thing this *hôtel* doesn't have is a room for rent. Well, they'll need to get rid of you somehow. Reservations recommended.

5171 blvd. St-Laurent (just south of av. Fairmount). www.hotelherman.com. ✆ **514/278-7000.** Small plates C$9–C$20. Mon, Wed–Sun 5pm–midnight. Métro: Laurier.

Inexpensive

Aux Vivres ★★ VEGAN In a town of meat—smoked meat, pig's feet, meat pie—it shouldn't be such a surprise that the veggie way hasn't taken firmer root. Thankfully, Aux Vivres has been hitting all the right notes since 1997, and with an especially open spirit. It's set up like a diner, with flavors from every continent: gyro with souvlaki-style seitan, baked-to-order chapati with vegelox and tofu cream, a BLT with bacon made from coconut. There are also salads, rice bowls, soups, desserts, and a daily chef's special. The default recipes are vegan made with organic vegetables, local whenever possible. The high-octane juice bar runs all year although the patio out back, even for this crowd, is seasonal.

4631 boul. St-Laurent (north of av. du Mont-Royal). www.auxvivres.com. ✆ **514/842-3479.** Most items under C$15. Cash only. Mon–Fri 11am–11pm; Sat–Sun 10am–11pm. Métro: Mont Royal.

Bilboquet ★★ DESSERT Slowly and surely this little ice cream joint has been taking over Montréal. The more artful and fitting term for it is an *artisan glacier,* and it's the real deal of handmade ice cream and sorbet, no powder flavor additives. This Outrement location is the original and out of the typical tourist's geographic reach, but there are now six additional storefronts, including one on Plateau Mont-Royal at 1600 Laurier east (✆ **514/439-6501**). But let's get to the good part: the flavors. Maple taffy, honey-lavender, Cassis sorbet (seedless) Raspberry, and Moka-Fouilli (chocolate and coffee ice cream with bits of salty caramel crunch), to

Eat Local Foods

Restaurants throughout the region tout locally sourced food on their menus, with much of the region's food grown, raised, or caught within 161km (100 miles). On menus, *terroir* refers to soil and the restaurant's allegiance to products grown in the immediate region. You can also often find "biodynamic," or organic, wines at many restaurants.

name a few. Bilboquet ice cream is also served in select restaurants and kiosks in the heart of Vieux-Port in warm months. All ages adore these treats.

1311 rue Bernard ouest (at av. Outremont). www.bilboquet.ca. ✆ **514/276-0414.** Most ice cream dishes under C$8. Cash only. March–mid-May daily 11am–9pm; Summer daily 11am–midnight; Mid-Sept–Dec daily 11am–10pm. Closed Jan–Mar. Métro: Outremont.

Fairmount Bagel ★★★ BAKERY There's only so much convincing one can do: Visitors must try a bagel while in Montréal! It's a whole different ballgame from bagels elsewhere. Bagels here are thinner and closer to a pretzel in appearance compared to the fluffy stand-ins you may be used to. Bakers hand-roll each bagel from an enormous slab of dough, then they're dropped in boiling water sweetened with a touch of honey, and baked in big wood-fired ovens on the premises. Poppyseed is the original flavor, though sesame may be the most popular. Founded in 1919, Fairmount offers nearly 20 types, including the Bozo (three bagels twisted to one, which Fairmount calls "a bagel for lovers") and the sweet bagel, comparable to biscotti. The shop is small, to-go only, but absolutely worth popping into to see the bakers in action. No planning needed since it's always open—24 hours a day, 7 days a week—even on Jewish holidays.

74 av. Fairmount ouest (near rue St-Urbain). www.fairmountbagel.com. ✆ **514/272-0667.** Most bagels under C$1. Cash only. Daily 24 hr. Métro: Laurier.

Green Panther ★★ LIGHT FARE This sunny vegan and vegetarian pita spot has something called "hippie sauce" on the menu. Need we say more? Now in two locations (the other is downtown at 2153 Mackay; ✆ **514/903-4744**), Green Panther does veggies up right with traditional falafel and a variety of other healthy combos, with a choice of healthy-sounding sauces, or tahini, or the aforementioned "hippie." The nice thing about going green is that you don't need to wonder about the ingredients. It's also nice to have the option of a half or full-size sandwich. Kombucha and other organic beverages are available as well as vegan baked goods and smoothies. On a recent visit, the soundtrack was all Bob Marley.

66 St-Viateur (near rue St-Urbain). www.thegreenpanther.com. ✆ **514/508-5564.** Most items less than C$8. Cash only. Mon–Sat 11am–10pm; Sun 11am–9pm. Métro: Rosemont or Laurier.

Magpie Pizzeria ★ PIZZA Come to Magpie for wood-fired pizza in a rustically hip atmosphere. Schoolhouse-style chairs surround thick pine tables and industrial pendants light the space. Simplicity rules the menu with Italian-sourced and fresh ingredients. There are nine different thin-crust options with mouth-watering toppings like caramelized onions and ricotta, and always a'Za of the week. It's fine to bring kids (service is friendly, but can be slow) and adults can opt to make a meal of oysters, salad, and charcuterie if they are pizza-ed out. In addition to beer and wine, there are a few apertifs, including Chinotto punch and a house Bloody Mary, oyster optional. Unlike most pizza joints, this one is serious about dessert. *Tarte tatin* with lemon *crème anglaise* over almond shortbread? Yes, please! Reservations recommended.

16 rue Maguire (near boul. St-Laurent). www.pizzeriamagpie.com. ✆ **514/507-2900.** Pizzas C$13–C$19. Tues 5:30–10pm; Wed–Fri noon–3pm and 5:30–10pm; Sat 5:30–11pm; Sun 5:30–10pm. Métro: Laurier.

St-Viateur Bagel & Café ★★ LIGHT FARE Myer Lewkowicz brought his bagel recipe from eastern Europe in 1957 and it's still being followed to a T at St-Viateur's many outposts. Like **Fairmount Bagel,** above, the process includes shaping each bagel by hand, dressing with seeds or spices, and baking in a wood-fired oven (there's a great photo spread of this on the St-Viateur website). Let's be clear: both bakeries make darn good bagels, though some locals would stake their fortune on one versus the other. In addition to taking bagels to go, at this location you can eat in, with bagel sandwiches, soup, or salad. The original, flagship bakery is still located at 263 rue St-Viateur ouest in the Mile End neighborhood. As a sign of the evolving times, St-Viatuer has joined the food-truck revolution and can be followed on Twitter at @StViateurBagel.

1127 av. du Mont-Royal est (at av. Christophe-Colomb). www.stviateurbagel.com. ✆ **514/528-6361.** Most items under C$12. Cash only. Daily 6am–10pm. Métro: Mont Royal.

Wilensky Light Lunch ★★ DINER The thought that comes to mind when you step through the doors here is "time travel." Every year that Wilensky's adds to its history, the more devoted people become to it's remaining exactly as-is. The interior is spare and so, well, 1952. That's when it moved to this locale, though Harry Wilensky started the business in 1932. Either way, it's not hard to imagine the Jewish immigrants who used to sit at one of nine counter stools and order a Moe, better known as the Special: a grilled, all-beef salami and bologna with mustard. It's a crowd-pleaser to present day. (***Insider tip:*** don't ask to hold the mustard and don't ask to have your sandwich cut in two.) The old prices are still on the wall and the new prices remain miraculously low. Another miracle? Genuine, old-time egg cream or cherry cola sodas made in house.

34 rue Fairmount ouest (1 block west of boul. St-Laurent). www.wilenskys.com. ✆ **514/271-0247.** All items less than C$5. Cash only. Mon–Fri 9am–4pm; Sat 10am–4pm. Métro: Laurier.

GAY VILLAGE

Expensive

Mezcla ★★★ SOUTH AMERICAN Word spread like wildfire when this *nuevo latino* bistro opened in 2012. It could've been the novelty—to prepare traditional Peruvian recipes with European cooking techniques—but more likely it was the outstanding results. Start with a Pisco Sour, a South American cocktail topped with egg white, a rare treat since this city is still catching on to the cocktail renaissance. If ordering a la carte, the ceviche, served with mix-ins of spicy fried corn, yucca, and carrot (*mezcla* is Spanish for mixture) is a must. But a majority of the mature and smartly dressed patrons order the C$49 five-course tasting menu, which includes with two seafoods (all from environmentally responsible fisheries) and two meats. Thin slices of milk-fed veal tongue arrive with truffled peaches and a concoction of lime, maple, black sesame, and aji Amarillo—a pepper unique to Peru and frequently used by this kitchen. Servers astutely describe each course and leave ample time in between. For better or worse, voices carry in this relaxed space, making a weeknight feel like Saturday. Reservations are strongly recommended. Mezcla is tucked away in an unexpected spot for a restaurant, let alone for a meandering tourist, and finding it will require dedication. It's worth it.

1251 rue de Champlain (at rue Sainte-Rose). www.restaurantmezcla.com. ✆ **514/525-9934.** Main courses C$19–C$33. 5-course tasting menu C$49. Tues–Sat 5–10pm. Métro: Papineau.

LITTLE BURGUNDY

Expensive

Joe Beef ★★ SEAFOOD/STEAK Foodies will have heard of the glutton-inducing Joe Beef before arriving in Montréal, and it's likely that some of them will have planned their trip around dining here. Co-founder David McMillan and the restaurant—think boisterous diner with adventurous food—have been profiled everywhere since the 2005 opening, and Vacay.ca named it the top restaurant in Canada in 2013. Like David Chang's teeny Momofuku in New York City, reservations for the limited seats here are essential. Most guests start with oysters or the Foie Gras Double Down: two slabs of deep-fried foie sandwiching bacon, cheddar, and maple syrup (no one seems to care that "Food & Wine" magazine quoted McMillan saying that the dish was a joke that took on a life of its own and that "I would never eat it. I think it's disgusting.") The chalkboard menu often includes chicken, grits, and crayfish; cornflake sturgeon nuggets; *saucisse de lapin* (rabbit and pork sausage); a selection of meats such as pork chop, BBQ ribs, and steak; and Spaghetti Homard-Lobster. The restaurant describes itself as "an homage to Charles'Joe-Beef' McKiernan, 19th century innkeeper and Montréal working class hero" and "a drunken crawl away from the Historic Atwater market."

2491 rue Notre-Dame ouest (near rue Vinet). www.joebeef.ca. ✆ **514/935-6504.** Main courses C$27–C$50. Tues–Sat 6:30pm–close. Métro: Lionel-Groulx.

EXPLORING MONTRÉAL

7

Montréal is a feast of choices, able to satisfy the desires of physically active and culturally curious visitors. Hike up the city's mountain, Mont Royal, in the middle of the city; cycle for miles beside 19th-century warehouses and locks on the Lachine Canal; take in artworks and ephemera at more than 30 museums and as many historic buildings; attend a Canadiens hockey match; party until dawn on rue Crescent, the Main, or in Old Montréal; or soak up the history of 400 years of conquest and immigration. It's all here for the taking.

Getting from hotels to attractions is easy. Montréal has an efficient Métro system, a logical street grid, and wide boulevards that all aid in the largely uncomplicated movement of people from place to place.

If you're planning to check out several museums, consider buying the Montréal Museums Pass (see the "Money Savers" box on p. 79). ***Tip:*** Some museums have good restaurants or cafes. Remember, too, that most museums—though not all—are closed on Mondays.

MONTRÉAL'S ICONIC SIGHTS

- Basilique Notre-Dame ★★★, p. 83
- Biodôme de Montréal ★★★, p. 89
- Centre des Sciences de Montréal ★★, p. 84
- Jardin Botanique ★★★, p. 90
- Musée d'Art Contemporain de Montréal, p. 78
- Musée des Beaux-Arts ★★★, p. 79
- Parc du Mont-Royal ★★, p. 94
- Pointe-à-Callière (Museum of Archaeology) ★★★, p. 85
- Vieux-Port ★★★, p. 94

OTHER TOP ATTRACTIONS

- Basilique-Cathédrale Marie-Reine-du-Monde, p. 78
- Centre Canadien d'Architecture ★, p. 78
- Insectarium de Montréal, p. 90
- La Ronde Amusement Park ★, p. 98
- L'Oratoire St-Joseph ★, p. 87
- Montréal Canadiens Hockey ★, p. 78
- Musée du Château Ramezay ★, p. 85
- Musée McCord ★★, p. 80
- Parc La Fontaine ★, p. 94
- Rio Tinto Alcan Planétarium ★, p. 90
- Stade Olympique, p. 91
- Underground City, p. 81

Montréal Attractions

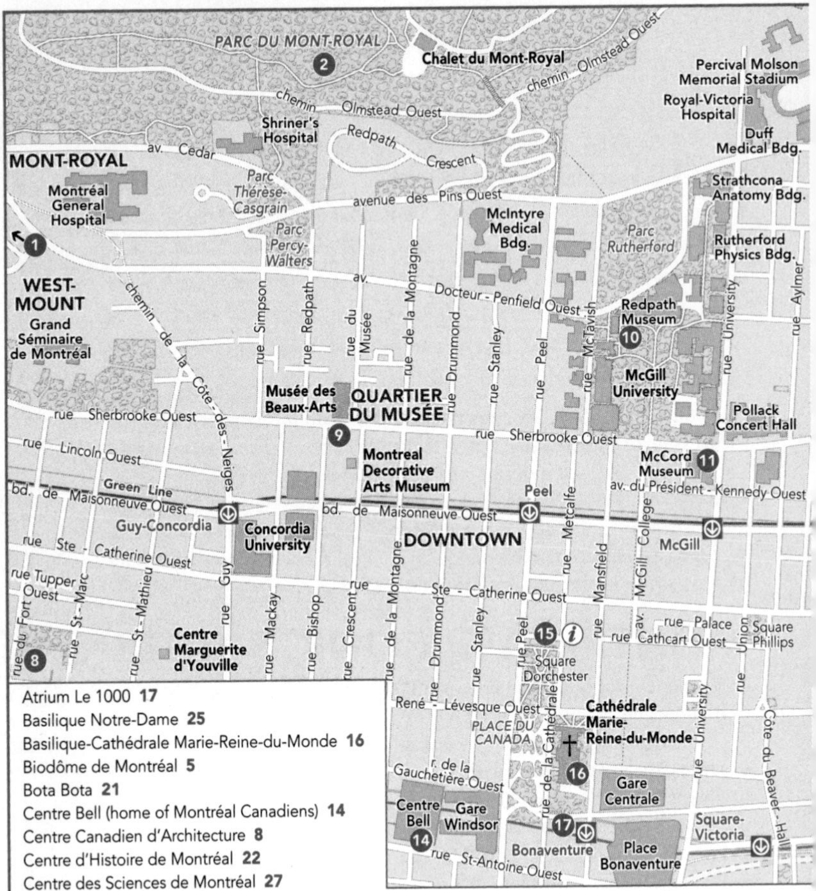

Atrium Le 1000 **17**
Basilique Notre-Dame **25**
Basilique-Cathédrale Marie-Reine-du-Monde **16**
Biodôme de Montréal **5**
Bota Bota **21**
Centre Bell (home of Montréal Canadiens) **14**
Centre Canadien d'Architecture **8**
Centre d'Histoire de Montréal **22**
Centre des Sciences de Montréal **27**
Chapelle Notre-Dame-de-Bon-Secours **32**
Croisières AML Cruises departure point **27**
Fantômes Ghost Walks **24**
Hôtel de Ville **18**
IMAX Theater **27**
Infotouriste Centre (Tourist Information Center) **15**
Insectarium de Montréal **3**
Jardin Botanique **3**
La Ronde Amusement Park **20**
Le Bateau-Mouche departure point **29**
Les Sautes-Moutons departure point **34**
L'Oratoire St-Joseph **1**
Marché Bonsecours **31**
Musée d'Art Contemporain de Montréal **12**
Musée des Beaux-Arts **9**
Musée du Château Ramezay **19**
Musée Marguerite-Bourgeoys **33**
Musée McCord **11**
Musée Redpath **10**
Navettes Fluviales Maritime Shuttles departure point **29**
Parc du Mont-Royal **2**
Parc La Fontaine **7**
Place Jacques-Cartier **30**
Pointe-à-Callière (Montréal Museum of Archaeology and History) **23**
Rio Tinto Alcan Planétarium **6**
Scandinave Les Bains **26**
Stade Olympique **4**
Underground City **13**
Vieux-Port **28**

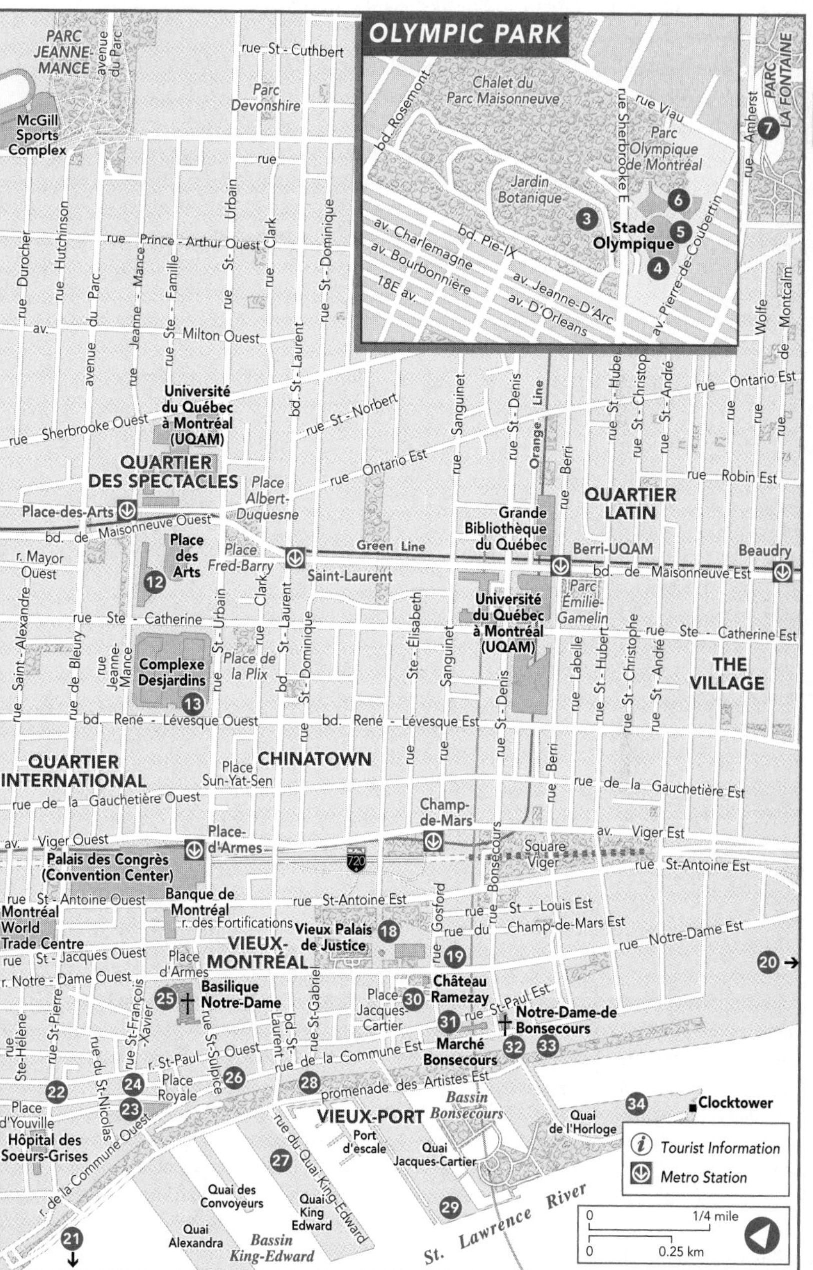
OLYMPIC PARK
Chalet du Parc Maisonneuve
bd. Rosemont
rue Sherbrooke E
rue Viau
Parc Olympique de Montréal
Jardin Botanique
Stade Olympique
bd. Pie-IX
av. Charlemagne
av. Bourbonnière
18E av.
av. Jeanne-D'Arc
av. D'Orleans
av. Pierre-de-Coubertin
PARC LA FONTAINE
rue Amherst
PARC JEANNE-MANCE
avenue du Parc
McGill Sports Complex
rue St-Cuthbert
Parc Devonshire
rue Prince-Arthur Ouest
rue Durocher
rue Hutchinson
rue Jeanne-Mance
rue Ste-Famille
rue St-Urbain
rue Clark
rue St-Dominique
av. Milton Ouest
bd. St-Laurent
rue Sherbrooke Ouest
Université du Québec à Montréal (UQAM)
rue St-Norbert
rue Ontario Est
QUARTIER DES SPECTACLES
Place Albert-Duquesne
Place-des-Arts
bd. de Maisonneuve Ouest
r. Mayor Ouest
Place des Arts
Place Fred-Barry
Saint-Laurent
Green Line
Orange Line
rue Sanguinet
rue St-Denis
rue Berri
rue St-Hubert
rue St-Christophe
rue St-André
rue Wolfe
rue de Montcalm
rue Robin Est
QUARTIER LATIN
Grande Bibliothèque du Québec
Berri-UQAM
Beaudry
bd. de Maisonneuve Est
Parc Émilie-Gamelin
rue Ste-Catherine
rue Ste-Catherine Est
rue Saint-Alexandre
rue de Bleury
Complexe Desjardins
Place de la Plix
rue Ste-Élisabeth
rue Labelle
THE VILLAGE
bd. René-Lévesque Ouest
bd. René-Lévesque Est
QUARTIER INTERNATIONAL
Place Sun-Yat-Sen
CHINATOWN
rue de la Gauchetière Ouest
rue de la Gauchetière Est
Champ-de-Mars
av. Viger Ouest
av. Viger Est
Place-d'Armes
Palais des Congrès (Convention Center)
720
Square Viger
rue Bonsecours
rue St-Antoine Est
rue St-Antoine Ouest
Banque de Montréal
Montréal World Trade Centre
r. des Fortifications
rue Gosford
rue St-Louis Est
rue du Champ-de-Mars Est
rue Notre-Dame Est
Vieux Palais de Justice
VIEUX-MONTRÉAL
rue St-Jacques Ouest
Place d'Armes
r. Notre-Dame Ouest
Basilique Notre-Dame
Château Ramezay
Place Jacques-Cartier
rue St-Paul Est
Notre-Dame-de Bonsecours
Marché Bonsecours
rue Ste-Hélène
rue St-Pierre
rue St-François-Xavier
rue St-Sulpice
bd. St-Laurent
rue St-Gabriel
rue du St-Nicolas
r. St-Paul Ouest
Place Royale
rue de la Commune Est
promenade des Artistes Est
Bassin Bonsecours
Place d'Youville
Hôpital des Soeurs-Grises
r. de la Commune Ouest
VIEUX-PORT
Port d'escale
rue du Quai King-Edward
Quai Jacques-Cartier
Quai de l'Horloge
Clocktower
Quai des Convoyeurs
Quai King Edward
Quai Alexandra
Bassin King-Edward
St. Lawrence River
Tourist Information
Metro Station
0 1/4 mile
0 0.25 km
2 3 4 5 6 7 12 13 18 19 20 21 22 23 24 25 26 27 28 29 30 31 32 33 34

DOWNTOWN ATTRACTIONS

If this is your first trip to Montréal, consider starting with the downtown walking tour in chapter 9.

Basilique-Cathédrale Marie-Reine-du-Monde No one who has seen both will confuse Montréal's "Mary Queen of the World" cathedral with St. Peter's Basilica in Rome, but a scaled-down homage was the intention of Bishop Ignace Bourget, who oversaw its construction after the first Catholic cathedral here burned to the ground in 1852. Most impressive is the 76m-high (249-ft.) dome, about a third of the size of the Italian original. The statues standing on the roofline represent patron saints of the region, providing a local touch. The interior is less rewarding visually than the exterior, but the ceiling and high altar are worth a look.

1085 rue de la Cathédrale (at rue Mansfield). www.cathedralecatholiquedemontreal.org. ✆ **514/866-1661.** Free admission; donations accepted. Mon–Fri 7am–6:15pm; Sat–Sun 7:30am–6:15pm. Métro: Bonaventure.

Centre Canadien d'Architecture ★ The CCA is a "bucket-list" destination museum for anyone interested in architecture, professional or not. The massive building also serves as a research center and is recognized internationally as a leader in public awareness, scholarship, and innovation in architecture. Exhibitions aim to connect how we think about architecture, how it is practiced in the modern day, and how societies and cultural differences influence changes over time. There are usually several temporary exhibitions on display (they change regularly), plus permanent collections that include prints and drawings, sketches, artifacts, and publications, some of which date back more than 600 years. Nearly all captions and text are in English and French. Across the street on the opposite side of boulevard René-Lévesque is a sculpture garden that provides a serene contrast to the hustle and bustle of the surrounding city.

1920 rue Baile (at rue du Fort). www.cca.qc.ca. ✆ **514/939-7026.** Admission C$10 adults, with discount for seniors and free for students and children; free admission Thurs after 5:30pm. Wed–Sun 11am–6pm; Thurs 11am–9pm. Métro: Guy-Concordia.

Montréal Canadiens Hockey ★ The city's beloved hockey team plays downtown at the Centre Bell arena. The Canadiens have won 24 Stanley Cups (the last one in 1992–93), and the season runs from October to April, with playoff games potentially continuing into June.

Centre Bell arena, 1909 ave des Canadiens-de-Montréal (at rue de la Montagne). www.canadiens.com. ✆ **877/668-8269** or 514/790-2525. Tickets C$43–C$263. Métro: Bonaventure or Lucien-L'Allier.

Musée d'Art Contemporain de Montréal ★★ The Museum of Contemporary Art is a must for art lovers with an interest in modern-day artistic movements. The collection is primarily Québec-centric, with works by the likes of Paul-Émile Borduas, Alfred Pellan, and Jean-Paul Riopelle among others, but there are also many works by international artists. This is no stodgy museum of the old-school: although you'll still see plenty of artwork hanging on walls, you're just as likely to encounter video installations, abstract sculptures, and studio glass creations that can make you believe inanimate objects are in fact quite alive. Onsite is a restaurant and a gift shop selling a variety of items such as jewlery, watches, stationery, and ceramics, nearly all handmade by local artisans.

185 rue Ste-Catherine ouest. www.macm.org. ✆ **514/847-6226.** Admission C$12 adults, with discounts for students and seniors; free for children 12 and under; free admission Wed 6–9pm.

MONEY savers

- **Buy the Montréal Museums Pass.** This pass grants entry to 38 museums and attractions, including most of those mentioned in this chapter. The C$75 pass is good for any 3 days of your choice in the 3 weeks following your first visit (one visit per museum). For a little more, the C$80 pass is good for 3 consecutive days plus unlimited access to public transportation (including the airport shuttle, bus no. 747) along with the museums. There are no separate rates for seniors or children. The pass is available at all participating museums, many hotels, the tourist offices at 1255 rue Peel (downtown) and 174 rue Notre-Dame (in Vieux-Montréal), and online at www.montrealmuseums.org.
- **Visit La Vitrine for last-minute ticket deals.** Regular priced and same-day discount tickets for a huge variety of cultural events are available at La Vitrine's high-tech ticketing center at 2 Ste-Catherine Es (✆ **866/924-5538** or 514/285-4545). Check the website, www.lavitrine.com, for a list bargain events; they are indicated by a distinctive red dot, under the "last minute" section.
- **Flash your AAA card.** Members of the American Automobile Association (AAA) get the same discounts as members of its Canadian sister organization, the CAA. That includes reduced rates at many museums, hotels, and restaurants.
- **Time your trip to coincide with Montréal Museums Day.** On the last Sunday in May, more than 30 museums welcome visitors for free in a citywide open house. Free shuttle buses run between the venues, as well. Visit www.montrealmuseums.org and click on "Montréal Museums Day" to see participating museums.

Tues and Thurs–Sun 11am–6pm; Wed and first Fri of the month (except Jan and Aug) 11am–9pm. Métro: Place des Arts.

Musée des Beaux-Arts ★★★ In recent years, Montréal's glorious Museum of Fine Arts has undergone dramatic new growth, sprouting new buildings and taking over an adjacent church. What was once one building on the north side of rue Sherbrooke is now a five-pavilion complex spilling over onto both sides of the city's grand boulevard (and directly onto the small ave Du Musée). All this enhances the museum's position as top museum in the province. If you can get to only one museum on your trip, make it this one. The permanent collection is always free to visit; only temporary exhibitions have an entry fee.

Recent shows have ranged from the dazzling and ginormous glassworks of Dale Chihuly to photography from the last 40 years by Québec auteurs. Exhibitions in 2014 represent painter Peter Doig (Jan–June 2014), the jewel-like Russian Fabergé eggs (summer 2014), and "From Van Gogh and Gauguin to Kirchner and Kandinsky: German Expressionism and France" (fall 2014). The museum has an expansive permanent collection that travels from the Old Masters to modern art—El Greco to Renoir to Rodin and beyond.

The buzz about the museum today, though, is its spectacular new Claire and Marc Bourgie Pavilion of Québécois and Canadian Art, which debuted in 2011. The collection of more than 3,000 works includes 500 Inuit works and 180 Amerindian artifacts; 600 of them are on display on six levels. Particularly engaging is the "Age of the Manifesto" gallery, featuring modernist works from the 1940s through 1960s by important Québécois including Alfred Pellan, Paul-Émile Borduas, and Jean-Paul Riopelle. A free audioguide for the Québec and Canadian wing includes commentary on 75 works, clips of artist interviews, and a musical soundtrack.

The museum also inaugurated the Bourgie Concert Hall inside the renovated 1894 church that it incorporated as part of the recent renovation. The hall features 20 stained-glass windows by Louis Comfort Tiffany. However, the church/concert hall is only open to visitors on tours or when attending a concert.

The entire complex linked by underground galleries. The street-level museum store, **M Boutique and Bookstore,** has an impressive selection of signature products, exhibition products, and posters from the artwork of Québécois painter Marc-Aurèle Fortin. Bistro **Café des Beaux-Arts** is an elegant dining option.

1380 rue Sherbrooke ouest (at rue Crescent). www.mmfa.qc.ca. ✆ **514/285-2000.** Free admission to the permanent collection. Admission to temporary exhibitions C$20 adults 31 and over, C$12 ages 13 to 30, free for children 12 and under. Wed 5–9pm C$10 ages 13 and up. Permanent collection Tues–Sun 10am–5pm; temporary exhibition same hours plus Wed until 9pm. Métro: Guy-Corcordia.

Musée McCord ★★ This museum is fresh at each visit, and it even boasts two appealing new permanent exhibitions: "Montréal: Points of View," touching on everything from first inhabitants to the liveliness of boulevard St-Laurent today, and "Wearing Our Identity: The First People's Collection," which presents a respectful look at how members of the region's First Nations thinking about their relationship to their clothing, which often is made of animal pelts. Says one sign: the clothes transform the wearer, "allowing them to acquire the strength, wisdom and spiritual power of the animals the garments are made from." A good museum shop features a small collection of locally made bags and fur hats from **Harricana** (p. 87), aboriginal artwork, and children's toys. Each exhibition is small, and won't take most visitors more than 15 minutes each, but there usually are four shows on display.

690 rue Sherbrooke ouest (at rue University). www.mccord-museum.qc.ca. ✆ **514/398-7100.** Admission C$14 adults, C$10 seniors, C$8 students, free for children 12 and under; free admission every Wed 5–9pm. Tues and Thurs–Fri 10am–6pm; Wed 10am–9pm; Sat–Sun 10am–5pm; Mon (Late June through Labour Day) 10am–6pm. Métro: McGill.

Musée Redpath Run by McGill University, this engaging, but slightly outdated museum focuses on natural history, but is best known for its Egyptian collection—including mummies and a sarcophagus—and a small but impressive display of fully constructed dinosaur skeletons. The kind of stuff kids love. There's an impressive collection of minerals from Québec province as well as an outdoor geological garden displaying examples of minerals and fossils from all parts of Canada. The museum is in a nice part of downtown on the McGill campus, and is free.

859 rue Sherbrooke ouest (rue University). www.mcgill.ca/redpath. ✆ **514/398-4086.** Free admission (donations suggested). Mon–Fri 9am–5pm; Sun noon–5pm. Closed public holidays and long weekends. Métro: McGill.

Shopping in Downtown

Among natives, shopping ranks right up there with dining out as a prime activity. Many Montréalers are of French ancestry, after all, and impeccable taste must bubble up through the Gallic gene pool. The city has produced a thriving fashion industry, from couture to ready-to-wear, with a history that reaches back to the earliest trade in furs and leather.

THE BEST BUYS

While not cheap, **Canadian Inuit sculptures** and 19th- to early-20th-century **country furniture** are handsome and authentic. Less expensive crafts are also available, including quilts and drawings by First Nation and other folk artists. The province's daring **high-fashion designers** produce appealing clothing at prices that are often reasonable. And while demand has diminished, superbly constructed **furs and leather goods** that recall Montréal's long history as part of the fur trade remain high-ticket items.

THE BEST SHOPPING AREAS

In downtown, **rue Sherbrooke** is a major high-end shopping street, with international and domestic designers, luxury shops, art galleries, and the Holt Renfrew department store. Also downtown, **rue Ste-Catherine** is home to the city's top department stores and is the heart of mid-priced shopping—it's the central commercial artery. From the cross street rue Aylmer, where the department store La Baie is located, Ste-Catherine offers a 12-block stretch of stores heading west that includes super-high-end jeweler Henry Birks, the moderately priced Simons department store, and the swank Ogilvy department store, where a bagpiper still announces the noon hour amid glowing chandeliers and wide aisles. International labels including Tommy Hilfiger, Kiehl's, Mango, HMV, and H&M are all represented. Streets are crowded, and the atmosphere is frenetic. Note that Ste-Catherine also has a smattering of adult strip clubs and sex shops (usually on the second floor) right alongside the family-friendly fare. For better and for worse, the mixed use of the street is a Montréal signature.

DOWNTOWN'S UNDERGROUND CITY

A unique shopping opportunity in Montréal is the **underground city,** also known, somewhat less dramatically, as the underground pedestrian network, and officially called RÉSO (from *réseau,* which means network in French). It's a warren of passageways connecting more than 1,700 shops in 10 shopping malls that have levels both above and below street level. Typical is the **Complexe Desjardins** (www.complexedesjardins.com; ✆ **514/845-4636**), a downtown mall with entrances at street level and underground, bounded by rues Ste-Catherine, St-Urbain, and Jeanne-Mance, and boulevard René-Lévesque. It has waterfalls and fountains, trees and hanging vines, and lanes of shops in every direction.

Another intriguing hub is **Les Cours Mont-Royal** at 1455 rue Peel (www.lcmr.ca; ✆ **514/842-7777**). It feels like a regular mall on the Métro level, where food courts, shoe shines, and scarf kiosks, but upstairs, you'll find shops suitable for outfitting indie rock bands—at least, ones that have sold (many) albums. Here C$300 jeans are *de rigueur* at independently owned boutiques, sunglasses are worn indoors, and a giant chandelier harkens back to the building's former life as the Mont-Royal Hotel.

Navigating the underground city is a challenge, as maps, signage, and even numbering of levels can differ from one section to the next. The main thing to remember is that when you enter a street-level shopping emporium downtown, it's likely that you'll be able to head to a lower level and connect to the tunnels and shopping hallways that lead to another set of stores.

FAVORITE DOWNTOWN STORES

We love **bookstores** (naturally) and many of our favorites are downtown: **Archambault** specializes in children's books along with CDs and musical instruments and is at Place des Arts at 1501 rue Jeanne-Mance (www.archambault.ca; ✆ **514/281-0367**). **Chapters** is the biggest bookstore chain in Canada (its sister store is **Indigo Musique & Café,** below), and is in the middle of the shopping hubbub at 1171 rue Ste-Catherine ouest (✆ **514/849-8825**). **Paragraphe** has a long storefront popular with students from McGill and is at 2220 avenue McGill College (www.paragraphbooks.com; ✆ **514/845-5811**). And **Ulysses**—ah, Ulysses—focuses on travel books of all shapes and sizes, in both English and French; its located at 560 avenue President Kennedy (www.ulyssesguides.com; ✆ **514/843-7222**). Finally, west of downtown, at 52 avenue Westminster North, the folks at **Bonder Bookstore** (www.bonder.com; ✆ **514/484-7131**) will happily take your special order by phone.

Guilde Canadienne des Métiers d'Art ★ In English, it's called the Canadian Guild of Crafts. A small, but choice collection of items is displayed in a meticulously arranged gallery setting: blown glass, tapestries, wooden bowls. The store is particularly strong in avant-garde jewelry and Inuk sculpture. A small carving might be had for C$100 to C$300, while larger, more important pieces go for thousands. 1460 rue Sherbrooke ouest (near rue Mackay), downtown. www.canadianguild.com. ✆ **866/477-6091.**

Harry Rosen For more than 50 years, this well-known retailer of designer suits and accessories has been making men look good in its own Harry Rosen line as well as name brands like Armani. Les Cours Mont-Royal, 1455 rue Peel (at boul. de Maisonneuve), downtown. www.harryrosen.com. ✆ **514/284-3315.**

Indigo Musique & Café ★ Occupying a street-level space in the downtown mall Place Montréal Trust, this very complete store sells music, books, magazines, and gifts, and operates a cafe upstairs. 1500 av. McGill College (at rue Ste-Catherine), downtown. www.chapters.indigo.ca. ✆ **514/281-5549.**

Musée des Beaux-Arts Boutique ★ An unusually large and impressive shop (which goes by the name M Boutique and Bookstore) that sells everything from folk art to furniture. The expected art-related postcards and prints are at hand, along with ties, watches, scarves, toys, games, jewelry, and Inuit crafts, with special focus on work by Québec artisans. The boutique is also online. 1380 rue Sherbrooke ouest (at rue Crescent), downtown. www.mbam.qc.ca/en/boutique. ✆ **514/285-1600.**

VIEUX-MONTRÉAL ATTRACTIONS

Vieux-Montréal's central plaza is **Place Jacques-Cartier,** the focus of much activity in the warm months. The plaza consists of two repaved streets bracketing a center promenade that slopes down from rue Notre-Dame to Old Port, with venerable stone buildings from the 1700s along both sides. Horse-drawn carriages gather at the plaza's base, and outdoor cafes, street performers, and flower sellers recall a Montréal of a century ago. Locals insist they would never go to a place so overrun by tourists—which makes one wonder why so many of them do, in fact, congregate here. They take the sun and sip sangria on the terraces just as much as visitors do, enjoying the unfolding pageant.

If this is your first trip to Montréal, consider the Vieux-Montréal walking tour in chapter 9. It leads past most of the sites listed here and can help you get your bearings.

Basilique Notre-Dame ★★★ Breathtaking in the richness of its interior furnishings and big enough to hold 4,000 worshipers, this magnificent structure was designed in 1824 by James O'Donnell, an Irish-American Protestant architect from New York—who was so profoundly moved by the experience that he converted to Catholicism after its completion. The impact is understandable. Of Montréal's hundreds of churches, Notre-Dame's interior is the most stunning, with a wealth of exquisite details, most of it carved from rare woods that have been delicately gilded and painted. O'Donnell, clearly a proponent of the Gothic Revival style, is the only person honored by burial in the crypt. The main altar was carved from linden wood, the work of Québécois architect Victor Bourgeau. Behind it is the **Chapelle Sacré-Coeur (Sacred Heart Chapel),** much of which was destroyed by an arsonist in 1978; it was rebuilt and rededicated in 1982. The altar displays 32 bronze panels representing birth, life, and death, cast by Montréal artist Charles Daudelin. A 10-bell carillon resides in the east tower, while the west tower contains a single massive bell, nicknamed **"Le Gros Bourdon,"** which weighs more than 12 tons and emanates a low, resonant rumble that vibrates right up through your feet. A 35-minute sound-and-light show called "Et la lumière fut" ("And Then There Was Light") is presented Tuesday through Saturday evenings from the last week in June through the first week of January, but not on holidays. Legendary tenor Luciano Pavarotti performed his famous Christmas concert here in 1978, the same place where French-Canadian songstress Céline Dion had her Cinderella wedding some 16 years later.

110 rue Notre-Dame ouest (on Place d'Armes). www.basiliquenddm.org. ✆ **514/842-2925.** Basilica C$5 adults, C$4 children 7–17, free for children 6 and under; includes 20-min. guided tour. Light show C$10 adults, C$9 seniors, C$5 children 17 and younger. Basilica Mon–Fri 8am–4:30pm, Sat 8am–4pm, Sun 12:30–4pm; light show late June–Sept Tues–Fri 6:30 and 8:30pm, Sat 7 and 8:30pm. Oct–early Jan Tues–Thurs 6:30pm, Fri 6:30 and 8:30pm, Sat 7 and 8:30pm. Métro: Place d'Armes.

Bota Bota ★ Converted from a real boat, Bota Bota's highly modern, all-season spa offers a luxurious water circuit of dry saunas, steam rooms, and three Jacuzzis, two of which are outside and offer stunning northern views of the Old Port. You can also come for relaxing body treatments in one of the many well-appointed private rooms or enjoy a manicure or pedicure in the boat's bow that also gives lovely views through its panoramic windows. Access to the "boat" starts at C$35 (depending on time of day) for 3 hours of play (or relax) time in all the water facilities, lounges, and bistro. Additional treatments include the "Tribal Journey" for C$135, which is 90 minutes and includes a "coffee grain scrub" and Tahitian massage.

Corner of rue de la Commune ouest and rue McGill. www.botabota.ca. ✆ **514/284-0333.** Daily 10am–10pm. Métro: Square-Victoria.

Centre d'Histoire de Montréal ★ Formerly a fire station, this 1903 building at Place d'Youville is now a well-run museum chronicling the history of Montréal. It includes a permanent exhibit that covers Montréal's beginings in the 16th-century all the way through to the modern day. You'll learn about the native people who first inhabited the region, the effect of European settlement, and how the city today manages to keep advancing in new and unique ways while still looking back to its storied past. There's also a well-curated collection of domestic artifacts spanning the 20th-century through today, including items that you'll probably remember from your own childhood, whether you grew up in Montréal or not.

335 Place d'Youville (at rue St-Pierre). www.ville.montreal.qc.ca/chm. ✆ **514/872-3207.** Admission C$6 adults, with discounts for students, children and seniors; free for children 5 and under. Jan–Nov Tues–Sun 10am–5pm. Métro: Square-Victoria.

Centre des Sciences de Montréal ★★ The Montréal Science Centre is a family-friendly complex that's arguably the most engaging and interactive experience a visitor will have in Montréal. Not just a museum, the CSM approaches science and technology in a hands-on way, so visitors can understand its applications in everyday life. Many of its exhibits and programs are geared toward adolescents and tweens (a show about sex was extremely straightforward and popular), but there's plenty to tap the inner kid in all visitors, young or old. Permanent exhibitions include Mission Gaia, a multimedia role-playing exhibit in which visitors work collectively to solve environmental and social problems, a technological showcase highlighting innovations that have dual purposes. Temporary exhibitions are a big draw; some recent ones include an exhibit of life-sized animatronic dinosaurs and an exhibit of props, costumes, and other materials from the "Star Wars" movies. Also onsite is an **IMAX theater** (p. 98), an international themed food court, multiple restaurants, a gift shop, and a summertime mall of boutiques at individual kiosks aligning the building.

Quai King Edward, Vieux-Port. www.montrealsciencecentre.com. ✆ **877/496-4724** or 514/496-4724. Admission for exhibitions C$14.50 adults, with discounts for children and seniors; free for children 3 and under. Exhibition tickets are $20 adults, with discounts for children and seniors; it includes admission to the permanent exhibitions. Combo packages are also available, go to the website for details and schedules. Daily 10am–5pm. Métro: Place d'Armes or Champ-de-Mars.

Chapelle Notre-Dame-de-Bon-Secours/Musée Marguerite-Bourgeoys ★ Just to the east of Marché Bonsecours, Notre-Dame-de-Bon-Secours Chapel is called the Sailors' Church because of the special attachment that fishermen and other mariners have to it. Their devotion is manifest in the several ship models hanging from the ceiling inside. There's also an excellent view of the harbor from the church's tower.

The first building, which no longer stands, was the project of an energetic teacher named Marguerite Bourgeoys (1620–1700) and built in 1675. Bourgeoys had come from France to undertake the education of the children of the colonists and, later, the native peoples. She and other teachers founded the Congregation of Notre-Dame, Canada's first nuns' order. The pioneering Bourgeoys was canonized in 1982 as the Canadian church's first female saint, and in 2005, for the chapel's 350th birthday, her remains were brought to the church and interred in the left-side altar.

A restored 18th-century crypt under the chapel houses the museum. Part of it is devoted to relating Bourgeoys's life and work, while another section displays artifacts from an archaeological site here, including ruins and materials from the colony's earliest days. An Amerindian campsite on display dates back more than 2,400 years.

400 rue St-Paul est (at the foot of rue Bonsecours). www.marguerite-bourgeoys.com. ✆ **514/282-8670.** Free admission to chapel. Museum (includes archaeological site) C$10 adults, C$7 seniors and students, C$5 kids ages 6–12, free for children 5 and under. C$20 families. May to mid-Oct Tues–Sun 10am–6pm; mid-Oct to mid-Jan and Mar–April 11am–4pm. Closed mid-Jan through Feb. Métro: Champ-de-Mars.

Hôtel de Ville City Hall, finished in 1878, is relatively young by Vieux-Montréal standards, and it's still in use, with the mayor's office on the main floor. The French Second Empire design makes it look as though it was imported, stone by stone, from the mother country: Balconies, turrets, and mansard roofs decorate the exterior. The details are particularly visible when the exterior is illuminated at night. The Hall of Honour is made of green marble from Campan, France, and houses Art Deco lamps from Paris and a bronze-and-glass chandelier, also from France, that weighs a metric ton. It was from the balcony above the awning that, in 1967, an ill-mannered Charles de Gaulle, then president of France, proclaimed, "Vive le Québec Libre!" ("Long live free Québec!")—a gesture that pleased his immediate audience, but strained relations with the Canadian government for years.

275 rue Notre-Dame est (at the corner of rue Gosford). www.ville.montreal.qc.ca. ✆ **514/872-0311.** Free admission. Mon–Fri 8am–5pm. Closed public holidays. Several 1-hr. guided tours July to late Aug Mon–Fri 10am–5pm; call or check website for schedule. Métro: Champ-de-Mars.

Marché Bonsecours Bonsecours Market is an imposing neoclassical building with a long facade, a colonnaded portico, and a silvery dome that can be seen from many parts of Vieux Montréal. It was built in the mid-1800s—the Doric columns of the portico were cast of iron in England—and first used as the Parliament of United Canada, and then as Montréal's City Hall until 1878. The architecture alone makes a brief visit worthwhile. For many years after 1878, it served as the city's central market. Essentially abandoned for much of the 20th century, it was restored in 1964 to house city government offices. Today, it contains restaurants, art galleries, and high-end, but affordable boutiques featuring Québécois products. The market is also a good landmark to keep in mind in case you find yourself in need of public restrooms.

350 rue St-Paul est (at the foot of rue St-Claude). www.marchebonsecours.qc.ca. ✆ **514/872-7730.** Free admission. Fall–spring daily 10am–6pm; summer daily 10am–9pm. Métro: Champ-de-Mars.

Musée du Château Ramezay ★ Named for Claude de Ramezay, governor of Montréal from 1704 to 1724, the château was built in 1705. It served as home to Ramezay and then the city's other governors until it was sold in the mid-1700s. It became the local headquarters to the American Continental Army in 1775 when revolutionary forces took control of the city from the British. Benjamin Franklin stayed here for a time in 1776 as he tried to convince the Québécois to side with the Americans in revolt against the British—to no avail. The building was subsequently used for a variety of purposes, including home to the English governors of Lower Canada, as a faculty building for Laval University's school of medicine, and as a government office building. In 1895 it was turned into a museum, and today it provides an excellent primer on the history of Montréal. In summertime, costumed interpreters help enlighten visitors on what life was like in early Montréal. There's also a historically accurate garden containing medicinal herbs, vegetables, and ornamental flowers that were popular around the time the château was built. There are several permanent exhibits on site, including one that outlines what life was like in the city in the 18th century. Special hands-on programs take place throughout the year, and may include spinning textiles, making soap or candles, and bread baking on a brick hearth.

280 rue Notre-Dame est. www.chateauramezay.qc.ca. ✆ **514/861-3708.** Museum admission C$10 adults, with discounts for students, children, and seniors; free for children 4 and under. Free admission to governor's garden. June to mid-Oct daily 10am–6pm; mid-Oct to May Tues–Sun 10am–4:30pm. Métro: Champ-de-Mars.

Pointe-à-Callière (Montréal Museum of Archaeology and History) ★★★ Several Montréal museums provide a thorough history of the city, but none quite match the heft of this one. For starters, Pointe-à-Callière consists of six buildings spread out exactly where the original colonists settled in the 1640s and is a bona fide archaeological site. Permanent exhibits include a multimedia show, and self-guided tour through the heart of the building. A series of underground tunnels wind their way to the Custom House, a path along which you'll see the centuries-old foundations of the original buildings that once stood here. As you go, you'll see illumiated displays showing off artifacts found during the excavations that took place, as well as the city's first Catholic cemetery, dating to 1643. The design of the newest building—the Éperon building—is a perfect example of contrasts, with a contemporary exterior and triangular shape reminiscent of the Victorian-era Royal Insurance building that stood here until 1951. Much of the museum is better for adults than children, but a new "Archaeo-Adventure" space opened in 2012 in the museum's Mariners' House, targeting kids 8 to 14; it simulates an archaeological dig for children and families, including a chance to role-play in the head archaeologist's tent and lab space. In addition, and somewhat inexplicably, an exhibit about The Beatles, who played Montréal in 1964, runs here through March 2014. The cafe is open for lunch only and the gift shop is located in the Mariners' House. To sample the collection before or after a visit, find the museum at www.google.com/artproject.

350 Place Royale (at rue de la Commune). www.pacmuseum.qc.ca. ✆ **514/872-9150.** Admission C$20 adults, with discounts for students, children, and seniors; free for children 5 and under. Late June to early Sept Mon–Fri 10am–6pm, Sat–Sun 11am–6pm; mid-Sept to mid-June Tues–Fri 10am–5pm, Sat–Sun 11am–5pm. Closed some holidays, so check online. L'Arrivage Café Mon 11:30am–2pm, Tues–Sun 11:30am–4pm. Métro: Place d'Armes.

Scandinave Les Bains ★ Bath complexes are common throughout Scandinavia, but less so in North America. This center brings Euro-style relaxation-through-water to Montréal's locals and guests. Visitors check in, change into bathing suits, and then have the run of the complex for the visit. There's a warm bath the size of a small swimming pool with jets and a waterfall, a steam room thick with the scent of eucalyptus oil, and a Finnish-style dry sauna. Peppered throughout the hallways are sling-back chairs, and one room is set aside just for relaxing or having a drink from the juice bar. The recommended routine is to heat your body for about 15 minutes, cool down in one of the icy rinse stations, and relax for 15 minutes—and then repeat the circuit a few times. Call to reserve a spot.

71 rue de la Commune ouest. www.scandinave.com. ✆ **514/288-2009.** Admission C$54. Bathrobe rental C$12. Packages available with massage. Must be 16 or older. Daily 8:30am–9pm. Métro: Champ-de-Mars.

Shopping in Vieux-Montréal

Stroll along the western end of cobblestoned **rue St-Paul** in Vieux-Montréal for avant-garde fashion and art set in a most picturesque corner of Canada.

Marché Atwater (www.marche-atwater.com), or Atwater market, west of Vieux-Montréal, is an important indoor-outdoor farmer's market that's open daily. French in flavor, it features fresh fruits, vegetables, and flowers along with boulangeries, fromageries, and shops with easy-to-travel-with food. It's a 45-minute walk, a quick bike ride, or a Métro trip to Lionel-Groulx.

Some of the city's quirkier antiques shops have disappeared in recent years, but there are still tempting shops along **"Antique Alley,"** as it's nicknamed, on rue Notre-Dame about 20 minutes (by foot) west of Vieux-Montréal. They're concentrated between rue Guy and avenue Atwater.

Here are favorite shops where you can find uniquely Québécois goods:

Galerie Le Chariot Galleries featuring Inuit art are found throughout the city, but few are as accessible as this one, located on Place Jacques-Cartier, in the heart of Vieux-Montréal. Here, shoppers can find handmade pieces by Inuk artists from Cape Dorset, Lake Harbour, and Baffin Island—carved bears, seals, owls, and tableaus of mothers and children. Pieces range in price from about C$150 to C$25,000 and are certified by the Canadian government. 446 Place Jacques-Cartier (in the center of the plaza), Vieux-Montréal. ✆ **514/875-4994.**

CIRQUE DU SOLEIL: MONTRÉAL'S HOMETOWN circus

The whimsical, talented band of artists that became Cirque du Soleil began as street performers in Baie-St-Paul, a river town an hour north of Québec City. These stilt walkers, fire breathers, and musicians had one pure intention: to entertain. The troupe formally founded as Cirque du Soleil (Circus of the Sun) in 1984 has matured into a spectacle like no other. Using human-size gyroscopes, trampoline beds, trapezes suspended from massive chandeliers, and the like, Cirque creates worlds that are spooky, sensual, otherworldly, and beautifully ambiguous. More than 1,300 of the company's acrobats, contortionists, jugglers, clowns, and dancers tour the world, and there are resident shows in Las Vegas and Orlando.

The company's offices are in Montréal in the Saint-Michel district, not far beyond the Mile End neighborhood. And they're not just offices. Cirque has been developing a small campus of buildings in this industrial zone since 1997. All new artists come here to train for a few weeks to a few months and live in residences on-site. The complex has acrobatic training rooms, a dance studio, workshops in which the elaborate costumes and props are made, and a space large enough to erect a circus tent indoors. Some 1,800 people are employed at the Montréal facility, including more than 400 who work on costumes alone.

The company doesn't have regular performances in Montréal, alas. For information about when they're coming to the province and where else in the world you can find a show, visit **www.cirquedusoleil.com**.

Galerie Zone Orange ★ Angry sock monkeys, creative jewelry, and colorful ceramics from regional artists are on display at the small Zone Orange, which also has a teeny espresso bar in its center. Perhaps the coolest products are the lightweight bags made from recycled billboards and street lamp banners by the eco-focused Atelier Entre-Peaux, a Montréal company. There are also sweet dolls for infants made from organic cotton by the local company Raplapla (look for the doll named Monsieur Tse-Tse). 410 rue St-Pierre (near rue St-Paul), Vieux-Montréal. http://shop.galeriezoneorange.com. ✆ **514/510-5809.**

Harricana ★ One designer taking a unique cue from the city's long history with the fur trade is Mariouche Gagné. Her company recycles old fur into funky patchwork garments. A leader in the *ecoluxe* movement, Gagné also recycles silk scarves, turning them into tops and skirts. Her workshop-boutique is close to the Marché Atwater (p. 86) and the Lionel-Groulx Métro station. 3000 rue St-Antoine ouest (at av. Atwater), west of Vieux-Montréal. www.harricana.qc.ca. ✆ **877/894-9919** or 514/287-6517.

MONT ROYAL & PLATEAU MONT-ROYAL ATTRACTIONS

L'Oratoire St-Joseph ★ This huge Catholic church—dominating Mont Royal's north slope—is seen by some as inspiring, by others as forbidding. It's Montréal's highest point, with an enormous dome 97m (318 ft.) high. Consecrated as a basilica in

2004, it came into being through the efforts of Brother André, a lay brother in the Holy Cross order who earned a reputation as a healer. By the time he had built a small wooden chapel in 1904 on the mountain, he was said to have performed hundreds of cures. His powers attracted supplicants from great distances, and he performed his work until his death in 1937. His dream of building a shrine to honor St. Joseph, patron saint of Canada, became a reality in 1967. In 1982, he was beatified by the pope—a status one step below sainthood—and on October 17, 2010, he earned the distinction of sainthood, too. A new exhibit was created shortly thereafter to commemorate this honor.

The church is largely Italian Renaissance in style, its giant copper dome recalling the shape of the Duomo in Florence, but of greater size and lesser grace. Inside is a sanctuary and exhibit that displays Brother André's actual heart in a formalin-filled urn. His original wooden chapel, with its tiny bedroom, is on the grounds and open to the public. More than two million pilgrims visit annually, many of who seek intercession from St. Joseph and Brother André by climbing the middle set of 99 steps on their knees. The 56-bell carillon plays Wednesday to Friday at noon and 3pm, Saturday at noon at 2:30pm, and Sunday at 12:15 and 2:30pm. Also on-site is an oratory museum featuring 264 nativity scenes from 111 countries. A modest 14-room hostel on the grounds is called the **Jean XXIII Pavilion.** Single rooms with shared bathroom start at C$50 and include breakfast (www.saint-joseph.org/en/visit-us/lodging).

Since 2002, the oratory has been implementing a multi-phase renovation project to improve overall accessibility for the ever-increasing number of visitors. Most recent completions include additional elevators, an elevator to the basilica, and a new vehicle entrance. In coming years, a new visitor's center and an observatory will be unveiled. The current phase of renovations is expected to complete in 2017.

3800 chemin Queen Mary (on the north slope of Mont Royal). www.saint-joseph.org. ✆ **877/672-8647** or 514/733-8211. Free admission to most sights, donations requested; oratory museum C$4 adults, C$3 seniors and students, C$2 children 6–17. Oratory museum daily 10am–4:30pm. C$5 for parking. Métro: Côtes-des-Neiges or Snowdon. Bus: 165 or 51.

Shopping in Plateau Mont-Royal & Mile End

In Plateau Mont-Royal, **rue St-Denis** north of Sherbrooke has blocks of shops filled with fun, funky items. **Boulevard St-Laurent** sells everything from budget practicalities to off-the-wall handmade fashions. Further north, **avenue Laurier,** between boulevard St-Laurent and avenue de l'Epée, is where to head for French boutiques, furniture and accessories shops, and products from the ateliers of young Québécois designers. This is a vibrant, upscale street, with a rich selection of restaurants, too. A trip to the shops in the bohemian Plateau and Mile End neighborhoods should send you home with a dash of local style.

Montréal boasts a heavenly network of **vintage boutiques**—it's no secret that this is where many of Montréal's artsy style-mavens procure their looks. Many *friperies,* as they're called in French, are scattered in the Plateau Mont-Royal, especially on boulevard St-Laurent near the cross street avenue Duluth. In Mile End, wander along rue Bernard or St-Viateur.

Other special shops where you can find uniquely Québécois goods:

Arthur Quentin Doling out household products of quiet taste and discernment since 1975, this St-Denis stalwart sells chic tableware, leather goods, kitchen gadgets, and home decor. That means linens and Limoges china, carafes and Le Creuset casseroles, and English tea trays and French barrettes. 3960 rue St-Denis (south of av. Duluth), Plateau Mont-Royal. www.arthurquentin.com. ✆ **514/843-7513.**

Fruits & Passion Founded in Québec in 1992, this popular chain features "personal care and ambience products"—fruity lotions, hand soaps, bubble bath, home cleaning agents, and more. 4159 rue St-Denis (at rue Rachel), Plateau Mont-Royal. www.fruits-passion.ca. ✆ **514/840-0778.**

Kanuk ★ One of the top Canadian manufacturers of high-end winter jackets makes its clothes right in Montréal and has a warehouse-like factory store in the heart of Plateau Mont-Royal. Like L.L. Bean in the U.S., the first customers for Kanuk's heavy parkas were outdoor enthusiasts. Today, clientele includes the general public. Heavy-duty winter coats cost upwards of C$700, but they're extremely popular. More modestly priced winter caps make nice (and cozy) souvenirs. Look, too, for end-of-season sales. 485 rue Rachel est (near rue Berri), Plateau Mont-Royal. www.kanuk.com. ✆ **877/284-4494** or 514/284-4494.

Les Chocolats de Chloé ★ If you approach chocolate the way certain aficionados approach wine or cheese—that is, on the lookout for the best of the best—then the teeny Chocolats de Chloé will bring great delight. Perhaps a basil-chocolate bonbon? Or one with fig and balsamic vinegar? 546 rue Duluth est (near rue St-Hubert), Plateau Mont-Royal. www.leschocolatsdechloe.com. ✆ **514/849-5550.**

Marché Jean-Talon ★★ Gourmands will want to make a pilgrimage to the north part of the city to this market. It's surrounded on all sides by the buzz and energy of the city, and is full of fresh fruits and vegetables and a host of gourmet shops. The market isn't near any of the sites, restaurants, or hotels listed in this guidebook, but it's an easy ride on the Métro—just head north to the Jean-Talon stop. 7070 av. Henri-Julien (at rue Jean-Talon est), north of Mile End. www.marche-jean-talon.com.

Zone A Québec company now with half a dozen locations, this housewares stores features colorful bowls and plates, clocks and frames, furnishings, and vases. Think clean lines of Ikea products, but several steps up in style and flair. 4246 rue St-Denis (at rue Rachel est), Plateau Mont-Royal. www.zonemaison.com. ✆ **514/845-3530.**

OLYMPIC PARK ATTRACTIONS

A 20-minute drive east of downtown on rue Sherbrooke or an easy Métro ride is **Olympic Park,** located in a neighborhood called Hochelaga-Maisonneuve. It has five attractions: **Stade Olympique** (Olympic Stadium), **Biodôme de Montréal, Insectarium de Montréal, Jardin Botanique** (Botanical Garden), and the new **Rio Tinto Alcan Planétarium,** which opened in 2013. All attractions are walking distance from each other, and in summertime there's a free shuttle bus that travels in a loop and passes all five attractions. Kids especially love the Biodôme and Insectarium. Combination ticket packages are available, and the Biodôme, Insectarium, and Jardin are all included in the **Montréal Museum Pass** (see the "Money Savers" box on p. 79). Underground parking at the Olympic Stadium is C$15 per day, with additional parking at the Jardin Botanique and Insectarium (C$12 at either location).

Biodôme de Montréal ★★★ A terrifically engaging attraction for children of nearly any age, the delightful Biodôme houses replications of four ecosystems: a tropical rainforest, a Laurentian forest, the St. Lawrence marine system, and the Labrador Coast and sub-polar regions. Visitors walk through each and hear the animals, smell the flora, and (except in the polar region, which is behind glass) feel the changes in temperature. The rainforest area is the most engrossing (the subsequent rooms increasingly less so), so take your time here. Animals here include the capybara, which looks like a large guinea pig, and golden lion tamarin monkeys that swing on branches only an arm's length away. Bats, fish, and penguins are among the few creatures behind glass. In 2013, visitors got to watch three newborn Canadian Lynx kittens at play. The facility also has a hands-on activity room called Naturalia, a shop, a bistro, and a cafeteria.

4777 av. Pierre-de-Coubertin (next to Stade Olympique). www.espacepourlavie.ca/en/biodome. ✆ **514/868-3000.** Admission C$18.75 adults, C$17.50 seniors, C$14 students, C$9.50 children 5–17. Check the website for hours, which change seasonally. Métro: Viau.

Insectarium de Montréal The Insectarium is part of the Jardin Botanique (below) and admission is included in the (rather steep) joint ticket price for the gardens. If you are already planning a trip to the gardens, this is worth taking in; otherwise, it's pretty small to justify a trip and a ticket on its own. That said, it's the place to be if bugs and spiders make you squirm with delight. There are live exhibits of insects from scorpions and tarantulas to ants and hissing cockroaches. Alongside the crawly little creatures are thousands of mounted ones, including butterflies and beetles. An outdoor playground is well designed for children 12 and under.

4581 rue Sherbrooke est. www.espacepourlavie.ca/en/insectarium. ✆ **514/872-1400.** Tickets can only be purchased in a package with the Jardin Botanique (see below). Check the website for hours, which change seasonally. Métro: Pie-IX.

Jardin Botanique ★★★ Spread across 75 hectares (185 acres), Montréal's Botanical Garden is a fragrant oasis all year round. Ten large exhibition greenhouses each have a theme: One houses orchids; another has tropical food and spice plants, including coffee, cinnamon, and ginger; another features rainforest flora. In a special exhibit each spring, live butterflies flutter among the nectar-bearing plants, occasionally landing on visitors. In September, visitors can watch monarch butterflies being tagged and released for their annual migration to Mexico.

Outdoors, spring is when things really kick in: lilacs in May, lilies in June, and roses from mid-June until the first frost. During the summer, the garden presents a spectacular and wildly popular competition and exhibition called **Mosaïcultures internationals**, with flora sculpted into gigantic, otherworldly topiary creatures. The **Chinese Garden,** a joint project of Montréal and Shanghai, evokes the 14th- to 17th-century era of the Ming Dynasty and was built according to the landscape principles of yin and yang. It incorporates pavilions, inner courtyards, ponds, and plants indigenous to China. A serene **Japanese Garden** fills 2.5 hectares (6.25 acres) and has a stone garden, a tea garden used for tea ceremonies, and a stunning bonsai collection with miniature trees as old as 350 years. The grounds are also home to the **Insectarium** (above).

4101 rue Sherbrooke est (opposite Olympic Stadium). www.espacepourlavie.ca/en/botanical-garden. ✆ **514/872-1400.** When Mosaïcultures internationals is on display (June–Sept) tickets are C$30 adults, C$28 seniors, C$23 students, C$15 children 5–17. Admission at other times is C$19 adults, C$18 seniors, C$14 students, C$9.50 children 5–17. Admission includes access to the Insectarium. Hours change throughout the year, but are at least daily from 9am–6pm. Check the website for exact schedules. No bicycles or dogs. Métro: Pie-IX.

Rio Tinto Alcan Planétarium ★ The planetarium moved from downtown to Olympic Park in 2013. Together with the Biodôme (next door), the Botanical Garden, and the Insectarium, the four attractions are being billed as "the Space for Life, the largest natural sciences museum complex in Canada." The planetarium has two theaters: one show is focused on science, and the other is focused on the poetic majesty of the stars. When we visited shortly after its opening, there were only one or two shows a day in English, so plan ahead. Architecturally, it's a stunning building, with arcs and curves and a metal exterior that evoke Frank Gehry's Guggenheim Museum Bilbao.

4801 ave Pierre-de Coubertin. www.espacepourlavie.ca/en/rio-tinto-alcan-planetarium-1. ✆ **514/868-3000.** Apr–Dec C$19 adults, C$18 seniors, C$14 students, C$9.50 children 5–17. Check the website for hours, which change seasonally. Shows begin every half hour starting from 9:30am; check website for which show times are in English. Métro: Viau.

Stade Olympique Montréal's space-age Olympic Stadium, the centerpiece of the 1976 Olympic Games, looks like a giant stapler. The main event is the 175m (574-ft.) inclined tower, which leans at a 45-degree angle and does duty as an observation deck, with a *funiculaire* that whisks passengers to the top in 95 seconds. On a clear day, the deck bestows an expansive view over Montréal and into the neighboring Laurentian mountains. At C$23, though, the admission price is as steep as the tower.

The complex includes a stadium that seats up to 56,000 for sporting events and music concerts (it was home to the Montréal Expos before that baseball team relocated to Washington, D.C., in 2005). The Sports Centre houses five swimming pools open for public swimming and classes, including one deep enough for scuba diving. There's also a gym, hot tub, and a wading pool with a water fountain and slides for toddlers. (Take note that the Sports Centre began renovations recently, leaving some areas closed. To avoid any disappointments, call ahead of time to check which areas are open.)

A 20-minute guided "quick tour" describing the 1976 Olympic Games and use of the center today are available daily for C$5. The roof doesn't retract anymore—it never retracted well anyway. That's one reason why it was first known as "the Big O" was scorned as "the Big Woe" and then "the Big Owe" after cost overruns led to heavy tax increases.

4141 av. Pierre-de-Coubertin. www.parcolympique.qc.ca. ✆ **514/252-4141**. Tower admission C$23 adults, C$20 seniors and students, C$12 children 5–17. Prices cheaper for residents. Public swimming admission C$7.25 adults, C$6.25 students and seniors, C$5.50 children 15 and under. Tower summer Mon 1–10pm, Tues–Sun 9am–10pm; winter Mon 1–6pm, Tues–Sun 9am–6pm. See website for fall and spring hours, which change often. Métro: Viau.

ORGANIZED TOURS

An introductory guided tour is often the best—or, at least, most efficient—way to begin exploring a new city and can certainly give you a good lay of the land and overview of Montréal's history. Tours take you past many of the attractions listed in this chapter and can give you a better sense of which ones to spend time exploring. For complete listings of prices and schedules, check the websites for tours listed below.

Most land tours leave from the Square Dorchester, right at the tourist office. Most boat tours depart from Vieux-Port (Old Port), the waterfront bordering Vieux-Montréal. There's parking at the dock, or take the Métro to the Champ-de-Mars or Square Victoria Station, and then walk toward the river.

Boat Tours

Among numerous opportunities for experiencing Montréal and environs by water, here are a few of the most popular:

Croisières AML Cruises (www.croisieresaml.com; ✆ **866/856-6668**): One of the more popular cruise operators, with options including a weekend brunch cruise for adults (C$51), with discounts for children and seniors. There are also guided history trips throughout the day, as well as a "Red Carpet" VIP dinner cruise, fireworks cruise, gourmet dinner cruises, and a whole host of other options. Boats depart from the King Edward Pier, in Vieux-Port.

Le Bateau-Mouche (www.bateau-mouche.com; ✆ **800/361-9952** or 514/849-9952): An air-conditioned, glass-enclosed vessel reminiscent of those on the Seine in Paris, Le Bateau-Mouche plies the St. Lawrence River from mid-May to mid-October. The shallow-draft boat takes passengers on a route inaccessible by traditional vessels, passing under several bridges and providing sweeping views of the city, Mont-Royal, and the St. Lawrence and its islands. Cruises run for 60 minutes and 90 minutes, and there's an evening dinner cruise. The 60-minute tours cost C$24 adults, with discounts for children and seniors. The tours depart from the Jacques-Cartier Pier, opposite Place Jacques-Cartier.

Les Descentes sur le St-Laurent (www.raftingmontreal.com; ✆ **800/324-7238** or 514/767-2230): Also provides hydro-jet rides on the white water. This departure point is a little closer to the rapids than the others, so a bit more of an adventure. Rafting and jet-boat options are available for C$43 and C$53 adults, with discounts for children (though kids must be at least 6 years old to go rafting and at least 8 years old to go jet-boating). Reservations are required. Métro: Angrignon. Bus: 110.

Les Sautes-Moutons (also known as **Lachine Rapids Tours;** www.jetboatingmontreal.com; ✆ **514/284-9607**): Provides an exciting—and wet—experience. Operating from May through October, its wave-jumper powerboats take on the St. Lawrence River's roiling Lachine Rapids. The streamlined jet boat makes the trip in about an hour. It takes a half-hour to get to and from the rapids, which leaves 30 minutes for storming along the 2.4m to 3.7m (8–12-ft.) waves. Reservations are required. Plan to arrive 45 minutes early to obtain and don rain gear and a life jacket. Bring a towel and change of clothes, as you almost certainly will get splashed or even soaked. Fares are C$67 adults, with discounts for children. Inquire about children 5 and under. The jet boats depart from the Clock Tower Pier (quai de l'Horloge) in Vieux-Port.

Navettes Fluviales Maritime Shuttles (www.navettesmaritimes.com; ✆ **514/281-8000**): From Jacques-Cartier Pier in Vieux-Montréal to either Ile Ste-Hélène or Longueuil, these are much milder water voyages, but still offer great views. It's one way to begin or end a picnic outing or extend a bike ride beyond Old Montréal. Both ferries operate from mid-May to mid-October, with daily departures every hour in the high season, and cost C$7.50 per person (free for children 5 and under). Your ticket stub gets you a discount at an array of partners.

Land Tours

Gray Line (www.grayline.com/things-to-do/canada/montreal; ✆ **800/472-9546**) offers commercial guided tours in air-conditioned motorcoach buses daily year-round. The basic city tour takes a little over 3 hours and costs C$49 for adults, with discounts for children and seniors, or free for children 4 and under. Tours depart from 1001 Dorchester Square in downtown. The motorcoach tours offer an option to pick you up at selected hotels. There's a shorter 2-hour "Hop-on-Hop-Off" tour on a double-decker bus that departs from the Dorchester Square location only.

Amphi-Bus (www.montreal-amphibus-tour.com; ✆ **514/849-5181**) is something a little different: It tours Vieux-Montréal much like any other bus—until it waddles into the waters of the harbor for a dramatic finish. Departures are hourly during the summer, with four departures daily in May and October. Check website for schedules. Fares are C$35 adults, with discounts for children and seniors. Reservations are required. The bus departs from the intersection of rue de la Commune and boul. St-Laurent.

Montréal's ***calèches*** (www.calechesluckyluc.com; ✆ **514/934-6105**) are horse-drawn open carriages whose drivers serve as guides. They operate year-round, and in winter, the horse puffs steam clouds in the cold air as the passengers bundle up in lap rugs. Reserved rides for up to four persons can be arranged from downtown for C$150 per hour and from Vieux-Montréal for C$125 per hour. During summer months, visitors can find the carriages waiting at Place Jacques-Cartier and rue de la Commune, and at Place d'Armes opposite Basilique Notre-Dame, where a 30-minute ride costs C$48 and an hour costs C$80. All of the guides speak French and English.

Walking & Cycling Tours

Guidatour (www.guidatour.qc.ca; ✆ **800/363-4021** or 514/844-4021) developed its walking tour of Vieux-Montréal in collaboration with the Centre d'Histoire de Montréal (p. 83). The 90-minute circuit costs C$21 for adults, with discounts for children and seniors; it's free for children 5 and under. Guidatour also offers a variety of bicycle tours in conjunction with **Ça Roule Montréal** that go through different parts of the city. Rides last approximately 4 hours and cover up to 16 miles, so although they're described as "easy" rides, be sure you're able and willing. The C$65 fee includes rental of a bike, helmet, and lock for the day. Tours start at the bike shop at 27 rue de la Commune est in Vieux-Port (also see "Bicycling & In-Line Skating," below). Reservations are required.

Food & Wine Trips

VDM Global offers two foodie tours, one through Vieux-Montréal and another in Little Italy. The Vieux-Montréal tour departs from the **Europea Espace Boutique** at 33 rue Notre-Dame ouest and makes stops at four different locations, primarily focusing on the city's French heritage. The Little Italy tour starts at la **Librairie Gourmande** at 7070 ave Henri Julien and includes stops at several restaurants as well as the **Jean Talon market** (p. 89), the largest open-air market in North America. All tours are bilingual and cost C$55 per person, which includes food tastings.

École de cuisine Mezza Luna offers Italian cooking classes by Elena Faita. She runs the packed-to-the-rafters cookware (and sportswear) shop **Quincaillerie Dante,** 6851 rue St-Dominique (✆ **514/271-2057**). In 2008, Faita-Venditelli was named "l'Ordre national," the most prestigious honorary distinction in the province. Visit www.ecolemezzaluna.ca or call ✆ **514/272-5299** to inquire.

If you have a car, the **Route des Vins (Wine Route),** 103km (64 miles) southeast of Montréal, is a pleasant vineyard tour. See the Day Trip on p. 133.

The Gourmet Route, online at www.parcoursgourmand.com, is a must for food lovers. The site promotes "gourmet tourism" and lists some 30 growers, processors, gourmet restaurants, and stores. An interactive map is especially useful for seeing what places are nearest.

OUTDOOR ACTIVITIES

After such long winters, locals pour outdoors to get sun and warm air at every possible opportunity (though there's also lots to do when there's snow on the ground). **Parc du Mont-Royal** and **Parc La Fontaine** (both listed below) are the city's biggest parks. The **Jardin Botanique** (p. 90) is also a beautiful oasis to spend a day strolling.

This is a walking city, and in the warm months, Montréal closes off large sections of main streets for pedestrian-only traffic, including rue Ste-Catherine both in the Village and adjacent to Quartier des Spectacles. For special events, rue St-Paul in Vieux-Montréal and rue St-Laurent in the Plateau get shut down as well.

Parc du Mont-Royal ★★ Montréal is named for this 232m (761-ft.) hill that rises at its heart—the "Royal Mountain." Walkers, joggers, cyclists, dog owners, and in-line skaters all use this largest of the city's green spaces throughout the year. In summer, **Lac des Castors (Beaver Lake)** is surrounded by sunbathers and picnickers (no swimming allowed, however). In winter, cross-country skiers and snowshoers follow miles of paths and trails laid out for their use through the park's 200 hectares (494 acres). Ice-skates, skis, poles, and snowshoes can all be rented for adults and children at the Beaver Lake Pavilion, the glass windowed building with a rippled roof. **Chalet du Mont-Royal** near the crest of the hill is a popular destination, providing a sweeping view of the city from its terrace. A few snack and beverage vending machines are there in case you get hungry or thirsty. **Maison Smith,** which houses the information center at the middle the park, includes a cafe serving light fare. Up the hill behind the chalet is the spot where, legend says, Paul de Chomedey, Sieur de Maisonneuve, erected a wooden cross after the colony sidestepped the threat of a flood in 1643. The present incarnation of the steel **Croix du Mont-Royal** was installed in 1924 and is lit at night. See chapter 9 for a walking tour through the park.

Downtown (entrances include one at rue Peel and av. des Pins). www.lemontroyal.qc.ca. ✆ **514/843-8240** (the Maison Smith information center in the park's center). Métro: Mont Royal. Bus: 11.

Parc La Fontaine ★ The European-style park in Plateau Mont-Royal is one of the city's oldest and most popular. Illustrating the traditional dual identities of the city's populace, half the park is landscaped in the formal French manner, the other in the more casual English style. A central lake is used for ice-skating in winter, when snowshoe and cross-country trails wind through trees. In summer, these trails become bike paths, and tennis courts become active. An open amphitheater, the **Théâtre de Verdure,** features free outdoor theater, music, and tango dancing. The northern end of the park is more pleasant than the southern end (along rue Sherbrooke), which attracts a seedier crowd.

Bounded by rue Sherbrooke, rue Rachel, av. Parc LaFontaine, and av. Papineau. www.ville.montreal.qc.ca and www.espacelafontaine.com. ✆ **514/280-2525** for park, 514/872-3626 for tennis reservations. Free admission to the park; C$9 per hr. for use of tennis courts. Park daily 6am–midnight; tennis courts Mon–Fri 9am–11pm, Sat–Sun 9am–9pm. Métro: Sherbrooke.

Vieux-Port ★★★ Montréal's Old Port at the base of Vieux-Montréal was transformed in 1992 from a dreary commercial wharf area into a 2km-long (1¼-mile), 53-hectare (131-acre) promenade and public park with bicycle paths, benches, and lawns. The wharfs house exhibition halls, summertime cafes, a wintertime ice skating rink, and a variety of other family activities, including the **Centre des Sciences de Montréal** (p. 84). It stretches along the waterfront, parallel to rue de la Commune, from rue McGill to rue Berri.

The area is most active from mid-May through October, when harbor cruises take to the waters and bicycles, in-line skates, and family-friendly quadricycle carts are available to rent. The summertime-only **Origine Bistro** (www.origine-bistro.com) is an appealing terrace/bar in front of Centre des Sciences de Montréal. In winter, things are quieter, but the outdoor ice-skating rink is a big attraction. At the port's far eastern end, in the last of the old warehouses, is a 1922 clock tower, **La Tour de l'Horloge,** with 192 steps leading past the exposed clockworks to observation decks overlooking the St. Lawrence River (admission is free).

Quai King Edward (King Edward Pier). www.oldportofmontreal.com. ✆ **800/971-PORT** (7678). Métro: Champ-de-Mars, Place d'Armes, or Square Victoria.

Warm-Weather Activities

BICYCLING & IN-LINE SKATING

Bicycling and rollerblading are hugely popular in Montréal, and the city helps people indulge these passions with an expanding network of more than 560km (348 miles) of cycling paths and year-round bike lanes. In warm months, car lanes in heavily biked areas are blocked off with concrete barriers, creating protected bike-only lanes.

In 2009, the city launched the wildly popular self-service bicycle rental program called BIXI, where users pick up bikes from designated bike stands in the city and drop them off at other stands for a small fee. See p. 38 in chapter 4 for details and p. 11 for one woman's experience.

Keep in mind, though, that BIXI rentals are designed for short-term use. If you want to rent a bike for a few hours or more, you are better off going to a bike shop. The shop **Ça Roule/Montréal on Wheels** (www.caroulemontreal.com; ✆ **877/866-0633** or 514/866-0633) at 27 rue de la Commune est, the waterfront road in Vieux-Port, rents bikes and skates from March to November. Rentals are by the hour or by the day on the weekend, with a deposit required. The company offers high-performance road bikes, and helmets and locks are included. The staff will set you up with a map (also downloadable from their website) and likely point you toward the peaceful **Lachine Canal,** a nearly flat 11km (6¾-mile) bicycle path, open year-round and maintained by Parks Canada from mid-April through October, that travels alongside locks and over small bridges. The canal starts just a few blocks away. **La Bicycletterie J.R.** (www.labicycletteriejr.com; ✆ **514/843-6989**) at 201 rue Rachel est in the Plateau offers 4-hour or 24-hour bike rentals, with longer options by the week. New bikes used for rentals are purchased each spring, so you'll never be stuck riding a rickety old jalopy.

Also for rent at Vieux-Port in warm months are **quadricycles** (www.oldportofmontreal.com/quadricycle-en.html; ✆ **514/465-0594**), or "Q-cycles"—four-wheeled bike-buggies that can hold up to six people. You can ride them only along Vieux-Port, and the rental booth is in the heart of the waterfront area, next to the Pavillian Jacques-Cartier. Rentals are by the half-hour and cost C$30 for a three-seater with spots for two small children, and C$40 for a six-seater.

If you're serious about cycling, get in touch with the nonprofit biking organization **Vélo Québec** (www.velo.qc.ca; ✆ **800/567-8356** or 514/521-8356). Vélo (which means bicycle) was behind the development of a 5,000km (3,107-mile) bike network called **Route Verte (Green Route)** that stretches from one end of the province of Québec to the other. The route was officially inaugurated in summer 2007. Many inns and restaurants along the route actively work to accommodate the nutritional, safety, and equipment needs of cyclists. (See the Day Trip "Biking the Route Verte (Green Route)" in chapter 10.) The Vélo website has the most up-to-date information on the state of the paths, the Montréal Bike Fest, road races, new bike lanes, and more. It also offers **guided tours** throughout the province.

GRAND PRIX AUTO RACING

The **Grand Prix** came back to Montréal in 2010 after a 1-year hiatus (the result of contract negotiations between the city and Formula One, which puts on the race), and the international auto race is slated to return to the city each summer through at least 2014. It attracts more than 100,000 people to the city's track (and to hotels and restaurants), bringing in as much as C$100 million in tourism dollars and making it the biggest tourism event of the year. In 2014, it will take place from June 6 to 8. Tickets range from C$49 to C$139 for general admission, C$299 to C$635 for grandstand seats.

HIKING

The most popular hike is to the top of **Mont Royal.** There are a web of options for trekking the small mountain, from using the broad and handsome pedestrian-only **chemin Olmsted** (a bridle path named for Frederick Law Olmsted, the park's landscape architect), to following smaller paths and sets of stairs. The park is well marked and small enough that you can wander without getting too lost, but the walking tour on p. 124 suggests one place to start and a number of options once you're inside.

JOGGING

There are many possibilities for running. In addition to the areas described above for biking and hiking, consider heading to the city's most prominent parks: **Parc La Fontaine** in the Plateau Mont-Royal neighborhood (p. 94), or **Parc Maisonneuve** in the city's east side, adjacent to the **Jardin Botanique** and across the street from **Olympic Park** (p. 89). Both parks are formally landscaped and well used for recreation and relaxation.

KAYAKING & ELECTRIC BOATING

It's fun to rent kayaks, large Rabaska canoes, pedal boats, or small eco-friendly electric boats on the quiet **Lachine Canal,** just to the west of Vieux-Port. **H2O Adventures** (www.h2oadventures.com; ✆ **514/842-1306**) won a Grand Prix du tourisme Québécois award for being a standout operation. Their rentals start at C$10 per half-hour. For a fee, they also offer 2-hour introductory kayak lessons, on Wednesday nights and Sunday afternoons. From June to August, the shop is open daily from 9am to 9pm. Cross the footbridge past Marché Atwater (p. 86), where you can also pick up lunch from the inside *boulangerie* and *fromagerie,* adjacent to the canal.

KSF (www.ksf.ca; ✆ **514/595-7873**), which also won a Grand Prix du tourisme Québécois award, is in the same geographic area and rents Stand Up Paddleboards along with kayaks.

SWIMMING

On Parc Jean-Drapeau, a man-made island park just across the harbor of Vieux-Port, there is an outdoor swimming pool complex and a lakeside beach, the **Plage des Iles** (www.parcjeandrapeau.com; ✆ **514/872-2323**). It is small, but very popular and open to the public from mid-June to mid-August. Admission to the beach is C$8 adults, with discounts for children, and free for kids 2 and under. Métro: Jean-Drapeau.

Plage de l'Horloge (Clock Tower Beach) is a new "urban beach" at quai de l'Horlage in Vieux-Port that debuted in the summer of 2012, complete with sand, sun umbrellas, and lounge chairs. It's open June through August. See www.vieuxportdemontreal.com for updates and details.

Cold-Weather Activities

CROSS-COUNTRY SKIING

Parc du Mont-Royal has an extensive cross-country course, as do many of the other city parks, though skiers have to supply their own equipment. Just an hour from the city, north in the Laurentides and east in the Cantons de l'Est, there are numerous options for skiing and rentals.

DOWNHILL SKIING

There are no options for downhill skiing in the city, mountains in the Laurentians or Cantons are just a couple hours drive away. See chapter 10 and the Day Trip "Skiing at Mont-Tremblant."

ICE SKATING

In the winter, outdoor skating rinks are set up in Vieux-Port, Lac des Castors (Beaver Lake), and other spots around the city; check tourist offices for your best options. One of the most agreeable venues for skating any time of the year is **Atrium Le 1000** (p. 97) in the downtown skyscraper at 1000 rue de la Gauchetière ouest. It's indoors and warm, and it's surrounded by cafes at which to relax after twirling around the big rink. And yes, it's even open in the summer.

IGLOOFEST

Held every winter during select Thursdays, Fridays, and Saturdays in January and February, this electronic music fest is literally a rave beneath the stars. A temporary outdoor dance club is erected along the quays of Vieux-Port, where revelers can dance until midnight to live DJs. See p. 94.

SNOW VILLAGE

This wintertime attraction was first unveiled in 2012. From January through March, a snow village is erected on Parc Jean-Drapeau and includes a bar, restaurant, and hotel, all carved out of ice. There are heated outdoor spas as well, not made from ice but decorated to look like they are. Events include karaoke, live DJs, and in years past, dog sledding. It perfectly represents the Montréalais penchant for throwing a good party any time, regardless of the temperature. See **www.snowvillagecanada.com** for details.

ESPECIALLY FOR KIDS

For families, few cities assure children will have as good a time as this one does. There are riverboat rides (p. 91), summer fireworks at **La Ronde Amusement Par**k (below), the **Centre des Sciences de Montréal** (p. 84), and magical circus performances by the many troupes that come through this circus-centric city. When in doubt, just head to **Olympic Park** (p. 89) and start at the **Biodôme** (p. 89). Plenty of attractions throughout this chapter will appeal to the under-18 crowd, but below are additional venues and programs that cater to them primarily.

Atrium Le 1000 ★ This medium-size indoor ice-skating rink in the heart of downtown offers skating year-round under a glass ceiling. Skate rentals are available, and a food court surrounds the rink. It attracts a full mix of patrons: groups of giggling teenage girls, middle-aged friends chatting and skating side by side, and young children teetering in helmets. Tiny Tots Time, typically Saturday and Sunday from 11:00am to 12:30pm, are reserved for children 12 and younger, and their parents.

1000 rue de la Gauchetière ouest. www.le1000.com. ✆ **514/395-0555.** Admission C$7.50 adults, with discounts for children and seniors. Skate rental C$7. Open daily; check website for schedules. Métro: Bonaventure.

Fantômes Ghost Walks ★ Evenings at 8:30pm, join with other intrepid souls for a ghost walk of Vieux-Montréal. The 90-minute tour heads down back alleys to places where gruesome events occurred, and actors appear as phantoms to tell about the historical crimes of the city. Because their stories include tales of sorcery, hangings, and being burned and tortured, it's recommended for children 12 and older.

360 rue St-François-Xavier. www.fantommontreal.com. ✆ **800/363-4021** or 514/844-4021. Admission C$22 adults, with discounts for students and children. July–Oct various evenings at 8:30pm; call or go online for exact days. Métro: Place d'Armes.

IMAX Theater ★ Images and special effects are way larger than life and visually dazzling on this screen in the **Centre des Sciences de Montréal** (p. 84). Recent films have highlighted NASA's Hubble Space Telescope, Sharks (in 3-D), and the migration of butterflies. Running time is usually less than an hour. One or two screenings per day are in English, and tickets can be ordered online. Check the schedule online.

Quai King Edward, Vieux-Port. www.montrealsciencecentre.com. ✆ **877/496-4724** or 514/496-4724. Movie tickets C$12 adults, with discounts for children and seniors, and free for children 3 and under. Shows daily. Métro: Place d'Armes or Champ-de-Mars.

La Ronde Amusement Park ★ Part of the American-owned Six Flags theme-park empire. Rides here are categorized, like hot sauces, by "thrill rating": mild, moderate, or max. Young children also have ample selection, including a carrousel, the Tchou Tchou Train and Air Papillon, which looks like a giant butterfly. Other attractions include a Ferris wheel, acrobatic shows, and front row seats in an open-air theater to the huge fireworks competition that takes place over nine evenings (see **L'International des Feux Loto-Québec,** p. 101). La Ronde is located on Parc Jean-Drapeau, a park comprising the small Île Ste-Hélène and adjacent Île Notre-Dame, which sit in the St. Lawrence River near Vieux-Port's waterfront and are connected by two bridges. The park is mostly car-free and accessible by Métro, bike, foot, or car.

22 chemin. Macdonald, Parc Jean-Drapeau on Île Ste-Hélène. www.laronde.com. ✆ **514/397-2000.** Admission prices (by height) C$47 patrons 1.4m (54 in.) or taller, with discounts for seniors and those under 1.4m (54 in.), free for children 2 and under. Special rates available online. Parking C$20–C$25. Summer Sun–Fri 11am–9pm, Sat 11am–11:30pm; spring and fall Sat–Sun only (call or check website to confirm hours). Métro: Papineau, then bus no. 769; Parc Jean-Drapeau, then bus no. 767.

FESTIVALS & NIGHTLIFE IN MONTRÉAL

8

From the esteemed annual summer jazz fest to the winter *Fête des Neiges,* Montréal's festivals and nightlife pull locals and visitors out of their private spaces and into the streets, public squares, concert halls, nightclubs, and restaurant terraces of the city. Snow is no deterrent, arctic temperatures merely a barometer for how many layers to wear. It's a city where people come together to celebrate life and the seasons with gusto. The city boasts an outstanding symphony, dozens of French- and English-language theater companies, a calendar with over 100 festivals, and the incomparable Cirque du Soleil.

Montréal's reputation for effervescent nightlife reaches back to the Roaring Twenties—specifically, to the 13-year period of Prohibition in the U.S. from 1920 to 1933. Americans streamed into Montréal for relief from alcohol deprivation (while Canadian distillers and brewers made fortunes). Montréal already enjoyed a sophisticated and slightly naughty reputation as the Paris of North America, which added to the allure.

Nearly a century later, packs of Americans still travel across the border to go to the city's bars and strip clubs (as do Canadians from other provinces) for bachelor and bachelorette weekends. Clubbing and barhopping are hugely popular activities, and nightspots stay open until 3am—much later hours than in many U.S. and Canadian cities, which still heed Calvinist notions of propriety and early bedtimes. The legal drinking age is also only 18.

That said, the city's nocturnal pursuits are often as sophisticated and edgy as anywhere else. The city is on the standard concert circuit that includes Chicago and New York, so internationally known entertainers, music groups, and dance companies pass through frequently. A decidedly French enthusiasm for film, as well as the city's reputation as a movie-production center, ensures support for film festivals and screenings of offbeat and independent movies.

Where to Play, Night & Day

Here's a quick look at the neighborhoods best known for nightlife, the performing arts, and Montréal's many festivals:

Vieux-Montréal, especially along rue St-Paul, has a universal quality, with many of its bars and clubs showcasing live jazz, blues, and folk music. The up-and-coming **Little Burgundy** hub, just west of Vieux-Montréal, has a sophisticated mix of bars and restaurants.

Last-Minute Tickets for Less

A ticket office for Montréal cultural events is centrally located at the Place des Arts, in the Quartier des Spectacles district. **La Vitrine** (www.lavitrine.com; ✆ **866/924-5538** or 514/285-4545) is at 2 rue Ste-Catherine est and sells last-minute deals, as well as full-price tickets.

Quartier des Spectacles is where many of the performing arts venues are located. It's also where many of the outdoor festivals take place.

In **Plateau Mont-Royal,** boulevard St-Laurent, known locally as "the Main," is a miles-long haven of hip and hipster restaurants and clubs. It starts roughly from rue Sherbrooke and goes all the way north into **Mile End** up to rue Laurier. It's a good place to wind up in the wee hours, as there's always someplace with the welcome mat still out, even after the official 3am closings. If you've still got steam after that, there are after-hours dance clubs in the **Gay Village.** Head to rue Ste-Catherine est in the Village, which closes in summer to cars and becomes flush with people as the cafes and bars that line the street build temporary terraces.

Downtown's parallel blocks of rue Crescent, rue Bishop, and rue de la Montagne north of rue Ste-Catherine are where much of the city's hard-core partying takes place, with rows of bars with outdoor terraces. Especially on summer weekend nights, the streets swarm with people careening from bar to restaurant to club. It's young and noisy—and also considered to be a tourist trap to locals, although many still tend to end up there. This area has a pronounced Anglophone (English-speaking) character.

Francophones, on the other hand, dominate the area known as the **Quartier Latin,** with college-age patrons most evident along the lower reaches of rue St-Denis, and their elders gravitating to the nightspots on the slightly more uptown blocks of the same street.

Most bars and clubs don't charge a cover, and when they do, it's rarely more than C$10. Happy hour is locally known as *cinq à sept,* although many venues offer specials that start earlier than 5pm and go later than 7pm. On Thursdays, many bars and restaurants offer some sort of food and drink special.

Festivals: Montréal's Big, Welcoming Personality

Once known as the city of 100 churches, Montréal is now the city of 100 festivals. The biggest festival on the calendar is the annual summer jazz fest, or **Festival International de Jazz de Montréal,** an internationally celebrated heavyweight offering lots of ticketed performances but hundreds of free shows at outdoor spots in the city's streets and plazas, too. See p. 102 for more.

Year-round, it's nearly impossible to miss a celebration of some sort. For an exhaustive list of festivals beyond those listed here, check the "What to Do" section of Tourisme Montréal's website, at www.tourisme-montreal.org/What-To-Do/Events. At last check, it had 120 festival entries. Below is a selection of some of the most popular events on the annual calendar.

JANUARY

La Fête des Neiges (The Snow Festival). Montréal's answer to Québec City's February winter Carnaval (see p. 186) features dog-sled runs, a human foosball court, and tobogganing. It's held on weekends from 10am to 5pm in January and the beginning of February. Visit www.parcjeandrapeau.com and search for "Fête des Neiges" or call ✆ **514/872-6120.** January 15 to February 15, 2014 (dates to be confirmed).

Igloofest. An electronic dance festival. Outdoors. In the arctic cold of winter. (The heartiness of the Québécois truly knows no bounds.) The dancing takes place at night, at a stage along the river, in Vieux Port. Runs from Thursdays through Saturdays for four weekends, and features local and international DJs. Visit **igloofest.ca/en**. January 16 to February 8, 2014.

FEBRUARY

Festival Montréal en Lumière (Montréal High Lights Festival). At the heart of this winter celebration are culinary competitions and wine tastings. There are also multimedia light shows, classical and pop concerts, outdoor activities for children at the Quartier des Spectacles, and the "*Nuit blanche*" all-night party where everyone dresses in white and heads to a free breakfast at dawn. Did we mention that the average monthly temperature in February is 24 degrees high Farenheit (-4 C) and 10 degrees low Farhenheit (-12)? Visit www.montrealhighlights.com or call ✆ **855/864-3737** or 514/288-9955, for details. February 20 to March 2, 2014.

APRIL

Bal en Blanc Party Week. Drawing crowds of an estimated 15,000 people, this 5-day "White Ball" rave/dance party is one of the biggest such events in the world. Everyone wears white and grooves to house and trance D.J. events at Palais des Congrès and the W Hotel. Visit **www.balenblanc.com**. Check the website for exact dates.

MAY

Montréal Museums Day. This event is an open house for most of the city's museums, with free admission and free shuttle buses. Visit www.museesmontreal.org or call the tourism office (✆ **877/266-5687**) for details. Last Sunday in May.

Montréal Bike Fest. For 8 days, tens of thousands of enthusiasts converge on Montréal to participate in cycling competitions that include a nocturnal bike ride (Tour la Nuit) and the grueling Tour de l'Île, a 52km (32-mile) race around the island's rim. It draws some 30,000 cyclists, shuts down roads, and attracts more than 100,000 spectators. The nonprofit biking organization Vélo Québec (✆ **800/567-8356** or 514/521-8356) lists details at www.velo.qc.ca. Late May into early June.

JUNE

Les FrancoFolies de Montréal. Since 1988, this music fest has featured French-language pop, hip-hop, electronic, world beat, and *chanson*. It's based at the Quartier des Spectacles downtown, with shows both outdoors on the plaza and inside the many theater halls in and around the area. Check www.francofolies.com or call ✆ **855/372-6267** or 514/876-8989. June 13 to 21, 2014.

Mondial de la Bière. Yes, beer fans, this is a 5-day festival devoted to your favorite beverage. Admission at the Palais des congrès (Convention Center) is free, and tasting coupons are C$1 each, with most tastings costing two to six coupons for 3- or 4-ounce samples. Showcased are world brands and boutique microbreweries. For details, check www.festivalmondialbiere.qc.ca or call ✆ **514/722-9640.** June 11 to 15, 2014.

Jean-Baptiste Day. Honoring St. John the Baptist, the patron saint of French-Canadians, this day is marked by far more festivities and enthusiasm throughout Québec than is Canada Day on July 1 (see below). It's Québec's own *fête nationale* with fireworks, bonfires, music in the parks, and parades. Visit www.fetenationale.qc.ca or call ✆ **514/527-9891** for details. June 24.

Les International des Feux Loto-Québec (International Fireworks Competition). Great fun, starting at 10pm at night on 9 summer evenings. These fireworks are presented in an Olympics-style competition, with countries vying for best in show. You can either enjoy the pyrotechnics for free from almost anywhere overlooking the river, or buy tickets to watch from the open-air theater in La Ronde amusement park on Île Ste-Hélène (tickets have the added benefit of admission to the amusement park). Kids, needless to say, love the whole explosive business. ***Insider tip:*** The Jacques Cartier bridge closes to traffic during the fireworks and offers an unblocked, up-close view. Go to www.internationaldesfeuxloto-quebec.com or call ✆ **514/397-2000** for details. In 2013, shows were held on selected Wednesdays, Fridays, and Saturdays from late June to early August. Check the Web for 2014 dates.

JULY

Canada Day. On July 1, 1867, three British colonies joined together to form the federation of Canada, with further independence from Britain coming in stages in the 1880s. Celebrations of Canada's birthday are biggest in Ottawa, though there are concerts, flag raisings, and family festivities in Montréal and Québec City. July 1.

Festival International de Jazz de Montréal. Since Montréal has a long tradition in jazz, this is one of the monster events on the city's calendar, celebrating America's art form since 1979. The 2013 edition featured performances by Holly Cole, the Jazz at Lincoln Center Orchestra Featuring Wynton Marsalis, Feist, the Joshua Redman Quartet, Trombone Shorty & Orleans Avenue, and hundreds more. It costs serious money to hear the big stars, and tickets often sell out months in advance, but hundreds of free or nearly free performances also take place during the party, many right on downtown's streets and plazas. Visit www.montrealjazzfest.com or call ✆ **855/299-3378** or 514/871-1881. The 35th edition will be held June 27 to July 6, 2014.

Festival Juste pour Rire (Just for Laughs Festival). Billed as the largest comedy festival in the world, this big annual event is going on its 32nd year. It runs for two and a half weeks and always creates a buzz. In 2013, Dave Chappelle had a ten-show run that broke festival records for number of tickets sold. The festival also awarded its Comedy Person of the Year designation to Amy Poehler, and had gala events hosted by Sarah Silverman, Seth Meyers, Joan Rivers, Eddie Izzard, and others. Over 250 comedians from nine countries performed, with hundreds more offering free street theater. Check www.hahaha.com or call ✆ **888/244-3155** or 514/845-2322 for details. Check the website for 2014 dates.

Divers/Cité Festival. In partnership with government agencies and sponsored by major corporations, Divers/Cité is one of North America's largest parties for gay, lesbian, bisexual, and transgendered people. It's 7 days of dance, drag, art, and music concerts, based in Vieux-Port on Quai Jacques-Cartier. For details, visit www.diverscite.org or call ✆ **514/285-4011.** Held July 29 to August 4 in 2013; check for 2014 dates.

THE PERFORMING ARTS

Circus

The extraordinary circus company **Cirque du Soleil** (p. 87) is based in Montréal. Each show is a celebration of pure skill and nothing less than magical, with acrobats, clowns, trapeze artists, and performers costumed to look like creatures not of this world—iguanas crossed with goblins, or peacocks born of trolls. Cirque performs internationally, with as many as 20 shows playing across the globe simultaneously. Although there isn't a permanent show in Montréal, the troupe usually comes through the city at least once a year; it will be at the Centre Bell December 20 to 30, 2013. Check **www.cirquedusoleil.com** for the current schedule.

Pavillon de la TOHU ★ Adjacent to Cirque du Soleil's training complex and company offices, TOHU is a performance space devoted to the circus arts. TOHU features an intimate in-the-round hall done up like an old-fashioned circus tent, and an exhibit space displays more than 100 circus artifacts. The annual May to June shows by students of the National Circus School present many of the top rising stars. The entire venue was built with recycled pieces of an amusement-park bumper-car ride and wood from a dismantled railroad. The facility is in the lower-income Saint-Michel district well north of downtown, but is accessible by Métro and bus, as well as taxi. Most of its programming information is in French. 2345 rue Jarry est (corner of rue

Don't Miss a Thing

For details about performances or special events when you're in town, "**Hour**" (www.hour.ca), in English, and "**Voir**" (www.voir.ca), in French, offer rich, up-to-date previews. One particularly fun blog about city happenings is **Midnight Poutine** (www.midnightpoutine.ca), a self-described "delicious high-fat source of rants, raves, and musings." The city's tourism office hosts a blog called **Montréal Buzz,** written by a team of locals (www.tourisme-montreal.org/blog).

d'Iberville, at Autoroute 40). www.tohu.ca. ✆ **888/376-8648** or 514/376-8648. Free to view facility and exhibits. Performances from C$25 adults, from C$15 children 12 and under. 8km (5 miles) from downtown, up rue St-Denis and east on rue Jarry to where it meets Autoroute 40. Métro: Jarry or Iberville. Bus: 94 nord.

Classical Music & Ballet

Many churches have exemplary classical music programs. At **Cathédrale Christ Church,** 635 rue Ste-Catherine ouest (www.montrealcathedral.ca; ✆ **514/843-6577,** ext. 369), a top-notch choir sings Sundays at 10am and 4pm with programs that often include modernists such as Benjamin Britten.

Les Grands Ballets Canadiens ★★ The prestigious touring company, performing both a classical and a modern repertoire, has developed a following far beyond national borders in its 50-plus years (it was founded in 1957). In the process, it has brought prominence to many gifted Canadian choreographers and composers. The troupe's production of "The Nutcracker" is always a big event each winter. Performances are held October through May. Place des Arts, 175 rue Ste-Catherine ouest (main entrance), downtown. www.grandsballets.qc.ca. ✆ **514/849-0269.** Tickets from C$53. Métro: Place-des-Arts.

Opéra de Montréal ★ Founded in 1980, this outstanding opera company mounts six productions per year in Montréal, with artists from Québec and abroad participating in such shows as Gershwin's "Porgy and Bess" and Puccini's "Turandot." Video translations are provided from the original languages into French and English. Performances are held from September through May. Place des Arts, 175 rue Ste-Catherine ouest (main entrance), downtown. www.operademontreal.com. ✆ 877/385-2222 or **514/985-2258.** Tickets from C$21. Métro: Place-des-Arts.

Orchestre Symphonique de Montréal (OSM) ★★ The orchestra got a gorgeous new home in 2011, **Maison symphonique de Montréal,** which is designed "shoebox" style, with seats on multiple balcony levels surrounding the performers. Music director Kent Nagano focuses the symphony's repertoire on programs featuring works by Beethoven, Bach, Brahms, and Mahler. It has programs for children 5 to 12 and special prices for people 34 and under, 25 and under, and 17 and under. Place des Arts, 1600 rue St-Urbain, downtown. www.osm.ca. ✆ **514/842-9951** for tickets. Tickets from C$28; discounts available for various age groups. Métro: Place-des-Arts.

Concert Halls & Auditoriums

Centre Bell Seating 21,273 for most events, Centre Bell is the home of the Montréal Canadiens hockey team and host to the biggest international rock and pop stars traveling through the city, including Québec native Céline Dion. There are guided tours and a Montréal Canadiens Hall of Fame (**www.hall.canadiens.com**). Centre Bell's street was renamed in 2009 for the 100th anniversary of the Canadiens; the former address was 1260 rue de la Gauchetière ouest. 1909 avenue des Canadiens-de-Montréal, downtown. www.centrebell.ca. ✆ 877/668-8269 or 514/790-2525. Métro: Bonaventure.

Métropolis After starting life as a skating rink in 1884, the 2,300-capacity Métropolis is now a prime showplace for both traveling rock groups—it has recently hosted Thirty Seconds to Mars and Franz Ferdinand—and annual events such as the summer jazz festival. 59 rue Ste-Catherine est, downtown. www.montrealmetropolis.ca/metropolis. ✆ **855/790-1245.** Métro: St-Laurent or Berri-UQAM.

Place des Arts ★★★ Since 1992, Place des Arts has been the city's central entertainment complex, presenting performances of musical concerts, opera, dance, and theater in seven halls, including **Salle Wilfrid-Pelletier** (2,982 seats, where the Opéra de Montréal and Les Grands Ballets Canadiens both perform), and the new **Maison symphonique de Montréal** (2,100 seats), where the Orchestre Métropolitain du Grand Montréal performs. Portions of the city's many arts festivals are staged in the halls and outdoor plaza here, as are traveling productions of Broadway shows. Place des Arts is at the center of the larger cultural hub known as the Quartier des Spectacles. Place des Arts, 175 rue Ste-Catherine ouest (main entrance and ticket office), downtown. www.pda.qc.ca. ✆ **866/842-2112** or 514/842-2112 for information and tickets. Métro: Place-des-Arts.

BARS & NIGHTCLUBS

Some nightclubs, restaurants, and bars position themselves as **supper clubs:** all-in-one venues where you go for drinks, stay for dinner, and then hang around drinking and possibly dancing until closing. Nightclubs can be exclusive—waiting in line is an unfortunate reality—and while there aren't dress codes for women (except what seems to be an unwritten rule that the shorter the dress, the more likely you are to be let in), some clubs have rules for men prohibiting baseball caps, sneakers, T-shirts, and messy jeans. Regular bars stay open until 3am; still others keep the fire burning after hours.

Downtown

Bar Furco ★ Industrial-chic Berlin meets an old Montréal fur warehouse. That's the inspiration for this downtown hotspot for cocktails and wine (the food menu kicks in after 5pm). Attractive 20- and 30-somethings gather after work and will even wait in line to soak up Furco's vintage-mod vibe. 425 rue Mayor (near Quartier des Spectacles). www.barfurco.com. ✆ **514/764-3588.** Métro: Place-des-Arts or McGill.

Brutopia ★ This pub pulls endless pints of its own microbrews, which might include maple cream or java stout on a given day. With three levels, a terrace in back, and a street-side balcony, it draws a mixed crowd, students with laptops, and old friends just hanging out. Unlike other spots on rue Crescent, where the sound levels can be deafening, here you can actually have a conversation. Bands perform most evenings. 1219 rue Crescent (north of boul. René-Lévesque). www.brutopia.net. ✆ **514/393-9277.** Métro: Lucien L'Allier.

Hurley's Irish Pub In front is a street-level terrace, and in back are several semi-subterranean rooms. Celtic instrumentalists perform nightly, usually starting around 9:30pm. There are 22 beers on tap and more than 50 single-malt whiskeys to choose from. 1225 rue Crescent (at rue Ste-Catherine), downtown. www.hurleysirishpub.com. ✆ **514/861-4111.** Métro: Guy-Concordia.

Maison de Jazz Right downtown, this New Orleans–style jazz venue has been on the scene for decades. Lovers of barbecued ribs and jazz arrive early to fill the room, which is decorated in mock–Art Nouveau style with tiered levels. Live music starts around 8pm most nights and continues until closing time. The ribs are OK, and the jazz is of the swinging mainstream variety, with occasional digressions into more esoteric forms. 2060 rue Aylmer (south of rue Sherbrooke). www.houseofjazz.ca. ✆ **514/842-8656.** Cover C$10. Métro: McGill.

Newtown A tri-level club in the center of rue Crescent nightlife, the shmancy Newtown is an appealing spot for *cinq-à-sept* (5-to-7pm) drinks, especially on the rooftop terrace in the warm months. The square bar in the middle of the main barroom is a friendly place, too. 1476 rue Crescent (at boul. de Maisonneuve), downtown. www.lenewtown.com. ✆ **514/284-6555.** Métro: Peel.

Pullman ★★ This sleek wine bar has dozens of wines as well as aperitifs and ports by the glass and offers both 2- and 4-oz. pours, so you can sample a number of vintages. In summer, try a Coimbra, a sangria-like drink with *porto blanco,* tonic, and lime. A competent tapas menu with standards like charcuterie and fun oddballs like grilled cheese bedazzled with port are prepared with the precision of a sushi chef. Pullman is a smartly designed multilevel space with pockets of ambience, from cozy corners to tables drenched in natural light. It's open daily from 4:30pm to 1am. 3424 av. du Parc (north of Sherbrooke). www.pullman-mtl.com. ✆ **514/288-7779.** Métro: Place-des-Arts.

Sir Winston Churchill Pub ★ The three levels of bars and cafes here are rue Crescent landmarks, and the New Orleans–style sidewalk and first-floor terraces (open in warm months) make perfect vantage points from which to check out the pedestrian traffic. With English ales on tap, the pub attempts to imitate a British public house and gets a mixed crowd of young professionals. 1459 rue Crescent (near rue Ste-Catherine). www.swcpc.com. ✆ **514/288-3814.** Métro: Guy-Concordia.

Upstairs Jazz Bar & Grill ★ The Upstairs Jazz Bar, actually *down* a few steps from the street, has been hosting live jazz music nightly since 1995. Big names are infrequent, but the groups are more than competent. Sets begin as at 8:30pm, and there are usually three each night, 7 days a week. Food ranges from bar snacks to more substantial meals. It's more of a mid-aged crowd, but a younger jazz-curious crew has been settling in, too. The cover charge is usually C$5 to C$20. 1254 rue Mackay (south of rue Ste-Catherine). www.upstairsjazz.com. ✆ **514/931-6808.** Métro: Guy-Concordia.

Vieux-Montréal

Le Deux Pierrots This has traditionally been one of the best known of Montréal's *boîtes-à-chansons* (song clubs), but its more visible personality these days is as a sports bar. The sports posters are what you'll mostly see when you walk by, but look for the smaller posters of musicians. On Friday and Saturday nights, a French-style cabaret still brings in singers who interact animatedly, and often bilingually, with the crowd. Arrive by 9pm or make a reservation because tables can fill up. 104 rue St-Paul est (west of Place Jacques-Cartier). www.lespierrots.com. ✆ **514/861-1270.** Métro: Place d'Armes.

Le Jardin Nelson ★★ In the summer, the outdoor dining options that line Place Jacques Cartier are tempting but touristy. Le Jardin Nelson has a people-watching porch adjacent to the plaza, but you're better off tucking into its large tree-shaded garden court, which sits behind a stone building dating from 1812. It's still touristy, but a pleasant hour or two can be spent listening to live jazz, played every afternoon and evening. Food takes second place, but the kitchen does well with its pizzas and *crêpes,* with *crêpe* options both sweet and savory. There are heaters outdoors to cut the chill and a few tables indoors, too. When the weather's nice, it's open as late as 1am; but it's closed November through mid-April. 407 Place Jacques-Cartier (at rue St-Paul est). www.jardinnelson.com. ✆ **514/861-5731.** Métro: Place d'Armes or Champ-de-Mars.

Philémon ★ The look here is chalet-chic, while the crowd is urban single professional. As one blogger put it, "you can always count on its strong quick 'n' dirty drinks, relaxed vibe, fashionable and goodlooking 20–40 year old crowd . . . Oh, and being hit on." The oysters are good and there's a great charcuterie platter. 111 rue St-Paul ouest (at rue St-Urbain). www.philemonbar.com. ✆ **514/289-3777.** Métro: Place d'Armes.

Suite 701 When Place d'Armes Hôtel converted its lobby and wine bar into this spiffy lounge, young professionals got the word. It's a beautiful hotel bar in a central location (right on Place d'Armes), and it makes a point of catering to the so-called *cinq-à-sept* (5-to-7pm) after-work crowd, especially on Thursdays. 711 Côte de la Place d'Armes (at rue St-Jacques). www.suite701.com. ✆ **514/904-1201.** Métro: Place d'Armes.

Velvet ★ This cavernous nightclub cultivates the feel of an underground speakeasy, courtesy of its virtually nonexistent signage and its tunnel entrance through the bar of Auberge St-Gabriel. Some of the bartenders here are models and many of the patrons have deep pockets, so, yes, come dressed to impress. Music ranges from house, hip-hop to electro. 420 rue St-Gabriel (near rue St. Paul est). Enter through the hotel bar. www.velvetspeakeasy.ca. ✆ **514/995-8754.** Metro: Place d'Armes.

Plateau Mont-Royal & Mile End

Baldwin Barmacie ★ The split-level space of this all-white bar attracts more of a young professional than starving-artist crowd. Sometimes there's a DJ, sometimes it's just owner Alex Baldwin's iTunes library, consisting of classic rock and old-school hip hop. Bottles line the walls as they would in an old-time pharmacy. This is a place to give a fancy cocktail a try. 115 av. Laurier ouest (at rue St. Urbain). www.baldwinbarmacie.com. ✆ **514/276-4282.** Métro: Laurier.

Bílý Kůň ★★ Pronounced "Billy Coon," this popular bar is a bit of Prague right in Montréal, from the avant-garde decor (mounted ostrich heads ring the room) to the full line of Czech beers, local microbrews, and dozen-plus scotches. Martini specials include the Absinthe Aux Pommes. Students and professionals jam in for the relaxed candle-lit atmosphere, which includes twirling ceiling fans and picture windows that open to the street. There's live jazz or DJs spinning upbeat pop most nights. Get here early to do a little shopping in the hipster boutiques along the street. 354 av. du Mont-Royal est (near rue St-Denis). www.bilykun.com. ✆ **514/845-5392.** Métro: Mont Royal.

Buvette Chez Simone ★ Simone is one of a group of friends who own this popular bar. The terrace (framed by greenery in summer) is a coveted spot in sunny weather. Stripped-down industrial chic in the interior envelops a central, oval-shaped bar. The menu has a satisfying selection of small eats, including *charcuterie* and cheeses, as well as a strong selection of wines by the glass. 4869 av. du Parc (at boul. St. Joseph ouest). www.buvettechezsimone.com. ✆ **514/750-6577.** Métro: Mont Royal or Laurier.

Casa del Popolo Set in a scruffy storefront, Casa del Popolo serves vegetarian food, operates a laid-back bar, and has a small first-floor stage. Across the street is a larger, sister performance space, **La Sala Rossa** (below). The two venues constitute the heart of the Montréal indie music scene. 4873 boul. St-Laurent (near boul. St-Joseph). www.casadelpopolo.com. ✆ **514/284-3804.** Cover C$5–C$15. Métro: Laurier.

Champs You like sports? Looking for a particular soccer/hockey/baseball/football game? Chances are good that it will be on here, in this three-story sports emporium. Games from around the world are fed to walls of TVs, and more than a dozen athletic events might be showing at any given time. Food is what you'd expect—burgers, steaks, and such. 3956 boul. St-Laurent (near av. Duluth). ✆ **514/987-6444.** Métro: Sherbrooke.

Dieu Du Ciel ★★★ Tucked into a corner building on rue Laurier, this neighborhood artisanal brewpub offers an alternating selection of some dozen beers, including house brews and exotic imports. The place buzzes, even midweek. With good conversation and some friends to sample the array, what more do you need? If it's guidance on where to begin, how about starting with the Première Communion (First Communion), a Scottish ale; moving on to the Rosée d'Hibiscus, which is less sweet than feared; and finishing with the Rigor Mortis ABT. Dieu du Ciel beers are also bottled and sold throughout the province. 29 av. Laurier ouest (near boul. St. Laurent). www.dieuduciel.com. ✆ **514/490-9555.** Métro: Laurier.

La Sala Rossa ★ A bigger venue than its sister performance space **Casa del Popolo** (see above), La Sala Rossa has a full calendar of interesting rock, experimental, and jazz music. The attached Sala Rossa restaurant serves up hearty Spanish food with a big card of tapas and paella—and, every Thursday, live flamenco music with dancing and singing. Reserve your spot a week or more in advance. 4848 boul. St-Laurent (near boul. St-Joseph). www.casadelpopolo.com. ✆ **514/844-4227.** Cover C$5–C$30. Métro: Laurier.

Vices & Versa ★ This *bistro au terroir* has featured microbrews on draft and in cask as well as chow from the region since 2004. It's a low-key, local joint with occasional musical acts and a lovely backyard beer garden. 6631 bd. St-Laurent (near rue St-Zotique). www.vicesetversa.com. ✆ **514/272-2498.** Métro: Beaubien.

Gay Village & Quartier Latin

Cabaret Mado ★ The glint of the sequins can be blinding! Inspired by 1920s cabaret, this drag theater has a dance floor, performances most nights, and is considered a premiere venue. We're still kicking ourselves for missing the "Spice Girls Drag World Tour" show. Look for the pink-haired drag queen on the retro marquee. 1115 rue Ste-Catherine est (near rue Amherst). www.mado.qc.ca. ✆ **514/525-7566.** Cover C$10. Métro: Beaudry.

Club Soda The long-established rock club in a seedy part of the Latin Quarter (and on the edge of the hotter Quartier des Spectacles) hosts Nirvana cover bands, fashion shows, and parts of the city's music and comedy festivals. 1225 boul. St-Laurent (at rue Ste-Catherine), Quartier Latin. www.clubsoda.ca. ✆ **514/286-1010.** Tickets from C$17. Métro: St-Laurent.

Les Foufounes Electriques From the outside, this Latin Quarter club looks goth and vaguely threatening, with a spider the size of a Smart Car hanging over the front gate. Inside, it's a multilevel rock club that features hard-core and punk bands and DJs. It's open daily 3pm to 3am. 87 Ste-Catherine est (near boul. St-Laurent). www.facebook.com/foufouneselectriques. ✆ **514/844-5539.** Métro: St-Laurent.

Sky Club & Pub A complex that includes drag performances in the cabaret room, a pub serving dinner daily, a hip-hop room, a spacious dance floor that's often set to house music, and a popular roof terrace, Sky is thought by many to be the city's hottest spot for the gay, young, and fabulous. It's got spiffy decor and pounding music. Did we mention there's also a pool and a hottub on the terrace? 1474 rue Ste-Catherine est (near rue Plessis). www.complexesky.com. ✆ **514/529-6969.** Métro: Beaudry.

Little Burgundy & Outer Districts

Burgundy Lion This Brit pub is a no-nonsense kind of place with banquettes and tavern-type wooden chairs. The Lion welcomes a slightly younger crowd on weekends than the regulars that come during the week. Television screens and sports team flags ensure that this is a lively spot to take in footie (soccer) and hockey games. The food menu is respectable, although the restaurant **Joe Beef** (p. 74) is across the street. 2496 rue Notre-Dame ouest (at rue Charlevoix). www.burgundylion.com. ✆ **514/934-0888.** Métro: Lionel-Groulx.

Piknic Electronik ★★ From late May to late September on sunny Sunday afternoons and into the evenings, it's a dance party at Parc Jean-Drapeau. Hipster kids, families with young children, and dancing queens who just didn't get enough on Saturday night gather and shake it outdoors under the Alexander Calder sculpture, *Man and His World,* located on the Belvedere on the north shore of Ile Sainte-Hélène, facing the river. There's usually a DJ and, sometimes, live acts. Music starts early afternoon and runs until about 8pm, but sometimes as late as 10:30pm. To find the outdoor locale, the website suggests taking the Métro and just following the rhythms when you exit! Belvedere in Parc Jean-Drapeau (Ile Ste-Hélène). www.piknicelectronik.com. ✆ **514/904-1247.** Admission C$14 adults, free for children 12 and under. May–Oct Sun 2–9pm. Métro: Jean-Drapeau.

MORE ENTERTAINMENT

Casino

The **Casino de Montréal** (www.casinosduquebec.com; ✆ **800/665-2274** or 514/392-2746), Québec's first, is housed in recycled space: The complex reuses what were the French and Québec pavilions during Expo 67. Asymmetrical and groovy, the buildings provide a dramatic setting for games of chance. As casinos go, this one is pretty nice. Four floors present roulette, craps, blackjack, baccarat, and varieties of poker, and there are more than 3,000 slot machines. There are four restaurants at the full range of price points. The casino is entirely smoke-free, with outside smoking areas. It's open 24 hours a day, 7 days a week, with overnight packages available at nearby hotels. No one under 18 is admitted, even to the restaurants. The casino is on Parc Jean-Drapeau. You can drive there or take the Métro to the Parc Jean-Drapeau stop and then walk or take the casino shuttle bus (no. 777, labeled CASINO).

Cinema

When movie-going in the province of Québec, check the film's original language and whether or not it's subtitled. In Montréal, English-language films are usually presented with French subtitles. However, when the initials "VF" (for *version française*) follow the title of a non-Francophone movie, it means that the movie has been dubbed into French.

In addition to the **Festival des Films du Monde held** in August (see above), the **Festival du Nouveau Cinéma** (www.nouveaucinema.ca) in October and **Rencontres Internationales du Documentaire de Montréal** (or RIDM, www.ridm.qc.ca) in November attract industry attention and visitors from far beyond Canada's borders. Theaters that specialize in contemporary and retrospective art house cinema include **Cinéma Excentris,** 3536 boul. St-Laurent near rue Prince Arthur (www.cinemaexcentris.com; ✆ **855/331-3303** or 514/847-2206) and **Cinémathèque Québécoise,** 335 bd.

de Maisonneuve est near l'Université du Québec à Montréal (UQAM; www.cinematheque.qc.ca; ✆ **514/842-9763**). Imposing, fantastically huge images confront viewers of the seven-story **IMAX Theatre** screen in the Centre des Sciences de Montréal (p. 84). Many of the films are suitable for the entire family.

Comedy

Comedy is hot in Montréal, mostly because the city is the home to the highly regarded **Juste pour Rire (Just for Laughs) Festival** every July (see p. 102). Throughout the year, **Comedyworks,** at 1238 rue Bishop (www.comedyworksmontreal.com; ✆ **514/398-9661**), feeds the comedy audiences. Monday is open mic, Tuesday is stand up, Wednesday is improv nights (a comedy troupe works off the audience's suggestions), and Thursday through Saturday feature international headliners. Reservations are recommended. Shows are in English and happen nightly at 8:30pm, with additional shows at 10:30pm on Friday and Saturday. If it's your first trip to a comedy club, know that profanity, bathroom humor, and ethnic slurs are common. Don't sit near the stage unless you're prepared to get picked on by the performer.

MONTRÉAL WALKING TOURS

9

Cities best reveal themselves on foot, and Montréal is one of North America's most pedestrian-friendly locales. There's much to see in the concentrated districts—cobblestoned Vieux-Montréal, downtown and its luxurious "Golden Square Mile," and Mont Royal itself—and in this chapter are strolls that will take you through the highlights of all of them.

The city's layout is mostly straightforward and simple to navigate, and the extensive Métro system gets you to and from neighborhoods with ease. These strolls will give you a taste of what's best about old and new Montréal, and send you off to discover highlights of your own. In the following tour we mention lots of great eating stops along the way. We know you couldn't possibly take us up on all our recommendations, but perhaps one or two of them will suit you when hunger strikes!

WALKING TOUR 1: VIEUX-MONTRÉAL

GETTING THERE: **If you're coming from outside Vieux-Montréal, take the Métro to the Place d'Armes station, which lets off next to the Palais des Congrès, the convention center. Follow the signs up the short hill 2 blocks toward Vieux-Montréal (Old Montréal). You'll find yourself in a central outdoor plaza.**

START: **Place d' Armes, opposite the Notre-Dame Basilica**

FINISH: **Vieux-Port**

TIME: **2 hours**

BEST TIMES: **Almost any day the weather is decent. Vieux-Montréal is lively and safe, day or night. Note that most museums are closed on Monday. On warm weekends and holidays, Montréalers and visitors turn out in full force, enjoying the plazas, the 18th- and 19th-century architecture, and the ambience of the most picturesque part of their city.**

WORST TIMES: **Evenings, days that are too cold, and times when museums and historic buildings are closed. Sunny days in winter are known to be particularly cold (as opposed to those when it is snowing and temperatures are notably warmer), but you can take advantage of the bright light. Do as the locals do and wear a warm coat, hat, mitts, and good boots.**

Walking Tour 1: Vieux-Montréal

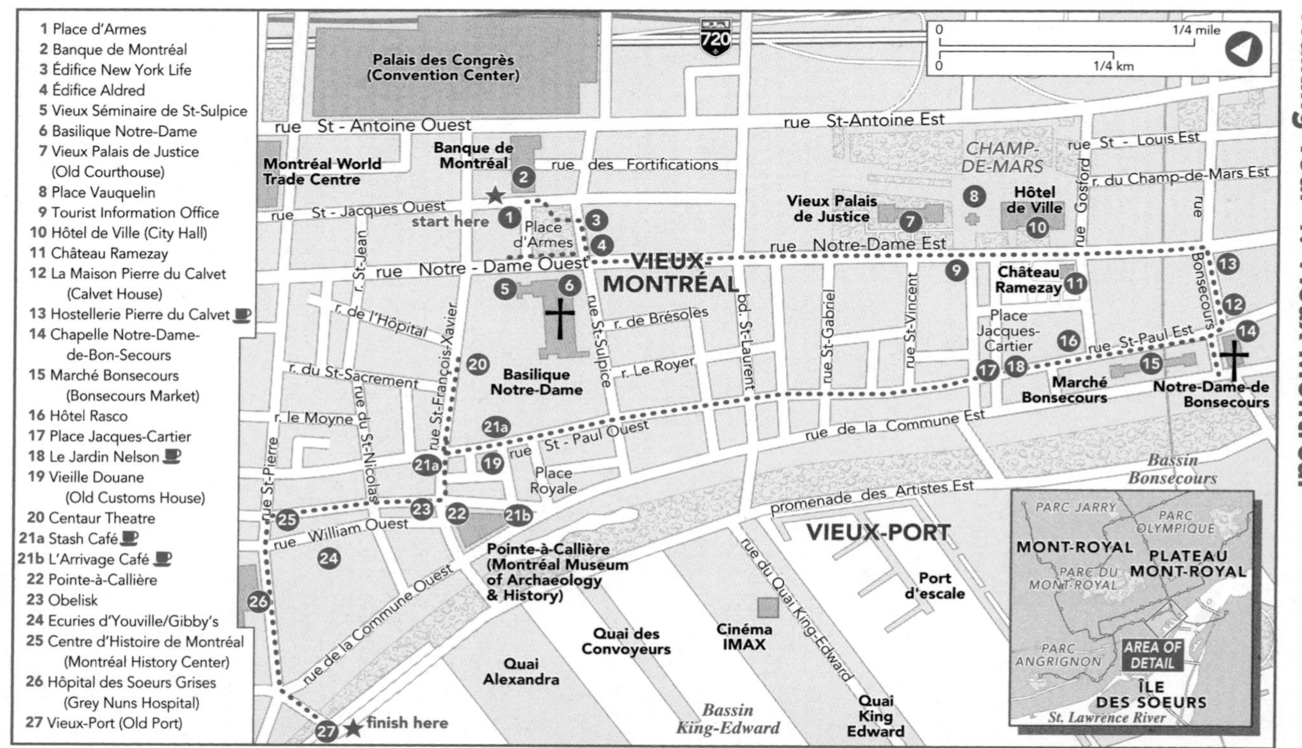

Vieux-Montréal is where the city was born. Its architectural heritage has been substantially preserved, and restored 18th- and 19th-century structures now house shops, boutique hotels, galleries, cafes, bars, and apartments. This tour gives you a lay of the land, passing many of the neighborhood's highlights and some of its best and most atmospheric dining spots.

Start at:

1 Place d'Armes

The architecture of the buildings that surround this plaza is representative of Montréal's growth: the Sulpician residence of the 17th century (see no. 5, below); the Banque de Montréal (see no. 2) and Basilique Notre-Dame (see no. 6) of the 19th century; and the Art Deco Edifice Aldred (see no. 4) of the 20th century.

The centerpiece of the square is a monument to city founder Paul de Chomedey, Sieur de Maisonneuve (1612–1676). The five statues mark the spot where settlers defeated Iroquois warriors in bloody hand-to-hand fighting, with de Maisonneuve himself locked in combat with the Iroquois chief. De Maisonneuve won and lived here another 23 years. The inscription on the monument reads (in French): YOU ARE THE BUCKWHEAT SEED WHICH WILL GROW AND MULTIPLY AND SPREAD THROUGHOUT THE COUNTRY.

The sculptures at the base of the monument represent other prominent citizens of early Montréal: Charles Lemoyne (1626–1685), a farmer; Jeanne Mance (1606–1673), a woman who founded the city's first hospital; Raphael-Lambert Closse (1618–1662), a soldier and the mayor of Ville-Marie; and an unnamed Iroquois brave. Closse is depicted with his dog, Pilote, whose bark once warned the early settlers of an impending Iroquois attack.

On the north side of the plaza, at 119 St-Jacques, is the domed, colonnaded:

2 Banque de Montréal

Montréal's oldest bank building dates from 1847. From 1901 to 1905, American architect Stanford White (1853–1906) extended the original building, and in this enlarged space, he created a vast chamber with green-marble columns topped with golden capitals. The public is welcome to stop in for a look. Besides being lavishly appointed inside and out, the bank also houses a small and quirky **banking museum,** which illustrates early operations. It's just off the main lobby to the left and admission is free.

Facing the Notre-Dame Basilica from the square, look over to the left. At the corner of St-Jacques is the:

3 Edifice New York Life

This red-stone Richardson Romanesque building, with a striking wrought-iron door and clock tower, is at 511 Place d'Armes. It's also known as the Québec Bank Building. At all of eight stories, this became Montréal's first skyscraper in 1888, and it was equipped with a technological marvel—an elevator.

Next to it, on the right, stands the 23-story Art Deco:

4 Edifice Aldred

If this building looks somehow familiar, there's a reason: Built in 1931, it clearly resembles New York's Empire State Building, also completed that year. The building's original tenant was Aldred and Co. Ltd., a New York–based finance company with other offices in New York, London, and Paris.

Facing the Notre-Dame Basilica again, just to its right is the:

5 Vieux Séminaire de St-Sulpice

The city's oldest building is surrounded by equally ancient stone walls. It feels almost like you've traveled back in time. This seminary was erected by Sulpician priests who arrived in Ville-Marie in 1657, 15 years after the colony was founded (the Sulpicians are part of an order founded in Paris in 1641). The clock on the facade dates from 1701, and its gears are made almost entirely of wood. The seminary is not open to the public.

After a look through the seminary's iron gate, head to the magnificent Gothic Revival–style church itself:

6 Basilique Notre-Dame

This brilliantly crafted church was designed in 1824 by James O'Donnell, an Irish Protestant living in New York. Transformed by his experience, he converted to Roman Catholicism and is the only person interred here. The main altar is made from a hand-carved linden tree. Behind it is the Chapel of the Sacred Heart (1982), a perennially popular choice for weddings (Québec-born singer Céline Dion married René Angélil here in 1994). The chapel's altar, 32 bronze panels by Montréal artist Charles Daudelin, represents birth, life, and death. Some 4,000 people can attend mass at a time, and the bell, one of North America's largest, weighs 12 tons. There's a small museum beside the chapel. Come back at night for a romantic take on the city, when more than a score of buildings in the area, including this one, are illuminated. During the Christmas season, three white angels are suspended at the entrance with ethereal blue lighting. See p. 83 for more about the church.

Exiting the basilica, turn right (east) on rue Notre-Dame. Cross rue St-Sulpice. On the north side of rue Notre-Dame is Claude Postel, a great place for sandwiches and pastries. Walk 4 blocks, passing chintzy souvenir shops, until you reach, on the left side, the grand:

7 Vieux Palais de Justice (Old Courthouse)

Most of this structure was built in 1856. The third floor and dome were added in 1891, and the difference between the original structure and the addition can be easily discerned with a close look. A second city courthouse, designed by Ernest-Cormier, was built in 1925 and is across the street, with a long colonnade. Since 1971, all legal business has been conducted in a third courthouse, the glass-encased building 1 block back, at 1 rue Notre-Dame est. The statue beside the Old Courthouse, called *Homage to Marguerite Bourgeoys,* depicts a teacher and nun and is the work of sculptor Jules LaSalle.

Also on your left, just past the courthouse, is:

8 Place Vauquelin

This small public square, with a splashing fountain and view of the Champ-de-Mars park, was created in 1858. The statue is of Jean Vauquelin (1728–1772), commander of the French fleet in New France. Renovations were going on around his statue when we last visited. Vauquelin stares across rue Notre-Dame at his counterpart, the English admiral Horatio Nelson (1758–1805). The two statues are symbols of Montréal's French and British duality.

On the opposite corner is a small but helpful:

9 Tourist Information Office

A bilingual staff stands ready to answer questions and hand out useful brochures and maps. It's open daily from April 1 to November 15 and closed in winter. The famed Silver Dollar Saloon once stood on this site. It got its name from the 350 silver dollars that were embedded in its floor.

Around the corner, on the right, is the Place Jacques-Cartier, a magnet for citizens and visitors year-round, which we will visit later in the stroll. Rising on the other side of rue Notre-Dame, opposite the top of the square, is the impressive, green-capped:

10 Hôtel de Ville (City Hall)

Built between 1872 and 1878 in the florid French Second Empire style, the edifice is seen to particular advantage when it is illuminated at night. In 1922, it barely survived a disastrous fire. Only the exterior walls remained, and after substantial rebuilding and the addition of another floor, it reopened in 1926. Take a minute to look inside at the generous use of French marble, the Art Deco lamps, and the bronze-and-glass chandelier. The sculptures at the entry are "Woman with a Pail" and "The Sower," both by Québec sculptor Alfred Laliberté. See p. 84 for more details.

Exiting City Hall, across rue Notre-Dame, you'll see a small, terraced park with orderly ranks of trees. The statue inside the park honors Montréal's controversial longtime mayor, Jean Drapeau (1916–1999). Next to it is:

11 Château Ramezay

Beginning in 1705, this was the home of the city's French governors for 4 decades, starting with Claude de Ramezay, before being taken over and used for the same purpose by the British. In 1775, an army of American rebels invaded and held Montréal, using the house as their headquarters. Benjamin Franklin was sent to try to persuade Montréalers to join the American revolt against British rule, and he stayed in this château. He failed to sway Québec's leaders to join the radical cause. Today, the house shows off furnishings, oil paintings, costumes, and other objects related to the economic and social activities of the 18th century and the first half of the 19th century. In past summers, nearby restaurant **Le Club Chasse et Pêche** (www.leclubchasseetpeche.com) has served an haute cuisine lunch in the garden under a posh white tent; ask if this is still a dining option. See p. 85 for more about the museum.

Continue in the same direction (east) along rue Notre-Dame. In the far distance, you'll see the Molson beer factory. At rue Bonsecours, turn right. Near the bottom of the street, on the left, is a house with a low maroon roof and an attached stone building on the corner. This is:

12 La Maison Pierre du Calvet (Calvet House)

Built in the 18th century and sumptuously restored between 1964 and 1966, this house was inhabited by a fairly well-to-do family in its first years. Pierre du Calvet, believed to be the original owner, was a French Huguenot who supported the American Revolution. Calvet met with Benjamin Franklin here in 1775 and was imprisoned from 1780 to 1783 for supplying money to the Americans. With a characteristic sloped roof meant to discourage snow buildup and raised end walls that serve as firebreaks, the building is constructed of Montréal gray stone. It is now a restaurant and *hostellerie* with an entrance at no. 405.

13 Hostellerie Pierre du Calvet

There is a voluptuously appointed dining room inside the Hostellerie Pierre du Calvet, 405 rue Bonsecours, called Les Filles du Roy (✆ 866/544-1725 or 514/282-1725), and it's a real splurge (we're talking C$25–C$46 mains). In the warm months, lunches, dinners, and Sunday brunches (a relative steal at C$25) are served in an outdoor courtyard. Take a peek to see the greenhouse and parrots that lead to the stone-walled terrace.

The next street, rue St-Paul, is Montréal's oldest thoroughfare, dating from 1672. The church at this intersection is the small:

14 Chapelle Notre-Dame-de-Bon-Secours

Called the Sailors' Church because so many seamen made pilgrimages here to give thanks for being saved at sea, this chapel was founded by Marguerite Bourgeoys, a nun and teacher who was canonized in 1982. Excavations have unearthed foundations of her original 1675 church—although the building has been much altered, and the present facade was built in the late 18th century. A **museum** (p. 84) tells the story of Bourgeoys's life and incorporates the archaeological site. Climb up to the tower for a view of the port and Old Town.

Head west on rue St-Paul. Just beyond the Sailors' Church is an imposing building with a colonnaded facade and silvery dome, the limestone:

15 Marché Bonsecours (Bonsecours Market)

Completed in 1847, this building was used first as the Parliament of United Canada and then as the City Hall, the central market, a music hall, and then the home of the municipality's housing and planning offices. It was restored in 1992 for the city's 350th birthday celebration to house temporary exhibitions and musical performances. It continues to be used for exhibitions, but it's more of a retail center now, with an eclectic selection of local art shops, clothing boutiques, and sidewalk cafes. When Bonsecours Market was first built, the dome could be seen from everywhere in the city and served as a landmark for seafarers sailing into the harbor. Today, it is lit at night.

Continue down rue St-Paul. At no. 281 is the former:

16 Hôtel Rasco

An Italian, Francisco Rasco, came to Canada to manage a hotel for the Molson family (of beer-brewing fame) and later became successful with his own hotel on this spot. The 150-room Rasco was the Ritz-Carlton of its day, hosting Charles Dickens and his wife in 1842, when the author was directing his plays at a theater that used to stand across the street. The hotel lives on in legend, if not in fact, as it's devoid of much of its original architectural detail and no longer hosts overnight guests. Between 1960 and 1981, the space stood empty, but the city took it over and restored it in 1982. It has contained a succession of eateries on the ground floor. The current occupant is **L'Autre Version** restaurant, whose inner courtyard/al fresco dining space is a hidden gem (www.restoversion.com).

Continue heading west on rue St-Paul, turning right when you reach:

17 Place Jacques-Cartier

Opened as a marketplace in 1804, this is the most appealing of Vieux-Montréal's squares, even with its obviously touristy aspects. The square's cobbled cross streets, gentle downhill slope, and ancient buildings set the mood, while outdoor cafes, street entertainers, itinerant artists, and assorted vendors invite lingering in warm weather. The Ben & Jerry's ice-cream shop doesn't hurt either. Calèches (horse-drawn carriages) depart from both the lower and the upper ends of the square for tours of Vieux-Montréal.

Walk slowly uphill, taking in the old buildings that bracket the plaza (plaques describe some of them in French and English). All these houses were well suited to the rigors of life in the raw young settlement. Their steeply pitched roofs shed the heavy winter snows, rather than collapsing under the burden, and small windows with double casements let in light while keeping out wintry breezes. When shuttered, the windows were almost as effective as the heavy stonewalls in deflecting hostile arrows or the antics of trappers fresh from nearby taverns. At the plaza's northern end stands a monument to Horatio Nelson, hero of Trafalgar, erected in 1809. This monument preceded London's much larger version by several years. After years of vandalism, presumably by Québec separatists, the statue had to be temporarily removed for restoration. The original Nelson is now back in place at the crown of the column.

18 Le Jardin Nelson

Most of the old buildings in and around the inclined plaza house restaurants and cafes. For a drink or snack during the warm months, try to find a seat in Le Jardin Nelson (no. 407), near the bottom of the hill. It's extremely popular with tourists, and for good reason. The tiered-level courtyard in back often has live jazz, while tables on the terrace overlook the square's activity. See p. 105 for details.

Return to rue St-Paul and continue west. Take time to window-shop the many art galleries that have sprung up alongside the loud souvenir shops on the street. If time permits, enjoy a drink at one of the bars along the way. The street numbers will get lower as you approach boulevard St-Laurent, the north-south thoroughfare that divides Montréal into its east and west halves. Numbers will start to rise again as you move onto St-Paul ouest (west). At 150 rue St-Paul ouest is the neoclassical:

19 Vieille Douane (Old Customs House)

Erected from 1836 to 1838, this building was doubled in size when an extension to the south side was added in 1882; walk around to the building's other side to see how the addition is different. That end of the building faces Place Royale, the first public square in the 17th-century settlement of Ville-Marie. It's where Europeans and Amerindians used to come to trade.

Continue on rue St-Paul to rue St-François-Xavier. Turn right for a short detour; up rue St-François-Xavier, on the right, is the stately:

20 Centaur Theatre

The home of Montréal's principal English-language theater is a former stock-exchange building. The Beaux Arts architecture is interesting in that the two entrances are on either side, rather than in the center, of the facade. American architect George Post, who was also responsible for designing the New York

Stock Exchange, designed this building, erected in 1903. It served its original function until 1965, when it was redesigned as a theater with two stages.

Return back down rue St-François-Xavier to rue St-Paul.

21 Stash Café & L'Arrivage Café

One possibility for lunch or a pick-me-up is the moderately priced Stash Café at 200 rue St-Paul ouest (at the corner of rue St-François-Xavier). It specializes in Polish fare and opens daily at noon. Another option is the glass-walled, second-floor L'Arrivage Café at the Pointe-à-Callière museum, your next stop. Its lunchtime "express menu" starts at C$12.

Continue on rue St-François-Xavier past St-Paul. At the next corner, the gray wedge-shaped building to the left is the:

22 Pointe-à-Callière

Known in English as the **Museum of Archaeology and History,** Pointe-à-Callière (p. 84) is a top-notch museum, packed with artifacts unearthed during more than a decade of excavation at the spot, where the settlement of Ville-Marie was founded in 1642. An underground connection also incorporates the **Old Customs House** you just passed.

A fort stood here in 1645. Thirty years later, a château was built on the site for Louis-Hector de Callière, the governor of New France, from whom the museum and triangular square that it's on take their names. At that time, the St. Pierre River separated this piece of land from the mainland. It was made a canal in the 19th century and later filled in. The museum's gift shop is located at the **Mariner's House building** at 165 Place d'Youville.

Proceeding west from Pointe-à-Callière, near rue St-François-Xavier, stands an:

23 Obelisk

Commemorating the founding of Ville-Marie on May 18, 1642, the obelisk was erected here in 1893 by the Montréal Historical Society. It bears the names of the city's early pioneers, including French officer Paul Chomedey de Maisonneuve, who landed in Montréal in 1642, and fellow settler Jeanne Mance, who founded North America's first hospital, l'Hôtel-Dieu de Montréal.

Continuing west from the obelisk 2 blocks to 296–316 Place d'Youville, you'll find, on the left, the:

24 Ecuries d'Youville (Youville Stables)

Despite the name, the rooms in the iron-gated compound, built in 1825 on land owned by the Grey Nuns, were used mainly as warehouses, rather than as horse stables (the actual stables, next door, were made of wood and disappeared long ago). Like much of the waterfront area, the U-shaped Youville building was rundown and forgotten until the 1960s, when a group of enterprising businesspeople bought and renovated it. Today, the compound contains offices and a steakhouse, **Gibby's,** 298 Place d'Youville (✆ **514/282-1837**), which is an institution, although not as hip with locals as Moishes (p. 66). If the gates are open, go through the passage toward the restaurant door to see the inner courtyard.

Continue another block west to the front door of the brick building on your right, 335 Place d'Youville and the:

25 Centre d'Histoire de Montréal (Montréal History Center)

Built in 1903 as Montréal's central fire station, this building now houses exhibits about life in Montréal, past and present. Visitors learn about traditions of the Amerindians, early exploration, and the evolution of industry, architecture, and professions in the city from 1535 to current day. See p. 83 for details.

Head down rue St-Pierre toward the water. Midway down the block, on the right at no. 138, is the former:

26 Hôpital des Soeurs Grises (Grey Nuns Hospital)

The hospital was founded in 1693 by the Charon Brothers to serve the city's poor and homeless. Bankrupt by 1747, it was taken over by Marguerite d'Youville, founder in 1737 of the Sisters of Charity of Montréal, commonly known as the Grey Nuns. It was expanded several times, but by 1871, the nuns had moved away and portions were demolished to extend rue St-Pierre and make room for commercial buildings. A century later, the Grey Nuns returned to live in their original home. From the sidewalk, visitors can see a very cool contemporary sculpture of inscribed bronze strips that cover the surviving chapel walls. The text on the sculpture comes from a letter signed by Louis XIV in 1694, incorporating the hospital. There are three exhibition rooms open to the public, by appointment only (✆ **514/842-9411**).

Continue down rue St-Pierre and cross the main street, rue de la Commune, and then the railroad tracks to this tour's final stop:

27 Vieux-Port (Old Port)

Montréal's historic commercial wharves have been reborn as a waterfront park, which, in good weather, is frequented by cyclists, in-line skaters, joggers, walkers, strollers, and couples. Across the water is the distinctive 158-unit modular housing project **Habitat 67,** built by famed architect Moshe Safdie for the 1967 World's Fair, which Montréal called Expo 67. Safdie's vision was to show what affordable community housing could be. Today, it's a higher-end apartment complex and not open to the public (aerial photos are at Safdie's website, www.msafdie.com). River surfers are known to "hit the waves" in a not-so-publicized spot just in back of this building.

Walk to your right. The triangular building you see is the entrance to **Jardin des Ecluses (Locks Garden),** a canal-side path where the St. Lawrence River's first locks are located. From here, you have several options: If the weather's nice, consider entering the Jardin des Ecluses to stroll the path along **Lachine Canal.** Only open in the summer season, **Café des Eclusiers,** 400 rue de la Commune ouest (✆ **514/496-0109**), offers a nice, scenic break. In under an hour, you'll arrive at Montréal's colorful **Marché Atwater** (p. 86), which is 3.8km (2¼ miles) down the path. If you walk the other direction, you'll take in the busiest section of the waterfront park and end up back at Place Jacques-Cartier.

To get to the subway, walk north along rue McGill to the Square-Victoria Métro station, the staircase to which is marked by an authentic Art Nouveau portal, designed by Hector Guimard for the Paris subway system.

Or return to the small streets parallel to rue St-Paul, where you'll find more boutiques and one of the highest concentrations of art galleries in Canada.

WALKING TOUR 2: DOWNTOWN MONTRÉAL

START:	**Bonaventure Métro station**
FINISH:	**Musée des Beaux-Arts and the lively rue Crescent**
TIME:	**2 hours**
BEST TIMES:	**Weekdays in the morning or after 2pm, when the streets hum with big-city vibrancy but aren't *too* busy.**
WORST TIMES:	**Weekdays from noon to 2pm, when the streets are crowded with businesspeople on lunch-break errands; Monday, when museums are closed; and Sunday, when many stores are closed and much of downtown is nearly deserted.**

After a tour of Vieux-Montréal, a look around the commercial heart of the 21st-century city will highlight the ample contrast between these two areas. To see the city at its contemporary best, take the Métro to the Bonaventure stop to start this tour.

After you've emerged from the Métro station, the dramatic skyscraper immediately to the west (or directly above you, depending on which exit you take) is:

1 1000 rue de la Gauchetière

Also called "Le 1000," this contribution to downtown Montréal is easily identified along the skyline by its copper-and-blue pyramidal top, which rises to the maximum height permitted by the municipal building code. Although it's mostly offices inside, it also has a year-round indoor skating rink (p. 97) under a glass dome.

Walk west on rue de la Gauchetière. Ahead is Le Marriott Château Champlain, whose distinctive facade of half-moon windows inspired its nickname "the Cheese Grater." Turn right on rue de la Cathedrale, heading north. At the next corner, you reach:

2 Boulevard René-Lévesque

Formerly Dorchester Boulevard, this street was renamed in 1988 following the death of René Lévesque, the Parti Québécois leader who led the movement for Québec independence and the province's use of the French language. Boulevard René-Lévesque is the city's broadest downtown thoroughfare.

Across bd. René-Lévesque is:

3 Square Dorchester

This is one of downtown's central locations. It's a gathering point for tour buses and horse-drawn calèches, and the square's shade trees and benches invite lunchtime brown-baggers. This used to be called Dominion Square, but it was renamed for Baron Dorchester, an early English governor, when the adjacent street, once named for Dorchester, was changed to boulevard René-Lévesque. The square was built over an old cemetery for 1832 cholera epidemic victims. Along the square's east side is the **Sun Life Insurance building,** built in three stages between 1914 and 1931, and the tallest building in Québec from 1931 until the skyscraper boom of the post–World War II era.

At the north end of the square is:

4 Montréal's Central Tourist Office

The Infotouriste Centre at 1255 rue Peel has maps and brochures and bilingual attendants, who are eager to answer questions, point you in the right direction, or give advice about hotels or tours. It's open daily (p. 32).

On bd. René-Lévesque at the corner of Square Dorchester is the:

5 Basilique-Cathédrale Marie-Reine-du-Monde

Suddenly get the feeling you're in Rome? This cathedral is a copy of St. Peter's Basilica, albeit a fraction of the size. It was built as the headquarters for Montréal's Roman Catholic bishop. The statue in front is of Bishop Ignace Bourget, the force behind the project. Construction lasted from 1875 to 1894, its start delayed by the bishop's desire to place it not in Francophone east Montréal, but in the heart of the Protestant Anglophone west. Read more at p. 78.

Continue on bd. René-Lévesque past the cathedral. In the next block, on the right, is:

6 Fairmont the Queen Elizabeth (Le Reine Elizabeth)

Montréal's largest hotel is right above **Gare Centrale,** the main railroad station. The Fairmont (www.fairmont.com/queenelizabeth; ✆ **866/540-4483** or 514/861-3511) is where John Lennon and Yoko Ono had their famous weeklong "Bed-in for Peace" in 1969.

On the other side of bd. René-Lévesque, directly across from the hotel, is:

7 Place Ville-Marie

One thing to keep in mind is that the French word *place,* or plaza, sometimes means an outdoor square, such as Place Jacques-Cartier in Vieux-Montréal. Other times, it refers to a building or complex that includes stores and offices. Place Ville-Marie is in this category. Known as PVM, the glass building was considered a gem of the 1960s urban redevelopment efforts. Its architect was I.M. Pei, who also designed the glass pyramid at the Louvre in Paris. Pei gave the skyscraper a cross-shaped footprint, recalling the cross atop Mont Royal. The underground houses a large shopping mall (**www.placevillemarie.com**).

Continue on bd. René-Lévesque to the end of the block and turn left on rue University. As you walk, look to the top of the skyscraper a few blocks down; this pink, postmodern glass office building is Tour KPMG and was completed in 1987. The two-peaked top is meant to resemble a bishop's miter, or cap, but many see the ears and mask of a certain DC Comics superhero. In 2 blocks, you'll reach:

8 Rue Ste-Catherine

This is one of the city's prime shopping streets, with name brands, local businesses, and department stores. Among them, to the right, is **La Baie**—or "the Bay"—successor to the famous fur-trapping firm Hudson's Bay Co., founded in the 17th century. Also here is **Henry Birks et Fils,** a preeminent jeweler since 1879, whose Birks Café is a decidedly posh spot to enjoy lunch, high tea, or buy some super-premium chocolates or macaroons.

If you're in the mood to shop, stroll west on this main shopping drag. (Be aware that there are adult shops here, too, most of which are above street level.) If you were to turn right and walk 5 short blocks to the east, you would reach Quartier des Spectacles, the city's central arts district. To continue the tour, return to this corner and the:

Walking Tour 2: Downtown Montréal

1 1000 rue de la Gauchetière
2 Boulevard René-Lévesque
3 Square Dorchester
4 Montréal's Central Tourist Office
5 Basilique-Cathédrale Marie-Reine-du-Monde
6 Fairmont the Queen Elizabeth (Le Reine Elizabeth)
7 Place Ville-Marie
8 Rue Ste-Catherine
9 Cathédrale Christ Church
10 Java U
11 Musée McCord
12 McGill University
13 Musée Redpath
14 Site of the Amerindian Hochelaga Settlement
15 Café Vasco da Gama
16 Maison Alcan
17 Musée des Beaux-Arts (Museum of Fine Arts)
18 Rue Crescent
19 Sir Winston Churchill Pub

9 Cathédrale Christ Church

Built from 1856 to 1859, this neo-Gothic building stands in glorious contrast to the city's downtown skyscrapers and is the seat of the Anglican bishop of Montréal. The church garden is modeled on a medieval European cloister. It offers a Sunday 10am Sung Eucharist and 4pm Choral Evensong, and weekday services at 8:15am, 12:15, and 5:15pm. **www.montrealcathedral.ca**.

Walk east on rue Ste-Catherine to avenue Union, where the La Baie department store is. Turn left on av. Union and go north 3 blocks, to rue Sherbrooke. As you cross boulevard de Maisonneuve, note the prominent bike lanes the city has installed, part of its massive biking network. At rue Sherbrooke, you'll be in front of McGill University's Schulich School of Music.

10 Java U

This casual eatery offers fresh and healthy options: sandwiches, quiche, fresh fruit, ice cream, and pastries. The atmosphere is collegiate and slightly upscale (p. 59).

Head left (west) on rue Sherbrooke. This is the city's grand boulevard, and the rest of the tour will take you past the former mansions, ritzy hotels, high-end boutiques, and special museums that give it its personality today. One block down on the left is:

11 Musée McCord

This museum of Canadian history opened in 1921 and was substantially renovated in 1992. Named for its founder, David Ross McCord, the museum maintains an eclectic collection of photographs, paintings, and First Nations folk art. Its special exhibits make it especially worth a visit. Hours and other details are on p. 80.

Continue west. On your right is:

12 McGill University

The gate is usually open to Canada's most prestigious university. It was founded in 1821 after a bequest from a Scottish-born fur trader, James McGill. The central campus mixes modern concrete and glass structures alongside older stone buildings and is the focal point for the school's 38,000 students.

On campus is the:

13 Musée Redpath

This quirky natural history museum is housed in an 1882 building with a grandly proportioned and richly appointed interior. Its main draws—worth a half-hour visit—are the mummies and coffin that are part of Canada's second-largest collection of Egyptian antiquities, and skeletons of whales and prehistoric beasts. Admission is free. See p. 80.

Continue on rue Sherbrooke. About 9m (30 ft.) past McGill's front gate, note the large stone on the lawn. This marks the:

14 Site of the Amerindian Hochelaga Settlement

Near this spot was the village of Hochelaga, a community of Iroquois who lived and farmed here before the first Europeans arrived. When French explorer Jacques Cartier stepped from his ship onto the land and visited Hochelaga in 1535, he noted that the village had 50 large homes, each housing several families. When the French returned in 1603, the village was empty. Read more about this history on p. 19 in chapter 3.

15 Café Vasco da Gama

Downtown is full of restaurants both fancy and casual. Right in between is Café Vasco Da Gama, 1472 rue Peel (1 block south of rue Sherbrooke), a sleek, high-ceilinged eatery with a Portuguese feel—the owners also run the esteemed Ferreira Café (p. 55) on the same block. It features big breakfasts, pastries, sandwiches, and tapas.

Two blocks farther down on rue Sherbrooke, at no. 1188, just past rue Stanley, is:

16 Maison Alcan

Rue Sherbrooke is the heart of what's historically been known as the "Golden Square Mile." This is where the city's most luxurious residences of the 19th and early 20th centuries were, and where the vast majority of the country's wealthiest citizens lived. (For a period of time, 79 families who lived in this neighborhood controlled 80 percent of Canada's wealth.) Maison Alcan is an example of a modern office building that has nicely incorporated one of those 19th-century mansions into its late-20th-century facade. In 2013 longtime residents Rio Tinto Alcan announced they would be moving out of the building; plans for the building's future have not yet been announced. On the opposite side of the street are Maison Louis-Joseph Forget at no. 1195 and Maison Reid Wilson at no 1201, both designated historic monuments.

Continue on rue Sherbrooke, passing on your left the newly renovated Ritz Carlton and the high-end Holt Renfrew department store. At the corner of rue Crescent is:

17 Musée des Beaux-Arts (Museum of Fine Arts)

This is Canada's oldest museum and Montréal's most prominent. Enter through the modern annex on the left side of rue Sherbrooke, which was added in 1991. It is connected to the original stately Beaux Arts building (1912) on the right side by an underground tunnel that doubles as a gallery. The adjacent church, which has Tiffany windows, was converted in 2011 into an addition to the museum, although it can only be visited on guided tours or when attending a classical concert there. See p. 79 for details.

There are several options at this point. If you have time to explore the museum, take the opportunity—a visit to the Musée des Beaux-Arts should be part of any trip to Montréal. For high-end boutique shopping, continue on rue Sherbrooke. For drinking or eating, turn left onto:

18 Rue Crescent

Welcome to party central. Rue Crescent and nearby streets are the focal point of the downtown social and dining district. The area is largely yuppie-Anglo in character, if not necessarily in strict demographics. Crescent's first block has small boutiques and jewelers, but the next 2 blocks are a gumbo of terraced bars and dance clubs, inexpensive pizza joints, and upscale restaurants, all drawing enthusiastic consumers looking to party the afternoon and evening away. It's hard to imagine that this was once a run-down slum slated for demolition. Luckily, buyers saw potential in these late-19th-century row houses and brought them back to life.

19 Sir Winston Churchill

Lively spots for food and drink are abundant along rue Crescent. Sir Winston Churchill Pub (no. 1459) is one. If you can, find a seat on the balcony.

WALKING TOUR 3: PARC DU MONT-ROYAL

START: **At the corner of rue Peel and avenue des Pins**

FINISH: **At the cross on top of the mountain (la Croix du Mont-Royal)**

TIME: **1 hour to ascend to the Chalet du Mont-Royal and its lookout over the city and come back down by the fastest route; 3 hours to take the more leisurely chemin Olmsted route and see all the sites listed below. It's easy to leave out some sites to truncate the walk. There's a city bus (no. 11) that travels along chemin de la Remembrance (Remembrance Rd.) at the top of the mountain.**

BEST TIMES: **Spring, summer, and autumn mornings**

WORST TIMES: **During the high heat of midday in summer, or on winter days when there is more ice than snow on the ground**

Join the locals: With a reasonable measure of physical fitness, the best way to explore the jewel that is Parc du Mont-Royal is simply to walk up it from downtown. It's called a mountain, but it is a very small one. A broad pedestrian-only road and smaller footpaths form a web of options for strollers, joggers, cyclists, and in-line skaters of all ages. Anyone in search of a little greenery and space heads here in warm weather, while in winter, cross-country skiers follow miles of paths and snowshoers tramp along trails laid out especially for them.

The 200-hectare (494-acre) urban park was created in 1876 by American landscape architect Frederick Law Olmsted, who also designed Central Park in New York City and parks in Philadelphia, Boston, and Chicago (although in the end, relatively little of Olmsted's full design for Mont Royal actually came into being). If you're carrying a smartphone, you can pull up a terrific interactive map at **www.lemontroyal.qc.ca/carte/en/index.sn**. You can also download podcasts for guided audio-video walks at the same website.

Start at the corner of rue Peel and av. des Pins, at the:

1 Downtown Park Entrance

After years of construction, this entrance is finally a thing of beauty, with broad steps and beautiful plantings. From here, it's possible to reach the top of this small mountain by a variety of routes. Hearty souls can choose the quickest and most strenuous approach—taking the steepest sets of stairs at every opportunity, which go directly to the Chalet du Mont-Royal and its lookout at the top (see no. 9). Those who prefer to take their time and gain altitude slowly can use the switchback bridle path. Or mix and match the options as you go along. Don't be too worried about getting lost; the park is small enough that it's easy enough to regain your sense of direction no matter which way you head.

Head up the footpath at this entrance. You'll soon reach the broad bridle path:

2 Serpentin & Chemin Olmsted (Olmsted Rd.)

The road zigzags here, giving this short stretch the name "Serpentin." It passes some beautiful stone houses to the left. If you want to bypass some of the switchbacks, use any of a number of paths for a shortcut—but stay only on established trails to prevent erosion. After about the fourth switchback, you'll reach an intersection with the option to go left or right. Turn left. This is chemin Olmsted (Olmsted Rd.), designed by Frederick Law Olmsted. It was built at a gradual

Walking Tour 3: Parc du Mont-Royal

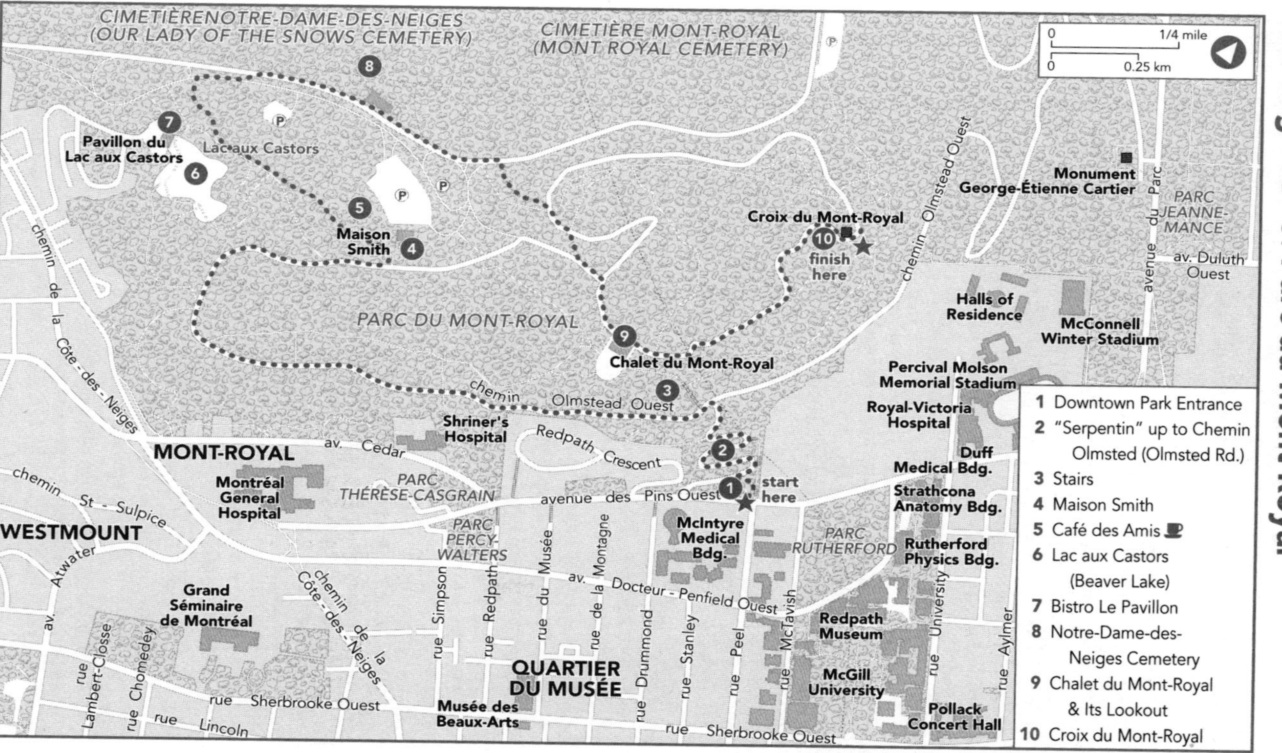

grade for horse-drawn carriages, so that horses could pull their loads up the hill at a steady pace and not be pushed from behind by the weight of the carriage on the way down. This road remains closed to automobiles even today. Following this shaded, pleasant road in the woods will get you to Maison Smith (see no. 4, below) in about 45 minutes.

Another option is to take the:

3 Stairs

There are numerous sets of stairs through the woods that let you bypass the Serpentin's broad switchbacks. These steps get walkers to the Chalet du Mont-Royal and its lookout (see no. 9) more quickly. ***Fair warning:*** The last 100 or so steps go almost straight up. On the plus side, you'll get to share sympathetic smiles with strangers you pass. Taking the steps bypasses sites no. 4, 5, and 6.

If you're taking chemin Olmsted, you eventually arrive at:

4 Maison Smith

Built in 1858, this structure has been used as a park rangers' station and park police headquarters. Today, it's a year-round information center (✆ **514/843-8240**) with a small exhibit about the park, a cafe (May–Oct), and a gift shop.

5 Café des Amis

From May through October, Café des Amis (✆ 514/843-8240), inside Maison Smith, offers sandwiches, sweets, and beverages including beer, wine, and hot chocolate.

From Maison Smith, walk through the field of sculptures, away from the radio tower, until you reach:

6 Lac des Castors (Beaver Lake)

This lake's name refers to the once-profitable fur industry, not to the actual presence of the long-gone animals. In summer, the lake is surrounded by sunbathers and picnickers, and you can rent a paddleboat. In the winter, it becomes an ice skater's paradise and, after the snow, a cross-country ski retreat and tobogganing wonder.

7 Bistro Le Pavillon

This 140-seat French restaurant that looks out on Beaver Lake and features seafood and steak. It's open throughout the year although sometimes just for lunch and sometimes just for dinner; call or check the website for the current schedule (www.pavillonmontroyal.com; ✆ 514/849-2002). Bus no. 11 stops at the restaurant if you're ready to head back into the city from here.

Walk across the road behind the pavilion, called chemin de la Remembrance (Remembrance Rd.), to enter:

8 Notre-Dame-des-Neiges Cemetery

This is the city's predominantly Catholic cemetery, and from here, you can visit the adjacent Protestant Mount Royal graveyard. Behind it (to the north), if you're up for a longer walk, is the small adjoining Jewish and Spanish-Portuguese cemetery. Notre-Dame-des-Neiges Cemetery reveals much about Montréal's ethnic mix: Headstones, some with likenesses in photos or tiles, are engraved with surnames as diverse as Zagorska, Skwyrska, De Ciccio, Sen, Lavoie, O'Neill, Hammerschmid, Fernandez, Müller, Haddad, and Boudreault.

This is another spot where you have the option of picking up the no. 11 bus on chemin de la Remembrance to head east toward the Guy Métro station. To continue the tour, head back toward Maison Smith and follow the signs on the main path for:

9 Chalet du Mont-Royal & Its Lookout

The front terrace here offers the most popular panoramic view of the city and the river. The chalet itself was constructed from 1931 to 1932 and has been used over the years for receptions, concerts, and various other events. Inside the chalet, take a look at the 17 paintings hanging just below the ceiling. They relate the region's history and the story of the French explorations of North America.

Facing the chalet from the terrace, locate the path running off to the right, marked by a sign that says CROIX, which means "cross." Follow it for about 10 minutes to the giant:

10 Croix du Mont-Royal

Legend has it that Paul de Chomedey, Sieur de Maisonneuve, erected a wooden cross here in 1643 after the young colony survived a flood threat. The present incarnation, installed in 1924, is made of steel and is 31.4 m (103 ft) tall. It is lit at night and visible from all over the city. Its lights were converted to LEDs in 2009. Beside the cross is a plaque marking where a time capsule was interred in August 1992, during Montréal's 350th-birthday celebration. Some 12,000 children ages 6 to 12 filled the capsule with messages and drawings depicting their visions for the city in the year 2142, when Montréal will be 500 years old and the capsule will be opened.

To return to downtown Montréal, you can go back along the path to the chalet terrace. On the left, just before the terrace, is another path. It leads to the staircase described in no. 3 and descends to where the tour began. The walk down by this route takes about 15 minutes. The no. 11 bus runs from the summit to the Mont Royal Métro. There are bus stops at Beaver Lake and along chemin de la Remembrance.

DAY TRIPS FROM MONTRÉAL

10

You don't have to travel far from Montréal to reach mountains, bike trails, or vineyards. In fact, great touring regions are a mere 30-minute drive from the city. The **Laurentian Mountains** (to the north) and **Cantons-de-l'Est** (also known by its British name, the Eastern Townships, to the southeast) both are developed with year-round vacation retreats, with skiing in winter, biking and boating in summer, maple sugaring in spring, and vineyard touring and leaf peeping in fall.

The pearl of the Laurentians (also called les Laurentides) is **Mont-Tremblant,** eastern Canada's highest peak and a winter mecca for skiers and snowboarders from all over North America. The bucolic Cantons-de-l'Est were known as the Eastern Townships when they were a haven for English Loyalists and their descendants.

Because both regions rely heavily on tourism for their livelihoods, knowledge of at least rudimentary English is widespread, even outside hotels and restaurants. Still, having at least a few phrases of French at your disposal will help immensely as you tour these Francophone-centric regions.

SKIING AT MONT-TREMBLANT ★★★

145km (90 miles) N of Montréal

Don't expect spiked peaks or high, ragged ridges. The Laurentian Shield's rolling hills and rounded mountains average between 300m and 520m (984 ft.–1,706 ft.) in height, with the highest being Mont-Tremblant, at 875m (2,871 ft.). These are not the Alps or the Rockies, but they're welcoming and embracing to most levels of skier. There are 13 ski centers within a 64km (40-mile) radius, but Mont-Tremblant itself is the most popular, with a vibrant pedestrian village at its base that is a kind of Aspen-meets-Disneyland. Skiers can usually expect reliable snow from early December to late March. The busiest times are February and March.

Essentials

GETTING THERE

BY CAR The fast and scenic **Autoroute des Laurentides,** also known as **Autoroute 15,** goes straight from Montréal to the Laurentians. About 15km (9 miles) before Mont-Tremblant, 15 ends and merges with the older **Route 117,** which also runs parallel with Autoroute 15. (If you have the time to meander, you can exit 15 at St-Jérôme and pick up the smaller

Route 117, which passes through many appealing small towns.) Montréalers fill the highways when they "go up north" on weekends, particularly during the top skiing months, so try to avoid driving on Friday afternoons.

There are four exits to the Mont-Tremblant ski area from Route 117. The first is exit 113, which takes visitors through Centre-Ville Mont-Tremblant (formerly the village of St-Jovite), a pleasant small town with a main street, rue de St-Jovite, lined with cafes and shops. From the center of town, Route 327 heads to the mountain.

The fourth exit, exit 119, bypasses Centre-Ville and goes directly to the mountain. Watch for signs with the resort's logo, which turns the "A" in "Tremblant" into a graphic of a ski mountain.

BY BUS **Galland** buses (www.galland-bus.com; ✆ **514/333-9555**) depart from **Station Centrale D'autobus,** 505 bd. de Maisonneuve est, and stop in the larger Laurentian towns, including Mont-Tremblant. The ride to Mont-Tremblant takes just under 3 hours.

VISITOR INFORMATION

Tourist offices are plentiful throughout the Laurentians—just look for the blue "?" signs. A major information center is at exit 51 off Autoroute 15. It shares a building with a McDonald's. Called **Tourisme Laurentides** (www.laurentides.com; ✆ **800/561-6673** or 450/224-7007), it has racks of brochures and a helpful staff. It's open daily. Closer to the ski mountain, there's an office at 5080 Montée Ryan (✆ **877/425-2434** or 819/425-2434), open daily 9am to 5pm. You can also check **www.tourismemont tremblant.com**, an official tourism site, and **www.tremblant.ca**, the Mont-Tremblant ski resort's website.

GETTING AROUND

You can certainly settle in for a day of skiing, eating, and shopping at the Mont-Tremblant ski center and resort village and get around by foot. If you want to visit Scandinave Spa (below), you'll need a car.

If you drive through the area, keep this in mind: The abundant use of the name "Tremblant" can be very confusing. There is Mont-Tremblant, the mountain. There's the resort village that is sometimes called the pedestrian village, sometimes called Tremblant, and sometimes called Mont-Tremblant Station. There's the old village of Mont-Tremblant about 5km (3 miles) northwest of the resort, which long ago was the region's center. There's Centre-Ville Mont-Tremblant, the cute commercial district about 12km (7½ miles) south of the mountain that used to be known as St-Jovite. Feeding the confusion is the fact that, in 2005, the villages of St-Jovite and Mont-Tremblant and the pedestrian village combined to become a single entity named Ville de Mont-Tremblant—but many maps and residents still refer to the areas by their old names. You'll also see signs for a lake, Lac Tremblant, next to the pedestrian village, and the large national park, Parc National du Mont-Tremblant. Clear as mud, right?

PARKING

There are parking lots right at the pedestrian village, and, if those are full, you'll find others close by (and well marked) that are served by shuttles to the village.

Hitting the Slopes (& the Spa)

The **Mont-Tremblant ski resort** (www.tremblant.ca) draws the biggest downhill crowds in the Laurentians and for 15 years running has been ranked as the top ski resort in eastern North America by "Ski Magazine." Founded in 1939, it's one of the oldest in North America. It pioneered creating trails on both sides of a mountain and was the second mountain in the world to install a chairlift. The vertical drop is 645m (2,116 ft.). When the snow is deep, skiers here like to follow the sun around the mountain, making the run down slopes with an eastern exposure in the morning and down the western-facing ones in the afternoon. There are higher mountains with longer runs and steeper pitches, but something about Mont-Tremblant compels people to return time and again. The resort has snowmaking capability to cover almost three-quarters of its skiable terrain (265 hectares/654 acres). Of its 95 downhill runs and trails, half are expert terrain, about a third are intermediate, and the rest beginner. The longest trail, Nansen, is 6km (3¾ miles).

For after-skiing (or instead of skiing), there's an appealing European-style Nordic spa nearby, built adjacent to a river and featuring both outdoor and indoor spaces. You can easily spend at least 3 hours at **Scandinave Spa,** 4280 Montée Ryan, Mont-Tremblant (www.scandinave.com; ✆ **888/537-2263**), open year-round. It's a rustic-chic complex of small buildings among evergreen trees on the Diable River shore. Few activities are more magical than being in a warm outdoor pool as snow falls, the sun sets, and the temperature plummets. For C$48, visitors (18 and older only) have run of the facility. Options include outdoor hot tubs designed to look like natural pools (one is set under a man-made waterfall); an indoor Norwegian steam bath thick with eucalyptus; indoor relaxation areas with supercomfortable, low-slung chairs; and the river itself, which the heartiest of folk dip into even on frigid days. (A heat lamp keeps a small square of river open, even through the iciest part of winter.) The idea is to move from hot to cold to hot, which supposedly purges toxins and invigorates your skin. Bathing suits are required, and men and women share all spaces except the changing rooms. Massages are available for extra fees.

If you visit in warm weather, a downhill dry-land alpine **Skiline luge run** is set up right on the ski mountain at the pedestrian village. The engineless sleds are gravity-propelled, reaching speeds of up to 48kmph (30mph), if you so choose (it's easy to go down as a slowpoke, too). Rides are priced by number of descents, starting at C$12 for one ride (C$3 for kids 6 and under). The village has other games and attractions, such as bungee trampoline, outdoor climbing walls, and forest ziplines. Find a listing at www.tremblant.ca/activities-and-events/summer-activities/index.aspx.

Where to Eat & Shop

The pedestrian-only resort village on Mont-Tremblant's slope (www.tremblant.ca/lodging-and-village/village/index.aspx) is the social hub of the region. The village has the prefabricated look of a theme park, but at least planners used the Québécois architectural style of pitched or mansard roofs in bright colors, not ersatz Tyrolean or Bavarian Alpine flourishes. For a sweeping view of the entire complex, take the **free gondola** from the bottom of the village to the top; it zips over the walkways, candy-colored hotels, and outdoor swimming pools.

Otherwise, you can stroll the village easily. Small lanes lead up past 32 clothing shops and 42 restaurants and bars.

Crêperie Catherine, at 113 chemin Kandahar (www.creperiecatherine.ca; ✆ **819/681-4888**) has both savory and sweet *crêpes* and something many of the restaurants in the village can lack—cozy ambience. If you go with a sweet *crêpe,* don't hesitate to smother it with the house specialty, *sucre a la crème* (a concoction of brown sugar and butter). You can order from any part of the menu any time of day. **Bistro Au Grain de Café** (www.augraindecafe.com; ✆ **819/681-4567**), tucked into a corner of the upper village just off the main plaza called Place St-Bernard, is another favorite for coffee and sandwiches (open daily 7:30am–11pm during ski season).

Like most ski mountains, beer, steak, and roast chicken are abundant. Slope-side drink palaces **Le Shack** (www.leshack.com; ✆ **819/681-4700**) and **La Forge** (www.laforgetremblant.com; ✆ **819/681-4900**) are full of TVs and music and feature perfectly agreeable family-friendly cuisine. The smaller microbrewery **Microbrasserie La Diable** (www.microladiable.com; ✆ **819/681-4546**), housed in a free-standing chalet at 117 chemin Kandahar, is more laid back and offers seven home brews and a menu that includes veggie and salmon burgers along with the expected burgers, salads, chili, and good homemade sausage. Be warned that it's a bit of a walk down chemin Kandahar from the base of the ski mountain, especially in those clunky boots, but the location makes it easier to get a table.

BIKING THE ROUTE VERTE (GREEN ROUTE) ★

Start at Val-David, 80km (50 miles) N of Montréal

Québec is bike crazy, and it's got the goods to justify it. In 2007, the province inaugurated the Route Verte (Green Route), a now-5,000km (3,107-mile) bike network that stretches from one end of the province to the other, linking all regions and cities. It's modeled on the Rails-to-Trails program in the U.S. and cycling routes in Denmark, Great Britain, and along the Danube and Rhine rivers, and was initiated by the non-profit biking organization Vélo Québec with support from the Québec Ministry of Transportation. Route Verte won the prestigious Prix Ulysse, one of the grand prizes given annually by the Québec tourist office, right out of the gate. The National Geographic Society went on to declare it one of the 10 best bicycle routes in the world.

Route Verte has a lot of sections, including paths all through the city of Montréal. But if you want to enjoy some countryside, head north out of the city to bike the popular **P'tit Train du Nord bike trail.** It goes through the Laurentians to Mont-Tremblant and beyond. It's built on a former railway track and passes through the scenic villages of Ste-Adèle, Val-David, and Ste-Agathe-des-Monts. Cyclists can easily hop on and off for a day trip. Food and bike repairs are offered at renovated railway stations along the path.

This day trip is based out of Val-David, one of the prettiest villages in the region. The town conjures up images of cabin hideaways set among hills rearing above ponds and lakes, and of creeks tumbling through fragrant forests. There is a prominent entrance to the bike path here.

Essentials

GETTING THERE

BY CAR Follow the directions above for "Mont-Tremblant for Skiing." At exit 76 of Autoroute 15 (and also along Rte. 117) is the village of Val-David (pop. 4,387), the region's faintly bohemian enclave.

VISITOR INFORMATION

The **Route Verte website** (www.routeverte.com) provides maps of all the paths by region (look for the "Laurentides" map). Advance planners might want to get the English-language guidebook "Cycling in Québec: Official Guide to Bicycling on Québec's Route Verte," which is published by Route Verte and can be ordered from the site.

Details specifically about the P'tit Train du Nord trail are at the **Tourisme Laurentides** website, at www.laurentides.com/en/linear-park-le-ptit-train-du-nord-230-km. The tourism office also publishes a **P'tit Train du Nord trail guide.** You can find it online at www.

myvirtualpaper.com/doc/tourisme-laurentides/official-guide-linear-park-2013-2014/2013070901/#0.

Val-David's **tourist office** is on the main street in the Petite Gare, or old train station, at 2525 rue de l'Église (www.valdavid.com; ✆ **888/322-7030,** ext. 4235, or 819/324-5678, ext. 4235). The building is adjacent to the bike path. It's open daily from 9am to 5pm from mid-May to mid-October and then again from mid-December to mid-March, with variable opening hours the rest of the year (call first).

PARKING

There is a parking lot next to the tourist office on rue de l'Église, adjacent to the bike path. There is a second parking lot on the opposite side of the bike path.

Hopping onto the Bike Path

First, some additional details about the P'tit Train du Nord bike trail: It is 232km (145 miles) long and passes through forests and some lovely villages (Val-David among them), and offers breathtaking mountain vistas. Since it was built on a former railway line, it is relatively flat. Former train stations have been repurposed into cafes, bistros, and covered refuges. Most have people who can help with bike repairs. Since the trail is shared by walkers and skaters, bikers are limited to a speed of 22 km/h (14m/h)—fast for casual bikers, medium speed for road warriors. The trail is free to ride on.

So, which direction to head? You can't go wrong either way. Again, take a look through Tourisme Laurentides' 32-page guidebook specifically about the trail, online (see Visitor Information, above). You'll see that Val-David is at km 42. Ste-Adèle (pop. 11,912), which has a popular lake, Lac Rond, is just 9km (5.6 miles) south. (In Ste-Adèle, the main drag, rue Valiquette, is lined with cafes, galleries, and bakeries.) Heading the other direction on the trail, Mont-Tremblant's splashy pedestrian village (see Day Trip 1) is at km 91, 49km (30 miles) north. The guidebook lists services along each km of the trail, from bars to bike repairs to banks to supermarkets. The folks at the tourist office in Val-David and at the region's central tourist office at exit 51 off Autoroute 15 can offer suggested itineraries depending on whether you want a leisurely or more challenging ride and on how much time you have.

If you didn't bring your own bike, **bike rentals** are available in Val-David at the tourist office and at **Roc & Ride Sports de Montagne** (2444 rue de l'Église; www.rocnride.com; ✆ **819/322-7978**).

Where to Eat & Shop

For a relaxing picnic, get fixings in Val-David at the **Metro Supermarket** across from the tourist office on the main street or around the corner at **Boulangerie La Vagabonde,** 1262 chemin de la Rivière (www.boulangerielavagabonde.com; ✆ **819/322-3953**), a bakery and tea room offering soups, salads, sandwiches, and pastries. If you're in town on a Saturday morning from late June to late September, look for the organic **farmer's market** on rue de l'Académie (opposite the church).

There's a lovely picnic spot right in the village: From the tourist office, turn left onto the bike path and walk 5 minutes to the North River and the teeny **Parc des Amoureux.** Look for the sign that says SITE PITTORESQUE.

For a more substantial meal, **Au Petit Poucet,** on Route 117 just south of Val-David (1030 Rte. 117; ✆ **888/334-2246** or 819/322-2246), evokes a Québec of hunting cabins and hearty sugar-shack cuisine. A floor-to-ceiling fireplace anchors the interior, and the menu features tourtière (meat pie), pea soup, baked beans, and sugar pie. There's a shop here for food to go.

Val-David is small, but it has many artist studios. You're in luck if you're visiting in mid-summer: the village hosts a huge **ceramic art festival** (www.1001pots.com; ✆ **819/322-6868**) daily from mid-July to mid-August (July 11–Aug 10 in 2014). Sculptors and ceramicists, along with painters, jewelers, and pewter smiths display their work, and there are concerts and art demonstrations.

TOURING VINEYARDS IN CANTONS-DE-L'EST ★

Start at Dunham, 95km (59 miles) SE of Montréal, toward Sherbrooke

The rolling countryside of Cantons-de-l'Est to the southeast of Montréal has long served as the province's breadbasket, and that includes grape and apple orchards (for wine and cider, natch). Still referred to by many English-speakers as the **Eastern Townships,** the region is largely pastoral, marked by billowing hills and small villages. Except for a few disheartening signs for fast-food stops, the region is largely advertisement-free.

Canada is known more for its beers and ales than its wines, but that hasn't stopped agriculturists from planting vines and transforming fruit into drinkable clarets, chardonnays, and Sauternes. The most successful efforts have blossomed along southern Ontario's Niagara Frontier and in British Columbia's relatively warmer precincts, but in the Cantons-de-l'Est, which enjoys the mildest microclimates in the province, apples grow, as do grapes. Most vintners and fruit growers are concentrated around Dunham, about 103km (64 miles) southeast of Montréal, with several vineyards along Route 202. The region also produces a special variety of wine known as ice cider *(cidre de glace).* It's an aperitif made from apples that have frosted over and is produced by vineyards such as Domaine Pinnacle, which is included on this tour.

Autumn presents particular attractions. In addition to the glorious fall foliage (usually best from early Sept to early Oct), the orchards around here sag under the weight of apples of every variety, and cider mills hum day and night. Visitors are invited to help with the harvest and can pay a low price to pick their own baskets of fruit. Cider mills open their doors for tours and tastings.

Essentials

GETTING THERE

BY CAR Leave Montréal by Pont Champlain, the bridge which funnels into arrow-straight Autoroute 10. Go east toward Sherbrooke. Within 20 minutes, you'll be passing fields, clusters of cows, and in summer, meadows strewn with wildflowers. The exit numbers represent the distance in kilometers that the exit is from Montréal. To get to Dunham, take exit 48 and pick up QC-233 south. Take that 9.5km (6 miles) to Rte. 104 E. Take that 25km (15.5 miles) to Rte. 202 West and signs for Dunham.

VISITOR INFORMATION

Tourisme Cantons-de-l'Est (www.easterntownships.org; ✆ **800/355-5755**) provides a slew of information. Driving from Montréal, the first regional **tourist information office** (www.granby-bromont.com; ✆ **866/472-6292** or 450/375-8774) is at exit 68 off Autoroute 10. It's open daily.

MAPLE heaven IN CABANES À SUCRE

For a purely Québec experience that shouldn't be missed, reserve a spot for a meal at a sugar shack. Called *cabanes à sucre* or *érablières* in French, they were once places that merely processed sap from maple trees. When producers realized that they were drawing large audiences, some began offering wider experiences to keep the customers reaching for their wallets, putting in bars and dining rooms where bountiful spreads of simple country food are served at long communal tables. Some even put in dance floors and booked live entertainment. Originally open only during sugaring-off season (roughly Feb–Apr), a few now stay open much longer, even all year. There are hundreds across the province, with small directional signs often positioned at roadsides or on highways. Total cost rarely exceeds C$30 per person, though seats can be hard to come by, so make reservations well in advance. At most shacks, you can see the rendering room, where sap gathered from maple-tree taps is boiled in a trough called an evaporator and then cooked further on a stove. Some sites have interpretative trails that wind through maple groves.

An in-season visit to **Cabane du Pic-Bois,** 1468 Gaspé Rd., off Route 241 south of Bromont (www.cabanedupicbois.com; ✆ **450/263-6060**), which offers "typical sugar-party meals" on spring weekends, exceeded every expectation. Locals packed long rows of tables in an adorable split-wood cabin under maple trees up a muddy road. There isn't a menu—you just sit down, and food starts arriving. In our case, thick pea soup and warm bread arrived, and then we helped ourselves to a buffet of ham, maple-tinged sausages, sweetly spiced baked beans, home fries, and mixed green salad and coleslaw lightly dressed with maple vinegar. Jugs of maple syrup stood at the ready for an extra dousing. Dessert of *grand-père* dumplings baked in maple syrup, thinly rolled pancakes, and maple taffy lollipops—made by wiggling a line of syrup onto a narrow tray of snow and rolling the taffy onto a popsicle stick—finished off the memorable meal. Signature products are often sold in a variety of sizes and forms, from syrup to maple candies to spreadable maple butter. Some folks, like PicBois's André Pollender, a fourth-generation maple producer, consider the lighter Grade A, from the first run of sap, the best syrup. Others prefer the darker, denser Grade B from later in the season. There's only one way to decide, of course: Taste and see for yourself!

Touring the Vineyards

A drive through this area and a stop for one vineyard tour makes for a pleasant afternoon, but if you're really gung-ho, you can follow the established **Route des Vins,** which passes 20 vintners. A map and travel information is at **www.laroutedesvins.ca**.

You can start anywhere, but a popular option is **Vignoble de l'Orpailleur,** at 1086 Rte. 202 in Dunham (www.orpailleur.ca; ✆ **450/295-2763**). It has guided tours every day from June through October for C$7. Its white wines, such as the straw-colored L'Orpailleur, are regulars on Montréal restaurant menus.

Ice cider and ice wine are two regional products that may be new to visitors: They're made from apples and grapes, respectively, left on the trees and vines past the first frost, and served ice-cold with cheese or dessert. One top producer is **Domaine Pinnacle,** at 150 Richford Rd. in Frelighsburg (www.icecider.com; ✆ **450/298-1226**), about 13km (8 miles) south of Dunham. Its *cidre de glace* is a regular gold medalist in international competitions (it avoids the risk of being cloyingly sweet, which is hard to do for ice cider). The farm's tasting room and boutique are open daily May through December and Thurs-Sun January through April.

Where to Eat & Shop

Many of the vineyards, including the two listed above, have either restaurants or gourmet food boutiques on site. For a wider variety of food and shopping, we like the village of **Knowlton.** It's at the southern tip of Lac Brome, on Rte 104 East (about 40km, or 25 miles, from Frelighsburg, above). At no. 39 on historic Victoria Street, **Barne's General Store** (© **450/243-6840**), has been in business since 1890 and is a spot for organic food, tube socks, colored poster board, penny candy, and a spicy red dip made with pomegranate and walnuts called *muhammara.* Mmm! Also here is the **Boutique Gourmet de Canards du Lac Brome,** producer of Lac Brome's famous (in this area, anyway) Peking duck meat. Though no live ducks are in view, there are more duck products here than the average non-Québécois can fathom. Located at 40 chemin du Centre (www.canardsdulacbrome.com; © **450/242-3825**), the store is open daily.

If you're touring in the spring, you'll be in the region at the time when every sugar-maple tree is being tapped and "sugared off." The result? **Maple festivals** and farms hosting sugaring parties, with guests wolfing down prodigious country repasts capped by traditional maple-syrup desserts. Montréal newspapers and the regional tourist offices keep up-to-date lists of what's happening and where during the sugaring; many of the festivals and "sugar shacks" are right in this area.

11 SETTLING INTO QUÉBEC CITY

Québec City seduces from first view. Situated along the majestic Fleuve Saint-Laurent (St-Lawrence River), much of the oldest part of the city—Vieux-Québec (Old Québec)—sits atop a rock bluff that once provided military defense. Fortress walls still encase the upper city, and the soaring Château Frontenac, a hotel with castlelike turrets, dominates the landscape. Hauntingly evocative of a coastal town in the motherland of France, the tableau is as romantic as any in Europe.

This was Canada's first European settlement, christened La Nouvelle France in the 16th century. Today, the Québec City clings to its French-speaking heritage and Gallic traditions: as it becomes more chic and current, it keeps one foot rooted proudly in the past. It also keeps one foot tapping year round: No matter the season, it seems there is always a party or festival going on somewhere. From the outdoor-activity-filled Winter Carnaval to the rich calendar of music and theater offerings in summer, the city's *joie de vivre* is ever in the air. While most theater is in French, even non-Francophones can enjoy the artistry of Québécois productions.

ESSENTIALS

Arriving

Served by highways, transcontinental trains and buses, and several airports, Québec City is easily accessible from within Canada, the U.S., or overseas.

BY PLANE

In Québec City, the teeny **Jean Lesage International Airport** (airport code YQB; www.aeroportdequebec.com; ✆ **877/769-2700**) is served by a number of major airlines. Most air traffic comes by way of Montréal, although there are some direct flights from Canadian and U.S. cities, including Toronto, Ottawa, Chicago, New York (Newark and JFK airports), and Philadelphia. Some direct flights are seasonal only.

From the airport, a taxi to downtown is a fixed-rate C$34. (Likewise, a taxi from downtown to the airport is also C$34.) There is a public bus, no. 78, but it runs only to the Les Saules bus terminal, at the corner of boulevard Massona and rue Michelet, which is well outside the tourist area. You'll need to transfer from there. The bus runs Monday through Friday, though typically adds weekends during the summer, and costs C$3, exact change only. Ask at the airport for the best route; you can also visit www.rtcquebec.ca or call ✆ **418/627-2511.**

BY BUS

Québec City's bus terminal, at 320 rue Abraham-Martin (© **418/525-3000**), is just beside the Gare du Palais train station. As from the train station, it's an uphill climb or short cab ride to Upper Town or other parts of Lower Town.

BY CAR

See p. 141 for general driving information and general directions into the province.

When driving between Montréal and Québec City, there are two options: Autoroute 40, which runs along the St. Lawrence's north shore, and Autoroute 20, on the south side (although not hugging the water at all). The trip takes about 3 hours.

Québec City is 867km (539 miles) from New York City and 644km (400 miles) from Boston. From New York, follow the directions to Montréal, and then pick up Autoroute 20 to Québec City. From Boston, follow the directions to Montréal, but at Autoroute 10, go east instead of west to stay on Autoroute 55. Get on Autoroute 20 to Québec City and follow signs for the Pont Pierre-Laporte, the major bridge into the city. Turn right onto Boulevard Wilfrid-Laurier (Rte. 175) shortly after crossing the bridge. It changes names first to Boulevard Laurier and then to Grande-Allée, a main boulevard that leads directly into the central Parliament Hill area and the Old City. Once the street passes through the ancient walls that ring the Old City, it becomes rue St-Louis, which leads straight to the famed Château Frontenac on the cliff above the St. Lawrence River.

Another appealing option when you're approaching Québec City from the south is to follow Route 132 along the river's southern side to the town of Lévis. A car ferry there, **Traverse Québec-Lévis** (www.traversiers.gouv.qc.ca; © **877/787-7483**), provides a 10-minute ride across the river and a dramatic way to see the city, especially for the first time. The schedule varies substantially through the year, but the ferry leaves at least every hour from 6am to 2am. One-way costs C$7.75 for a car and driver, C$3.25 for each additional adult, and C$15 for a car with up to six passengers.

BY TRAIN

Québec City's train station, Gare du Palais, is in Lower Town at 450 rue de la Gare-du-Palais. Many of the hotels listed in this book are up an incline from the station, so a short cab ride might be necessary.

The train ride between Montréal and Québec City takes about 3 hours.

BY BOAT

Québec City is a stop for cruise ships that travel along the St. Lawrence River. Ships dock in a neighborhood called Vieux-Port. As in Montréal, there is an abundance of restaurants and shops in walking distance.

Visitor Information

High season in Québec City is from June 24 (Jean-Baptiste Day, a provincial holiday) through Labour Day (the first Mon in Sept, as in the U.S., a national holiday). For those 11 weeks, the city is in highest gear. Tourist offices, museums, and restaurants all expand their operating hours, and hotels charge top dollar. This book notes the changes in hours and prices throughout the year for many venues, but it's best to call and confirm open hours before making a special trip to an attraction or restaurant outside of the high season.

The most central tourist information center is in Upper Town, across from the Château Frontenac and directly on Place d'Armes. **Centre Infotouriste de Québec,** 12 rue Ste-Anne (www.bonjourquebec.com; © **877/266-5687**), is run by the province of Québec's tourism department and is open from 8:30am to 7pm daily from late June

LONG MAY THEY WAVE: THE flags OF CANADA

With a relatively small population spread over a territory larger than the continental U.S., Canadians' loyalties have always tended to be directed to the cities and regions in which they live, rather than to the nation at large. Part of this comes from the semicolonial relationship the nation retained with England after the British North America Act made it self-governing in 1867 (Queen Elizabeth II is still on all the currency). Part comes from the fact that Canada has two official languages. Canadians didn't even have an official national anthem until "O Canada" was given the honor in 1980.

Local loyalties are reflected in the flags. Québécois began asserting themselves and declaring their regional pride after World War II and officially adopted their national flag, the Fleurdelisé, in 1950. It employs blue-and-white crossbars with four fleurs-de-lis (one in each resulting quadrant) and is flown prominently in Québec City.

In 1965, the red-and-white maple leaf version of the Canadian flag was introduced across all of Canada, replacing a previous ensign that featured a Union Jack in the upper-left corner.

In the face of decades of hurt and outright hostilities between French and English Canada, there must be occasional sighs of longing in some quarters for the diplomatic display of the flag of Montréal. Adopted way back in 1832, it has red crossbars on a white background. The resulting quadrants have depictions of a rose, a fleur-de-lis, a thistle, and a shamrock. They stand, respectively, for the founding groups of the new nation—the English, French, Scots, and Irish.

through to August and from 9am to 5pm daily the rest of the year. It has brochures, a lodging reservation service, a currency-exchange office, and information about tours by foot, bus, or boat. Also in front of the Château on Dufferin Terrace, is **Kiosk Frontenac**, operated by **Parks Canada** (www.pc.gc.ca; ✆ **888/773-8888** or 418/648-7016). Guided tours of the Fortifications of Québec start here. It's open late May to mid-October from 9:30am to 5:30pm.

From early June to early September, service agents for **Québec City Tourism** (www.quebecregion.com; ✆ **877/783-1608** or 418/641-6290) ride throughout the tourist district on motor scooters to answer any questions you have. In French, they're called the *service mobile,* and their blue mopeds bear flags with a large question mark. Just hail them as they approach—they're bilingual.

City Layout

BASIC LAYOUT Because of its beauty, history, and unique stature as a walled city, Québec City's historic district was named a UNESCO World Heritage Site in 1985. Almost all of a visit to Québec City can be spent on foot in the old Lower Town, which hugs the river below the bluff, and in the old Upper Town, atop Cap Diamant (Cape Diamond). Many accommodations, restaurants, and tourist-oriented services are based in these places.

The colonial city was first built right down by the St. Lawrence River. It was here that the earliest merchants, traders, and boatmen earned their livelihoods. Unfriendly fire from the British and Amerindians in the 1700s moved residents to safer houses atop the cliffs that form the rim of the Cap. The tone and atmosphere of the 17th and 18th centuries still suffuse these areas today.

Basse-Ville (Lower Town) became primarily a district of wharves and warehouses. That trend has been reversed, with small hotels and many attractive bistros and shops bringing life to the area. It maintains the architectural feel of its origins, however, reusing old buildings and maintaining the narrow cobbled streets.

Haute-Ville (Upper Town) turned out to not be immune to cannon fire, as the British General James Wolfe proved in 1759 when he took the city from the French. Nevertheless, the division into Upper and Lower towns persisted for obvious topographical reasons. Upper Town remains enclosed by fortification walls, with a cliff-side elevator (*funiculaire*) and several steep streets connecting it to Lower Town.

MAIN AVENUES & STREETS In Basse-Ville (Lower Town), major streets are **St-Pierre, Dalhousie, St-Paul,** and (parallel to St-Paul) **St-André.** Within the walls of Haute-Ville (Upper Town), the principal streets are **St-Louis** (which becomes **Grande-Allée** outside the city walls), **Ste-Anne,** and **St-Jean.** Detailed maps of Upper and Lower towns and the metropolitan area are available at the tourist offices.

FINDING AN ADDRESS If it were larger, the historic district's winding and plunging streets might be confusing to negotiate. However, the area is very compact. Most streets are only a few blocks long, making navigation and finding a specific address fairly easy.

Neighborhoods in Brief

HAUTE-VILLE

Old Québec's Upper Town, surrounded by thick ramparts, occupies the crest of Cap Diamant and overlooks the Fleuve St-Laurent (St. Lawrence River). It includes many of the sites for which the city is famous, among them the **Château Frontenac** and the **Basilique Cathédrale Notre-Dame.** At a still-higher elevation, to the south of the Château and along the river, is **La Citadelle,** a partially star-shaped fortress built by the French in the 18th century and augmented often by the English (after their 1759 capture of the city) well into the 19th century.

With most buildings at least 100 years old and made of granite in similar styles, Haute-Ville is visually harmonious, with few jarring modern intrusions. When they added a new wing to the Château Frontenac, for instance, they modeled it after the original—standing policy here.

Terrasse Dufferin is a pedestrian promenade atop the cliffs that attracts crowds in all seasons for its magnificent views of the river and its water traffic, which includes ferries gliding back and forth, cruise ships, and Great Lakes freighters putting in at the harbor below.

BASSE-VILLE & VIEUX-PORT

Old Québec's Lower Town encompasses **Vieux-Port,** the old port district; the impressive **Musée de la Civilisation,** a highlight of any visit; **Place-Royale,** perhaps the most attractive of the city's many small squares; and the pedestrian-only **rue du Petit-Champlain,** which is undeniably touristy, but not unpleasantly so, and has many agreeable cafes and shops. Visitors travel between Lower and Upper towns by the cliff-side elevator *(funiculaire)* at the north end of rue du Petit-Champlain, or by the adjacent stairway.

PARLIAMENT HILL, INCLUDING MONTCALM

Once you pass through the Upper Town walls at St-Louis Gate, you're still in Haute-Ville, but no longer in Vieux-Québec. Rue St-Louis becomes **Grande-Allée,** a wide boulevard that passes the stately Parliament building and runs parallel to the broad expanse of the Plains of Abraham, where one of the most important battles in the history of North America took place between the French and the British for control of the city. This is also where the lively Carnaval de Québec is held each winter. Two blocks after Parliament, Grande-Allée becomes lined on both sides with terraced restaurants and cafes. The city's large modern hotels are in this area, and the **Musée National des Beaux-Arts** is a pleasant 20-minute walk up the Allée from the Parliament. Here, the neighborhood becomes more residential and flows into the Montcalm district.

ST-ROCH

Northwest of Parliament Hill and enough of a distance from Vieux-Québec to warrant a cab ride, this newly revitalized neighborhood has some of the city's trendiest restaurants and bars. Along the main strolling street, **rue St-Joseph est,** sidewalks have been widened, new benches added, and artists hired to renovate the interiors and exteriors of industrial buildings. It has all brought a youthful pop and an influx of new technology and media companies to the neighborhood.

Much of St-Roch, including what's referred to as Québec's "downtown" shopping district, remains nondescript and a little grubby. But rue St-Joseph, radiating both directions from rue du Parvis (a nice little street for nightlife), is home to an ever-growing number of top-notch restaurants and cute boutiques. ***Note:*** On older maps, rue du Parvis was called rue de l'Église.

FAUBOURG ST-JEAN

This area is the continuation of Upper Town's rue St-Jean after you exit the walled city and go through the central square called Place d'Youville. It is definitely a route less travelled by tourists, but it is a vibrant area, packed with shops, bars, and restaurants where many locals work, live, and play.

GETTING AROUND

By Foot

Once you're within or near the walls of Québec City's Old Town, virtually no restaurant, hotel, or place of interest is beyond walking distance. In bad weather, when you're traversing between opposite ends of Lower and Upper towns, a taxi might be necessary. But, in general, walking is the best way to explore.

Travelers in wheelchairs or using strollers will find the city generally accommodating, although challenging in the winding, steep, and often cobblestoned Upper and Lower Towns. All streets have sidewalks, though, and there are curb cuts for easy passage onto the streets. See p. 213 in Chapter 18 for more information about navigating the city by wheelchair.

By Funiculaire

To get between Upper and Lower towns, you can take streets, staircases, or a cliff-side elevator known as the *funiculaire,* which has long operated along an inclined 64m (210-ft) track. The upper station is near the front of the city's visual center—Château Frontenac and Place d'Armes—while the lower station is at the northern end of the teeny rue du Petit-Champlain, a pedestrian-only shopping street. The elevator offers excellent aerial views of the historic Lower Town on the short trip and runs daily from 7:30am until 11pm all year and until midnight in high season. Wheelchairs and strollers are accommodated. The one-way fare is C$2.25. Read about its history at **www.funiculaire-quebec.com**.

By Taxi

Taxis are everywhere: cruising, parked in front of the big hotels, and in some of Upper Town's larger squares. In theory, they can be hailed, but they are best obtained by locating one of their stands, as in the Place d'Armes or in front of Hotel-de-Ville (City Hall). Restaurant managers and hotel bell captains will also summon them upon request. The starting rate is C$3.45, each kilometer costs C$1.70, and each minute of waiting adds up to C63¢. Tip 10 to 15 percent. Companies include **Taxi Coop** (**✆ 418/525-5191**) and **Taxi Québec** (**✆ 418/525-8123**).

By Bus

For travel within the most touristed areas, take the C$2 Ecolobus (www.rtcquebec.ca). It makes a loop through the city, including stops at Musée de la Civilisation in Lower Town and the Château Frontenac, Hotel-de-Ville (City Hall), Place D'Youville, and Centre des Congress in Upper Town. Get on and off at any stop. The buses run on electricity, so they're quiet and eco-friendly.

By Car

Québec City is compact, but driving can be tricky because there are so few roads between Upper and Lower Town and because many streets are one-way.

On-street parking is very difficult in Québec City's old, cramped quarters. When you find a rare space on the street, be sure to check the signs for hours when parking is permissible. Meters cost C50¢ per 15 minutes, and some meters accept payment for up to 5 hours. Meters are generally in effect Monday through Saturday from 9am to 9pm and Sunday 10am to 9pm. But double-check: Spots along Parc des Champs-des-Batailles (Battlefields Park) have to be paid for 24 hours a day. Disabled parking permit holders may park their vehicle in front of a parking meter free of charge as long as they do not exceed the maximum parking time permitted, usually 2, 5, or 10 hours. Handicapped permits from outside Canada are accepted.

Many of the smaller hotels and B&Bs that don't have their own parking lots maintain special arrangements with local garages, with discounts for guests of a few dollars off the usual C$16 or more per day. Check with your hotel.

If a particular hotel or *auberge* (French word for "inn") doesn't have access to a garage or lot, plenty of public ones are available and clearly marked on the foldout city map available at tourist offices and local businesses. Two common choices for visitors are, in Upper Town, the underground lot beneath Hotel-de-Ville (City Hall), with entrances on rue Ste-Anne and côte de la Fabrique; and, in Lower Town, the lot across the street from Musée de la Civilisation on rue Dalhousie. The tech-savvy can search for Québec City and download a parking app to GPS devices at www.vincipark.ca.

Prepare for snow to affect driving, and possibly parking conditions from November to April. Cars that impede snow removal can be fined and towed so underground parking is optimal. Provincial law requires snow tires for Québec plated vehicles between December 15 and March 15; vehicles plated from the U.S. or other provinces are exempt.

Names and contact information for **rental-car** agencies doing business in the province of Québec are listed on p. 213. In addition to renting cars at the Jean Lesage International Airport, Hertz has an office in Upper Town on Côte du Palais at rue St-Jean. Avis has a desk in the Hilton Quebec lobby, 1100 René-Lévesque est and Budget is in the same complex; and Enterprise has multiple locations, including 690 René-Lévesque est.

Unlike in Montréal, drivers in Québec City are permitted to turn right at red traffic lights after coming to a full stop and yielding to pedestrians in the crosswalk. Look out for the occasional sign at busy intersections prohibiting right turns on red. See p. 40 in chapter 4 for additional driving rules.

By Bike

Given Vieux-Québec's hilly topography and tight quarters, cycling isn't the most obvious choice to get from sight to sight either within the walls or in Lower Town. But beyond the walls, or bike touring for the fun of it, is another story. Québec has a great network of cycling paths—nearly 400km (249 miles) in the Greater Québec Area alone. Downloadable maps are available at www.quebecregion.com; search for "bike map." For longer treks, look into the province's **Route Verte** (Green Route)—see "Biking the Route Verte (Green Route)" on p. 131. Downloadable maps, trip calculators, suggested day trips and longer tours are available at www.routeverte.com.

Bicycle rentals are available in Lower Town, near the Gare du Palais train station, at **Cyclo Services** (289 rue St-Paul; www.cycloservices.net; ✆ **877/692-4050** or 418/692-4052), for C$25 for 4 hours, with daily and weekly rental also available. Choices include cruisers, road bikes, tandem, and kids' bikes. They also rent accessories and repair bikes. The shop is open daily from 8am to 8pm. **Vélo Passe-Sport Plein Air** (35 rue Dalhousie; http://velopasse-sport.com; ✆ **418/692-3643**) rents an assortment of bikes for periods of 2, 4, and 8 hours for C$20 to C$35 (no longer-term rentals). It is open daily in season (May–Oct) from 9am to 6pm. Both bike shops lead guided bike tours within Vieux-Québec or at locations outside the city, such as Île d'Orléans.

For a quick jaunt, especially along the non-hilly La promenade Samuel-De Champlain (see p. 180) west of the city along the St. Lawrence River, Québec City's only **BIXI** station is in the parking lot behind Hôtel Le Germain-Dominion on rue St-Paul in Lower Town. The hotel has contracted directly with Montréal's unique public bike-sharing system, which allows anyone to use a credit card to release a bike from the dock and pay only for the duration of the ride. (A one-time use costs C$3.50 for 61-90 minutes and adds C$7 for every half hour after that.) BIXI is designed for commuters and typically has dozens of stations throughout a dense urban area. In this case, there is only one station and you must return the bike to it in order to have your credit card deposit refunded. To learn more about BIXI, see p. 38.

The use of motorcycles is prohibited within the walls of Old Québec.

[FastFACTS] QUÉBEC CITY

Below are useful facts and phone numbers while you're traveling in the city. For more information about the province overall, see chapter 18.

ATMs/Banks Desjardins has a handy ATM near Hotel-de-Ville (City Hall) at 19 rue des Jardins (www.desjardins.com; ✆ **800/224-7737**) and RBC Royal Bank has a location at 700 Place D'Youville (www.rbc.com; ✆ **418/692-6800**). CIBC, TD Bank, and other Canadian banks also have ATMs in the greater area. In Canada, some debit cards require a four-digit pin and if your card has a longer one it can be declined. Calling your bank or credit card companies in advance of travel can prevent them from flagging your account. Also, as in other countries, it's common to be charged fees when withdrawing from ATMs.

Business Hours Most businesses are open Monday through Saturday from around 9 or 10am and close between 5 and 6pm; some stay open until 9pm on Thursday and Friday. On Sundays, businesses typically open between 10am and noon and close at 5pm. **Bank** hours in Québec City are Monday through Friday from 10am to 3pm; occasionally hours are extended on Thursday and Friday, and Saturday morning. Most **restaurants** serve until 9:30 or 10pm. **Bars** stay open until 3am with some "after hours" options. A list of holidays on which most businesses are closed can be found at www.quebecregion.com. In general, hours are longer in high season (May–Sept) and during Carnaval.

Dentists Tourisme Québec advises calling ✆ **418/666-4363** Monday through Friday or if an emergency on weekends.

Doctors & Hospitals In Québec City there's a five-hospital network called CHUQ which is affiliated with the University of Laval's medical school. The L'Hôtel-Dieu de Québec (www.chuq.qc.ca; ✆ **418/525-4444**) is in Upper Town at 11 côte du Palais. It's a teaching hospital (and a national historic site of Canada) and has an emergency room.

Embassies & Consulates See p. 214 in Chapter 18.

Emergencies Dial ✆ **911** for police, fire, or ambulance assistance.

Internet Access Many public spaces such as cafes have free Wi-Fi; hotel lobbies are often free Wi-Fi hotspots but many charge a daily access rate. **Zap Québec** tracks free Wi-Fi hotspots at www.zapquebec.org.

Mail & Postage Québec City's most centrally located postal station in the tourist area is at 5 rue du Fort, near Château Frontenac in Upper Town. See p. 216 in Chapter 18 for postage rates.

Newspapers & Magazines Québec's source for English-language news is the **Québec Chronicle-Telegraph**, published in print every Wednesday and online at www.qctonline.com. As the descendant of several newspapers published for more than 3 centuries, in June 2014 it will celebrate its 250th anniversary as North America's oldest newspaper.

Pets In public areas, owners must clean up after pets, and dogs must be on a leash no longer than 6 feet. In case of veterinary emergency, call ✆ **418/872-5355.** If traveling into Canada with a dog, be advised to have a rabies certificate on hand.

Pharmacies Brunet (110 rue St-Paul, Lower Town; www.brunet.ca; ✆ **418/694-1262**), Pharmaprix (698 rue St-Jean, Upper Town; www1.pharmaprix.ca; ✆ **418/529-2171**), and Uniprix (369 rue de la Couronne, St-Roch; www.uniprix.com; ✆ **418/529-2121**) are three chain pharmacies with multiple outlets in Québec City. Note that when searching for a location online, the pharmacy may be listed under the pharmacist's name, but is still a storefront.

Safety The tourist sections of Québec City are well-lit and pedestrian friendly. Generally, it's safe to walk after dark, particularly during one of the city's many festivals when people are out and about. However, always take the usual precautions. In a 2012 Canadian Centre for Justice Statistics study on police-reported crime, Canada's crime rate had dipped to its lowest level in 40 years with Québec City reporting the second lowest crime rate of the major cities.

Tipping Tipping practices in the province are similar to those in large Western cities. See p. 220 in Chapter 18 for more. Québecers are known to add up GST and QST taxes on their restaurant bills to get a quick tip amount of approximately 15 percent.

WHERE TO STAY IN QUÉBEC CITY

12

Staying in one of the small luxurious boutique properties within or below the walls of Vieux-Québec (or at the iconic Château Frontenac) can be one of your trip's most memorable experiences. On the other end of the size spectrum, the string of skyscrapers just outside Upper Town lack some of the city's historical charm, but offer high-end facilities and some of the best views of the city.

In addition to the descriptions that follow, "The Official Accommodation Guide" published by Québec City Tourism is a useful resource for planning your stay, as is its accompanying website at www.quebecregion.com. Both list every member of the Greater Québec Area Tourism and Convention Bureau, from campgrounds to homes for rent as well as B&Bs and the city's most upscale hotels. Free copies of the print guide are available at tourist offices (see p. 220). When choosing your destination, keep in mind that standards of amenities fluctuate wildly from one hotel to another, even from room to room within a single establishment. It's reasonable to ask to see two or three options before settling on one.

best HOTEL BETS

- **Best Splurge: Fairmont Le Château Frontenac** and its unforgettable spires soar above this gorgeous city. Nothing can beat it for proximity to all the sights. In fact, "the Château" is one of the sights. Even if you don't stay here, come by for a tour, a meal, or a drink. See p. 145.
- **Best Service:** The staff at **Auberge St-Antoine** is professional without being stuffy. They've been known to call all over town to help find "the big game" on TV and then ask later if your team won. The ancient walls and archaeological displays from lobby to bedside make for an exceptionally unique stay. See p. 150.
- **Best Romantic Hotel:** The sleek **Hôtel Le Germain-Dominion** is a favorite, infusing a pre–World War I building with the comforts of modern day. The bedding is hands-down gold star luxury. See p. 150.
- **Best Eclectic *Auberge:*** At **Auberge Place d'Armes,** every room is individually themed. Visitors can stroll the boardwalk in front of Frontenac, squeeze down the narrow, artwork lined rue du Trésor, and call it a night in a wholly original room. See p. 148.
- **Best Cultural Immersion:** The **Hôtel-Musée Premières Nations** in Wendake is modeled after a Huron longhouse. A stay here can include a Huron-Wendat museum visit, First Nations–inspired cuisine, spa massotherapy, and a balcony view of the Akiawenrahk River. See p. 153.
- **Best Location for Peace and Quiet:** The **Parc des Gouverneurs,** next to the Château, offers a tranquil respite that's still close to Upper Town's

Hotel Rates in Québec City

Following is an explanation of the hotel rates as we define them in this book:

Expensive	C$200 and up
Moderate	C$100–C$200
Inexpensive	Under C$100

As with Montréal's hotels, the prices listed here are by no means written in stone, and should be used more as a guideline for comparing properties. Rates provided are typical of Québec City's high seasons in summer (typically June–Aug) and winter (around Christmastime to Carnaval). They can be significantly lower when tourism is slow.

restaurants and shops. Many B&Bs and small hotels are on the park or nearby, including **Maison du Fort** and **Manoir Sur-le-Cap.** See both on p. 149.

- **Best Value: Auberge du Quartier** offers high-end accomodations for budge travelers. It's within walking distance of the Plains of Abraham and the shops on avenue Cartier. See p. 152.
- **Best Eco Hotel: Hôtel du Vieux-Québec** is carbon neutral and solar-powered, it recaptures energy from hot water, and has more enviro-friendly plans in the works for 2014. See p. 148.
- **Best Adventure Hotel:** Friends may call you crazy, or just plain cold. The **Hôtel de Glace (or Ice Hotel),** just 10 minutes from downtown Québec City, is built from scratch each year and open from January to late March. Sleep on a bed of ice or chillax as a daytripper. See p. 153.
- **Best for Families:** If you want to stay in the city, there's an indoor pool at **Hôtel Manoir Victoria,** just off rue St-Jean's shopping and dining scene and some of the in-house spa treatments are tailored to kids. See p. 148. In warm weather, the outdoor heated pool at **Loews Le Concorde Hotel** can't be beat. Views from the upper floors can captivate even the most distracted teens. See p. 151.

VIEUX-QUÉBEC: HAUTE-VILLE (UPPER TOWN)

Nestled under the wing of the magnificent Château Frontenac, boutique hotels in this lovely area can offer warm personal service and historical charm. That said, there's high demand to stay in this coveted area near the "castle," so prices at some properties can be steep for what they offer.

Expensive

Fairmont Le Château Frontenac ★★★ You will not and should not miss this incredible Québec landmark, fondly called the "castle" or *le château.* Its majestic spires and gabled rooftops have been visible along the cliff overlooking the St. Lawrence River since 1893. The interior is likewise grand, with deluxe furnishings in all 618 rooms. Some have fireplaces or whirlpool tubs. Rooms with river views are pricer than courtyard views; the priciest, on the Fairmont Gold floor, impress with a dedicated concierge, bar, and breakfast area. In the latter half of 2013, a limited number of rooms are available for a "scaffolding" rate while some exterior stonework undergoes

Québec City Hotels

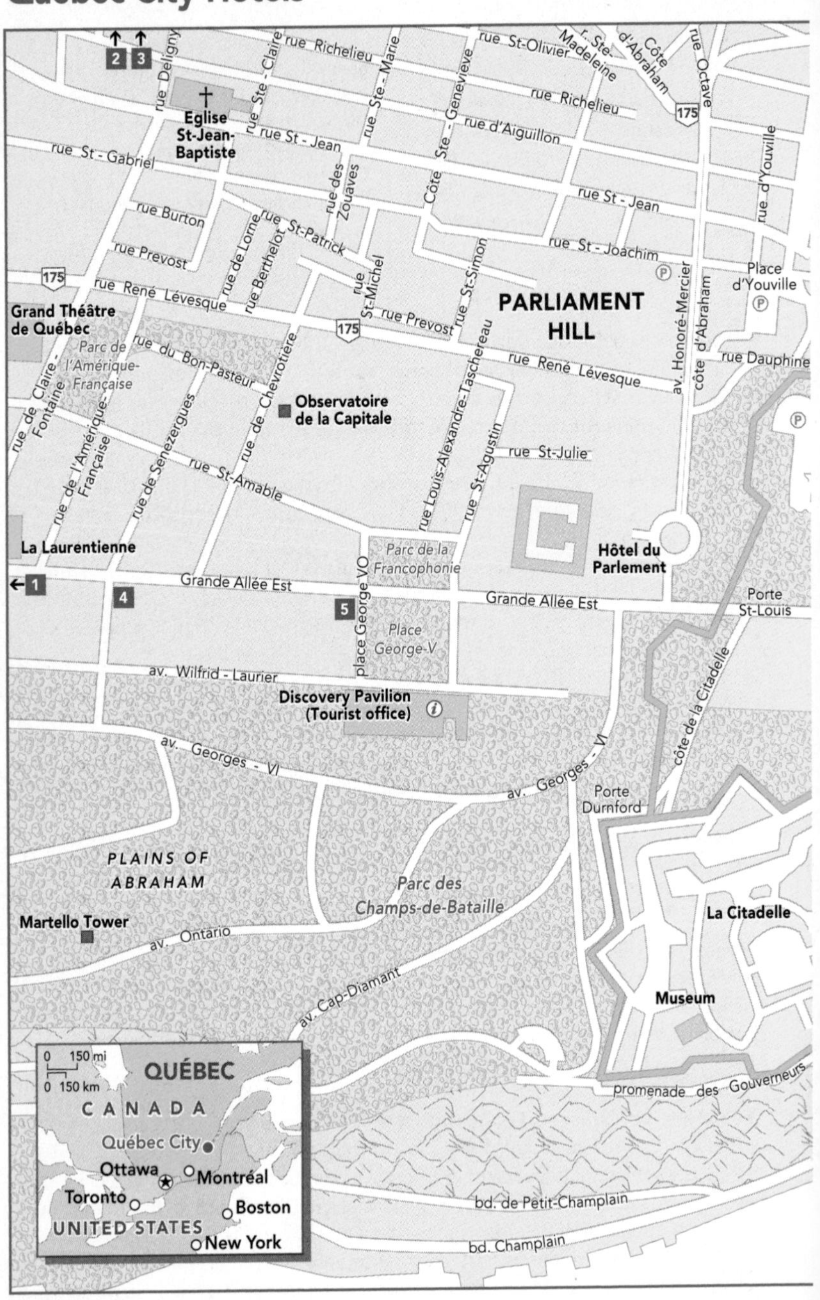

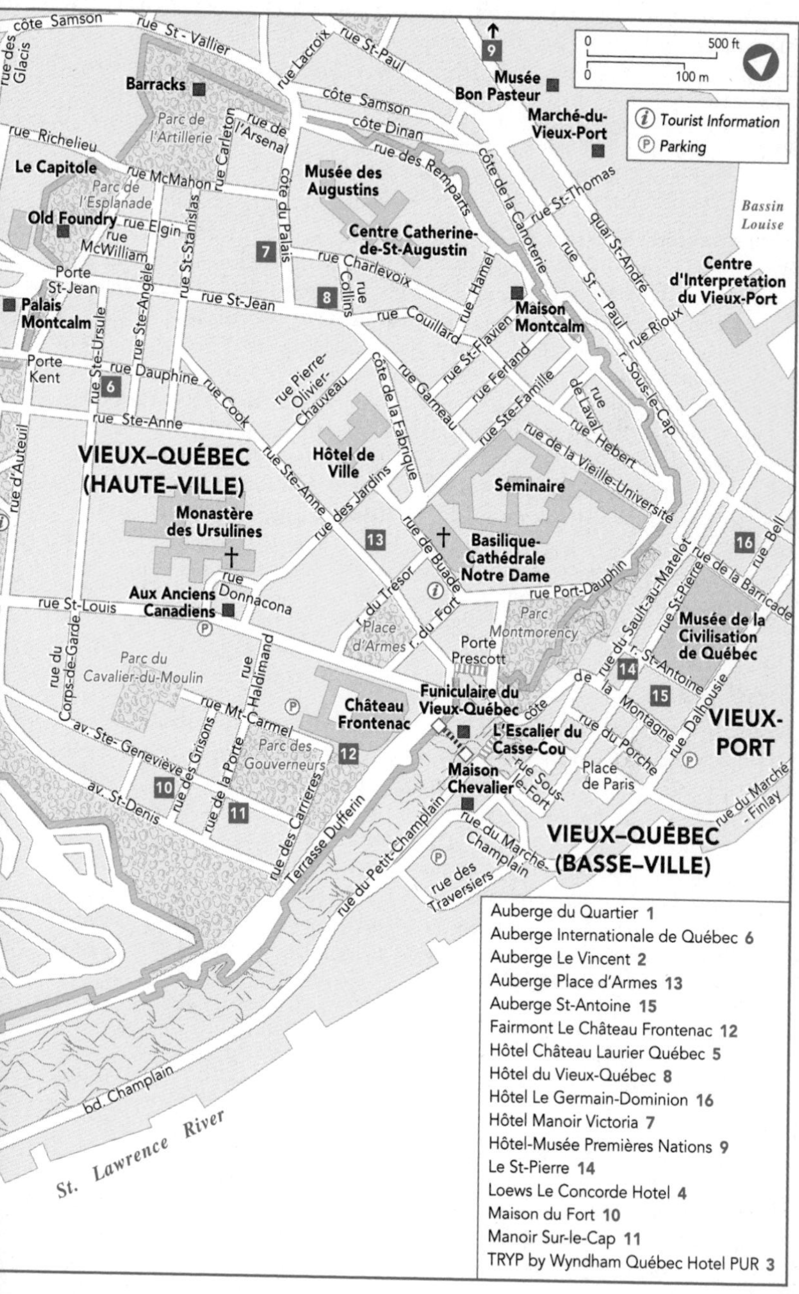
0 500 ft
0 100 m
Tourist Information
Parking
VIEUX–QUÉBEC (HAUTE–VILLE)
VIEUX–QUÉBEC (BASSE–VILLE)
VIEUX-PORT
Barracks
Parc de l'Artillerie
Le Capitole
Parc de l'Esplanade
Old Foundry
Porte St-Jean
Palais Montcalm
Porte Kent
Musée Bon Pasteur
Marché-du-Vieux-Port
Bassin Louise
Centre d'Interpretation du Vieux-Port
Musée des Augustins
Centre Catherine-de-St-Augustin
Maison Montcalm
Hôtel de Ville
Seminaire
Monastère des Ursulines
Basilique-Cathédrale Notre Dame
Aux Anciens Canadiens
Place d'Armes
Parc Montmorency
Porte Prescott
Musée de la Civilisation de Québec
Parc du Cavalier-du-Moulin
Château Frontenac
Funiculaire du Vieux-Québec
L'Escalier du Casse-Cou
Maison Chevalier
Parc des Gouverneurs
Place de Paris
Terrasse Dufferin
St. Lawrence River
côte Samson
rue des Glacis
rue St-Vallier
rue Lacroix
rue St-Paul
rue Richelieu
rue de l'Arsenal
rue Carleton
rue McMahon
côte du Palais
côte Dinan
rue des Remparts
côte de la Canoterie
rue St-Thomas
quai St-André
rue St-Paul
rue Elgin
rue McWilliam
rue St-Stanislas
rue Charlevoix
rue Collins
rue Hamel
rue St-Jean
rue Ste-Angèle
rue Ste-Ursule
rue Couillard
rue St-Flavien
rue Rioux
r. Sous-le-Cap
rue Dauphine
rue Cook
rue Pierre-Olivier-Chauveau
côte de la Fabrique
rue Garneau
rue Ferland
rue Ste-Famille
rue de Laval
rue Hebert
rue Ste-Anne
rue d'Auteuil
rue de la Vieille-Université
rue des Jardins
rue Ste-Anne
rue de Buade
rue du Trésor
rue du Fort
rue Port-Dauphin
rue du Sault-au-Matelot
rue St-Pierre
rue de la Barricade
rue Bell
rue Donnacona
rue St-Louis
rue du Corps-de-Garde
rue Haldimand
r. St-Antoine
côte de la Montagne
rue Dalhousie
rue Mt-Carmel
av. Ste-Geneviève
rue des Grisons
rue de la Porte
rue du Porche
rue Sous-le-Fort
av. St-Denis
rue des Carrières
rue du Petit-Champlain
rue du Marché-Champlain
rue du Marché-Finlay
rue des Traversiers
bd. Champlain
Auberge du Quartier 1
Auberge Internationale de Québec 6
Auberge Le Vincent 2
Auberge Place d'Armes 13
Auberge St-Antoine 15
Fairmont Le Château Frontenac 12
Hôtel Château Laurier Québec 5
Hôtel du Vieux-Québec 8
Hôtel Le Germain-Dominion 16
Hôtel Manoir Victoria 7
Hôtel-Musée Premières Nations 9
Le St-Pierre 14
Loews Le Concorde Hotel 4
Maison du Fort 10
Manoir Sur-le-Cap 11
TRYP by Wyndham Québec Hotel PUR 3

renovation (expected to be complete April 2014). Le Champlain Restaurant is also temporarily closed through the end of 2013. If staying over is out reach, anyone can enjoy the scenery from the **St-Laurent Bar et Lounge** (p. 188) or **Café de la Terrasse,** which serves an elegant afternoon tea on Saturdays from 1:30 to 3pm.

1 rue des Carrières (at Place d'Armes). www.fairmont.com/frontenac-quebec. ✆ **866/540-4460** or 418/692-3861. 618 units. From C$399 double; from C$499 suite. Packages available. Valet or self-parking C$32 per day; hybrid vehicles free. Pets accepted (C$35 per day per pet). **Amenities:** 3 restaurants; bar; babysitting; children's programs; concierge; executive-level rooms; gift shops; health club; pools (1 indoor and 1 kiddie pool w/outdoor terrace); room service; spa; Starbucks cafe; Wi-Fi (C$14 per day).

Hôtel Manoir Victoria ★★ At press time, this elegant, old-world hotel was in the midst of giving a modern renovation to its standard guest rooms (anticipated completion: early 2014). The once antique lobby has already been updated with purple, red, and gray mixed-century furniture and the suites are fashionably sleek. In addition, a new restaurant **Chez Boulay bistro boréal** (see p. 157) has become a magnet for local and visiting foodies. This is one of the more luxurious hotel choices within walking distance of rue St-Jean bar and shopping scene. Another feature that sets this hotel apart: there's a small indoor pool and an onsite, full-service spa that even serves kids and teens. Package options abound, and rebates are available for reserving 2 or more nights. Note that there's a steep staircase from the front door to the lobby, although elevators make the trip to most guest rooms.

44 Côte du Palais (at rue St-Jean). www.manoir-victoria.com. ✆ **800/463-6283** or 418/692-1030. 156 units. High season C$185–C$400 double; low season C$135–C$350 double. High season C$450–C$600 suite; low season C$350–C$500 suite. Packages available. Valet parking C$22. **Amenities:** 2 restaurants; bar; babysitting; concierge; exercise room; indoor pool; sauna; room service; spa; free Wi-Fi.

Moderate

Auberge Place d'Armes ★★ This high-end (yet well-priced) *auberge* has a long history and has taken great care preserving the structural elements from the buildings that are now the hotel. One section housed a former provincial prime minister and later became a wax museum; the other was the home of the co-founder of Holt Renfrew, still one of Canada's leading luxury stores. Now carefully renovated guest rooms—each one unique—feature everything from exposed stone walls dating back to 1640 to rain showers with jets, flatscreen TVs, and craft furniture. You can see each room online. This section of rue Ste-Anne is pedestrian-only and lined with outdoor dining, great for people-watching. Breakfast is included and is served at the very good in-house restaurant **Le Pain Béni** (p. 160).

24 rue Ste-Anne (at Place d'Armes). www.aubergeplacedarmes.com. ✆ **866/333-9485** or 418/694-9485. 21 units. Summer C$188–C$219 double; fall–spring from C$139 double. Rates include continental breakfast. Packages available. Valet parking C$22 (high season only); C$22 self parking. Pets accepted (C$25 per day). **Amenities:** Restaurant; bikes; babysitting; concierge; room service; free Wi-Fi.

Hôtel du Vieux-Québec ★★ Many hotels claim to be in the heart of Old Québec, this one really is, as it's on a prime corner in the rue St-Jean dining and shopping area (though admittedly all of upper and lower town is very walkable). Either way, it provides consistent accommodations and is increasingly eco-friendly. A rooftop garden lowers overall energy consumption and houses honeybees and solar power cells. Rainwater is captured and re-used as is the heat from drain water. Rooms feature custom furnishings made with carefully harvested local mahogany or maple and are

CONSIDERING A b&b

Vieux-Québec has about a dozen B&Bs and that number triples if the rest of the city is an option for you. With rates mostly in the C$80 to C$140 range, they don't necessarily offer substantial savings over the small hotels, but do give you the opportunity to get to know some of the city dwellers. If you discover one while exploring, a property is full if the sign says COMPLET and VACANT if rooms are available. "The Official Accommodation Guide" put out by Québec City Tourism lists every member of the Greater Québec Area Tourism and Convention Bureau, including B&Bs, with details about the number of rooms, the prices, and the facilities. It's available at tourist offices (p. 220). There's also a handy search feature for B&Bs at **www.quebecregion.com**.

equipped with mini fridges and coffeemakers. Families often choose this hotel for its location, value, and extras (free summer walking tours, many rooms have two queen beds, plus there's a lounge with a fireplace, board games, and library). The ground-level bistro, **Les Frères de la Côte** (✆ **418/692-5445**) offers a good value, too.

1190 rue St-Jean (at rue de l'Hôtel Dieu). www.hvq.com. ✆ **800/361-7787** or 418/692-1850. 45 units. May to late Oct: from C$158–C$218 double; late Oct to Apr from C$118 double. Rates include continental breakfast for rooms booked directly with hotel. Packages available. Self parking C$16. Pets accepted (C$25 per day). **Amenities:** Restaurant; fitness room; free Wi-Fi.

Maison du Fort ★ Guests just departing Maison du Fort nodded in agreement over their reason for coming back time and again: the friendly owner. Situated near Parc des Gouverneurs, this B&B starts your day nicely with muffins, tea, and coffee. With a nod to the posh Château Frontenac nearby, each room has a goose down duvet. The home was built in the Georgian style in 1851 by architect Charles Baillargé, and the high ceilings and older woodwork add a bit of romance. However, the spirit of the place is perhaps best represented by its two house cats, purring contentedly. (An aside: the Têtu House, just down the block at no. 25, was home to Antoine de St-Exupéry, author of "Le Petit Prince.") Note that you'll need to climb few stairs to get into the B&B, but guests rooms are also located up one, two, or three full flights of stairs.

21 av. Ste-Geneviève (at rue des Grisons). www.hotelmaisondufort.com. ✆ **888/203-4375** or 418/692-4375. 9 units. C$129–C$219 double. Rates include breakfast. Free Wi-Fi.

Manoir Sur-le-Cap ★ Inns on the charming Parc des Gouverneurs, opposite the Château Frontenac, are close to the action, but are quieter and more affordable. This inn distinguishes itself with friendly service and 14 comfy rooms, all unique. Many feature exposed stone or brick walls and some have balconies that overlook the river. If stairs are an issue, request a room on the main floor, but note that there are a few steps leading up to it, too.

9 av. Ste-Geneviève (near rue de la Porte). www.manoir-sur-le-cap.com. ✆ **866/694-1987** or 418/694-1987. 14 units. High season C$125–C$185 double; low season C$95–C$125 double. Self-parking C$22. Free Wi-Fi.

Inexpensive

Auberge Internationale de Québec ★ The city's hostel is a comfortable and affordable option. In addition to dorm housing—one room with several bunks, common for Hostelling International (HI)–designated properties—there are also modest rooms with either shared or private bathrooms. Interns coordinate group activities such as pub crawls, museum visits, and tours to Montmorency Waterfalls or across the St. Lawrence River. No need for a sleeping bag (they are not permitted); pillows, sheets, and blankets are provided. Lockers and laundry are available for a fee as well as a modest kitchen for meal prep. Reservations are strongly recommended in summer.

19 rue. Ste-Ursule (near rue Ste-Anne). www.aubergeinternationaldequebec.com. ✆ **866/694-0950** or 418/694-0755. 25 private rooms, 277 beds. C$75–C$90 private room for 2; C$30 per person for shared dorm room. Discount available for HI members. Rates for private rooms include breakfast. **Amenities:** Restaurant; self-service kitchen; free Wi-Fi in lobby.

VIEUX-QUÉBEC: BASSE-VILLE (LOWER TOWN)/VIEUX-PORT

Lower town is essentially an extension of the Upper Town, separated by a photogenic bluff that divides the two areas. A *funiculaire* conveniently connects the two areas, or you can take the adjacent *L'éscalier casse-cou* (Breakneck Steps)—which are not quite as scary or steep as they sound. In this area, travelers can count small hotels that are big on luxury. While the waterfront is lovely, it (along with some adjacent streets) can seem empty and lonely during off season.

Expensive

Auberge St-Antoine ★★★ This is one of the most memorable and splurge-worthy hotels in Québec City. Ancient walls, beams, and stone floors from the original buildings—used as a wharf, a cannon battery, and by British merchants—were incorporated into the current, cleanly modern design. Artifacts unearthed during a large-scale archeological dig are on display throughout—in the lobby, outside the door to each guest room, and by each bedside—all arranged with curatorial care. Rooms are luxurious and spacious. Fine linens, cozy bathrobes, and heated bathroom floors are standard; deep tubs, balconies, fireplaces, or kitchenettes are optional. Staff extends a warm welcome and will go out of their way to meet your needs, especially during the off-season. The **Café Artéfact** lounge, tucked between cathedral-like windows near the lobby, serves lunch, snacks, and drinks, and **Panache** (p. 162), where breakfast is served, offers some of the city's finest dining. This hotel picks up annual national and international awards and is a member of the prestigious Relais & Châteaux luxury group. Free tours are available to guests upon request.

8 rue St-Antoine (next to the Musée de la Civilisation). www.saint-antoine.com. ✆ **888/692-2211** or 418/692-2211. 95 units. C$189–C$439 double; from C$399 suite. Packages available. Valet parking C$25. Pets accepted (C$150 per visit). **Amenities:** Restaurant; bar; babysitting; cinema; concierge; exercise room; room service; spa treatments; free Wi-Fi.

Hôtel Le Germain-Dominion ★★★ Urban elegance is the ruling principle in one of the city's most refined boutique hotels. Built in 1912, the building formerly housed Dominion Fish & Fruit Limited and became a hotel in 1997. Part of a small chain with locations in Montréal, Toronto, and Calgary, the rooms here are furnished with exceptionally comfortable beds and sheets that are downright heavenly. About two-thirds of rooms have both tubs and showers, and bathrooms are well lit and stylish. The continental breakfast (which includes delicious espresso) can be taken on the leafy outdoor terrace in the summer or near the lobby fireplace in colder months. The parking lot out back has Québec City's only BIXI station (see p. 38) for easy bike borrowing and rental.

126 rue St-Pierre (at rue St-Paul). www.germaindominion.com. ✆ **888/833-5253** or 418/692-2224. 60 units. C$189–C$325 double. Rates include continental breakfast. Valet parking C$23. Pets accepted (C$30 per stay). **Amenities:** Espresso bar; babysitting; concierge; exercise room; room service; free Wi-Fi.

Moderate

Le St-Pierre ★ This is one of the homier options in Old Québec. Owned by the same people as the adjacent, upscale and more contemporary **Hôtel 71** (✆ **888/692-1171**), which we also recommend, the two properties share **Il Matto** (p. 161), a mod Italian restaurant on the first floor. Rooms at Auberge Le St-Pierre have a living room feel, with creamy walls, light brown wood floors, and an occasional exposed stone wall. It's a good choice for longer stays or families, as units offer room to spread out and some have modest kitchens. Jetted baths and bathrobes are standard. The breakfast here is a plus: always included and cooked to order.

79 rue St-Pierre (behind the Musée de la Civilisation). www.le-saint-pierre.ca. ✆ **888/268-1017** or 418/694-7981. 41 units. C$160–C$260 double; C$260–C$320 suite. Rates include full breakfast. Packages available. Valet parking C$21. **Amenities:** Restaurant, bar; babysitting; concierge; exercise room; free Wi-Fi.

PARLIAMENT HILL (ON OR NEAR GRANDE-ALLEE)

A flat land that extends away from Vieux-Québec, the area includes green spaces Parc des Champs-de-Bataille and the Plains of Abraham, as well as the Musée National des Beaux-Arts du Québec near the posh Montcalm residential neighborhood. This area is a good choice if touring by car or attending events in the area. Accommodations here have a more generic feel than the options in Vieux-Québec, but if you prefer the feel of a familiar chain hotel you'll have more choices here.

Expensive

Hôtel Château Laurier Québec ★ Sandwiched between the scenic oasis of the Plains of Abraham and the frenetic, club-lined Grande-Allée, Château Laurier is many different hotels in one. This may influence how you select your room. For example, there are six categories that vary in age, style, and price. The most affordable are in the "Express" category; the "Superior" rooms are the most up-to-date. There's an abundance of wheelchair-accessible rooms, too. Château Laurier distinguishes itself as a "Francoresponsible" hotel by playing French music and featuring photographs and paintings by French and Québécois artists in the hallways. It's also eco-responsible—the pool is saltwater, surplus food is delivered to food banks, and recycling is *de rigeur.* An electric car recharging station is on site.

1220 Place Georges-V ouest (at Grande-Allée). www.hotelchateaulaurier.com. ✆ **877/522-8108** or 418/522-8108. 291 units. From C$149–C$279 double. Packages available. Parking C$20. **Amenities:** Restaurant; bar; concierge; executive-level floors; exercise room; Jacuzzis (1 indoor, 2 outdoor); indoor saltwater pool; room service; Finnish sauna; spa; Wi-Fi (C$15 per day).

Loews Le Concorde Hotel ★ There's always something tantalizing about seeing spectacular views from the top of tall buildings, especially in an otherwise rural part of the province. Rooms on the fifth floor and above, as well as the hotel's revolving rooftop restaurant, **L'Astral** (p. 189), exceed that desire as the St. Lawrence and lights from Old Québec sparkle in the distance. Some rooms even have outdoor terraces. This hotel can be counted on for its overall quality of service and stay. Kids are treated to a lending library of toys and pets are welcome for a fee. Note that crowds can swallow this place up, either the ones partying on the Grande-Allée or the wedings or conventions held within. With a heated outdoor pool in summer, though, it could mean fun for the whole family.

1225 Cours du Géneral de Montcalm (at Grande-Allée). www.loewsleconcorde.com. ✆ **800/463-5256** or 418/647-2222. 406 units. High season C$199–C$299 double; low season C$109–C$219. Packages available. Valet parking C$29, self-parking C$24. Pets accepted (C$25 per stay). **Amenities:** Restaurant; bar; babysitting; concierge; health club; pool (outdoor heated); room service; sauna; Wi-Fi (free in lobby, C$12 per day).

Moderate

Auberge du Quartier ★★ New inside, affordable, and a stone's throw from any activity on the Plains of Abraham, including **summer festival** (see p. 186). Sounds perfect. So what gives? The clubs and sometimes high-decibel hubbub along Grande-Allée are not every visitor's cup of tea. This boutique *auberge* has recently updated guest rooms with down comforters, high-end sheets, and splashes of mod decor. The Musée National des Beaux-Arts du Québec (p. 176) is just down the street and avenue Cartier, right around the corner, has shopping and dining worthy of an afternoon, or breakfast (on a recent stay, the buffet breakfast, included during low season, did not match the quality of the hotel's other features). Staffers are friendly and willing to go out of their way to help.

170 Grande Allée ouest (near av. Cartier). www.aubergeduquartier.com. ✆ **800/782-9441** or 418/525-9726. 291 units. High season C$129–C$145 double; low season C$89–C$119 double. Packages available. Parking C$15. **Amenities:** Breakfast included in low season; free Wi-Fi.

ST-ROCH

Young restaurateurs, artists, media techies, and fashionistas have settled into Québec's St-Roch neighborhood, dubbing the area "Le Nouvo St-Roch" (pronounce it "Saint-Rock"). Each visit finds new boutiques and restaurants, so don't be surprised if people are talking about venues that aren't mentioned in this book; St-Roch is, however, slightly removed from the main attractions listed in this book.

Expensive

TRYP by Wyndham Québec Hotel PUR ★ What PUR offers is ultramod accommodations in the hip St-Roch neighborbood, just outside the hub of the main tourist draws but certainly not out of reach by car (or the very ambitious walker). It has been many things, including a Holiday Inn and a chic independently owned hotel tower, but now it's part of the extensive Wyndham hotel network. Rooms still have incredible views, especially on the highest floors, and the large indoor pool is still an attraction. Furnishings are super spare—white with a shock of orange—but comfy. Because of the large number of rooms, last-minute deals can be had. The ground-floor restaurant, **Table,** serves Asian and American cuisine and breakfast for hotel guests.

395 rue de la Couronne (at rue St-Joseph). www.hotelpur.com. ✆ **800/267-2002** or 418/647-2611. 242 units. C$189–C$249 double. Packages available. Pets accepted (C$25 per day). Valet parking C$21. **Amenities:** Restaurant; fitness center; indoor heated pool; sauna; free Wi-Fi.

Moderate

Auberge Le Vincent ★ For personal treatment in a cool part of town, this Vincent Van Gogh–inspired *auberge* is for you. Owners Sonia Tremblay and Antonio

THE coldest RECEPTION IN TOWN

How many chances do you get to sleep in a hotel built from 500 tons of ice? On a bed of ice, near a chandelier made of ice, after dancing in a disco made of ice, ice, ice? Québec's **Hôtel de Glace (Ice Hotel),** 9530 rue de la Faune (www.hoteldeglace-canada.com; ✆ **877/505-0423**), is built every winter on a site just 10 minutes from downtown. For C$17.50 you can visit, but for C$269 per person (and up), you can have a cocktail and spend the night. Tempted?

Nearly everything at the Hôtel de Glace is made of ice, from the ice chandelier in vaulted main hall, to the thick-ice shot glasses in which vodka is served, to the pillars and arches and furniture. That includes the frozen slabs that serve as beds; high-tech sleeping bags provide insulation (a how-to class explains how to zip yourself up correctly).

Nighttime guests get their rooms at 9pm after the last tour ends, and have to clear out by 9am, before the next day's arrivals. Some rooms are vaguely grand and some are designed according to the yearly theme: One year there was a Chess Room featuring solid-ice chess pieces the size of small children at each corner of the bed. Other rooms bring the words "monastic" or "cell block" to mind.

Bear in mind that, except for in the hot tub, temperatures everywhere hover between 23° and 27°F (–5° and –3°C). Refrigerators are used not to keep drinks cold, but to *keep them from freezing.*

The hotel has 44 rooms and suites, a wedding chapel, and a nightclub with DJ for guests to shake the chill from their booties. Open each January, it houses guests until late March—after that, it's destroyed.

Soares pull out all the stops for their guests with goose duvets, 400-thread-count sheets, in-room espresso, and a fridge for your goodies. There's always a homemade breakfast. Rooms are up either one or two flights of stairs, and the din from the streets below can be heard sublty in the background. Van Gogh-esque murals liven up the common spaces along with work by local artists.

295 rue St-Vallier est (corner of rue Dorchester). www.aubergelevincent.com. ✆ **888/523-5005** or 418/523-5000. 10 units. High season C$199–C$279 double; low season C$149–C$199 double. Rates include full breakfast. Packages available. Parking C$15. **Amenities**: Free Wi-Fi.

JUST OUTSIDE THE CITY

For travelers with agendas other than the century-old sights in the historic center—an interest in First Nations culture, perhaps—or those covering a lot of ground by car may want to stay outside the city for a night or two. Note that this is a bit of a trek if your interests lie in Québec City. In addition to this recommendation below, consult the Walking Tours in chapter 16.

Moderate

Hôtel-Musée Premières Nations ★ Every room in this relaxing, earthy resort features a private balcony that overlooks the Akiawenrahk River. The hotel is situated on a forested section of the First Nations reservation called Wendake, just fifteen minutes from Québec City by car. Once here, you'll find everything you need to decompress. The "multisensory" Nordic spa has a waterfall, heated sidewalks, a firepit, and a time-out yurt for quiet relaxation. Massage treatments can be booked on a whim or in advance. The high-end La Traite restaurant specializes in First Nations–inspired cuisine such as red deer, elk, or smoked mackerel. A three-course table d'hôte is priced at C$40 per person; more elaborate and costlier tasting menus are also available. Paintings and sculpture by First Nations artists are featured throughout the hotel and an on-site museum celebrates Huron-Wendat culture. An afternoon could be spent poking around the handful of shops and galleries in Wendake or touring the reconstructed

5 Place de la Rencontre, Wendake, Québec. www.hotelpremieresnations.ca. ✆ **866/551-9222** or 418/847-2222. 55 units. C$129–C$269 double. Packages available. Free parking. From Rte. 175 north, take exit 154 for rue de la Faune, enter Wendake reservation and follow signs. **Amenities:** Restaurant; bar; babysitting; bike rental; free Wi-Fi.

WHERE TO EAT IN QUÉBEC CITY

13

With a little research, it's possible to eat extraordinarily well in Québec City. It used to be that this gloriously scenic town had no *temples de cuisine* comparable to those of Montréal. That's all changed. There are now restaurants equal in every way to the most honored establishments of any North American city, with surprising numbers of creative, ambitious young chefs and restaurateurs bidding to achieve similar status.

best EATING BETS

- **Best Restaurants for a Special Evening: Le Saint-Amour** may be the most romantic restaurant in the city. **Initiale** is hushed and elegant. Both stellar restaurants woo you at the door. See p. 157 and 161.
- **Best Bistros:** In a city that specializes in the informal bistro tradition, **Chez Boulay** is a welcome addition to rue St-Jean and **Le Clocher Penché Bistrot** offers a cozy atmosphere and a reason to explore the trendy St-Roch neighborhood. See p. 157 and 165.
- **Best Bargains:** A main course at **Aux Anciens Canadiens** can set you back C$70 or more (yikes), but every day until 5:45pm the purveyor of classic Québécois fare offers a three-course meal with wine or beer for just C$20. The ritzy **Laurie Raphaël** also has a lunchtime deal of three courses for about C$29. See p. 157 or 161.
- **Best Idyllic Terrace:** The crimson-red main room *is* sexy, but try to have a dinner on the leafy enclosed back terrace of Lower Town's **Toast!** The terrace at the terrific **Panache** is also worth seeking out. See both on p. 162.
- **Best Hipster Night Out:** Let **Le Moine Échanson, L'Affaire est Ketchup,** and **Patente et Machin** duke it out for the cool-kid badge while you relax and enjoy their with-it, home-style cooking. See p. 164, p. 165, and 165.
- **Best for Families:** Large (it seats 180) and jovial, **Le Café du Monde** manages the nearly impossible: classic French food *and* fast service without a compromise in quality, even on crowded holiday weekends. Kids are not just welcomed at St-Roch's hip **Le Cercle,** the under-12 set eat free Saturday brunch from a menu designed for them. See p. 163 and 165.
- **Best Breakfast with Locals:** In the residential neighborhood of Montcalm, not far from the Musée des Beaux-Arts du Québec, **Café Krieghoff** gets a mix of families, singles, and artsy folks of all ages. See p. 164.
- **Best Sugar Pie:** We have to go with **Aux Anciens Canadiens** for this category as well. Québec's favorite dessert reaches its apogee at this admittedly tourist-heavy venue in central Upper Town. Think maple syrup with a crust, or pecan pie without the pecans. See p. 157.

THE REAL DEAL ABOUT meals

There are blatantly touristy restaurants along rue St-Louis in Upper Town and around the Place d'Armes, many of them with hawkers outside. They can produce decent meals and are entirely satisfactory for lunch.

At the better places, though, reservations are essential during holidays and festivals. Other times, it's necessary to book ahead only for weekend evenings. Dress codes are rarely stipulated, but "dressy casual" works almost everywhere.

The evening meal tends to be served earlier in Québec City than in Montréal, at 7pm rather than 8pm. In the winter months, when tourist traffic slows, restaurants can close early or reduce the number of days they're open, so confirm before heading out.

The best dining deals in Québec City are table d'hôte, fixed-priced meals. Nearly all full-service restaurants offer them. Generally, these meals include at least soup or salad, a main course, and a dessert. Some places add an extra appetizer and/or a beverage. The total price ends up being approximately what you'd pay for the main course alone. At lunchtime, table d'hôte meals are even cheaper (and you have more time to walk off the big meal).

RESTAURANTS BY CUISINE

BISTRO

Bistro B ★ ($$$, p. 163)
Chez Boulay ★★ ($$$, p. 157)
L'Affaire est Ketchup ★ ($$, p. 165)
L'Echaudé ★ ($$$, p. 162)
Le Clocher Penché Bistrot ★★★ ($$$, p. 165)
Patente et Machin ★ ($$, p. 165)

CONTEMPORARY QUÉBÉCOIS

Initiale ★★★ ($$$, p. 161)
Laurie Raphaël ★★ ($$$, p. 161)
Le Moine Échanson ★★ ($$, p. 164)
Le Pain Béni ★★ ($$, p. 160)
Le Saint-Amour ★★★ ($$$, p. 157)
Panache ★★★ ($$$, p. 162)
Toast! ★ ($$, p. 162)

FUSION

Le Cercle ★★★ ($$, p. 165)

ITALIAN

Il Matto ★ ($$$, p. 161)

LIGHT FARE

Café Krieghoff ★★★ ($, p. 164)
Chez Temporel ★ ($, p. 160)
Paillard ★★ ($, p. 160)

TRADITIONAL FRENCH

Le Café du Monde ★ ($$, p. 163)

TRADITIONAL QUÉBÉCOIS

Aux Anciens Canadiens ★★ ($$$, p. 157)

KEY TO ABBREVIATIONS:
$$$** = Expensive **$$** = Moderate **$ = Inexpensive

VIEUX-QUÉBEC: HAUTE-VILLE (UPPER TOWN)

In addition to the options listed below, food is also available in Upper Town at the jazz club **Charles Baillairgé** and the **Pub St-Patrick, Pub St-Alexandre** (p. 188), and **St-Laurent Bar et Lounge** (p. 188).

Expensive

Aux Anciens Canadiens ★★ TRADITIONAL QUÉBÉCOIS Situated within one of Upper Town's oldest homes (circa 1676), under a hard-to-miss, quaintly red roof, is the city's favorite destination for traditional Québécois cuisine. A dinner of pea soup, *tourtiere* (meat pie), baked beans, and maple syrup pie may sound basic, but these and the more contemporary adaptations of game (vacuum-cooked wild caribou filet mignon, for example) are prepared exceptionally well here. Small windows, low ceilings, checked tablecloths, and servers who dress in period costume add warmth and a smidge of whimsy to what is otherwise a fine dining (and expensive) night out. The three-course early-bird special (daily until 5:45pm) is a bargain for C$20—and it includes wine or beer.

34 rue St-Louis (at rue des Jardins). www.auxancienscanadiens.qc.ca. ✆ **418/692-1627.** Reservations recommended. Main courses C$39–C$79; table d'hôte lunch C$20. Mon–Wed 4:30–9pm; Thurs–Sun noon–9pm.

Chez Boulay bistro à boréal ★★ BISTRO It's almost as if chefs Jean-Luc Boulay and Arnaud Marchand anticipated reviews when naming their restaurant: "Chez Boulay bistro à boréal is more than a mouthful . . ." It's much more, actually (and it goes by Chez Boulay for short). Their airy, modern bistro opened in 2012 as part of renovation of **Hôtel Manoir Victoria** (see p. 148), and it fills a need in this part of Upper Town for an all-around reliably good meal in an upscale, but not over-the-top ambience. Boulay, who has been perfecting his craft for more than 35 years at **Le Saint-Amour** (see below), wouldn't stand for much less than perfection. The menu is Nordic-inspired with deer, duck, mackerel, Labrador tea spice, wintergreen, and birch syrup among the popular ingredients. Portions are generous, especially at brunch (Sat–Sun, 10am–3pm). Clientele is middle-aged locals with discriminating palettes and visitors looking for a much nicer alternative to the pub fare that seems ubiquitous on this street.

1100 rue St-Jean (near rue St-Stanislas). http://chezboulay.com. ✆ **418/380-8166.** Main courses brunch C$17–C$20; lunch C$15–C$21; dinner C$22–C$37. Mon–Fri 11:30am–10:30pm; Sat–Sun 10am–10:30pm.

Le Saint-Amour ★★★ CONTEMPORARY QUÉBÉCOIS The owners of this quirkily exquisite endeavor, Jacques Fortier and head chef Jean Luc Boulay, wouldn't want a neon arrow pointing to their restaurant. Since they opened Le Saint-Amour in 1978 they've hardly needed a shingle out front. It's tucked away on a quiet Upper Town side street—a sole black awning over an arched doorway—exactly where you'd want to step out of a horse-drawn carriage for a romantic dinner for two. Make the reservations. The interior speaks more to the 1970s than to present day, but the service is relentlessly adept and the dishes remain subtly complex. Foie gras is a specialty (seared, in terrine) and though the chef has long embraced the meats, his kitchen turns out incredible meatless options, especially when requested in advance (there's even

Québec City Restaurants

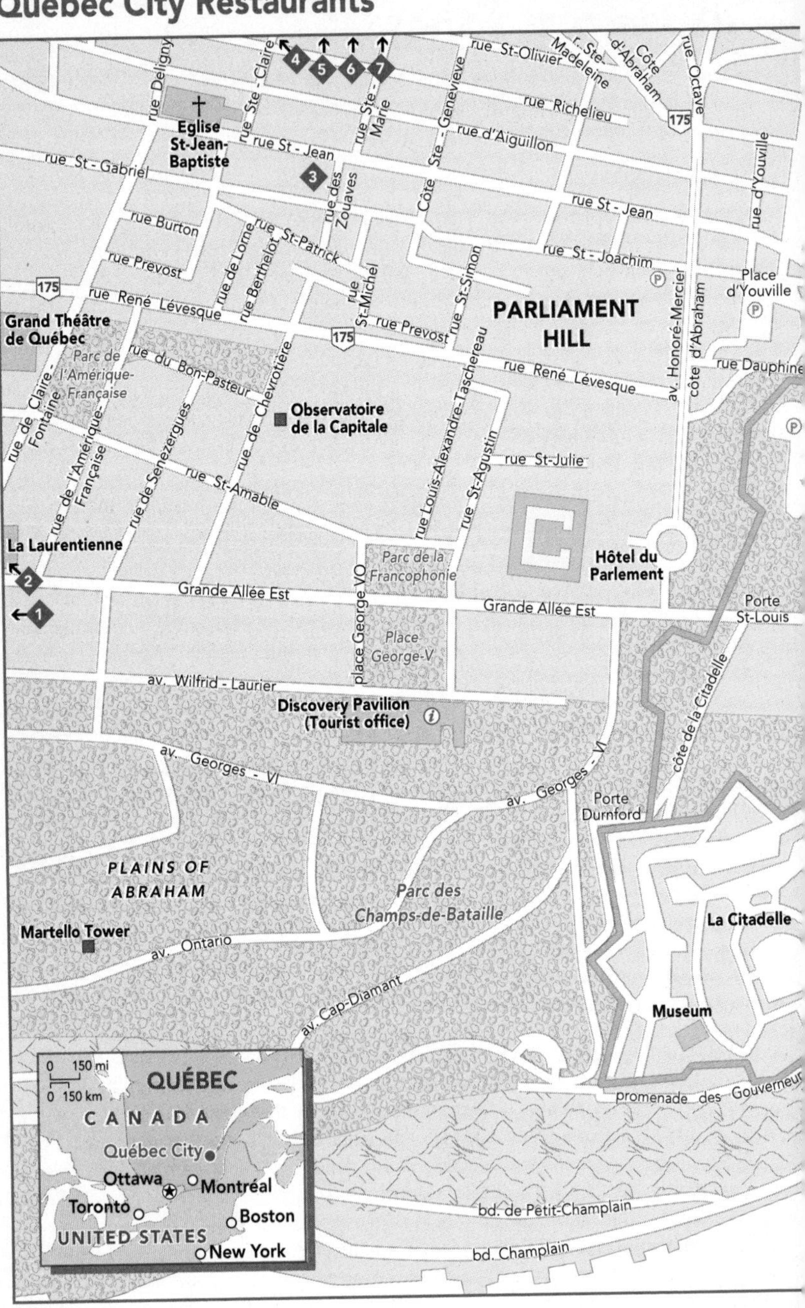

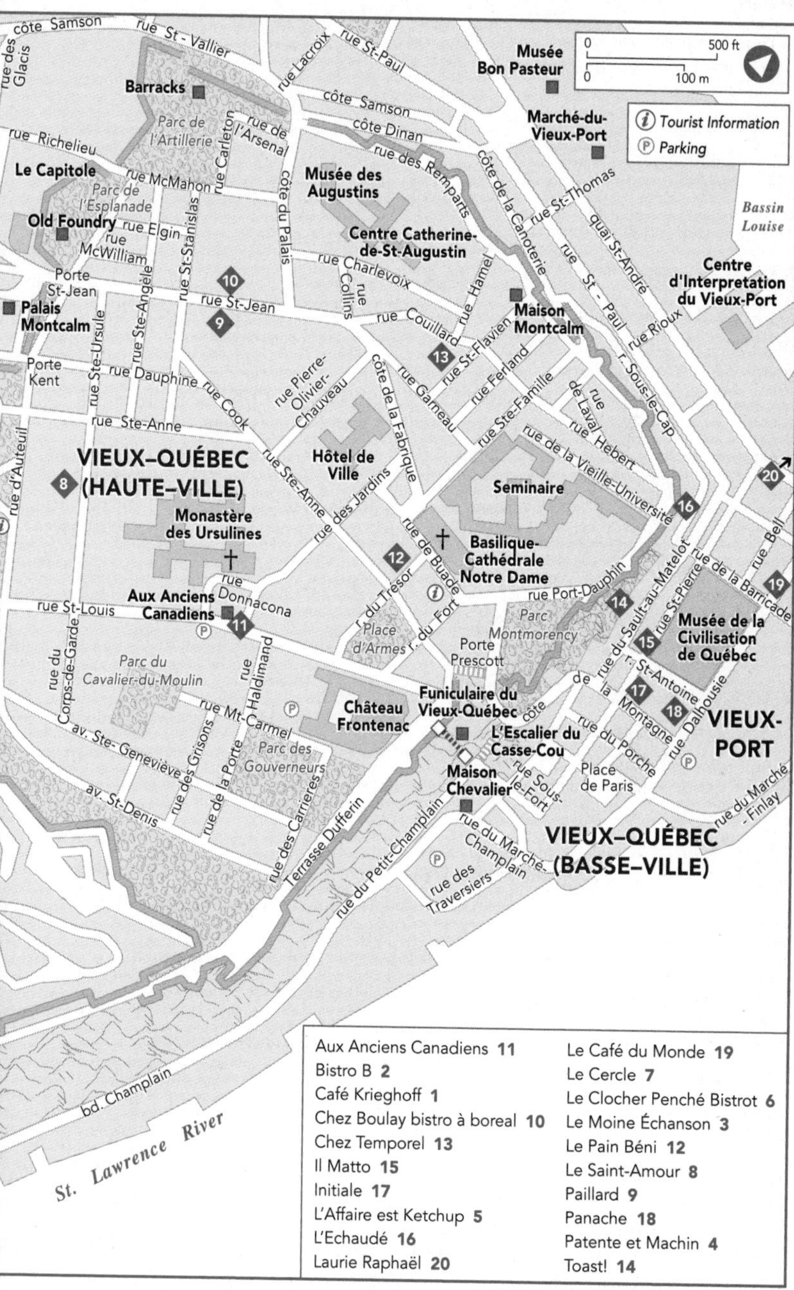
0 500 ft
0 100 m
Tourist Information
Parking
VIEUX–QUÉBEC (HAUTE–VILLE)
VIEUX–QUÉBEC (BASSE–VILLE)
VIEUX-PORT
Bassin Louise
St. Lawrence River
Musée Bon Pasteur
Marché-du-Vieux-Port
Barracks
Parc de l'Artillerie
Le Capitole
Parc de l'Esplanade
Old Foundry
Porte St-Jean
Palais Montcalm
Porte Kent
Musée des Augustins
Centre Catherine-de-St-Augustin
Centre d'Interpretation du Vieux-Port
Maison Montcalm
Hôtel de Ville
Seminaire
Monastère des Ursulines
Basilique-Cathédrale Notre Dame
Aux Anciens Canadiens
Parc du Cavalier-du-Moulin
Place d'Armes
Parc Montmorency
Porte Prescott
Musée de la Civilisation de Québec
Château Frontenac
Funiculaire du Vieux-Québec
L'Escalier du Casse-Cou
Maison Chevalier
Parc des Gouverneurs
Place de Paris
Terrasse Dufferin
côte Samson
rue des Glacis
rue St-Vallier
rue Lacroix
rue St-Paul
côte Dinan
rue de l'Arsenal
rue Richelieu
rue McMahon
rue Carleton
côte du Palais
rue des Remparts
côte de la Canoterie
rue St-Thomas
quai St-André
rue Elgin
rue McWilliam
rue St-Stanislas
rue Charlevoix
rue Collins
rue Hamel
rue St-Jean
rue Ste-Angèle
rue Ste-Ursule
rue Couillard
rue St-Flavien
rue Rioux
r. Sous-le-Cap
rue Dauphine
rue Cook
rue Pierre-Olivier-Chauveau
côte de la Fabrique
rue Garneau
rue Ferland
rue Ste-Famille
rue de Laval
rue Hebert
rue Ste-Anne
rue d'Auteuil
rue des Jardins
rue de la Vieille-Université
rue Bell
rue de Buade
rue Port-Dauphin
rue du Sault-au-Matelot
rue St-Pierre
rue de la Barricade
rue St-Louis
rue Donnacona
r. du Tresor
r. du Fort
r. St-Antoine
rue du Corps-de-Garde
rue Haldimand
rue Mt-Carmel
côte de la Montagne
rue du Porche
rue Dalhousie
av. Ste-Geneviève
rue des Grisons
rue de la Porte
rue des Carrieres
rue Sous-le-Fort
av. St-Denis
rue du Petit-Champlain
rue du Marché-Champlain
rue du Marché-Finlay
rue des Traversiers
bd. Champlain
Aux Anciens Canadiens 11
Bistro B 2
Café Krieghoff 1
Chez Boulay bistro à boreal 10
Chez Temporel 13
Il Matto 15
Initiale 17
L'Affaire est Ketchup 5
L'Echaudé 16
Laurie Raphaël 20
Le Café du Monde 19
Le Cercle 7
Le Clocher Penché Bistrot 6
Le Moine Échanson 3
Le Pain Béni 12
Le Saint-Amour 8
Paillard 9
Panache 18
Patente et Machin 4
Toast! 14

The Price You'll Pay

Here's what you can expect to pay for your main course at a restaurant in Québec City:

Expensive	C$20 and up
Moderate	C$10–C$20
Inexpensive	Under C$10

a vegetarian main on occasion). The now-infamous 2008 visit by Sir Paul McCartney (a vegetarian) to this establishment clearly had an impact. Desserts here may be the best in town.

48 Rue Sainte-Ursule (near rue St-Louis). www.saint-amour.com. ✆ **418/694-0667.** Reservations recommended. Main courses C$46–C$52; table d'hôte lunch C$18–C$33; discovery dinner C$115. Mon–Fri 11:30am–2pm; daily 6–10pm.

Moderate

Le Pain Béni ★★ CONTEMPORARY QUÉBÉCOIS If you want to sit outdoors on the touristy, pedestrian-only part of rue Ste-Anne (it can be abuzz with action), find an open table at Le Pain Béni. It pegs its menu as "bistronomique," a mix of high and low, with traditional French fare punctuated by avant-garde experimentation. Here's an example: smoked Québec deer carpaccio served with berries ketchup, mushroom and Parmesan espuma (foam), and a pickle. If that's too adventurous for you pulled pork mini burgers, or a choice of three kinds of pizza, may hit the spot. Indoor seating is also a fine choice, with exposed stone and brick walls from the 1600s. Le Pain Béni is located in the Auberge Place d'Armes (p. 148) and right next to the narrow art-lined walkway, rue du Trésor.

24 rue Ste-Anne (at rue du Trésor). www.painbeni.com. ✆ **866/333-9485** or 418/694-9485. Main courses C$18–C$35; table d'hôte cost of main plus C$10, or C$20 for a more elaborate version. May–Oct daily 11:30am–10pm; Nov–Apr daily 11:30am–2:30pm and 5:30–10pm.

Inexpensive

In addition to **Paillard,** below, children may like **Casse-Crêpe Breton,** 1136 rue St-Jean (www.cassecrepebreton.com; ✆ **418/692-0438**), for its savory and sweet crepes (C$6–C$9). Centrally located in the heart of Upper Town, it's usually packed at lunch. Go a little early or a little late to avoid the wait.

Chez Temporel ★ LIGHT FARE Québec's visitors often write up Chez Temporel as a "discovery," or as "authentically Québec" experience. That's what we like about it, too, especially in relation to this part of Upper Town near rue St-Jean, where non-chain restaurants can be hard to find. This modest, nine-table cafe covers the basics like coffee, quiche, and salad very well. For some reason tourists are unlikely to take a turn off the main drag (but not you!) so you may find yourself among local college students or a neighborhood dog-walker who stops in for a quick bite and orders in French. If you send the cafe a postcard that describes why you liked dining there, they may post it on the wall. In business since 1974, they're clearly doing something right.

25 rue Couillard (near rue Christie). ✆ **418/694-1813.** Most items under C$11. Mon–Fri 8am–10pm; Sat–Sun 9am–10pm.

Paillard ★★ LIGHT FARE Paillard has a high-end fast-food feel to it, but it's one of a kind, and thoroughly Québec. Frankly, it's what one wishes all fast food could be. The bread is crusty and sometimes piping hot, either used on sandwiches or served with soups that are (and taste) homemade. It's perfect for an affordable lunch or dinner that doesn't take hours, or for a coffee break with a formidable *macaron.* There are also salads and gelati. As a sign of its forward-thinking, Paillard unveiled the *crobeign* (half donut, half croissant; in English, called a cronut) before most other Eastern seaboard cities caught on to the trend.

1097 rue St-Jean (near rue St-Stanislas). www.paillard.ca. ✆ **418/692-1221.** All items under C$10. Daily 7am–10pm. Winter hours may be shorter.

VIEUX-QUÉBEC: BASSE-VILLE (LOWER TOWN)/VIEUX-PORT

This part of Lower Town is thick with hotels, and thus tourists, which means there are numerous dining options beyond what's listed below. Taken as a group, the establishments on or surrounding rue St-Paul and rue Sault-au-Matelot are expensive, but quite good, one to the next. You might have better luck happening upon a decent meal here than the restaurants clustered near Frontenac, or Lower Town near Petit-Champlain or Place Royale. In addition to the options listed below, food is also available in Lower Town at the bar **SSS** (p. 189), and the wine bar/music room **Le Pape-Georges** (p. 189).

Expensive

Il Matto ★ ITALIAN You might choose Il Matto because you're simply craving Italian or perhaps you want a change-up from Québécois bistro fare. Or maybe you want to sip cocktails among the fresh-faced after work crowd. The menu features Italian comfort food (Caesar salad, minestrone soup, pizza, spaghetti) in a high-energy, trendy atmosphere. (On a recent visit the house was jammed, midweek, early evening.) The young owner, Rocco Cortina, is gaining a following, with the resultant TV appearances.

71 rue St-Pierre (near rue St-Antoine). www.ilmatto.ca. ✆ **418/266-9444.** Reservations strongly recommended on weekends. Main courses C$17–C$30. Mon–Fri 11:30am–2pm and 5:30–11pm; Sat–Sun 5:30–11pm.

Initiale ★★★ CONTEMPORARY QUÉBÉCOIS Initiale sets the gold standard for dining in Québec City and in the province. Set on a charming corner amidst Lower Town's finest hotels, the entrance radiates an aura of serious decorum—the interior does as well. Ceilings are grandly high and there's enough distance between tables to privately gush as each course is expertly presented. That's why young and mature couples celebrate milestone anniversaries here. The menu is designed to hit complex notes in a minimum of four courses with the chef's strong preference being that you take the nine-course grand menu (C$129), which could start with locally caught turbot or mackerel with currant lemon sauce and move into new onion with rose vinegar or cream of corn and chanterelles. Duckling breast figures into the heartier dishes (still tiny by most standards), as does leg of lamb. Expect perfection with wine selection; you won't be disappointed. On that note, expect it of desserts, too, such as raspberries in clover sauce with milk *confiture* (a kind of thick, sweet caramel jam).

54 rue St-Pierre (corner of Côte de la Montagne). www.restaurantinitiale.com. ✆ **418/694-1818.** Reservations recommended on weekends. Table d'hôte lunch C$49; table d'hôte dinners C$69–C$89; grand tasting menu C$129. Tues–Fri 11:30am–2pm; Tues–Sat 6–9pm.

Laurie Raphaël ★★ CONTEMPORARY QUÉBÉCOIS Dining in this part of town can be very expensive, especially at accomplished restaurants like Laurie Raphaël. Here, there's an exceptional three-course "chef chef" lunch for C$29 per person. On sunny days, it's ideal to reserve a table on the corner terrace and let the server be your guide. Ask questions (Why "chef chef"?), savor starters like vichyssoise or mains like beef wonton with seared veggies, and ruminate about new methods to try at home. Hands-on learning may be an option because chef and owner Daniel Vézina frequently leads cooking classes on site. Dinner here can be an extraordinary culinary experience to add to a Québec City vacation.

117 rue Dalhousie (at rue St-André). www.laurieraphael.com. ✆ **418/692-4555.** Reservations recommended. Main courses C$43–C$50; 3-course chef-chef lunch C$29, dinner C$60; 10-course dinner C$115. Tues–Fri 11:30am–2pm; Tues–Sat 6–10pm. Note January closures.

L'Échaudé ★ BISTRO There are many menu combinations at this competent venue, such as table d'hôte and *carte d'hôte* (menu of the day) or additions to entrees or wine flights, which can make dining here a good value. The setting is confidently chic, as if the white linens and silver set themselves. The servers know bistro cuisine and the lengthy wine list like the backs of their hands. That's a good thing and why lots of locals frequent the place. The menu is classic—*tartares,* duck confit, steak frites, crème brûlée for dessert. Some diners may yearn for more excitement or innovation. A late-night discount kicks in after 9pm: A la carte menu items are 21 percent off.

73 rue Sault-au-Matelot (near rue St-Paul). www.echaude.com. ✆ **418/692-1299.** Reservations suggested on weekends. Main courses C$19–C$30; add C$12 for carte d'hôte or C$18 for table d'hôte. Mon–Fri 11:30am–2:30pm; Sat–Sun 10am–2:30pm; daily 5:30–10pm.

Panache ★★★ CONTEMPORARY QUÉBÉCOIS Panache is a superior restaurant housed in the repurposed buildings that make up the likewise superior hotel, **Auberge St-Antoine** (p. 150). Historic preservationists will appreciate that the massive wood beams and stone walls of a 19th century wharf have been incorporated into a rough-hewn, cleverly designed dining space (in summer, there's quite a terrace). Oenophiles, on the other hand, can choose from an extensive wine list (700+ labels from 14 countries). And locavores should know that the kitchen has an organic garden on the nearby Île d'Orléans. But let's talk meat: Beef, veal, and duck are locally sourced and served with the likes of chanterelles and garlic flower or blueberry reduction sauce. In recent years, Panache has taken its food on the road with a pop-up restaurant, a mobile food truck, and the casual **Café de la Promenade** on La Promenade Samuel-De Champlain (p. 180). All are versatile and seasonal; check the website for updates and open hours. Also inside the hotel and just down the hall from Panache is another dining option, **Café-Bar Artéfact,** which serves light meals and cocktails in cozy alcoves just off the main lobby.

10 rue St-Antoine (in Auberge St-Antoine). www.saint-antoine.com. ✆ **418/692-1022.** Reservations recommended. Main courses lunch C$20-C$26, dinner C$36–C$49; 7-course signature menu C$105. Mon–Fri 6:30–10:30am and noon–2pm; Sat–Sun 7–11am and 11:30am-2pm; daily 6–10pm.

Toast! ★ CONTEMPORARY QUÉBÉCOIS Chef and co-owner Christian Lemelin started cooking at age 17 and, now into his 30s, still seems young. His menu is agile and not afraid to reveal itself: "Duck breast from Canard Goulu farm, seared on its fat, comfit heart and gizzards" for example, served with "parsley root purée, fine green bean tempura with old balsamic & lardoons . . ." And so on. English-only speakers will appreciate such verbosity. Though prices are high (add seared foie gras to any entrée for C$20), the atmosphere is lively and laid-back. The outdoor terrace makes for memorable summer dining. The same owners run **SSS** around the corner (p. 189), which focuses on small plates and loud music.

17 rue Sault-au-Matelot (at rue St-Antoine). www.restauranttoast.com. ✆ **418/692-1334.** Reservations recommended on weekends. Mains C$29–C$39. Sun–Weds 6–10:30pm; Thurs–Sat 6–11pm.

EATING vegetarian IN A LAND THAT IS NOT

Vegetarians may be concerned about eating in Québec City, a destination with a rich regional cuisine, where calf brains are a delicacy and pies are made of meat.

Fortunately, many restaurants offer a standing veggie option, such as the *mezzelune* of homemade pasta, mascarpone cheese, and vegetables glazed with black garlic at **Toast!** (p. 162). Others will tweak an entrée if you call ahead and ask.

If you eat dairy products, a cheese plate traditionally served as a last course could become your main dish, although you'll have to ignore the raised eyebrows. You'll have limitless options, though, with the innovations of the province, which include Pied-de-Vent, Le Riopelle de l'Ile, and Le Migneron de Charlevoix. Those three cheeses, plus 150 more in summer, can be found at **La Fromagère du Marché** (✆ **418/692-2517,** ext. 238), in the **Marché du Vieux-Port.** While you're there, you'll find a generous selection of seasonally fresh fruits and vegetables, and freshly baked baguettes.

Tip: If the French language isn't your strong suit, assume that most dishes have meat and learn to recognize a few terms. Sorry to say, *saucisse* is sausage, not sauce, and *fruits de mer* do not grow on trees.

Moderate

Le Café du Monde ★ TRADITIONAL FRENCH This spacious waterfront restaurant simultaneously channels T.G.I. Friday's and traditional French cooking, with a long menu that truly has something for everyone. Count on the baby spinach salad, fries cooked in duck fat, or three-cheese fondue for starters and the black pudding as a main course. There's also super-tender rotisserie chicken and many options from the sea. Kids love the deep-fried ice cream with caramel sauce for dessert. It's one of few spots with outdoor seating that overlooks the St. Lawrence.

84 rue Dalhousie (next to the cruise terminal). www.lecafedumonde.com. ✆ **418/692-4455.** Reservations recommended. Main courses C$23–C$39; table d'hôte C$34–C$40. Mon–Fri 11:30am–11pm; Sat–Sun and holidays 9am–11pm.

PARLIAMENT HILL (ON OR NEAR GRANDE-ALLEE)

If you're a serious (or even a beginning) foodie, you might want to stroll rue St-Jean heading away from Old Town's gates. Along this stretch are artisan bread makers, baristas, tea purveyors and more (see also p. 175 in chapter 14). **La brûlerie de café de Québec** on 575 rue Saint-Jean (www.bruleriedecafe.com; ✆ **418/529-4769**) roasts its own beans and supplies area restaurants. In addition to the restaurant options listed below, food is also available on Grande-Allée at the bar/restaurant **Savini,** on p. 189.

Expensive

Bistro B ★ BISTRO This newish, open air, open kitchen bistro is a solid addition to city dining at large and to the Montcalm neighborhood just adjacent to Parliament Hill in particular. For one, it has cocktails that can be enjoyed out front in warm months and indoors at a cozy bar. (And it's not a mediocre, predictable list. Think daily specials with fresh local ingredients like basil gel or peach elixir.) The food menu follows suit. A recent visit started with a crisp yellow beet salad with apples and hazelnuts, followed by a main course of red deer with subtle (perhaps too much so) truffle sauce. Guinea fowl with roasted veggies looked appealing on the plates that sailed by. Menus on an iPad for the table augment the chalk on slate above the counter. The music was a bit amped and baseball shirts on servers a bit much (maybe that won't last the season), but all in all, an enjoyable spot.

1144 av Cartier (at rue Aberdeen). www.bistrob.ca. ✆ **418/614-5444.** Reservations recommended. Main courses C$20–C$32. Mon–Fri 11:30am–2pm; Sat–Sun 10am–2pm; daily 6–11pm.

Moderate

Le Moine Échanson ★★ CONTEMPORARY QUÉBÉCOIS This earthy, adventurous restaurant started as a kind of hole-in-the-wall kitchen, with a few oak barrels out front and lots of hanging plants. It served funky wines and food in jars and became the go-to for artsy, engaged eaters. Word spread (in part, by us) and it doubled in size and refined its overall look and feel. It still leads the pack for dishes cooked with butter, bacon, and intense cheeses and develops seasonal recipes to complement privately imported batches of wine. A source of pride is that guests can have a glass for C$6 to C$10 or a bottle for C$36 to C$60. Appetizers and cheese plates can start or end the night, served on house whim, between the hours of 5 and 6pm or 10pm and 1am.

585 rue St-Jean (at rue Ste-Marie). www.lemoineechanson.com. ✆ **418/524-7832.** Reservations recommended. Main courses C$16–C$30. Daily 6–11pm.

Inexpensive

For a quick snack, **Al Wadi,** 615 Grande-Allée est (✆ **418/649-8345**), is in the heart of the Grande-Allée party district and is open 10:30am till 4am Wednesday through Sunday (from 10:30am–11:30pm Mon–Tues). Gyros, *shawarma,* falafel, and other veggie options are on tap.

Café Krieghoff ★★★ LIGHT FARE Café Krieghoff can be habit-forming, especially if you visit Québec City often enough. It may not wow or woo those seeking haute cuisine, but it can make you feel like you're taking an afternoon off from tourists and settling in to a low-profile Québécois way of life. Partly it's the Montcalm neighborhood, just 10 minutes walk from the Parliament building down Grande-Allée, a right turn on avenue Cartier. (Set aside time to browse the 5-block street of gourmet food shops, clothing boutiques, and locally made goods; p. 176.) And partly it's the great coffee, reliable cooking, friendly service, and chance to sit outside.

1089 av. Cartier (north of Grande-Allée). www.cafekrieghoff.qc.ca. ✆ **418/522-3711.** Most items under C$19. Mon–Fri 7am–10pm; Sat–Sun 8am–10pm.

ST-ROCH

St-Roch's still-up-and-coming restaurant scene runs along a street with excellent bakeries, coffee shops, and ethnic food options. Two favorites include **Le Croquembouche** (225 rue Saint-Joseph est; www.lecroquembouche.com; ✆ **418/523-9009**), for baked goods, and the coffee shop **Brûlerie St-Roch** (375 rue St-Joseph est; www.brulerie-st-roch.com; ✆ **418/529-1559**).

Expensive

Le Clocher Penché Bistrot ★★★ BISTRO Clocher Penché has laid-back European sophistication down pat. Its early presence in the bohemian St-Roch neighborhood has paved the way for other experimental, down-home restaurants to take form and it has a loyal local following. The shifting menu relies on regional *terroir*—from homemade cavatelli with lobster cream to blood sausage over grilled hearts of romaine—and service is efficient and friendly. Definitely save room for a dessert!

203 rue St-Joseph est (at rue Caron). www.clocherpenche.ca. ✆ **418/640-0597.** Reservations recommended. Main courses C$21–C$26; table d'hôte lunch and weekend brunch C$16. Tues–Fri 11:30am–2pm; Sat–Sun 9am–2pm; Tues–Sat 5–10pm.

Moderate

L'Affaire est Ketchup ★ BISTRO The expression, "*l'affaire est ketchup*," is unique to the province (or so claim the locals) and means "it's all good" or "everything's cool." Rightly so at this boho slip of a restaurant (we are talking small and seriously homespun). You could walk past the half run-down exterior a few times, mistaking it for a soup kitchen. That's just part of the charm. Inside, the chef whips up magic like duck *magret* or scallops with celeriac purée from a kitchen that makes an Easy Bake Oven look like a six-burner Viking. It was the city's best-kept secret until American chef and TV host Anthony Bourdain brought the cameras around.

46 rue St-Joseph est (near boul. Langelier). www.laffaireestketchup.net. ✆ **418/529-9020.** Main courses C$14–C$25; table d'hôte lunch C$15 (plus dessert). Tues–Sat 11am–9pm.

Le Cercle ★★★ FUSION Here's a perfect spot to gather with friends, order "tapas mania" (small plates on chef's whim from C$10–C$50 per person), and choose a bottle or two from Le Cercle's carefully selected wines. Sommelier and co-owner Fréderic Gauthier really knows his stuff. Some tapas plates are built around sturgeon or salmon, smoked in-house, or incorporate wine into flavorful sauces. Many come with a side of pickled vegetables or other creative condiments. At brunch on the weekends, *le pain doré* (French toast) is topped with a mouth-watering combo of rhubarb compote, ricotta, pecans, and maple syrup. On Saturdays, kids under 12 eat free (from a designated menu) when accompanied by an adult. The bar is open late and there's a plethora of films and other live entertainment held in the adjacent space.

226½ rue St-Joseph est (near rue Caron). www.le-cercle.ca. ✆ **418/948-8648.** Reservations recommended on weekends. Tapas C$5–C$14; main courses C$15–C$34; tapas mania C$10–C$50 per person. Mon–Wed 11:30am–1:30am; Thurs–Fri 11:30am–3am; Sat 10am–3am; Sun 10am–1:30am.

Patente et Machin ★ BISTRO Not surprisingly, this way casual undertaking has ties to **L'Affaire est Ketchup** (see above, same owners). In this instance the name's rough translation is "thingies and gadgets" or maybe, food-wise, "nibbles and bites." That's how the menu is divided: *Machins* are small-ish: oysters, bisques, and such, while *Patentes* are main courses like red deer with juniper berries or giant roasted scallops. *Grosses patentes* are main courses built for two. Dining in this cramped, boisterous spot among folks in their 30s felt as close to going to a friend's house for dinner as we could imagine—that is, if the friend is crazy into high-quality food and goes the extra mile, but keeps it simple. No foam, gels, sprays, or pomades in sight here. Service is slow and inattentive but, then again, so are a lot of friends.

82 rue St-Joseph ouest (near rue St-Valier). www.facebook.com/Patente.et.Machin. ✆ **581/981-3999.** Main courses C$14–C$20. Daily 6–10pm.

EXPLORING QUÉBEC CITY

14

Wandering the streets of Vieux-Québec is a singular pleasure, comparable to exploring a provincial capital in Europe. You might happen upon an ancient convent, gabled houses with steeply pitched roofs, a battery of 18th-century cannons in a leafy park, or a bistro with a blazing fireplace on a wintry day.

Vieux-Québec (or the Old City) is so compact that it's hardly necessary to plan precise sightseeing itineraries. Most of the historic sights are within the city walls of Haute-Ville (Upper Town) and Basse-Ville (Lower Town). Start at Terrasse Dufferin alongside the Château Frontenac and go off on a whim, down L'Escalier du Casse-Cou (Breakneck Stairs) to the Quartier du Petit-Champlain and Place-Royale, or out of the walls to the military fortress of the Citadelle that overlooks the mighty St. Lawrence River and onto the Plains of Abraham, where generals James Wolfe of Britain and Louis-Joseph, marquis de Montcalm of France, fought to their mutual deaths in a 20-minute battle that changed the continent's destiny.

A few winding, somewhat steep roads (or the Breakneck Stairs or *funiculaire*) connect Upper and Lower Town. Upper Town it can also be hilly, with sloping streets, but only people with physical limitations are likely to experience difficulty. Other sights are outside Upper Town's walls, along or just off the boulevard called Grande-Allée. If rain or ice discourages exploration on foot, tour buses and horse-drawn *calèches* are options as well as an electric city bus that loops by most major sights.

QUÉBEC CITY'S ICONIC SIGHTS

- Basilique Cathédral Notre-Dame de Québec ★★★, p. 172
- Château Frontenac ★★★, p. 172
- Fortifications-de-Québec ★, p. 180
- Hôtel du Parlement ★, p. 176
- La Citadelle ★★, p. 173
- L'Escalier du Casse-Cou ★, p. 167
- Musée de la Civilisation ★★★, p. 167
- Musée National des Beaux-Arts ★★★, p. 176
- Parc des Champs-des-Bataille, p. 181
- Place-Royale ★★★, p. 170
- Quartier de Petit-Champlain, p. 171

OTHER TOP ATTRACTIONS

- La Promenade Samuel-De Champlain ★★, p. 180
- Marché du Vieux-Port ★★, p. 172
- Musée de l'Amérique Françopphone ★★, p. 174
- Observatoire de la Capitale, p. 177
- Rue du Trésor ★, p. 174

VIEUX-QUÉBEC: BASSE-VILLE (LOWER TOWN) ATTRACTIONS

If this is your first trip to Québec City, consider starting with the walking tour of this area in chapter 16.

L'Escalier du Casse-Cou ★ These stairs connect Terrasse Dufferin at the top of the cliff (in Upper Town) with rue Sous-le-Fort at the base (Lower Town). The name translates to "Breakneck Stairs," and they are, indeed, very steep, although hardly neck-break-inducing anymore. A stairway has existed here since the settlement began. Nestled along the northern side of the steps (to the right after you've come down) are good quality bistros, small shops, and even a chocolate store. In 1698, the town council had to explicitly forbid citizens from taking their animals up or down the stairway, and those who didn't comply were punished with a fine.

Maison Historique Chevalier ★★ As part of Les Musées de la Civilisation (see below), this and two neighboring homes evidence the urban architecture of New France. Built in 1752 and rebuilt 10 years later, Maison Chevalier's asymetrical design followed what used to be a shoreline. Walls, as well as window and door openings, are made of regional sandstone and limestone. Indoor tours process through rooms decorated with furnishings representative of Québec's different political regimes during the 18th and 19th centuries. For a bird's-eye view of the Old City's shifting layout and its facades, see the 45-minute 3-D movie, "In Our History's Footsteps."

50 rue du Marché-Champlain (at rue). www.mcq.org. ✆ **866/710-8031** or 418/643-2158. Admission C$5.50 adults, C$5.25 seniors, C$5.25 students, C$2 children 12–16, free for children 11 and under. Late June to early-Sept daily 9:30am–5pm; Mid-Sept to Oct Tues–Sun 10am–5pm; Oct–Dec and Jan–May Sat–Sun 10am–5pm.

Musée de la Civilisation ★★★ This engaging museum can be both a geographic and cultural touchstone for a visit to Québec City. It sits prominently in the center of Lower Town, between rue St-Paul and Dalhousie (entrance side) and promises info-packed, interactive permanent and touring exhibitions. Open since 1988, this is the lead of three related museums whose objectives include ethnographic collecting, preservation, and stimulation of an evolving cultural conversation about the history of Québec and its peoples. (The other two are Musée de l'Amérique Francophone and Musée de la place Royale; you can get a discount for purchasing admission to all three.) The permanent exhibit, "People of Québec . . . Then and Now," winds the clock back more than 400 years with audio recordings based on accounts from actual historic figures. Archival documents, flags, clothing, furniture, musical instruments, and toys are also on view with interpreation in French and English. Through March 2014, "Game Story" taps a more recent (and not uniquely Québécois) obsession, video games. The exhibit is organized by the technological leaps from 1970s to present day with a nod to the province's role in video game creation. Plan a few hours to a half day

Québec City Attractions

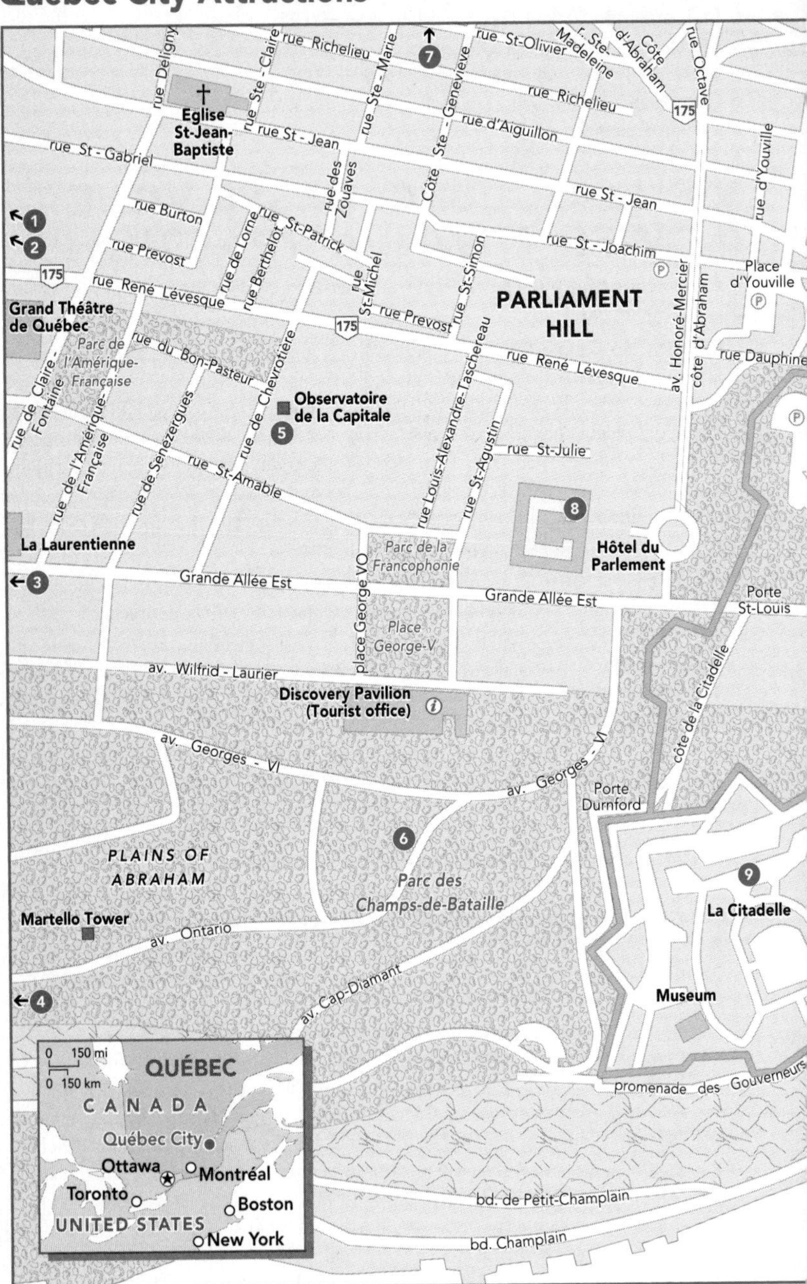

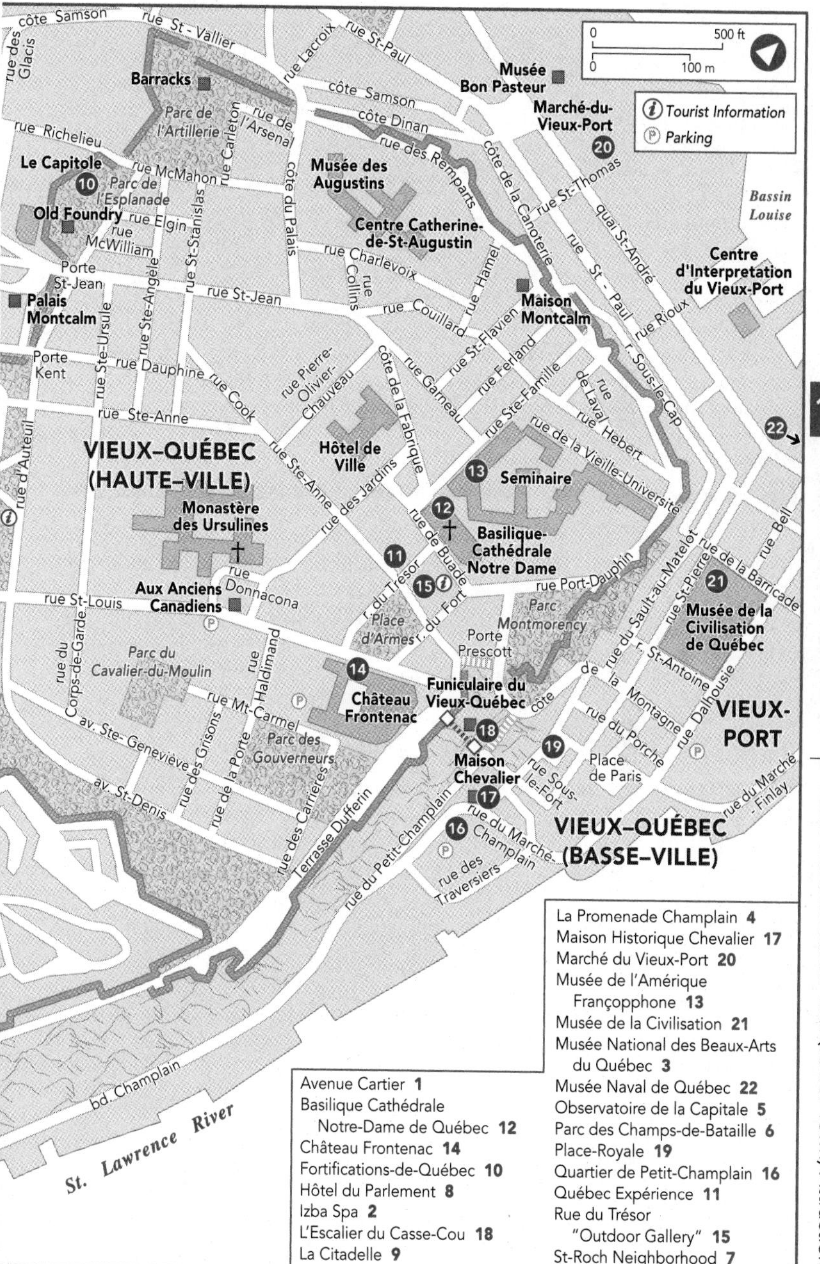

Vieux-Québec: Basse-Ville (Lower Town) Attractions

au revoir **FREE CIRQUE DU SOLEIL AND IMAGE MILL?**

Two groundbreaking events, launched to help celebrate Québec City's 400th anniversary in 2008, were so beloved they returned for five summer encores. The ever-innovative **Cirque du Soleil,** which got its start just north of Québec City, put on free—yes, free—outdoor performances every Tuesday through Saturday evening from June 24 to Labour Day. For many years the troupe performed under a highway intersection (gritty and très cool) then it moved to the harbor to share a double bill with artist Robert LaPage's ***Moulin des Images*** (Image Mill). Entirely unique to Québec City, LePage's three different multimedia shows were projected in Vieux-Port along 600m (over a third of a mile) of industrial grain silos and produced an outdoor community event, akin to nightly fireworks displays. As we go to print, there is no plan for either show to continue in 2014. However, since both were such spectacular jewels in Québec's already encrusted crown, our fingers are crossed that one or both might reappear. If so, you should make every effort to take in this top-notch entertainment for all ages. Check the city tourist office, www.cirquedusoleil.com or www.lacaserne.net/index2.php/other_projects.

for this museum as there are usually about five concurrent exhibits. The onsite cafe overlooks the St. Lawrence and serves wine and beer.

85 rue Dalhousie (at rue St-Antoine). www.mcq.org. ✆ **866/710-8031** or 418/643-2158. Admission C$15 adults, C$14 seniors, C$10 students, C$5 children 12–16, free for children 11 and under; free to all Nov–March Tues and Jan–Feb Sat 10am–noon. Three museum discount (Musée de la Civilisation, Musée de l'Amérique Francophone, and Musée de la place Royale), good for 2 weeks after purchase: C$23 adults, C$21 seniors, C$16 students, C$7 kids 12–16, free under 12. Late June to early-Sept daily 9:30am–6:30pm; mid-Sept to late June Tues–Sun 10am–5pm.

Musée Naval de Québec ★ This museum details the birth of the Canadian Navy and the military support provided by ships via the St. Lawrence, including supply and troop delivery to battles on the Plains of Abraham. On prominent display is the Silver Destroyer, a Naval trophy forged by goldsmiths, as well as a model privateer schooner. The website includes several "capsule" video clips with highlights and a virtual museum (www.privateers.ca) that examines the difference between pirates and "privateers," or, pirates in service to the King. Groups are advised to request tours in advance.

170 rue Dalhousie (near boul. Champlain). ✆ **418/694-5387.** www.navalmuseumofquebec.com. Free admission. June–Sept daily 10am–5pm; Sept–Oct Wed–Sun 10am–noon and 1–4pm. Call for hours Oct–May.

Place-Royale ★★★ This small, but picturesque plaza is considered by Québécois to be the literal and spiritual heart of Basse-Ville—in grander terms, the birthplace of French America. There's a **bust of Louis XIV** in the center. In the 17th and 18th centuries, Place-Royal, or "Royal Square," was the town marketplace, and the center of business and industry. **Eglise Notre-Dame-des-Victoires** (see the box on p. 173 about its parish's 350th anniversary) dominates the plaza. It's Québec's oldest stone church, built in 1688 after a massive fire in Lower Town destroyed 55 homes in 1682. The church was restored in 1763 and again in 1969. Its paintings, altar, and large model boat suspended from the ceiling were votive offerings brought by early settlers to ensure safe voyages. The church is open daily to visitors May through September, and admission is free. Sunday Masses are held at 10:30am and noon. During one visit there was a wedding that had just ended, and the whole square was there to greet the new couple as they exited their church.

Commercial activity here began to stagnate around 1860, and by 1950, this was a poor, rundown district. Rehabilitation began in 1960, and all the buildings on the square have now been restored, though only some of the walls are original. One building now houses the **Musée de la place Royale** on the ground floor, an affiliate of Les Musées de la Civilisation. Here, a 3-D movie about Samuel Champlain and other exhibitions detail the city's 400-year history. When you exit, turn left and, at the end of the block, turn around to view a *trompe l'oeil* mural depicting citizens of the early city.

Musée de la place Royale 27 rue Notre-Dame. www.mcq.org. ✆ **866/710-8031** or 418/646-3167. Centre admission C$7 adults, C$6 seniors, C$5 students, C$2 children 12–16, free for children 11 and under; free to all Nov–Mar Tues and Jan–Feb Sat 10am–noon. Three museum discount (Musée de la Civilisation, Musée de l'Amérique Francophone, and Musée de la place Royale), good for 2 weeks after purchase: C$23 adults, C$21 seniors, C$16 students, C$7 kids12–16, free under 12. Late June to early-Sept daily 9:30am–5pm; mid-Sept to late June Tues–Sun 10am–5pm.

Shopping in Lower Town

At the bottom of the Breakneck stairs and the *funiculaire* is the quaint **Quartier de Petit-Champlain,** an area of *petit* (small) winding cobblestone streets. The curved rue du Petit-Champlain is pedestrian-only and the main point of interest. Restored houses in the *quartier* have been turned into clothing boutiques, specialty shops, and galleries, some of which feature locally made products—but you'll find a substantial number of trinkets and T-shirts sold here, too. Petit-Champlain attracts more visiting shoppers than locals, tilting the products toward Québec-centric items.

About a half-dozen antiques shops line **rue St-Paul** near the waterfront on the opposite end of Lower Town. They're filled with knickknacks, Québec country furniture, candlesticks, old clocks, Victoriana, Art Deco and Art Moderne objects, and the increasingly sought-after kitsch and housewares of the early post–World War II period. **Machin Chouette,** 225 rue St-Paul (www.machinchouette.com; ✆ **418/525-9898**), hand selects antiques for homes with a modern flair and also makes custom storage units out of album covers, vinyl records, and wood butter boxes. At **Les Antiquités Bolduc,** 89 rue St-Paul (www.lesantiquitesbolduc.com; ✆ **418/694-9558**), brother-and-sister duo Stéphanie and Frédéric Bolduc sell vintage knickknacks, such as antique sconces and grandfather clocks.

These are other special shops where you can find uniquely Québécois goods:

Boutique des Métiers d'Art In a stone building at the corner of Place-Royale, this carefully arranged store displays works by scores of Québécois craftspeople, at least some of which are likely to appeal to almost any customer. Among these objects are wooden boxes, jewelry, graphics, and a variety of gifts. When departing, be sure to turn left, walk past the end of the building, and turn around—it's a surprise! 29 rue Notre-Dame. www.metiers-d-art.qc.ca. ✆ **418/694-0267.**

Les Fourrures du Vieux-Port The fur trade underwrote the development and exploration of Québec and the vast lands west, and continues to be important to the region to this day. This Lower Town merchant has as good a selection as any, including knit furs and shearlings, along with designer coats by Christia and Olivieri. The store was recently renovated and now boasts three floors. 55 rue St-Pierre (at Côte de la Montagne). www.quebecfurs.com. ✆ **866/692-6688** or 418/692-6686.

Marché du Vieux-Port ★★ Local produce, seafood, cheeses, baked goods, and other regional products such as maple syrup, *vin de cidre* (cider wine), and cassis are featured all year at this indoor farmer's market. A handy online guide specifies exactly what's in season when: *betteraves* (sugar beets) from July to November, for example, and *pétoncles* (scallops) every month of the year. Perfect for a stroll and snack. They open at 9am everyday and close at 6pm on weekdays, 5pm on weekends. 160 Quai Saint-André. www.marchevieuxport.com. ✆ **418/692-2517.**

Vert Tuyau Coop The fused-glass jewelry, turned-wood bowls, and felted wool garments here are all 100-percent Québec-made. This artist collective was founded to offer tourists an alternative to trinkets made and shipped from the other side of the globe. 46 rue du Petit-Champlain. www.verttuyau.com. ✆ **418/692-1111.**

VIEUX-QUÉBEC: HAUTE-VILLE (UPPER TOWN) ATTRACTIONS

One way to think of Upper Town's layout is to imagine what kind of structures you would build on higher ground, especially 400 years ago. Perhaps a glorious castle to welcome visitors as they enter the city? (Château Frontenac has that covered.) Some kind of military protection? (That would be La Citadelle.) How about the mother of all Catholic churches (Notre Dame Basilica, *merci.*)

And what would surround these historic landmarks in modern day? On the streets Côte de la Fabrique and rue St-Jean, there are shops, bars, and restaurants with a feel that is slightly more everyday than Lower Town's Petit-Champlain. In part, this means McDonald's. It also means that some of Canada's major clothing stores (Roots, Tristan, Bedo) have a presence in this area, which can be its own point of exploration.

A walking tour of the Old City's Upper Town is on p. 191.

Basilique Cathédrale Notre-Dame de Québec ★★★ Notre-Dame Basilica, representing the oldest Christian parish north of Mexico, has weathered a tumultuous history of bombardment, reconstruction, and restoration. In 2014 it celebrates 350 years as home to the mother parish to all of North America (see below). Parts of the existing basilica date from the original 1647 structure, including the bell tower and portions of the walls, but most of today's exterior is from the reconstruction completed in 1771. The interior, a re-creation undertaken after a fire in 1922, is flamboyantly neo-baroque, with glinting yellow gold leaf and shadows wavering by the fluttering light of votive candles. It's beautifully maintained, with pews buffed to a shine. Paintings and ecclesiastical treasures still remain from the time of the French regime, including a chancel lamp given by Louis XIV. More than 900 people are buried in the crypt, including four governors of New France. Groups should reserve the 1-hour guided visits to the cathedral and the crypt in advance by phone.

20 rue Buade (at Côte de la Fabrique). www.patrimoine-religieux.com. ✆ **418/694-0665.** Free; donations encouraged. Crypt tour C$5. Cathedral Mon–Sat 7am–close (4, 5, or 8:30pm depending on season); Mass Mon–Fri 8am and 12:05pm; Sat 8am and 5pm; Sun 9:30 and 11am (and 5pm May–Oct).

Château Frontenac ★★★ It used to be that visitors curious about the interior of Québec City's most iconic building could take guided tours of the hotel. No longer.

350 YEARS OF CATHOLIC faith

In 1664, Bishop François de Laval founded what is now considered the "mother-parish" of all North American Catholic parishes on the shores of the mighty St. Lawrence—**Notre-Dame de Québec.** In 2014, the parish celebrates its 350th anniversary. Through those many generations, the parish has had accomplishments that include establishing a convent of the Ursuline community (it got permission from Louis XIII, King of France) and a seminary to instruct the First Nations. It also established and oversees the **Basilica Cathedral of Notre-Dame de Québec** and the **Notre-Dame-des-Victoires** church, two active faith communities.

Celebratory events will run throughout the calendar year, within three sections: The Jubilee (a year of grace), The Pilgrimage (a journey of faith), and The Holy Door (a passage that leads to inner peace). These will take form as feasts, blessings, summits, conferences, special exhibits at local museums, musical performances, and a self-guided pilgrimage that persons of all faiths are encouraged to complete. For more information, or to commit to a pilgrimage visit http://notredamedequebec.org.

But you can still take in the plush lobby or any of its three restaurants, including the **St-Laurent Bar et Lounge** (p. 188) and **Café de la Terrasse,** which serves an afternoon tea on Saturdays ($37 per person, May–Oct). Designed as a version of a Loire Valley palace, the hotel opened in 1893 to house railroad passengers and encourage tourism. It's visible from almost every quarter of the city, commanding its majestic position atop Cap Diamant, the rock bluff that once provided military defense.

1 rue des Carrières, at Place d'Armes. www.fairmont.com/frontenac-quebec. ✆ **866/540-4460** or 418/692-3861.

La Citadelle ★★ The duke of Wellington had this partially star-shaped fortress built at the south end of the city walls in anticipation of renewed American attacks after the War of 1812. Some remnants of earlier French military structures were incorporated into the Citadelle, including a 1750 magazine. Dug into the Plains of Abraham high above Cap Diamant (Cape Diamond), the rock bluff adjacent to the St. Lawrence River, the fort has a low profile that keeps it all but invisible until walkers are actually upon it. The facility has never actually exchanged fire with an invader, but still continues its vigil for the state. It's now a national historic site and, since 1950, has been home to Québec's **Royal 22e Régiment,** the only fully Francophone unit in Canada's armed forces. That makes it North America's largest fortified group of buildings still occupied by troops. Admission includes a guided tour to the Citadelle and its 25 buildings, as well as the small regimental museums in the former powder house and prison. The long walk could test the patience of younger visitors and the legs of many older people, though. For them, it might be better simply to attend the 35-minute choreographed ceremony of the **Changing of the Guard,** which runs from daily at 10am from June 24 until the first Monday of September. It's an elaborate ritual inspired by the Changing of the Royal Guard in London and is included in the regular admission fee. Note that it can be cancelled if the weather's bad. The 22e celebrates its 100th anniversay in 2014 with new exhibits and free activities to be announced.

1 Côte de la Citadelle (at rue St-Louis). www.lacitadelle.qc.ca. ✆ **418/694-2815.** Admission C$10 adults, C$9 seniors and students, C$5.50 children 8–17, free for children 7 and under; families C$25. May–Sept daily 9am–5pm; Oct-April 10am-4pm.

Musée de l'Amérique Francophone ★★ The spoils of a 5-year archeological excavation on the Cap-Rouge Promontory are a noteworthy addition to this museum devoted to the migration of French speaking populations to Canada and the U.S. "The Rediscovered Colony: a Section of Our History Revealed!" features highlights from the nearly 6,000 objects brought to light from the first European colony north of Mexico, which dates back to 1541. Shards of pottery and corn kernels, for example, suggest that the colonists, led by Jacques Cartier and Jean-François de La Rocque de Roberval, bartered with local Amerindians. The exhibit is on view until 2015 along with a permanent exhibit about the Francophone odyssey and art culled from the collection of the Séminaire de Québec in celebration of its 350th anniversary. The museum is located on the site of the seminary and visitors can tour the now-secularized chapel, which still displays a few saint relics. The seminary's stunning inner courtyard is one of the most photographed nooks in the city.

2 Côte de la Fabrique (next to Basilique Notre-Dame). www.mcq.org. ✆ **866/710-8031** or 418/692-2843. Admission C$8 adults, C$7 seniors, C$5.50 students, C$2 children 12–16, free to all Nov–May Tues and Jan–Feb Sat 10am–noon. Three museum discount (Musée de la Civilisation, Musée de l'Amérique Francophone, and Musée de la place Royale), good for 2 weeks after purchase: C$23 adults, C$21 seniors, C$16 students, C$7 kids12–16, free under 12. Late June to early-Sept daily 9:30am–5pm; mid-Sept to late June Tues–Sun 10am–5pm.

Québec Expérience ★ This multisensory 3-D historical recap has action-seeking kids (or action movies) in mind. It promises "30 minutes of emotions" that will make you "pulsate to the greatest moments in the development of the city." There's the anticipated chronology of events—from the Amerindians to European explorers and their subsequent plagues, battles, and triumphs. And then there are the cannons that point at you in your seat and a simulated fire that seems to envelop the theater, screams and all. While not all viewers are convinced by the special effects, it is one way to pummel the lessons of history home.

8 rue du Trésor (second floor). www.quebecexperience.com. ✆**418/694-4000.** Admission C$9.50 adults, C$7 seniors and students, free for children 5 and under, C$26 family. Mid-May to Sept daily 10am–10pm; Oct to mid-May daily 10am–5pm. English- and French-language shows alternate throughout the day.

Rue du Trésor "Outdoor Gallery" ★ Sooner or later, everyone passes this small outdoor alley near the Place d'Armes. Artists gather along here much of the year to exhibit and sell their work. Most of the prints on view are of Québec scenes and can make attractive souvenirs. The artists seem to enjoy chatting with interested passersby.

Rue du Trésor (between rue Ste-Anne & rue Buade). www.ruedutresor.qc.ca.

Shopping in Upper Town

Upper Town shops cater to all ends of the spectrum, from high-end collectors of Inuit art to packs of teenagers on school vacations looking for T-shirts with crude jokes. As with Lower Town, Upper Town is small enough that you can wander at leisure without the risk of getting lost.

Crocs The recipe behind Crocs originated in Québec and this two-story store is chock full of the latest styles made in multicolored, marshmallow rubber. 1073 rue St-Jean (at rue St-Stanislas). www.crocs.com. ✆**418/266-0262.**

Galerie Brousseau et Brousseau ★ In 2005, the important Inuit art collection assembled over 50 years by Québécois Raymond Brousseau was acquired by the

RUE ST-JEAN: A feast OF FOOD

Take a walk along rue St-Jean and head several blocks past the city walls (and, technically, out of the Old City's Upper Town) and your tastebuds will quickly thank you. This section, called Faubourg St-Jean, has a reputation for its grocers, butchers, and gourmet foods. **Choco-Musée Érico** (634 rue St-Jean; www.chocomusee.com; ✆ **418/524-2122**), about 5 blocks outside Upper Town walls is an adorable chocolate shop that includes a small room with historical information about how chocolate is made. Flavors include Szechuan, jasmine, chai cardamom, and hibiscus sorbet. **Épicerie J.A. Moisan** (699 rue St-Jean, 4 blocks outside Upper Town walls; www.jamoisan.com; ✆ **418/522-0685**) is a can't-miss food emporium. It must stock close to 30 types of olives, for instance, and the case is full of delicious prepared goodies and cooking supplies like duck fat. It claims to be the oldest grocery store in North America (it dates back to 1871). You may be wondering where to find a bottle of wine to take back to your room? Liquor and other spirits can be sold only in stores operated by **Société des Alcools du Québec,** the provincial agency known as SAQ. There's one at 853 rue St-Jean (near aut Dufferin Montmorency; www.saq.com; ✆ **418/643-4337**) and another at 1059 avenue Cartier.

Musée des Beaux-Arts du Québec, and 285 works from the 2,635-piece collection are on display at that museum. Here, you can buy Native Canadian carvings selected by the same family to take home. This is the most prominent of the city's art dealers, and it offers certificates of authenticity. Prices are high, but competitive for merchandise of similar quality. The shop is set up like a gallery, so feel free just to browse. 35 rue St-Louis (at rue des Jardins). www.sculpture.artinuit.ca. ✆ **418/694-1828.**

Les Délices de l'Érable We were skeptics of this all-maple-to-all people storefront, too, and then we saw the sign for maple-drenched donuts. Served hot. Yum. It turns out this little shop has a tiny museum (as does its Montréal location) and admission is free. It describes the traditional maple sap harvest methods and the many different products made from the sweet stuff. Many are, of course, available to purchase and sample firsthand. Whether you stop here or some place else selling maple-infused goodies, you shouldn't leave town without some kind of maple experience. 1044 rue Saint-Jean (near rue Ste-Angele). www.mapledelights.com. ✆ **418/692-3245.**

LOGO Sport A fun stop for the sports-crazed. You can buy brand new Nordique gear here (though Quebec's beloved hockey team moved in 1995) and classic Canadian match-ups play on an overhead TV. 1028 rue St-Jean (at rue Ste-Ursule). www.logosport.ca. ✆ **418/692-1351.**

Sachem Fur hats, baby moccasins, carvings, music, and jewelry are all packed into this compact boutique, which specializes in *"art amérindien."* Included are a variety of miniature Inukshuk human figurines, which look like they've been made of stacked rocks. 17 rue des Jardins (near Hôtel-de-Ville). ✆ **418/692-3056.**

Simons ★ Vieux-Québec's only department store opened here in 1840. Small by modern standards, a recent expansion upped the ante at this trendy and generally inexpensive clothing retailer for women, men, and teens. 20 Côte de la Fabrique (near the Hôtel-de-Ville). www.simons.ca. ✆ **418/692-3630.**

PARLIAMENT HILL ATTRACTIONS

The imposingly grand Parliament building lies just outside the city walls on Grande-Allée. Where the politics end the party begins: the few blocks west of Parliament pulses with city nightlife. Compared to Vieux-Québec the buildings on Parliament Hill are taller and more modern, and there's open space to spare especially since the expansive park called the Plains of Abraham runs the length of this district.

Hôtel du Parlement ★ Since 1968, what the Québécois call their "National Assembly," has occupied this imposing Second Empire château constructed in 1886. Twenty-two bronze statues of some of the most prominent figures in the province's tumultuous history grace the facade. Inside, highlights include the Assembly Chamber and the Legislative Council Chamber, where parliamentary committees meet. Throughout the building, representations of the fleur-de-lis and the initials VR (for Victoria Regina) remind visitors of Québec's dual heritage. Free 30-minute guided tours are available weekdays year-round, and weekends in summer. Tours start at the Parliament building visitor center; enter at door no. 3. Note that during summer hours, tours of the gardens are also available.

The grand Beaux Arts–style restaurant **Le Parlementaire** (✆ **418/643-6640**) is open to the public, as well as parliamentarians and visiting dignitaries. Featuring Québec products and cuisine, it serves breakfast and lunch Monday through Friday most of the year, but you should check the schedule for closures (it is closed starting the second week of Dec until the second week of Jan). The much lower-key **Café du Parlement** (✆ **418/643-5529;** Mon–Fri 7:30am–2pm most of the year) is also an option for coffee, sandwiches, and eco-friendly takeaway. The massive fountain in front of the building, **La Fontaine de Tourny,** was commissioned by the mayor of Bordeaux, France, in 1857. It was installed in 2007 as a gift from the Simons department store to the city for its 400th anniversary. Also outdoors, to the right of the main entrance as you're facing it, is a large **Inukshuk** statue.

Entrance at corner of Grande-Allée est and av. Honoré-Mercier. www.assnat.qc.ca. ✆ **866/337-8837** or 418/643-7239. Free admission. Guided tours late June to Labour Day Mon–Fri 9am–4:30pm, Sat–Sun and holidays 10am–4:30pm; rest of the year Mon–Fri 9am–4:30pm. Reservations recommended.

Izba Spa Spas, especially Nordic spas, are serious business in this province but they are more conspicuous in the resorts surrounding ski mountains. This classy stone walk up, tucked among residences on boulevard René-Lévesque, draws on the Russian *banya* (steam bath) tradition. The signature Izba body treatment incorporates a light brushing of the skin with oak or birch leaves and a honey rub. With a wide array of massage services, as well as manicures, pedicures, body wraps, and more, this spa can suit either a brief or all-compassing desire to unwind.

36 boul. René-Lévesque est (near av. de Salaberry). www.izbaspa.qc.ca. ✆ **418/522-4922.** Mon–Wed and Sat–Sun 9am–5pm; Thurs–Fri 9am–9pm.

Musée National des Beaux-Arts du Québec ★★★ For almost 40 years, Québec's major art museum sat 100 meters from a prison. Designed by Charles Baillairgé in 1867, the prison was almost immediately overpopulated, but did not completely end service until the 1970s. By 1991 the museum had annexed the cell blocks and watchtower into gallery space to grow its presence as the world's leading collector of Québécois art.

Among that collection is "L'Hommage à Rosa Luxemburg," an enormous triptych by Québec abstract expressionist and surrealist Jean-Paul Riopelle (1923–2002). His permanent gallery is one of several stops on a circuit that could start with the dynamic Inuit collection and move through colonial, modernist, figurative, and abstract art, all created by artists from the province.

The museum leans somewhat contemporary, especially with visiting exhibitions. The ten recently acquired canvasses that make up "XXth Century," painstakingly date-stamped by conceptual artist Bill Vazan, will be on display through September 2014. It runs concurrent with "Les matins infidèles. L'art du protocole," featuring works by 15 Canadians who utilized similarly time-sensitive, or protocol-driven processes.

There's a 1-hour tour of the prison geared to 12- to 17-year-olds called "Behind Bars" and another geared toward adults called "Murders and Beggars;" both tours run year-round.

The museum is situated on the Parc des Champs-de-Bataille (Battlefields Park), at the fringe of the tourist orbit, and is about a half-hour walk from Upper Town.

Parc des Champs-de-Bataille (near where av. Wolfe-Montcalm meets Grande Allée). www.mnba.qc.ca. ✆ **866/220-2150** or 418/643-2150. Admission C$18 adults, C$16 seniors, C$10 ages 13-30, free for children 11 and under, C$40 family, half-price admission Wed 5–9pm. June to Labour Day Thurs–Tues 10am–6pm, Wed 10am–9pm; day after Labour Day to May Tues and Thurs–Sun 10am–5pm, Wed 10am–9pm. Bus: 11.

Observatoire de la Capitale Here's where a rough translation of French may be misleading: the views from here are gorgeous, but they're not of the stars. At 132m high and 221m above sea level, this *observatoire* offers a 360-degree view of the Québec City skyline, from the city's highest vantage point. Each year about 70,000 visitors take the 28-second ride up the elevator up to the 31st floor of the Marie-Guyart building. Views can stretch beyond the Laurentian mountains in one direction and the bridge to Île d'Orléans in another. For kids (and adults), there's also an interactive, touch-screen exhibit about the history of the capital city.

Edifice Marie-Guyart 1037, rue De La Chevrotière, Parliament Hill. www.observatoire-capitale.com. ✆ **888/497-4322** or 418/644-9841. Admission C$10 adults, C$8 students and seniors, free for children 11 and under. Feb to mid-Oct daily 10am–5pm; Mid-Oct to Jan Tues–Sun 10am–5pm.

ST-ROCH: SHOPPING

Want to know where the cool kids live? Or at least where smart Québécois buy croissants? Nouvo Saint-Roch is a long walk from the tourist zone, but well worth checking out. Most of the appeal is along rue St-Joseph. Grab a cup of coffee from **Brûlerie St-Roch** (375 rue St-Joseph est; www.brulerie-st-roch.com; ✆ **418/704-4420**), or a pain au chocolat from **Le Croquembouche** (225 rue Saint-Joseph est; www.lecroquembouche.com; ✆ **418/523-9009**) and dodge in and out of the high-end fashion retailers on rue St-Joseph's eastern end to the pawn shops and consignment stores on the western end. If you ask for directions, it's pronounced "Saint Rock."

Benjo ★★ This toy store is worth a special trip. A bronze frog welcomes kids into this floor-to-ceiling wonderland of toys, most of which are made in Canada. Think trains, race cars, and dolls as far as the eye can see. Kids could meet the life-sized robot Monsieur Bioule or catch a children's choir singing traditional Christmas songs in

SHOPPING: EXPLORE avenue cartier

When you exit the Old City on Grande-Allée est, you'll find hotels, restaurants, and clubs, but shopping doesn't kick in until Grande-Allée meets av. Cartier, a street with gourmet foods, boutique clothing, and few tourists—part of a neighborhood called Montcalm, just beyond Parliament Hill. There's nothing like a lazy afternoon here. You can feel as much like a city-dweller as possible by ordering a latte bowl at **Café Krieghoff** (see p. 164), then pop in and out of shops like **Zone** (999 av. Cartier at the corner of boul. René-Lévesque; www.zonemaison.com; ✆ **418/522-7373**) for mod housewares or **Boutique Ketto** (951 av. Cartier at Crémazie; www.kettodesign.com; ✆ **418/522-3337**) for impish pottery, ceramic jewelry, and stationery made in Québec. There's a fantastic bakery (or two—or is it three?) on this street and unique clothing stores for women young and less young.

French. An ice cream parlor tops it off April through September. Small visitors enter and exit through a tiny VIP door. 550 boul. Charest est (near rue du Parvis). www.benjo.ca. ✆**418/640-0001.**

Dubuc Get your Euro-look up to par with Canadian darling and Montréal-based fashion designer Philippe Dubuc's avant-garde menswear in urban shades of cement, steel, and charcoal. While most of the edgy suit styles compliment the slimmer male, there are also more universal shirts—always, however, with impeccable tailoring. 537 rue St-Joseph est (near rue du Parvis). www.dubucstyle.com. ✆**418/614-5761.**

Signatures Québécoises ★ Six thousand square feet, twenty-five cutting-edge clothing designers from Québec, all in an old church. Heavenly, yes, but it's pretty much St-Roch in a nutshell. Harricana fashions (www.harricana.qc.ca) created from recylced fur, silk, and old wedding dresses by Mariouche Gagné, who was born on Île d'Orléans, is just one example. Église Saint-Roch, 560 rue Saint-Joseph est. www.signaturesquebecoises.com. ✆**418/648-9976.**

SHOPPING COMPLEXES

Shopping malls on a grand scale aren't found anywhere near Old Town. For that, you need to visit the neighboring municipality of **Sainte-Foy.** Malls here differ little from their cousins throughout North America in terms of layout and available products. With 350 shops, **Laurier Québec,** 2700 boul. Laurier, in Sainte-Foy (www.laurierquebec.com; ✆ **800/322-1828**), is the biggest, and it claims some 13 million shoppers each year. The bookstore **La Maison Anglaise et Internationale** (www.lamaisonanglaise.com; ✆ **418/654-9523**) has been one of the region's leading sources of English and Spanish language books for more than 2 decades. It's located in **Place de la Cité** (www.placedelacite.com; ✆ **418/657-7015**), which is within walking distance of Laurier. From mid-May through mid-October, buses shuttle shoppers between Laurier and several hotel stops in Québec City; call ✆ **418/664-0460** for schedules. If you've go your own wheels, it's a 10-minute drive northwest of Vieux-Québec to **Galeries de la Capitale** (www.galeriesdelacapitale.com; ✆ **418/627-5800**), located at 5401 boul. des Galeries. It has an indoor amusement park, ice rink, and IMAX movie theater alongside its 280 shops.

ORGANIZED TOURS

Québec City is small enough that you can get around with a good map and a guidebook, but a tour is tremendously helpful for getting background information about the city's history and culture, for grasping the lay of the land, and in the case of bus tours, for seeing those attractions that are a bit of a hike or require wheels to reach.

Below are some agencies and organizations that have proved to be reliable. Arrange tours by calling the companies directly or by stopping by the large tourist center at the Place d'Armes in Upper Town.

Bus Tours

Buses are convenient if extensive, walking is difficult, especially in hilly Upper Town. Among the established tour operators, **Dupont,** which also goes by the name **Old Québec Tours** (www.tourdupont.com; ✆ **800/267-8687** or 418/664-0460), operates the city's only open-air double-decker bus. Passes allow for on-off access to 11 stops. The company also leads multiple day tours that differ by the season. Summer tours head north into the Charlevoix region for **whale-watching excursion,** a 10-hour day that includes a 3-hour cruise among the belugas (see p. 210). Winter tours head to ski areas or the **Hôtel de Glace** (see p. 153).

Horse-Drawn Carriage Tours

A romantic, if expensive, way to see the city at a genial pace is in a horse-drawn carriage, called a *calèche.* Carriages will pick you up or can be hired from locations throughout the city, including at Place d'Armes. A 40- to 45-minute ride costs C$90, plus tip, for four people maximum. Carriages operate year-round, rain or shine. Companies include **Calèches du Vieux-Québec** (www.calecheduvieuxquebec.com; ✆ **418/683-9222**) and **Calèches Québec** (www.calechesquebec.com; ✆ **418/692-0068**), which also has horse-drawn trams.

River Cruises

Croisières AML (www.croisieresaml.com; ✆ **800/563-4643** or 418/692-1159 in late-spring to mid-fall season) offers a variety of cruises. Its *Louis Jolliet* is a three-decked, 1930s ferry boat–turned–excursion vessel, which carries 1,000 passengers and is stocked with bilingual guides, full dining facilities, and a bar. The company offers brunch and dinner cruises, as well as jaunts that take in the fireworks. The boats dock at quai Chouinard, at 10 rue Dalhousie, in Vieux-Port.

Similar cruises are offered by **Croisières le Coudrier** (www.croisierescoudrier.qc.ca; ✆ **888/600-5554** or 418/692-0107). Their boats have a signature look—like a glass capsule—designed for panoramic views.

Walking Tours

Times and points of departure for walking tours change, so get up-to-date information at any tourist office (addresses are listed on p. 220). Many tours leave from the Place d'Armes in Upper Town, just in front of the **Château Frontenac.**

Tours Voir Québec (www.toursvoirquebec.com; ✆ **866/694-2001** or 418/694-2001) specializes in English-only guided tours of the Old City. "The Grand Tour," which is available year-round, is a 2-hour stroll that covers the architecture, events, and cultural history of the city. Tours are limited to 15 people. Cost is C$23 adults, C$20 students (ISIC, or International Student Identify Card, required), C$11 children 6 to

12, and free for children 5 and under. Foodies will want to note the many different "Food Tours," which stop at about seven different places, sampling local goodies such as cheese, ice cider, pâté, and chocolate. Cost is C$43 per adult. Private tours may also be arranged.

One way to split the difference between being out on your own and being on a guided tour is to use **Map Old Québec** (www.oldquebecmap.com), a website that offers a beautifully designed map and MP3 files. The audio files are free and a map can be ordered online or purchased for C$3 at a few dozen stores around town. Used together you can listen and learn at your own pace.

OUTDOOR ACTIVITIES

Inside the city, **Parc des Champs-de-Bataille** (**Battlefields Park;** below) is the most popular park for bicycling and strolling.

Just outside the city, lakes and hills provide countless opportunities for outdoor recreation, including swimming, boating, fishing, skiing, snowmobiling, and sleigh riding. There are three centers in particular to keep in mind, all within a 45-minute drive from the capital. The plateaus and glacial valleys of **Parc national de la Jacques-Cartier** (www.sepaq.com/pq/jac/en; ✆ **800/665-6527**) are off Route 175 north; **Station touristique Duchesnay** (www.sepaq.com/duchesnay; ✆ **877/511-5885**) is a state park resort on the shores of Lac Saint-Joseph, northwest of the city; and **Parc du Mont Ste-Anne** (www.mont-sainte-anne.com; ✆ **888/827-4579**) is northeast of the city. All three centers are mentioned in the listings below. From mid-November through March, the **Taxi Coop Québec** shuttle service (www.taxicoop-quebec.com; ✆ **418/525-5191**) picks up passengers at Québec City hotels in the morning to take them to alpine and cross-country ski runs, and to snowmobile trails, with return trips in the late afternoon.

La Promenade Samuel-De Champlain ★★ When Québec celebrated its 300th anniversary, the government of Québec gave the people **Parc des Champs-de-Bataille** (see above). For the 400th anniversary (in 2008) it created La Promenade Samuel-De Champlain, a scenic path approximately 2.5 km long (1½ miles) along the St. Laurent River between Quai des Cageux and Côte de Sillery. The space required shifted the road inland so that the public could bike, rollerblade, or walk along the water's edge all year long. With Pont de Québec and Pont Pierre Laporte framing the picturesque setting in the Ste-Foy-Sillery-Cap-Rouge *arrondissement,* Québec City has a beautiful new space, which involved planting 1,500 trees and outdoor contemporary art. There is a sports zone for activities such as soccer, quaint picnic nooks, lights at night for evening strolls, and at the Quai des Cageux there is modular 25m-high (82-ft.) observation tower next to a small cafe, run by **Panache** restaurant (see p. 162) where you can enjoy over-the-counter foods like paninis, wraps, hot dogs, ice cream, and beverages.

2795 boul. Champlain. www.quebecregion.com. ✆ **877/783-1608.** Free admission and parking. Observation tower daily 7am–11pm; Cafe daily 11am–8pm, depending on weather.

Lieu historique national des Fortifications-de-Québec ★ The walls and ramparts that once protected Vieux-Québec from its enemies are now under the protection of the national government as part of the **Fortifications of Québec National Historic Site.** The locations that make up this site include the Governors' Garden and Montmorency Park as well as other places of note such as the Québec Garrison Club,

Maillou House, Terrasse Dufferin and the **Promenade des Gouverneurs.** Visitors can tour the series of defensive buildings erected by the French in the 17th and 18th centuries that make up **Parc de l'Artillerie** (Artillery Park) in Upper Town. They include an ammunition factory that was functional until 1964. An iron foundry, officers' mess and quarters, and a scale model of the city created in 1806 are on view. It may be a blow to romantics and history buffs to learn that St-Jean Gate in the city wall was built in 1940, the fourth in a series that began with the original 1693 entrance, which was replaced in 1747, and then replaced again in 1867. Tickets can be purchased at two informational kiosks: in front of Frontenac on Dufferin Terrace and at 2 rue d'Autueil, near the St-Jean Gate.

2 rue d'Auteuil (near Porte St-Jean). www.pc.gc.ca/artillerie. ✆ **888/773-8888** or 418/648-7016. Admission C$3.90 adults, C$3.40 seniors, C$1.90 children 6–16, free for children 5 and under, C$9.80 for groups and families. Additional fees for audio guide, tea ceremony, and special activities. Early May to early June and early Sept to early Oct daily 10am–5pm; late June to early Sept daily 10am–6pm; April to mid-May by reservation.

Parc des Champs-des-Batailles ★★★ Known in English as Battlefields Park, this green gathering place of winding paths and the occasional fountain or monument was Canada's first national urban park. It covers 108 hectares (267 acres) and officials compare it to New York's Central Park or London's Hyde Park. A section called the **Plains of Abraham** is where Britain's General James Wolfe and France's Louis-Joseph, marquis de Montcalm, engaged in their short, but crucial battle in 1759, which resulted in the British defeat of the French troops. It's also where the national anthem, "O Canada," was first performed. From spring through fall, visit the **Jardin Jeanne d'Arc (Joan of Arc Garden),** just off avenue Wilfrid-Laurier, near the Loews le Concorde Hotel. This spectacular garden combines French classical design with British-style flower beds. In the rest of the park, nearly 6,000 trees of more than 80 species blanket the fields and include the sugar maple, Norway maple, American elm, and American ash. Also in the park are two Martello towers, cylindrical stone defensive structures built between 1808 and 1812 when Québec feared an American invasion.

The **Discovery Pavilion of the Plains of Abraham** (835 av. Wilfred-Laurier; ✆ **855/649-6157** or 418/649-6157) is the starting point for tours, hosts a multimedia show called The Odyssey, and houses a scale model of the park. Entrance fees during high season also provide access to activities such as the Martello Tower 1 and a tour on Abraham's Bus. Yet there's much to be said for simply taking in the landscape for exercise or to glimpse the exquisite vantage points of the St. Lawrence. There are groomed cross-country ski trails in the winter and the snow can pile higher than parking meters and last through March. In warmer weather, look for evidence of carpet-bedding, also called mosaiculture—an ornamental garden technique that creates lettering out of plants. This park's horticulturalists are experts and take great pride in creating stunning designs each growing season. The whole park is that, really, an emblem of the pride this city takes in its vivid history and vibrant present-day life.

Parc des Champs-des-Batailles. www.ccbn-nbc.gc.ca. ✆ **888/497-4322** or 418/644-9841. Discovery Pavilion admission C$14 adults, C$10 ages 13–17 and seniors, C$4 ages 5–12, free for children 4 and under. July to early Sept daily 9:30am–5:30pm; Early Sept to June daily 9:30am–5pm.

Warm-Weather Activities

BIKING

There's lots of good biking in the city, either along the river or up in Parliament Hill in Parc des Champs-de-Bataille. A marked path for cyclists (and in-line skaters) along the waterfront was new in 2008 and is well maintained. It extends both directions alongside the river and heading out of the city. Tourist information centers provide bicycle-trail maps and can point out a variety of routes. To rent bikes or join a guided tour, see the "Québec City by Bike" section on p. 141. Mountain bikers, meanwhile, head to **Mont Ste-Anne,** which has the most well-known mountain bike network in eastern Canada. It was host to the 2010 Mountain Bike and Trial World Championships, and every year to **Vélirium** (www.velirium.com), the International Mountain Bike Festival and World Cup. It's 42km (26 miles) northeast of Québec City. See the intro above for contact information.

CAMPING

The greater Québec City area has 18 campgrounds, most of which have toilets and showers. For a list of sites and their specs, go to **www.quebecregion.com** and search for "campground" or pick up a free copy of "The Official Accommodation Guide" published by Québec City Tourism.

GOLF

An 18-hole course, **Golf de la Faune** (www.golfdelafaune.com; ✆ **866/627-8008** or 418/627-1576), opened in June 2008, 10 minutes from downtown, at the **Four Points by Sheraton Québec** (www.fourpoints.com/quebec; ✆ **418/627-8008**). The course has eight water hazards and 45 sand traps. Green fees start at C$40.

About 40 minutes north of the city at Mont Ste-Anne, **Le Grand Vallon** (www.legrandvallon.com; ✆ **888/827-4579** or 418/827-4653) is an 18-hole, par-72 course with tree-lined stretches, 4 lakes, and 40 sand traps. Rates start at C$44 and include a golf cart, access to the driving range, and practice balls. Also a short drive west of Québec City, **Golf Le Grand Portneuf** (www.legrandportneuf.com; ✆ **866/329-3662** or 418/873-2000) offers 36 challenging holes in a peaceful, scenic environment. Other courses are located near Jacques-Cartier national park and on Île d'Orléans.

SWIMMING

Those who want to splash around during their visit have several hotel options with pools. Fairmont Le Château Frontenac has one, as do Hôtel Manoir Victoria, Loews Le Concorde, Hôtel Château Laurier, and Hotel PUR. They're all listed in chapter 12. Outside the city, the waterpark at **Village Vacances Valcartier** (p. 184) has more than 35 water slides, a wave pool, and themed rivers, such as the Tropical River or the Crazy Cascades.

For swimming in natural bodies of water less than 30 minutes drive from the city, two nearby lake options are **Lac Saint-Joseph** (www.la-plage.ca; ✆ **877/522-3224**) and **Lac Saint-Charles** (www.laccesnature.qc.ca; ✆ **418/849-6163**).

Cold-Weather Activities

CROSS-COUNTRY SKIING

With 47 ski centers and at least 2,500km (1,553 miles) of trails, the options to cross-country ski in Greater Québec are plentiful. Within the city, the **Parc des Champs-de-Bataille,** where Carnaval de Québec establishes its winter playground during February, has a network of free, groomed cross-country trails in winter. You can rent equipment at the **Discovery Pavilion** (p. 181), near the Citadelle. Thirty minutes outside the city, **Station touristique Duchesnay** (p. 180) offers extensive trails and ski rentals. This is where the **Hôtel de Glace** (p. 153) is built each winter. The resort also has a spa, other hotel accommodations, and a bistro. The **Association of Cross-Country Ski Centers of Québec Area's** website (www.skidefondraquette.com) has venue listings and maps.

DOG SLEDDING

Aventure Inukshuk (www.aventureinukshuk.qc.ca; © **418/875-0770**) is located in Station touristique Duchesnay, in the town of Ste-Catherine-de-la-Jacques-Cartier. Guides show you how to lead a sled pulled by six dogs. A 1-hour trip takes you deep into a hushed world of snow and thick woods, past rows of Christmas trees, and over a beaver pond. The dogs live in a field of individual pens and houses under evergreen trees. Guides train and care for their teams themselves. Overnight camping trips are available. The 1-hour trip, which includes an additional half-hour of training, costs C$95 in December, January, and March, and C$104 in February. Children 6 to 12 are half price, and children 2 to 5 go free (children 1 and younger aren't allowed). Expensive, especially for families, but the memory stays with you.

DOWNHILL SKIING

The coastal-hugging mountain, **Le Massif,** is famous for its "I'm about to drop into the St. Lawrence!" feeling as one shushes downhill. Over the years, Le Massif has steadily increased services on-mountain and well as transportation to the mountain. See p. 209 for Day Trip information. Also: **Mont Ste-Anne** offers eastern Canada's largest total skiing surface, with 66 trails (17 are lit for night skiing). See p. 211 for more information. Another option is **Stoneham Mountain Resort** (www.ski-stoneham.com; © **800/463-6888** or 418/848-2415), about 30 minutes north of the city.

ICE SKATING

From the end of October to mid-March, a mini outdoor rink is set up in Place d'Youville just outside the Upper Town walls. Admission is free, and skates can be rented. If you want to feel like a true northerner, and skate through trees to the sound of music, take a quick jaunt west of town to **Centre de plein air de Beauport** (www.centrepleinairbeauport.ca; © **877/641-6113** or 418/641-6112), where admission is free on weekdays.

SNOWMOBILES

Snowmobiles, known here as "ski-doos," are hugely popular. It's said, in fact, that there are more trails for snowmobiling than there is asphalt in Québec City. In addition to options for day trips, many restaurants and hotels outside the city accommodate snowmobile touring, making it possible to travel from locale to locale. **La Fédération des clubs de motoneigistes du Québec** (F.C.M.Q.; www.fcmq.qc.ca) has extensive information about snowmobiling in the province, including maps and trail permits. Also, check the tourist office for current options.

TOBOGGANING

An old-fashioned toboggan run called **Les Glissades de la Terrasse** (© **418/829-9898**) is set up right in the city on the steep wooden staircase at Terrasse Dufferin's south end in winter. The slide extends almost to the Château Frontenac. Next to the ticket booth, a little sugar shack sells sweet treats. Cost is C$2.50 per person.

ESPECIALLY FOR KIDS

Children who love Arthurian tales of fortresses and castles or Harry Potter's adventures will delight in walking around this storybook city and the **Château Frontenac** (p. 172). On **Terrasse Dufferin** in Upper Town, there are coin-operated telescopes, street entertainers, and ice-cream stands. Halfway down **Breakneck Stairs (L'Escalier du Casse-Cou;** see p. 167) are giant **cannons** ranged along the battlements. The gun carriages are impervious to the assaults of small humans, so kids can scramble all over them at will.

If military sites might be appealing, take them to see the colorful **Changing of the Guard** ceremony at **La Citadelle** (p. 173). Or just head for the **Parc des Champs-de-Bataille (Battlefields Park,** which features the **Plains of Abraham;** p. 181) adjacent to the La Citadelle if young ones need to run off excess energy. Acres of grassy lawn provide room to roam and are perfect for a family picnic. **Québec Expérience** (p. 174) is a flashy way to introduce some history of the region to kids, although it might be too vivid for younger children. In Lower Town, the **Musée de la Civilisation** (p. 167) presents exhibits for families and, given that it's free for children 11 and younger, it's great value. **The Musée du Fort** (www.museedufort.com; ✆ **418/692-2175**) contains a floor-sized diorama that depicts the French, British, and U.S. battles for control of Québec. It was built by a high school teacher in the 1960s and has had a few updates since; the presentation lasts 30 minutes.

When in doubt, head to the water. **Montmorency Falls** (p. 208) makes a terrific day trip for children of all ages during any season (in winter it's an icy wonderland). It's just 10 minutes north of the city by car, and there are bus tours to the site, as well. It costs to park, but walking around near the water is free. On Wednesdays and Saturdays from late July to mid-August, the falls are host to a grand fireworks competition, **Les Grand Feux Loto-Québec** (p. 186). It pits international pyrotechnical teams against each other in a contest for who can make the biggest and brightest presentation.

Village Vacances Valcartier (www.valcartier.com; ✆ **888/384-5524**) in St-Gabriel-de-Valcartier, about a half-hour northwest of the city, is a major man-made water park. In summer, it boasts 35 slides, a gigantic wave pool, a huge pirate ship, and a faux Amazon River to go tubing down. In winter, the same facilities are put to use for "snow rafting" on inner tubes and skating. Instead of carrying cash or credit cards, visitors can register their credit cards and then pay for food and other services by pressing a finger to a screen.

If sea life is of interest, block off time to see the more than 10,000 marine animals at **Aquarium du Québec** (www.sepaq.com/ct/paq; ✆ **866/659-5264** or 418/659-5264), about 15 minutes west from the city near the bridges. It covers 16 hectares (about 39 acres) with outdoor and indoor activities such as a walrus show, seal training, a touch basin—and, there are polar bears! Families can bring a picnic or grab a treat on-site.

Québec City is day-trip-distance to where whales come out to play each summer. See p. 210 for details about **whale watching**.

In March the **Red Bull Crashed Ice World Championship** event takes over Vieux-Québec. The newly invented sport brings athletes from all over the world. Dressed in hockey gear, four brave souls skate downhill in a rough and tumble roller derby–esque race with lots of leaps, drops, and sharp turns. The starting line is drawn in Upper Town and the finish line in Lower Town's Place-Royale. It is immensely exhilarating to watch—and free. See www.redbull.ca for details.

If you're going to the wintertime **Carnaval** (p. 185), kids won't want to miss the dog sled race through the old city streets or the canoe races, where teams push, pull, or paddle (depending on the state of the river) from one side to another. The best place to view the water competition is from the Terrasse Dufferin or from the lookout on the opposite bank in Lévis.

FESTIVALS & NIGHTLIFE IN QUÉBEC CITY

15

Though Québec City has fewer nighttime diversions than exuberant Montréal, there are more than enough to occupy visitors' evenings. Apart from theatrical productions, which are usually in French, knowledge of the language is rarely needed to enjoy the entertainment.

If you want to stroll around and take in the nightlife options, there are three principal streets to choose from in Upper Town: rue St-Jean inside and outside the walls, Grande-Allée outside the walls (where a beery collegiate atmosphere can sometimes rule as the evening wears on), and avenue Cartier in the Montcalm neighborhood. In St-Roch, the hot spots are on or near rue St-Paul.

Happy hour is locally known as *cinq à sept* (meaning 5–7pm) and specials are often written on a chalkboard out front as "*5 à 7.*" Many venues offer specials that start earlier or go later; some start after 10pm and include discounted late-night food menus.

Festivals: Québec City Celebrates Every Season

There are two major festivals to plan around in Québec City, one in summer (**Festival d'Eté**) and one in winter (**Carnaval**). Both include non-stop entertainment for all ages and a chance swirl among the tens of thousands who gather to celebrate this city's seasonal extremes—sun and snow (the latter being abundant and long-lasting).

But in every season, there's some kind of festival, anniversary, remembrance, or special event. For an exhaustive list beyond those listed here, check the Events tab of Québec City Tourisme's website, at **www.quebecregion.com**. There, you can conduct a basic search or an advanced search that sorts free events from ticketed ones and events by categories of interest.

JANUARY-FEBRUARY

Carnaval de Québec. This wintertime extravaganza takes over the city for more than 2 weeks each February and includes an insanely icy canoe race, dogsled competitions, parades, snow sculpture, and more. Purchase a C$15 badge to gain entrance to two stage areas and more than 300 activities for the duration of the festival. There are also free events and surprise appearances by an enormous, cheery, high-kicking snowman, called Bonhomme. Montréal celebrates its "Fête des Neiges" the previous 2 weeks (see p. 100). Visit www.carnaval.qc.ca or call ✆ **866/422-7628** or 418/626-3716. January 31 to February 16, 2014.

Pentathlon des Neiges. Skate, ski, snowshoe, run, bike long or short distances on the Plains of Abraham. There's something for everyone during this annual snow-sport competition that runs concurrent with Carnaval and after. Visit **www.pentathlondes neiges.com**. January 31 to March 2, 2014.

MARCH

Red Bull Crashed Ice. An elevated ice track winds from Vieux-Québec's Upper to Lower Town and men in hockey gear fight their way down to the bottom. The set-up alone for this crazy race is worth seeing firsthand. It's an international sport called ice-cross downhill, and it can be viewed for free. Visit **www.redbullcrashedice.ca** for details. March 2014 (check website to confirm date).

MAY

Carrefour International de Théâtre de Québec. Multilingual theater and song has come to venues throughout Québec each spring for 15 years running. Visit www.carre fourtheatre.qc.ca or call ✆ **888/529-1996** or 418/692-3131. May 20 to June 7, 2014.

JUNE

Festival Grand Rire. New and seasoned comedy talent descends on the city for the 15th year. More than 100 events are held at venues in Place D'Youville and its surrounds. Check www.grandrire.com or call ✆ **877/441-7473** or 418/640-2277. Runs for 10 days in mid-June.

Gran Fondo Mont-Ste-Anne. This road biking event is open to all riders over 14 who are physically fit. All routes start and finish in the Mont Ste-Anne ski area parking lot, 42km (26 miles) north of the city. Participants can choose from three different challenge levels. For details, visit **www.granfondoeco.com**. Mid- to late-June.

JULY

Canada Day. Canadian cities, including Québec, celebrate the formation of the federation of Canada with free music, flag raisings, and other activities. July 1.

Festival d'Été (Summer Festival). For 11 days, this city forgets all about winter—heck, it hardly remembers to sleep. This is one of the colossal musical events on the yearly calendar and hotels and entertainment venues fill up fast. Wristbands must be purchased to gain entrance to hear the likes of Stevie Wonder, Neko Case, Bruno Mars, or Guns N' Roses (who performed in 2013). Street acts and DJs are set up for free all around town. Billed as world music, the festival also gives Canadian and Québécois performers a decent share of the stages. Visit www.info festival.com or call ✆ **888/992-5200** or 418/529-5200. July 3 to 13, 2014.

AUGUST

Les Grand Feux Loto-Québec. On Wednesday and Saturday nights, crowds gather on the banks of the St. Lawrence for an international fireworks competition. Free for all. Check **www.lesgrandsfeux.com** for details. Early to late August.

Les Fêtes de la Nouvelle-France SAQ (New France Festival). The 17th and 18th centuries come to life during this annual celebration of the birth of New France. Events are held at more than a dozen points of interest in Vieux-Québec. One highlight is the Parade of Giants, where enormous puppets walk alongside tiny companions, all in period costume. (Worth a search for photos online!) A new theme—2013 was the year of the heroine—is chosen every year to illuminate that particular facet of history. Visit www.nouvellefrance.qc.ca or call ✆ **866/391-3383** or 418/694-3311. August 6 to 10, 2014.

Velirium and UCI Mountain Bike World Cup. It's the penultimate competition for professional cross-country and downhill mountain bikers, and spectators are invited. This multi-day mountain biking competition on Mont Ste-Anne 42km (26 miles) north of the city features professional women, men, and juniors racing on courses that would give beginners nightmares. Meanwhile, City8 brings dirt biking and free styling right into Québec City at its central Place d'Youville. There are also clinics, parties, and competitions for amateur bikers of all ages and bike preferences. Visit www.velirium.com or call ✆ **418/827-1122.** July 30 to August 4, 2014.

Festibière de Québec. A mug and tokens open up a world of beer at this annual festival. Taste the local and international goods from microbreweries, pubs, and cider houses. Giant hot dogs and of course *poutine* can be the break you take between cold ones. Believe it or not, education is a key component, with speakers lined up to talk history, brew process, distribution, and marketing. There are more modest events in fall and winter. Visit www.festibierede quebec.com or call ✆ **418/948-1166.** Four days in mid-August.

SEPTEMBER

Festival de Magie de Québec. Get out the top hats, hide the rabbits! More than 40 free magic shows and workshops are planned for this St-Roch festival. In 2013, escape artist Simon Pérusse extricated himself from a straight jacket while hanging upside down from a crane. For details, visit **www.festival demagie.ca**. Held late August to early September (Labour Day weekend).

Fête Arc-en-Ciel. Québec City's 5-day gay-pride fest attracts thousands of people to Place d'Youville and St-Roch. Drag shows, movies, happy hours, and dance parties are all part of the mix For details, visit **www. glbtquebec.org**. Held late August to early September (Labour Day weekend).

International des Musiques Sacreés de Québec. Heading into its 18th year, this celebration of sacred music takes place at 11 venues, including several historic churches. Globally known, artists perform spiritual (not necessarily religious) music that ranges from gospel to Buddhist chants to Corsican polyphonies. Passports for C$150 grant access to all events with a reserved seat up front. Children 12 and under, with an adult, attend free. Many other ticket options are available. Visit www.imsq.ca or call ✆ **866/525-9777** or 418/525-9777. Seven days in mid-September.

Grand Prix Cyclistes. The world's top cycling teams (as in the same guys in the Tour de France) spend 1 day competing in Québec and then head to Montréal for a race there. Both races are held on city streets (routes can be found online) and are free to spectators. The teams arrive a few days prior and can be spotted on training rides or having a bite at local restaurants. In 2013, Québec launched the first **Cyclo La Québécoisie** (www.cyclosquebecoises.com) to complement the Grand Prix. It features two cycling loops for riders of all levels. Visit www.gpcqm.ca or call ✆ **450/671-9090** for more information. Mid-September.

THE PERFORMING ARTS

Circus

Cirque du Soleil (p. 87) got its start just outside of Québec City and has a history of creating free public performances for major celebrations such as the 450th anniversary of Jaques Cartier's discovery of Canada (in 1984) or the 400th anniversary of the founding of Québec City (in 2008). The last event launched a spectacular 5-year, five-chapter aerial show called "The Harbor of Lost Souls," with one of five chapters performed every summer—again, for free, most evenings—through 2013. To find out if the troupe has plans to return in 2014 (nothing had been announced as this book went to press), visit **www. cirquedusoleil.com**. If Cirque is returning, put a visit at the top of your to-do list.

Classical Music, Opera & Dance

The region's premier classical groups are **Orchestre Symphonique de Québec** (www. osq.org; ✆ **877/643-8131** or 418/643-5598), Canada's oldest symphony, which performs at the Grand Théâtre de Québec (see below), and **Les Violons du Roy** (www. violonsduroy.com; ✆ **418/692-3026**), a string orchestra that is celebrating its 30th year. It features a core group of 15 musicians and performs at the centrally located Palais Montcalm (see below). Also in its 30th year, **Opéra de Québec** (www.opera dequebec.qc.ca; ✆ **877/643-8131**), has "The Tempest" and two other programs slated for the 2013–2014 season.

Concert Halls & Performance Venues

Many of the city's churches host sacred and secular music concerts, as well as special Christmas festivities. There are also a number of outdoor amphitheatres with full summer schedules. Look for posters on outdoor kiosks around the city and check with the tourist office (p. 220) for listings.

Colisée Pepsi This 15,000-seat arena is home to the Remparts, a popular junior hockey team. The stadium also hosts events such as monster truck extravaganzas, boxing matches, and occasional rock shows. It's a 10-minute drive northwest of Parliament Hill. 250 boul. Wilfrid-Hamel (ExpoCité), north of St-Roch. www.expocite.com. ✆ 800/900-7469 or **418/691-7110.**

Grand Théâtre de Québec ★★ Classical music concerts, opera, dance, jazz, klezmer, and theatrical productions are presented in two halls. Visiting conductors, orchestras, and dance companies perform here, in addition to resident companies such as the Orchestre Symphonique de Québec and Opéra de Québec. 269 boul. René-Lévesque est (near av. Turnbull), Parliament Hill. www.grandtheatre.qc.ca. ✆ **877/643-8131** or 418/643-8131.

Le Capitole ★ Big musical productions such as "Sweeney Todd" and "The Beatles Story," along with live musical performances, keep this historic 1,262-seat theater on Place d'Youville buzzing along (productions are in French). More intimate shows are put on in the attached Le Cabaret du Capitole. 972 rue St-Jean (at Place d'Youville), Parliament Hill. www.lecapitole.com. ✆ **800/261-9903** or 418/694-4444.

Palais Montcalm ★ Renovations have made this venue bigger and more modern, and it's now a hub of the city's cultural community. The main performance space seats 979 and presents a mix of dance programs, plays, and classical music concerts. More intimate recitals happen in a 125-seat cafe-theater. 995 Place d'Youville (near Porte Saint-Jean), Parliament Hill. www.palaismontcalm.ca. ✆ **877/641-6040** or 418/641-6040.

BARS & NIGHTCLUBS

In addition to regular bars and nightclub, look for *boîtes à chansons* (literally, "boxes with songs"), which are small clubs that feature casual evenings of music from singer-songwriters. They're a regional specialty and popular throughout Québec.

Vieux-Québec: Haute-Ville (Upper Town)

Pub St-Alexandre ★ Roomy and sophisticated, this is one of the best-looking bars in town. It's done in British-pub style: polished mahogany, exposed brick, and a working fireplace that's particularly comforting during the 8 cold months of the year. Bartenders serve more than 40 single-malt scotches and 250 beers, along with hearty bar food (*croque monsieur,* steak-and-kidney pie, fish and chips). Check the schedule for the occasional live music—rock, blues, jazz, or Irish. 1087 rue St-Jean (near rue St-Stanislas). www.pubstalexandre.com. ✆ **418/694-0015.**

Ristorante Il Teatro ★★ This friendly Italian restaurant directly on the Place d'Youville is open from 7am to at least 2am every day. It's part of a complex that includes **Le Capitole** theater (above), and actors, musical performers, and theater staff often come in for a drink or a meal after shows. 972 rue St-Jean (at Place d'Youville). www.lecapitole.com/en/restaurant.php. ✆ **418/694-9996.**

St-Laurent Bar et Lounge ★ A swank little room inside Québec's magical castle, the hotel Château Frontenac (see p. 145). Dark wood and marble lend an air of elegance, and a bank of windows overlooks the river. The crowd is older and well

DANCE, dance, DANCE!

The Parliament Hill neighborhood, on or near Grande-Allée, has the highest concentration of dance clubs. **Dagobert Night Club** (600 Grande-Allée est; www.dagobert.ca; ✆ **418/522-0393**) imports DJs from Montréal and as far away as the U.K. and is a rite of passage for many locals or others just of age who pack the 1,000-person patio. Just across the street is **Maurice Night Club** (575 Grande-Allée est; www.mauricenightclub.com; ✆ **418/647-2000**), a converted mansion with a couple of bars within (an older crowd gravitates toward its **Charlotte Lounge**). The nearby **Savini** (680 Grande-Allée est; www.savini.ca; ✆ **418/647-4747**), a self-dubbed *"vinothèque,"* combines wine, hostesses in teeny dresses, and nightly DJs. It's also a fine spot for late-night pizza or salad. Catering mostly to gay and lesbian clientele, **Le Drague Cabaret Club** (815 rue St-Augustin; www.ledrague.com; ✆ **418/649-7212**), or "the Drag," features two dance floors and a cabaret with drag shows on Thursday, Friday, and Sunday nights. It's located just off rue St-Jean in the Faubourg St-Jean neighborhood, within walking distance of the other clubs. See also **Boudoir** in St-Roch, below.

heeled, reflected in the drink options: the Winston Churchill, the F.D. Roosevelt, and the Maurice Duplessis—three martinis named after famous Château guests. There's a small food menu and an outdoor terrace. Château Frontenac, 1 rue des Carrières. www.fairmont.com/frontenac-quebec/dining/le-saint-laurent. ✆ **418/692-3861.**

Vieux-Québec: Basse-Ville (Lower Town)

Le Pape-Georges ★ A cozy wine bar in a 345-year-old stone-and-beamed room that features *chanson* (a French-cabaret singing style), along with other music, Friday through Sunday at 10pm (and Thurs in summer). Light fare is available, along with up to 15 choices of wine by the glass (the bar's motto: "Save water; drink wine!"). 8 rue Cul-de-Sac (near boul. Champlain). www.papegeorges.ca. ✆ **418/692-1320.**

SSS ★ SSS may be the only lounge and restaurant in Vieux-Québec that adopts the sleek, bigger-city approach of sounding its techno beats onto the sidewalk to lure cocktail seekers. Owned by the same team behind the upscale restaurant **Toast!** (p. 162), SSS brings French flair to American comfort foods—ribs, hot dogs, onion rings. Guests can opt for entrees or apps, dining room or bar. On busy nights, a snack menu kicks in after 10:30pm (and on busy afternoons between 2–5pm). 71 rue St-Paul (near rue Sault-au-Matelot). www.restaurantsss.com. ✆ **418/692-1991.**

Théâtre Petit-Champlain ★ Québécois and French singers alternate with jazz and blues groups in this roomy cafe and theater in Lower Town. Performances take place most Wednesdays through Saturdays at 8pm. Tickets run about C$20 to C$50. There's a pretty outdoor patio for preshow drinks. 68 rue du Petit-Champlain (near the funiculaire). www.theatrepetitchamplain.com. ✆ **418/692-2631.**

Parliament Hill (on or Near Grande-Allée)

L'Astral ★ Spinning slowly above the city, this restaurant and (sometimes) bar atop the **Loews Le Concorde Hôtel** (p. 151) unveils a breathtaking 360-degree panorama. L'Astral is mainly regarded as a restaurant, but on slower nights it sets aside a section for patrons to come just for drinks and the sunset view. 1225 Cours du Général de Montcalm (at Grande-Allée). www.lastral.ca. ✆ **800/463-256** or 418/780-3602.

La Ninkasi du Faubourg With a tagline *"bières et culture,"* Ninkasi features almost all Québécois wine and spirits, including 40 local microbrews. In warm months, there's an outdoor terrace. It's open daily from 1pm to 3am. 811 rue St-Jean (1 block west of av. Honoré-Mercier). www.laninkasi.ca. ✆ **418/529-8538.**

St-Roch

Boudoir Lounge The hottest club in St-Roch, Boudoir has two floors and books DJs on Thursday, Friday, and Saturday nights and live music on Sunday nights. Local hipsters generally hop between here, **Versa** across the street at no. 432 (www.versarestaurant.com), and **Yuzu** Sushi-Bar (www.yuzu.ca) at no. 438; the latter reopened in spring 2011 after a million-dollar reno and expansion. 441 rue du Parvis (at boul. Charest est). www.boudoirlounge.com. ✆ **418/524-2777.**

La Barberie Microbrasserie Coopérative de travail ★★ There's no better spot to hang out on a sunny afternoon with a carousel of house-made microbrews than in La Barberie's beer garden. Get there early on weekends because seats go fast and stay occupied. This place is so laid back that midweek you can bring your lunch and heat it up on the premises. 310 rue St-Roch (at rue de la Reine). www.labarberie.com. ✆ **418/522-4373.**

Le Cercle ★★ A unique gallery-bar-resto-concert venue, this spot in St-Roch can be a go-to for drinks, tapas (see p. 165), or good music. 228 rue St-Joseph est (near rue Caron). www.le-cercle.ca. ✆ **418/948-8648.**

QUÉBEC CITY WALKING TOURS

16

The many pleasures of walking in picturesque French Québec are easily comparable to walking in similar *quartiers* in northern European cities. Stone houses rub shoulders with each other, carriage wheels creak behind muscular horses, sunlight filters through leafy canopies, drinkers and diners lounge in sidewalk cafes, childish shrieks of laughter echo down cobblestone streets. Not common to other cities, however, is the bewitching vista of river and mountains that the higher elevations bestow.

In winter especially, Vieux-Québec takes on a Dickensian quality, with a lamp glow flickering behind curtains of falling snow. The man who should know—Charles Dickens himself—described the city as having "splendid views which burst upon the eye at every turn."

WALKING TOUR 1: UPPER TOWN (VIEUX-QUEBEC: HAUTE-VILLE)

START: **Château Frontenac, the castlelike hotel that dominates the city**

FINISH: **Hôtel du Parlement, on Grande-Allée, just outside the walls**

TIME: **2 to 3 hours, depending on whether you take all the optional diversions**

BEST TIMES: **Anytime, although early morning when the streets are emptier is most atmospheric, and the best time to take unobstructed photographs**

WORST TIMES: **None**

The Upper Town (Haute-Ville) of Old Québec (Vieux-Québec) is surrounded by fortress walls. This section of the city overlooks the St. Lawrence River and includes much of what makes Québec so beloved. Buildings and compounds along this tour have been carefully preserved, and most are at least a century old. ***Start:*** At the grand Château Frontenac, the visual heart of the city.

1 Château Frontenac

Reportedly the most photographed hotel in the world, and it's not hard to see why. A copper roof only needs replacing every 100 years,

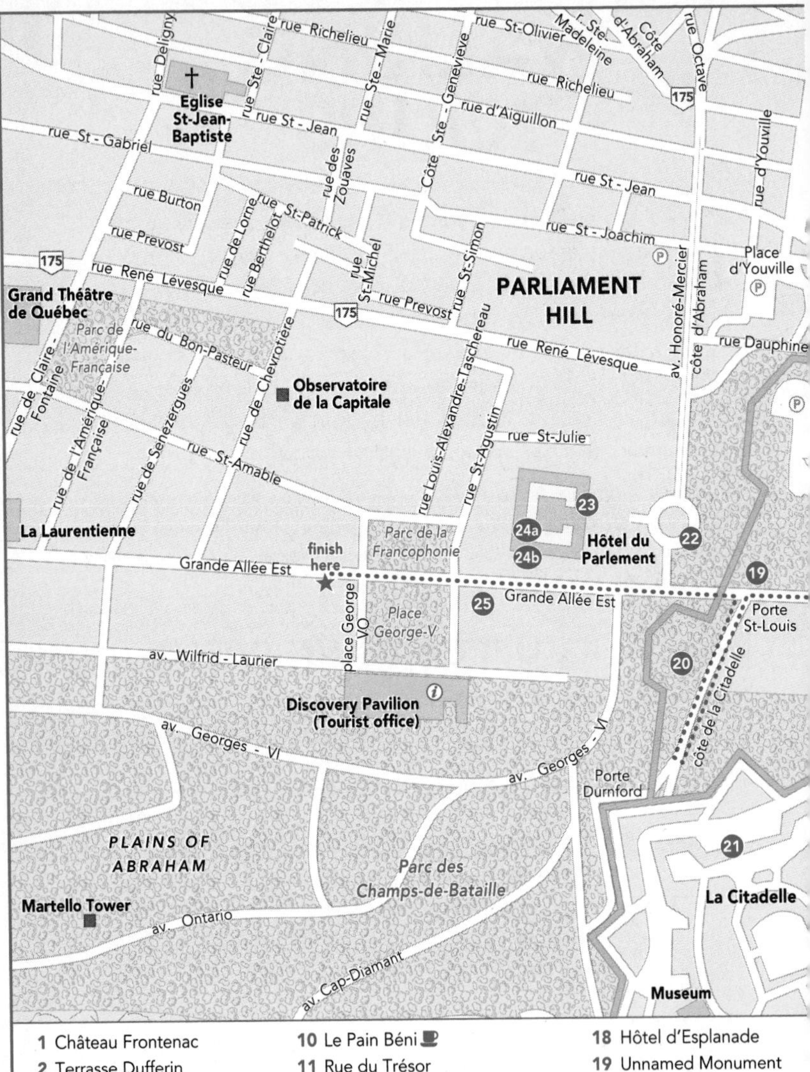

1 Château Frontenac
2 Terrasse Dufferin
3 Promenade des Gouverneurs
4 Parc des Gouverneurs
5 Maison Kent
6 Maison Jacquet
7 Aux Anciens Canadiens
8 Maison Maillou
9 Place d'Armes
10 Le Pain Béni
11 Rue du Trésor
12 Basilique Notre-Dame
13 Séminaire de Québec
14 Hôtel-de-Ville (City Hall)
15 Anglican Cathedral of the Holy Trinity
16 Chapelle/Musée des Ursulines
17 Cannonball
18 Hôtel d'Esplanade
19 Unnamed Monument
20 Stone Memorial
21 La Citadelle
22 Site of Winter Carnaval
23 Hôtel du Parlement
24a Le Parlementaire
24b Café du Parlement
25 Grand-Allée

VIEUX–QUÉBEC (HAUTE–VILLE)
VIEUX–QUÉBEC (BASSE–VILLE)
VIEUX-PORT
St. Lawrence River
Bassin Louise
Tourist Information
Parking
0 500 ft
0 100 m
Barracks
Parc de l'Artillerie
Le Capitole
Parc de l'Esplanade
Old Foundry
Porte St-Jean
Palais Montcalm
Porte Kent
Musée Bon Pasteur
Marché-du-Vieux-Port
Musée des Augustins
Centre Catherine-de-St-Augustin
Centre d'Interpretation du Vieux-Port
Maison Montcalm
Hôtel de Ville
Seminaire
Monastère des Ursulines
Aux Anciens Canadiens
Basilique-Cathédrale Notre Dame
Place d'Armes
Parc Montmorency
Porte Prescott
Musée de la Civilisation de Québec
Funiculaire du Vieux-Québec
Château Frontenac
L'Escalier du Casse-Cou
Maison Chevalier
Place de Paris
Parc du Cavalier-du-Moulin
Parc des Gouverneurs
Terrasse Dufferin
start here
côte Samson
rue St-Vallier
rue des Glacis
rue Lacroix
rue St-Paul
rue de l'Arsenal
rue Carleton
rue Richelieu
rue McMahon
rue Elgin
rue McWilliam
rue St-Stanislas
côte du Palais
côte Dinan
rue des Remparts
côte de la Canoterie
rue St-Thomas
quai St-André
rue Charlevoix
rue Collins
rue Hamel
rue St-Jean
rue Couillard
rue St-Flavien
rue Rioux
r. Sous-le-Cap
rue Ste-Ursule
rue Ste-Angèle
rue Dauphine
rue Cook
rue Pierre-Olivier-Chauveau
côte de la Fabrique
rue Garneau
rue Ferland
rue Ste-Famille
rue de Laval
rue Hebert
rue Ste-Anne
rue d'Auteuil
rue de la Vieille-Université
rue des Jardins
rue du Trésor
rue de Buade
rue Port-Dauphin
rue Bell
rue Sault-au-Matelot
rue St-Pierre
rue de la Barricade
rue Donnacona
rue St-Louis
r. du Fort
r. St-Antoine
rue Dalhousie
côte de la Montagne
rue du Corps-de-Garde
rue Haldimand
rue Mt-Carmel
av. Ste-Geneviève
rue des Grisons
rue de la Porte
rue du Porche
rue Sous-le-Fort
av. St-Denis
rue des Carrieres
rue du Petit-Champlain
rue du Marché-Champlain
rue des Traversiers
rue du Marché-Finlay
bd. Champlain
0 150 mi
0 150 km
QUÉBEC
CANADA
Québec City
Ottawa
Montréal
Toronto
Boston
UNITED STATES
New York

and, it seems, the time is now for Québec City's "castle." A major, multimillion-dollar renovation project is presently underway. This means that over 36 tonnes (about 80,000 lbs.) of new chocolate-brown metal will dominate the skyline—that is, until it oxidizes into its eventual green patina. The original section of the famous edifice that defines the Québec City skyline was built as a hotel from 1892 to 1893 by the Canadian Pacific Railway Company. Known locally as "the Château," the hotel today has 618 rooms (p. 145).

Walk around to the river side of the Château, where there is a grand boardwalk called:

2 Terrasse Dufferin

With its green-and-white-topped gazebos in warm months, this boardwalk promenade looks much as it did 100 years ago, when ladies with parasols and gentlemen with top hats strolled along it on sunny afternoons. It offers vistas of river, watercraft, and distant mountains, and is particularly romantic at sunset.

Walk south on Terrasse Dufferin, past the Château. If you're in the mood for some exercise, go to the end of the boardwalk and continue up the stairs—there are 310 of them—walking south along the:

3 Promenade des Gouverneurs

This path was renovated in 2007 and skirts the sheer cliff wall, climbing up and up past Québec's military **La Citadelle** (p. 173), a fort built by the British army between 1820 and 1850 that remains an active military garrison. The promenade/staircase ends at the grassy **Parc des Champs-de-Bataille** (p. 181), about 15 minutes away. If you go to the end, return back to Terrasse Dufferin to continue the stroll.

Walk back on the terrace as far as the battery of old (but not original) cannons on the left, which are set up as they were in the old days. Climb the stairs toward the obelisk into the:

4 Parc des Gouverneurs

Just southwest of the Château Frontenac, this park stands on the site of the mansion built to house the French governors of Québec. The mansion burned in 1834, and the ruins lie buried under the great bulk of the Château. B&Bs and small hotels now border the park on two sides.

The **obelisk monument** is dedicated to both generals in the momentous battle of September 13, 1759, when Britain's General James Wolfe and France's Louis-Joseph, marquis de Montcalm, fought for what would be the ultimate destiny of Québec (and, quite possibly, all of North America). The French were defeated, and both generals died. Wolfe, wounded in the fighting, lived only long enough to hear of England's victory. Montcalm died a few hours after Wolfe. Told that he was mortally wounded, Montcalm replied, "All the better. I will not see the English in Québec."

Walk up rue Mont-Carmel, which runs between the park and Château Frontenac. Turn right onto rue Haldimand. At the next corner, rue St-Louis, stands a white house with blue trim. This is:

5 Maison Kent

Built in 1648, this might be Québec's oldest building. It's most famous for being the building in which France signed the capitulation to the British forces. Its name comes from the duke of Kent, Queen Victoria's father. He lived here for a few years at the end of the 18th century, just before he married Victoria's mother in an arranged liaison. His true love, it is said, was with him in Maison Kent. Today, the building houses France's consulate general.

To the left and diagonally across from Maison Kent, at rue St-Louis and rue des Jardins, is:

6 Maison Jacquet

This small, white dwelling with crimson roof and trim dates from 1677 and now houses a popular restaurant called **Aux Anciens Canadiens** (p. 157). Among the oldest houses in the province, it has sheltered some prominent Québécois, including Philippe Aubert de Gaspé, the author of *Aux Anciens Canadiens,* which recounts Québec's history and folklore. He lived here from 1815 to 1824.

7 Aux Anciens Canadiens

Try Québécois home cooking right here at the restaurant named for de Gaspé's book, "Aux Anciens Canadiens," 34 rue St-Louis. Consider caribou in blueberry-wine sauce or Québec meat pie, and don't pass up the maple sugar pie with cream. See p. 181.

Leaving the restaurant, turn back toward Maison Kent (toward the river) and walk along rue St-Louis to no. 17:

8 Maison Maillou

This house's foundations date from 1736, but the house was enlarged in 1799 and restored in 1959. It's best seen from the opposite side of the street. Maison Maillou was built as an elegant luxury home and later served as headquarters of militias and armies. Note the metal shutters used to thwart weather and unfriendly fire.

Continue on rue St-Louis to arrive at the central plaza called:

9 Place d'Armes

This plaza was once the military parade ground outside the governors' mansion (which no longer exists). In the small park at the center is the fountain **Monument to the Faith,** which recalls the arrival of the Recollet monks from France in 1615. France's king granted them a large plot of land in 1681 on which to build their church and monastery.

Facing the square is the **monument to Samuel de Champlain,** who founded Québec in 1608. Created by French artist Paul Chevré and architect Paul Le Cardonnel, the statue has stood here since 1898. Its pedestal is made from stone that was also used in the Arc de Triomphe and Sacré-Coeur Basilica in Paris.

Near the Champlain statue is the diamond-shaped **UNESCO monument** designating Québec City as a World Heritage Site, a rare distinction. Installed in 1986, the monument is made of bronze, granite, and glass.

The city's major **tourist information center** faces the plaza, at 12 rue Ste-Anne.

10 Le Pain Béni

This part of town is a great place to sit and watch the world go by. Grab a sidewalk table and enjoy something to drink or eat. One option: Le Pain Béni (p. 160) in the first-floor of Auberge Place d'Armes at 24 rue Ste-Anne.

Just adjacent to Le Pain Béni is the narrow pedestrian lane called:

11 Rue du Trésor

Artists (or their representatives) hang their prints and paintings of Québec scenes on both sides of the walkway. In decent weather, it's busy with browsers and sellers. Most prices are within the means of the average visitor, but don't be shy about bargaining for a better deal.

Follow rue du Trésor down to rue Buade and turn left. On the right, at the corner of rue Ste-Famille is the:

12 Basilique Cathédrale Notre-Dame de Québec

The basilica's golden interior is ornate and its air rich with the scent of burning candles. Many artworks remain from the time of the French regime. The chancel lamp was a gift from Louis XIV, and the crypt is the final resting place for most of Québec's bishops. The basilica dates back to 1647 and has suffered a tumultuous history of bombardment and reconstruction; see p. 172 for more information, including the celebration of the parish's 350th anniversary throughout 2014.

As you exit the basilica, turn a sharp right to enter the grounds and, a few steps in, the all-white inner courtyard of the historic:

13 Séminaire de Québec

Founded in 1663 by North America's first bishop, Bishop Laval, this seminary had grown into Laval University by 1852 and priests are still in residence here. During summer, tours given by **Musée de l'Amérique Françopphone** (based inside the seminary's grounds), pass by some of the seminary's buildings, which reveal lavish decorations of stone, tile, and brass. An exhibit of gilt-framed oil paintings collected by the seminary throughout its 350 years will be on display at the **Musée** through 2015. For museum open hours and information, visit www.mcq.org, call © **866/710-8031,** or see p. 174.

Head back to the basilica. Directly across the small park from the church is:

14 Hôtel-de-Ville (City Hall)

The park next to City Hall is often converted into an outdoor event space in summer, especially during the **Festival d'Été** (Summer Festival, p. 186) when it is used for concerts and other staged programs.

As you face City Hall, the tall building to the left is **Edifice Price,** Old City's tallest building at 18 stories. It was built in 1929 in Art Deco style with geometric motifs and a steepled copper roof. When it was built, it inadvertently gave a bird's-eye view into the adjacent Ursuline Convent, and a "view tax" had to be paid to the nuns to appease them. It is dramatically lit at night.

Facing the front of Hôtel-de-Ville, walk left on rue des Jardins toward Édifice Price. On your left, you'll pass a small statue celebrating the city's connections to *le cirque* and its performers. Cross over rue Ste-Anne. On the left are the spires of the:

15 Anglican Cathedral of the Holy Trinity

Modeled after London's St-Martin-in-the-Fields, this building dates from 1804 and was the first Anglican cathedral to be built outside the British Isles. The interior is simple, but spacious and bright, with pews of solid English oak from the Royal Windsor forest and a latticed ceiling with a gilded-chain motif. Lucky visitors may happen upon an organ recital or choral rehearsal.

One block up rue des Jardins, turn right at the small square (triangle shaped, actually) and go a few more steps to 12 rue Donnacona, the:

16 Chapelle/Musée des Ursulines

Handiwork by Ursuline nuns from the 17th, 18th, and 19th centuries is on display here, along with Amerindian crafts and a cape that was made for Marie de l'Incarnation, a founder of the convent, when she left for New France in 1639.

Peek into the restored chapel if it's open. The tomb of Marie de l'Incarnation is here. She was beatified by Pope John Paul II in 1980. Two richly decorated altarpieces, created by sculptor Pierre-Noël Levasseur between 1726 and 1736, are also worth a look.

From the museum, turn right on rue Donnacona to walk past the **Ursuline Convent,** originally built in 1642. The present complex is actually a succession of different buildings added and repaired at various times until 1836, as frequent fires took their toll. A statue of Marie is outside. The convent is now a private girls' school and not open to the public.

Continue left up the hill along rue du Parloir to rue St-Louis. Turn right. At the next block, rue du Corps-de-Garde, note the tree on the left side of the street with a:

17 Cannonball

Lodged at the base of the trunk, one story says that the cannonball landed here during the Battle of Québec in 1759 and, over the years, became firmly embraced by the tree. Another story says that it was placed here on purpose to keep the wheels of horse-drawn carriages from bumping the tree when making tight turns.

Continue along rue St-Louis another 2 blocks to rue d'Auteuil. The house on the right corner is:

18 Hôtel d'Esplanade

Notice that many of the windows in the facade facing rue St-Louis are blocked by stone. This is because houses were once taxed by the number of windows they had, and the frugal homeowner who lived here found this way to get around the law—even though it cut down on his view.

Continue straight on rue St-Louis toward the Porte St-Louis, a gate in the walls. Before the gate on the right is the Esplanade powder magazine, part of the old fortifications. Just before the gate is an:

19 Unnamed Monument

This monument commemorates the 1943 meeting in Québec of U.S. President Franklin D. Roosevelt and British Prime Minister Winston Churchill. It remains a soft-pedaled reminder to French Québécois that it was the English-speaking nations that rid France of the Nazis.

Just across the street from the monument is a small road, Côte de la Citadelle, that leads to La Citadelle. Walk up that road. On the right are headquarters and barracks of a militia district, arranged around an inner court. Near its entrance is a:

20 Stone Memorial

This marks the resting place of 13 soldiers of General Richard Montgomery's American army, felled in the unsuccessful assault on Québec in 1775. Obviously, the conflicts that swirled for centuries around who would ultimately rule Québec didn't end with the British victory after its 1759 battle with French troops.

Continue up the hill to:

21 La Citadelle

The impressive star-shaped fortress just beyond view keeps watch from a commanding position on a grassy plateau 108m (354 ft.) above the banks of the St. Lawrence. It took 30 years to complete, by which time it had become obsolete. Since 1920, the Citadelle has been the home of the French-speaking **Royal 22e Régiment,** which fought in both world wars and in Korea. With good timing and weather, it's possible to watch a **Changing of the Guard** ceremony, or (as it's called) "beating the retreat." See p. 173 for more details.

Return to rue St-Louis and turn left to pass through Porte St-Louis, which was built in 1873 on the site of a gate dating from 1692. Here, the street broadens to become Grande-Allée. To the right is a park that runs alongside the city walls.

22 Site of Winter Carnaval

One of the most captivating events on the Canadian calendar, the 17-day **Carnaval de Québec** happens every February and includes outdoor games, snow tubing, dogsled races, canoe races along the St. Lawrence River, night parades, and more. A palace of snow and ice rises on this spot just outside the city walls, with ice sculptures throughout the field. Colorfully clad Québécois come to admire the palace and dance the nights away at outdoor parties. On the left side of Grande-Allée, a carnival park of games, food, and music is set up on Parc des Champs-de-Bataille. For an instant pick-me-up during the cold winter festival, try to find the Carnaval's signature drink, the caribou, which is an elixir of sherry, port wine, and hard liquors. See p. 185 for more about the festivities.

Across the street from the park, on your right, stands the province of Québec's stately:

23 Hôtel du Parlement

Constructed in 1884, this government building houses what Québécois call their "National Assembly" (note the use of the word "national" and not "provincial").

The massive fountain in front of the building, **La Fontaine de Tourny,** was commissioned by the mayor of Bordeaux, France, in 1857. Sculptor Mathurin Moreau created the dreamlike figures on the fountain's base.

In the sumptuous Parliament chambers, the fleur-de-lis symbol and the initials VR (for Victoria Regina) are reminders of Québec's dual heritage. If the crown on top is lit, Parliament is in session. Along the exterior facade are 22 bronze statues of prominent figures in Québec's tumultuous history.

Guided tours are available weekdays year-round from 9am to 4:30pm, and weekends in summer from 10am to 4:30pm. See p. 176 for more information.

24 Le Parlementaire & Café du Parlement

Le Parlementaire restaurant (✆ **418/643-6640**), in the Hôtel du Parlement (p. 176) at 1045 rue des Parlementaires, is done up in regal Beaux Arts decor and open to the public (as well as parliamentarians and visiting dignitaries) for breakfast and lunch Monday through Friday most of the year. The more casual Café du Parlement (✆ **418/643-5529**) has eat-in or takeout options in biodegradable containers, and is located on the ground floor. Or mosey on down Grande-Allée to find plenty of other options.

Walking Tour 2: Lower Town

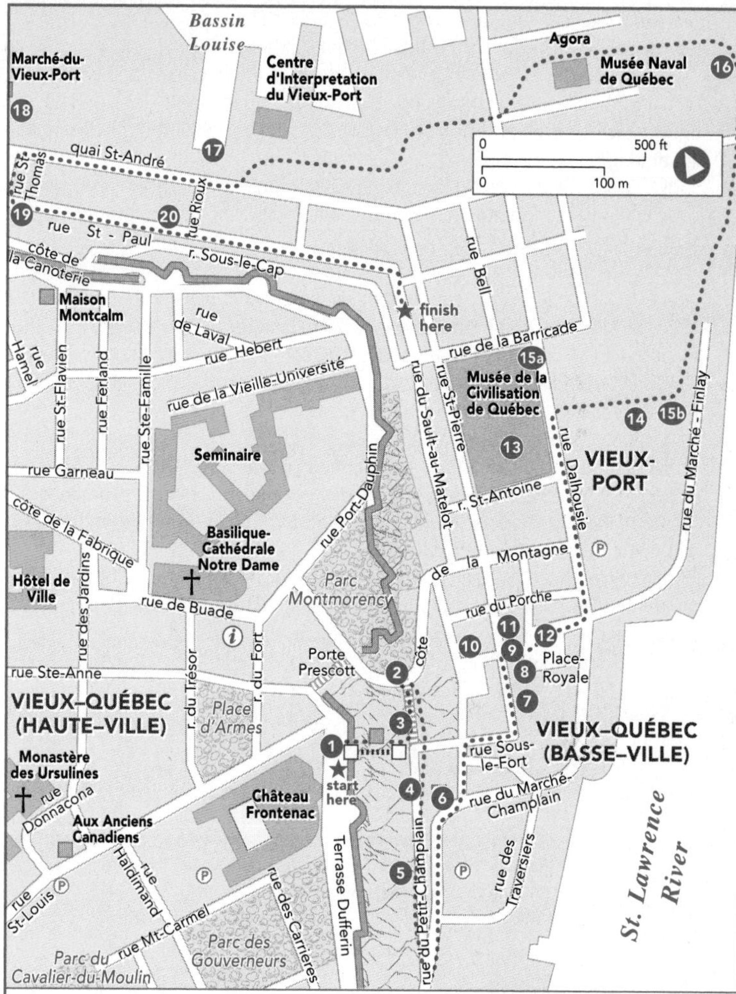

1 Funiculaire
2 L'Éscalier du Casse-Cou
3 Maison Louis Jolliet
4 Rue du Petit-Champlain
5 Le Lapin Sauté
6 Maison Chevalier
7 Royal Battery
8 Place-Royale
9 Église Notre-Dame-des-Victoires
10 Musée de la place Royale
11 Maison Lambert Dumont
12 Place de Paris
13 Musée de la Civilisation
14 Vieux-Port (Old Port)
15a Café 47
15b Café du Monde
16 Pointe-à-Carcy
17 Espace 400e Pavilion
18 Marché du Vieux-Port
19 Rue St-Paul
20 Mistral Gagnant

Continue down:

25 Grand-Allée

Just past Hôtel du Parlement is a park called Place George-V, and behind the park are the charred remains of the **1885 Armory.** A major visual icon and home to the country's oldest French-Canadian regiment, the Armory was all but destroyed in an April 2008 fire. The stone facade still stands. The destruction was a huge blow to the city, and discussions over what kind of rebuilding to do are still continuing.

To the left of the armory is a building that houses the **Discovery Pavilion** (p. 181), where a multimedia exhibit called "Odyssey: A Captivating Virtual Journey Covering 400 Years" is presented.

After the park, the street becomes lined with cafes, restaurants, and bars on both sides. This strip really gets jumping at night, particularly in the complex that includes **Maurice Night Club** and **Charlotte Lounge** (p. 189), at no. 575.

One food possibility is **Chez Ashton,** at 640 Grande-Allée est. The Québec fast-food restaurant makes what many consider the town's best *poutine*—French fries with cheese curds and brown gravy.

A great way to end the stroll is with a stop at **L'Astral,** the restaurant and bar atop Loews le Concorde Hotel, at the corner of Grande-Allée est and Cours du Général-De Montcalm. The room spins slowly (it takes about 1½ hours for a full rotation) and lets you look back at all the places you've been and all the places still to go. See p. 189 for information.

The city bus along Grande-Allée can return you to the Old City, or turn left at Loews and enter the **Parc des Champs-de-Bataille (Battlefields Park;** p. 181) at the Joan of Arc Garden. If you turn left in the park and continue along its boulevards and footpaths, you'll end up at the Citadelle. If you turn right, you'll reach the **Musée National des Beaux-Arts du Québec** (p. 176).

WALKING TOUR 2: LOWER TOWN (VIEUX-QUÉBEC: BASSE-VILLE & VIEUX-PORT)

START:	**Either in Upper Town at Terrasse Dufferin, the boardwalk in front of Château Frontenac, or if you're already in Lower Town, at the *funiculaire* (the cable car that connects the upper and lower parts of the Old City)**
FINISH:	**Place-Royale, the restored central square of Lower Town**
TIME:	**1½ hours**
BEST TIMES:	**Anytime during the day. Early morning lets you soak up the visual history, though shops won't be open**
WORST TIMES:	**Very late at night**

The Lower Town (Basse-Ville) part of Old Québec (Vieux-Québec) encompasses the city's oldest residential area—now flush with boutique hotels, high-end restaurants, and touristy shops—and Vieux-Port, the old port district. The impressive Musée de la Civilisation is here, and if you have time, you may want to pause from the tour for a visit. We start at the cliff-side elevator *(funiculaire)* that connects Upper and Lower towns.

If you're in Upper Town, descend to Lower Town by one of two options:

1 Funiculaire (Option A)

This cable car's upper terminus is on Terrasse Dufferin near the Château Frontenac. As the car descends the steep slope, its glass front provides a broad view of Basse-Ville (Lower Town).

Or, if you prefer a more active means of descent, use the stairs to the left of the *funiculaire,* the:

2 L'Éscalier du Casse-Cou (Option B)

"Breakneck Stairs" is the self-explanatory name given to this stairway (although truth be told, they're not *that* harrowing anymore). Stairs have been in place here since the settlement began. In 1698, the town council had to forbid citizens from taking their animals up and down the stairway.

Both Breakneck Stairs and the *funiculaire* arrive at the intersection of rues Petit-Champlain and Sous-le-Fort. Look at the building from which the *funiculaire* passengers exit:

3 Maison Louis Jolliet

This building is now the *funiculaire*'s lower terminus and full of tourist trinkets and gewgaws, but it has an auspicious pedigree. It was built in 1683 and was home to Louis Jolliet, the Québec-born explorer who, along with a priest, Jacques Marquette, was the first person of European parentage to explore the Mississippi River's upper reaches.

Walk down the pretty little street here:

4 Rue du Petit-Champlain

Allegedly North America's oldest street, this pedestrian-only lane swarms with restaurantgoers, cafe sitters, strolling couples, and gaggles of schoolchildren in the warm months. Some shops listed in the "Shopping in Lower Town" section of Chapter 14 are here. In winter, it's a snowy wonderland, with ice statues and twinkling white lights.

5 Le Lapin Sauté

Though it's early in the stroll, there are so many eating and shopping options here that you might want to pause for a while. Look for the sign with the flying rabbits for Le Lapin Sauté, at 52 rue du Petit-Champlain, a country-cozy bistro with hearty food in generous portions. A lovely terrace overlooks a small garden and, in the warm months, street musicians serenade diners.

At the end of Petit-Champlain, turn left onto boulevard Champlain. A lighthouse from the Gaspé Peninsula used to stand across the street, but it has been returned to its original home, leaving just an anchor and cannons to stand guard (rather forlornly) over the river.

Follow the street's curve; this block offers pleasant boutiques and cafes. At the corner is the crimson-roofed:

6 Maison Chevalier

Dating from 1752, this was once the home of merchant Jean-Baptiste Chevalier. Note the wealth of windows, more than 30 in front-facing sections alone. In 1763, the house was sold at auction to ship owner Jean-Louis Frémont, the grandfather of Virginia-born John Charles Frémont. John Charles went on to become an

American explorer, soldier, and politician who mapped some 10 Western and Midwestern territories.

The Chevalier House was sold in 1806 to an Englishman, who in turn rented it to a hotelier, who transformed it into an inn. In 1960, the Québec government restored the house, and it became a museum about 5 years later. It's overseen by the **Musée de la Civilisation,** which mounts temporary exhibitions. Entrance fees and hours are listed on p. 167.

Just past the maison's front door, turn left and walk up the short block of rue Notre-Dame, a carefully restored street of stone and brick buildings. There's a cozy boîtes à chansons (small clubs with live music) called Papes Georges, just around the corner at 8 rue Cul-De-Sac. Otherwise, turn right at Sous-le-Fort and walk 1 block to the:

7 Royal Battery

Fortifications were erected here by the French in 1691 and the cannons added in 1712 to defend Lower Town from the British. The cannons got their chance in 1759, but the English victory silenced them, and eventually, they were left to rust. Sunken foundations were all that remained by the turn of the 20th century, and when the time came for restorations, it had to be rebuilt from the ground up.

From the Royal Battery, walk back up rue Sous-le-Fort. This is a good photo opportunity, with the imposing Château Frontenac on the cliff above framed between ancient houses.

Turn right on rue Notre-Dame. Half a block up the grade is the heart of Basse-Ville, the small:

8 Place-Royale

Occupying the center of New France's first permanent colony, this small and still very much European-feeling enclosed square served as the town marketplace. It went into decline around 1860 and, by 1950, had become a derelict, run-down part of town. Today, it has been restored to very nearly recapture its historic appearance. The prominent bust is of Louis XIV, the Sun King, a gift from the city of Paris in 1928. The striking 17th- and 18th-century houses once belonged to wealthy merchants. Note the ladders on some of the steep roofs, used to fight fire and remove snow. See p. 170 for more information about the square.

Facing directly onto the square is:

9 Église Notre-Dame-des-Victoires

Named for French naval victories over the British in 1690 and 1711, Québec's oldest stone church was built in 1688 after a massive Lower Town fire destroyed 55 homes in 1682. The church was restored in 1763 after its partial destruction by the British in the 1759 siege. The white-and-gold interior has a few murky paintings and a large model boat suspended from the ceiling, a votive offering brought by early settlers to ensure safe voyages. On the walls, small prints depict the stages of the Passion. The church is open to visitors daily 9:30am to 5pm May to late June and until 8:30pm from late June through early September. The rest of the year it's open only for celebrations, concerts, and special events. See p. 173 for more information and details for events surrounding the parish's 350th anniversary in 2014.

Walk straight across the plaza, passing the:

10 Musée de la place Royale

For decades, this space was nothing but a propped-up facade with an empty lot behind it, but it has been rebuilt to serve as an interpretation center with shows and exhibitions about this district's history; it's good for kids, as well as adults (p. 171).

At the corner on the right is the:

11 Maison Lambert Dumont

This building now houses Geomania, a store selling rocks and crystals. In earlier years, though, it was home to the Dumont family and one of several residences in the square. To the right as you're facing it once stood a hotel where U.S. President William Taft would stay as he headed north to vacation in the picturesque Charlevoix region.

Walk about 15m (49 ft.) past the last building on your left and turn around; the entire end of that building is an amusing *trompe l'oeil* mural of streets and houses, and depictions of citizens from the earliest colonial days to the present. Have your photo taken here—nearly everyone does!

Return to Place-Royale and head left toward the water, down two small sets of stairs to the:

12 Place de Paris

This plaza contains a discordantly bland white sculpture that resembles three stacked Rubik's Cubes. It's called *Dialogue avec L'Histoire* and was a gift from the city of Paris in 1987.

Continue ahead to rue Dalhousie, a main street for cars, and turn left. A few short blocks up and on the left is the:

13 Musée de la Civilisation

This wonderful museum, which opened in 1988, may be housed in a lackluster gray-block building, but there is nothing plain about it once you enter. Spacious and airy, with ingeniously arranged multidimensional exhibits, it's one of Canada's most innovative museums. If there is no time now, put it at the top of your must-see list for later. See p. 167.

Across the street from the museum is:

14 Vieux-Port (Old Port)

In the 17th century, this 29-hectare (72-acre) riverfront area was the port of call for European ships bringing supplies and settlers to the new colony. With the decline of shipping by the early 20th century, the port fell into precipitous decline. But since the mid-1980s, it has experienced a rebirth, becoming the summer destination for international cruise ships. It got additional sprucing up for Québec's 400th anniversary in 2008.

15 Café 47 or Café du Monde

If you're doing this stroll in the colder months, you might want to head indoors at this point. Café 47, on the first floor inside the Musée de la Civilisation, offers a cafe menu from 10am to 5:30pm and a bistro menu from noon to 3pm. To continue the tour, head back to rue Dalhousie and cross over toward Terminal de Croisières to the waterfront. Another option awaits right on the harbor: Café du Monde, at 84 rue Dalhousie, offers traditional French cuisine in a fun-for-all atmosphere (see p. 163).

From the museum, head across the parking lot to the river and turn left at the water's edge. After Terminal de Croisières, the cruise terminal, you'll pass the Agora, an outdoor theater, and behind it, the city's Customs House, built between 1830 and 1839.

Continue along the river's promenade, past the Agora, to the small landscaped:

16 Pointe-à-Carcy

The bronze statue of a sailor here is a memorial to Canadian merchant seamen who lost their lives in World War II. From the point, you can look out across Louise Basin to the Bunge of Canada grain elevator, which stores wheat, barley, corn, and soybean crops that are produced in western Canada before they are shipped to Europe. The silos made up a massive "screen" upon which the nightly **"Image Mill"** show was projected on summer nights for 5 consecutive years (2008–2013). At press time it was uncertain whether the silos would be lit once again in 2014 (p. 170).

Follow the walkway left from Pointe-à-Carcy along the Louise Basin. You'll pass the **Musée Naval de Québec,** which was closed for years of renovation and reopened in the summer of 2010, in time to celebrate the navy's centennial birthday. See p. 170. In the warm months, you can board a scenic river cruise here.

At the end of the basin, take a short jog left, and then right to stay along the water's edge. Up ahead is a modern glass building, the:

17 Espace 400e Pavilion

This modern building was the central location for Québec's 400th-anniversary celebrations in 2008. It now hosts temporary exhibitions or events such as the **Festibière de Québec** (Québec Beer Festival; p. 186).

From the pavilion, continue 1 block to:

18 Marché du Vieux-Port

This colorful market at 160 quai St-André has jaunty teal-blue roofs and, in summer, rows and rows of booths heaped with fresh fruits and vegetables, regional wines and ciders, soaps, pâtés, jams, handicrafts, cheeses, chocolates, fresh fish, and meat. Cafes and kiosks offer options for a meal or sweet treat.

As you approach, you'll see, down the street, the city's grand train station, designed in 1916 by New York architect Bruce Price. He designed the Château Frontenac in 1893 and used his signature copper-turned-green spires here, too.

Leaving the market, cross rue St-André at the light and walk a short block to:

19 Rue St-Paul

Turn left onto this street, which is home to galleries, craft shops, and about a half-dozen antiques stores. They include **Machin Chouette** (no. 225), which sells antiques "restored, revamped" with a mid-century flair, and **Les Antiquités Bolduc** (no. 89), which has old fashioned photos, porcelain figures, antique lamps, and the like. Rue St-Paul manages to maintain a sense of unspoiled neighborhood.

20 Mistral Gagnant

Mistral Gagnant at 160 rue St-Paul, is a sunny Provençal restaurant that features hearty fare such as omelets, escargot, bouillabaisse, and outrageously good lemon pie. It offers one of the best values for a table d'hôte lunch—three courses for less than C$18.

From here, return to the heart of Lower Town—Place-Royale and the *funiculaire*—by turning right off rue St-Paul onto either rue du Sault-au-Matelot or the parallel rue St-Pierre. Both are quiet streets with galleries and restaurants.

DAY TRIPS FROM QUÉBEC CITY

17

Forests, mountains, waterfalls, and other natural treasures surround Québec City and can be reached in less than a few hours drive—spend a whole day, or weekend, if you wish. Bucolic **Île d'Orléans,** over a bridge just outside the city, is an unspoiled mini-oasis with farms, orchards, maple groves, and 18th- and 19th-century houses. The **waterfalls of Montmorency** make for dazzling fun, especially in the spring, when winter thaws make them thunder. **Le Massif** is a top destination for downhill sports enthusiasts, especially after a fresh snowfall.

You can easily combine the second Day Trip, to Montmorency waterfalls, with the first or third Day Trips to Île d'Orléans or Le Massif. The waterfalls are along the highway just across from Île d'Orléans and on the way north to Le Massif.

TOURING QUÉBEC'S BREADBASKET ON ÎLE D'ORLÉANS ★★★

16km (10 miles) NE of Québec City

Isolated from the mainland until 1935, the only way to get to the scenic, rolling hills of this little island in eyesight from the city used to by boat (in summer) or over the ice in sleighs (in winter). The highway bridge built that year has allowed the island's fertile fields to become Québec City's primary market garden. During harvest periods, fruits and vegetables are picked fresh on the farms and trucked in daily. Artisanal cheeses, ciders (both alcoholic and non), wines, and microbrews are produced, and the island proudly promotes agritourism for visitors. In warmer months, visitors go for the day or for extended sojourns.

Île d'Orléans was first inhabited by native people, and then settled by the French as one of their initial outposts of New France in the 17th century. (Jacques Cartier had landed here in 1535 and first named the island Bacchus, in celebration of its many grapevines, but renamed it later to honor the duke of Orléans.) The island has six tiny villages, originally established as parishes, and each has a church as its focal point. Some are stone churches that date from the days of the French regime, and with fewer than a dozen such churches left in all of the province of Québec, this is a particular point of pride for the islanders. Notable are the many red-roofed homes.

In mid-July, hand-painted signs posted by the main road announce FRAISES: CUEILLIR VOUS-MÊME (STRAWBERRIES: YOU PICK 'EM). The same invitation to pick your own is made during apple season, August through October. Other seasonal highlights include the visit of thousands of migrating snow geese, ducks, and Canada geese in April and May and again in late October. It's a spectacular sight when they launch in flapping hordes so thick that they almost blot out the sun.

Essentials

GETTING THERE

BY CAR Get on Autoroute 440 east, in the direction of Ste-Anne-de-Beaupré. In about 15 minutes, the Île d'Orléans bridge will be on your right. Take exit 325. If you'd like to hire a guide, **Maple Leaf Guide Services** (www.mapleleafservices.com; ✆ **877/622-3677** or 418/622-3677) can provide one in your car or theirs.

BY BUS **Dupont,** which also goes by the name **Old Québec Tours** (www.tourdupont.com; ✆ **800/267-8687** or 418/664-0460), offers a 4-hour island "food" tour and a 4½-hour "countryside" tour that, besides Île d'Orléans, includes a visit to the Montmorency Falls (p. 208) and the Basilica of Sainte-Anne-de-Beaupré.

BY BIKE Biking over the bridge is not recommended, given the bridge's narrow and precarious pedestrian sidewalk. Cyclists who arrive with their bikes on the back of their cars can park at the tourist office for a small fee, or in many of the parking lots of the island's churches for free. To rent a bike, **Ecolocyclo,** at 501 chemin Royal in Ste-Pétronille (www.ecolocyclo.net; ✆ **418/828-0370**), is open 10am to 6pm daily late-June to early September and on the weekends (or weekdays on-call) the rest of the warmer months.

VISITOR INFORMATION

After arriving on the island, turn right on Route 368 east toward Ste-Pétronille. The **Bureau d'Accueil Touristique,** or Tourist Information Center (www.tourisme.iledorleans.com; ✆ **866/941-9411** or 418/828-9411), is in the house on the right corner at 490 côte du Pont. Pick up the useful map that has most of the farms and restaurants. The bureau is open daily from about 9am to 5pm, with longer hours in the peak summer months and somewhat shorter hours in winter. Note that many attractions are closed or have limited hours from October through May.

Driving the Island's Perimeter

A coast-hugging road—Route 368, also called chemin Royal and, in a few stretches, chemin de Bout-de-l'Île—circles the island, which is 34km (21 miles) long and 8km (5 miles) wide. It's possible to make a circuit of Île d'Orléans by car in a half-day, but you can justify a full day if you eat a good meal, visit an orchard or cheese-making facility, or just skip stones at the edge of the river. We suggest making a **counterclockwise circuit on Route 368,** starting with Ste-Pétronille, only 3km (1¾ miles) after turning right from the bridge. If you're strapped for time, loop around as far as St-Jean, and then drive across the island on route du Mitan ("Middle Road"). You'll get back to the bridge by turning left onto Route 368.

Where to Eat

If you're hungry when you arrive, **Ste-Pétronille,** the first village on the driving tour, was a top vacation destination for the Québécois at the end of the 19th century and is

An Important Navigational Note for the Island

Street numbers on the ring road called chemin Royal start anew in each village. That means that as you loop around the perimeter of Île d'Orléans, you could pass a no. 1000 chemin Royal in one stretch and then another no. 1000 chemin Royal a few minutes later. Be sure that you know not just the number of your destination, but also which *village* it's in.

known for its Victorian inn and restaurant, **La Goéliche** (22 chemin du Quai; www.goeliche.ca; ✆ **888/511-2248** or 418/828-2248). All rooms face the water, and first-floor units have small terraces. Nonguests can come for breakfast, lunch, or dinner, or simply for the view of the mighty St. Lawrence. For a more modest snack, the nearby **Chocolaterie de l'Île d'Orléans,** 150 chemin du Bout-de-l'Île (www.chocolaterieorleans.com; ✆ **800/363-2252** or 418/828-2252), serves sandwiches, quiche, and pizza and specializes in homemade chocolates and ice cream.

You might plan your trip to time a meal at **Le Moulin de St-Laurent** (www.moulinstlaurent.qc.ca; ✆ **888/629-3888** or 418/829-3888) at 754 chemin Royal in the village of St-Laurent. It is one of Île d'Orléans's most romantic restaurants. It's housed in a flourmill that operated from 1720 to 1928. From May through October, lunch (11:30am–2:30pm) and dinner (5:30–8:30pm) are served daily; call to confirm hours and to make reservations.

You'll pass other restaurants and places for nibbles during the drive. Some are noted in the text below.

The village of **St-Jean,** at about the half-way point on the long south-eastern side of the island, was home to sea captains—that might be why the houses in the village appear more luxurious than others on the island. The creamy-yellow "Scottish brick" in the facades of several of the homes was ballast in boats that came over from Europe and was considered a sign of luxury and wealth. The village **church** was built in 1734, and the walled **cemetery** is the final resting place of many fishermen and seafarers. **Manoir Mauvide-Genest,** at 1451 chemin Royal (www.manoirmauvidegenest.com; ✆ **418/829-2630**), was the manor home of a French surgeon who settled here in 1720 and went on to become one of New France's leading figures. The building, open daily 10am to 5pm from mid-May to mid-October, is filled with authentic and reproduction furnishings and is classified as a historic monument. Heading east from here, you may be able to smell cinnamon rolls fresh out the oven at **La Boulange,** 2001 chemin Royal (www.laboulange.ca; ✆ **418/829-3162**). Across the street and through the church parking lot, steps lead to a picturesque spot where striated rocks line the St. Lawrence.

It's here in St-Jean that you can drive straight across the island on route du Mitan ("Middle Road"). This is a pretty road for a quick detour into the countryside, too.

Potatoes and leeks are grown at the island's most northeastern tip, which lead some to dub **St-François** "the village of vichyssoise." The St. Lawrence River is 10 times wider here than when it flows past Québec City and can be viewed especially well from the town's **observation tower,** in the rest area you'll pass on your right. After you've looped around the island's northern edge, the road stops being Route 368 east and becomes Route 368 west.

The next little village, **Ste-Famille,** was founded in 1661 and is the island's oldest parish. Just as you enter the village, you will pass 10 agritourism spots in quick order, including **Les Fromages de l'Îsle d'Orléans,** 4696 chemin Royal (www.fromagesdeliledorleans.com; ✆ **418/829-0177**), an artisanal dairy that makes a 17th century–style cheese called Paillasson. The village's **Parc des Ancêtres** is a riverside green space with picnic tables. Sharing the same parking lot is **Pub le Mitan,** 3887 chemin Royal (www.microorleans.com; ✆ **418/829-0408**), a microbrewery with a deck that overlooks the river, recommended more for its brews and views than its food.

When you cross into **St-Pierre,** you're nearly back to where you started. If you haven't stopped at any orchards yet, visit **Bilodeau,** 2200 chemin Royal in St-Pierre (www.cidreriebilodeau.qc.ca; ✆ **418/828-9316**). It produces some of Île d'Orléans's regular ciders and *cidre de glace,* a sweet wine made from apples left on the trees until after the first frost. Another wine option here is the appealing **Cassis Monna et Filles,** 721 chemin Royal (www.cassismonna.com; ✆ **418/828-2525**). Black currants, or *gadelle noire,* are grown here, and a chic shop features a display on how the berries are harvested and transformed into Crème de Cassis, the key element to a Kir cocktail. In season there is a charming cafe with a terrace where you can enjoy a light lunch. St-Pierre's central attraction is its original church at 1249 chemin Royal, the island's oldest (1717). Services are no longer held here, but there's a large **handicraft shop** with crafts made by locals in the back, behind the altar. The shop is open most days from May to October.

VISITING MONTMORENCY FALLS ★★★

11km (6¾ miles) NE of Québec City

Back on the mainland, the impressive Montmorency Falls are visible from Autoroute 440 and act as a hub for outdoor activity in all seasons. You can view the waterfalls from the bottom, from the top, from paths along the side, and even from above, on a bridge that crosses them a top. At 83m (272 ft.) tall, they're 30m (98 ft.) higher than Niagara Falls—a boast no visitor is spared. These falls, however, are far narrower. They were named by Samuel de Champlain for his patron, the duke of Montmorency, to whom he dedicated his voyage of 1603. The yellow cast of the falls comes from the high iron content of the riverbed. On summer nights, the plunging water and its surrounding cove is illuminated.

In winter, there's a particularly impressive sight: The freezing spray sent up by crashing water builds a mountain of white ice at the base, nicknamed *pain de sucre* (sugarloaf). It grows as high as 30m (98 ft.) and attracts ice climbers. Of course, you can simply come to observe.

Essentials

GETTING THERE

BY CAR Take Autoroute 440 east out of Québec City. After 10 minutes, watch for exit 325 for the falls and the parking lot. If you miss the exit, you'll see the falls on your left and will be able to make a legal U-turn.

BY BUS **Dupont,** which also goes by the name **Old Québec Tours** (www.tourdupont.com; ✆ **800/267-8687** or 418/664-0460), offers tours to the falls.

BY TRAIN Montmorency Falls is the Québec City departure point (or arrival point) for the **Train of Le Massif de Charlevoix** (www.lemassif.com/en/train; ✆ **877/536-2774**), which transports passengers along the corridor between the falls,

Baie-Saint-Paul and La Malbaie. The ski resort Le Massif is located just south of Baie-Saint-Paul, directly on the river's edge (see Day Trip below).

VISITOR INFORMATION

The address for the falls is 5300 boul. Ste-Anne in Québec City. Visitors can access the falls for free year-round. The cable car operates mid-April to October and late December to early January daily, and from February to mid-April on weekends. Visit www.sepaq.com/ct/pcm or call ✆ **418/663-3330** for rates, hours, and other park activities.

PARKING

There are three parking areas—at the base of the cable car at the bottom of the falls, at Manoir Montmorency at the top of the falls, and at Boischatel, northeast of the falls—and fees depend on season, size of vehicle, and in some cases, number of passengers.

Viewing the Falls

There are several ways to see the 83m (272-ft.) falls. A path from the lower parking area leads to the base of the falls, where the water comes crashing down. The view is spectacular from here in all seasons. Stairs ascend from here to the top, 487 in sum, with viewing platforms along the way. At the top, a footbridge spans the water where it flows over the cliff. If you don't want to walk to the top, a cable car runs from the parking lot to a terminal alongside the falls, with a pathway that leads close the water's edge. (Round-trip tickets are around C$13 for adults, C$6.50 for kids 6–17.) At that top terminal is **Manoir Montmorency,** a villa that contains an interpretation center, gift shop, cafe, and a restaurant—open year round. The dining room and porch have a side view of the falls; reservations are suggested. In winter, snowshoes can be rented from Manoir Montmorency.

In 2013 the park added two **via ferrata circuits** in the Boischatel fault, for visitors who want to combine a little rock climbing with a little hiking. Anchored by a safety tether, visitors are led on group hikes by a professional guide along the cliffs with aerial views of the cove that surrounds the falls. The beginner route is 200m long and takes just over an hour to complete; the intermediate is 60m longer and takes 2½ hours. Minimum age to participate is 12.

Where to Eat

In addition to the restaurant at Manoir Montmorency (above), picnicking is a good option. The falls are surrounded by the provincial **Parc de la Chute-Montmorency** (www.sepaq.com/Montmorency; ✆ **800/665-6527** or 418/663-3330), where visitors can take in the view. The grounds are accessible year-round and include hiking trails, playgrounds, and historic guided tours.

SKIING AT LE MASSIF ★★

75km (46 miles) NE of Québec City

The area's most dramatic ski mountain is **Le Massif.** Located in Petite-Rivière-St-François, about 1 hour drive from Québec City, its fans wax rhapsodic over its Zen qualities, including quiet ski lifts, healthy food options, and runs that give the illusion of heading directly into the icy and expansive St. Lawrence River. It claims the highest vertical east of the Canadian Rockies with 52 trails, including one that's 5.1km (3.2 miles). Check www.lemassif.com for the current year's pricing. There are day rates for adults, seniors, and children of different ages, and no fee for children 6 and under. There's a daily shuttle bus from Québec City to the mountain (see below).

Le Massif is in the heart of the **Charlevoix region**, where the stunning expanse of the river, high-end inns, and a wide variety of outdoor activities, including whale-watching in summer and fall, invite an overnight stay. Check www.tourisme-charlevoix.com for possible accommodations.

Cirque du Soleil co-founder Daniel Gauthier owns Le Massif and has been working for years to develop both the ski operations and the outlying area. The most recent additions include the urban-meets-rural Hôtel La Ferme (the farm), located in Baie-St-Paul, and a concept train (concept: luxury transit meets gastronomic dining, in a combination so exquisite you can't say no, until you see the rates) that makes stops in towns along the St. Lawrence between Québec City and La Malbaie; there are stations at the mountain base and hotel. Gauthier calls the region "a place where tranquility and energy coexist in perfect harmony." That's true. He also says that the project is necessary for the long-term survival of his mountain. That may be true, too. Whether he'll achieve the second without soiling the first is the essential question. Locals are watching with great interest and more than a little nervousness.

Essentials

GETTING THERE

BY CAR Take Autoroute 440 east toward Sainte-Anne-de-Beaupré, continue on 138 east for about 45km, turn right at sign for **Le Massif.** The ride to Le Massif takes just over 1 hour.

BY CARPOOL As a way to encourage eco-responsibility, Le Massif suggests finding a carpool via **Allo Stop** (www.allostop-quebec.com).

BY BUS Le Massif offers two-way ski **bus shuttles** that depart from the shopping complex Place Ste-Foy and the Place d'Armes near Château Frontenac for C$25. Book seats by calling ✆ **418/664-0460.**

BY TRAIN To travel in sleekly high-style, the **Train of Le Massif de Charlevoix** (www.lemassif.com/en/train; ✆ **877/536-2774**), picks up skiers in Montmorency Falls, feeds them a gourmet breakfast and provides an après-ski cocktail on the ride home, for a pretty penny (summer 2013 adult rate: C$175 roundtrip).

VISITOR INFORMATION

Le Massif de Charlevoix (www.lemassif.com; ✆ **877/536-2774** or 418/632-5876) is a growing resort complex that includes the mountain, the train, and Hôtel La Ferme, located in Baie-St-Paul. Representatives or the website can answer your questions to help plan a stay. You can also check **www.tourisme-charlevoix.com**, an official tourism site for the region, and **www.quebecregion.com**, the Québec City Tourisme's website. The mountain is typically open early December through early April from 8:30am to 4pm on weekends and 9am to 4pm (sometimes earlier) on weekdays.

PARKING

There are parking lots at both the summit chalet and the mountain's base.

Hitting the Summit (Then the Base)

Unlike most ski mountains, at **Le Massif,** it's most common to park at the summit (as opposed to the base), snap on the skis or board, and descend. *La Goélette* is the easiest trail down. Le Massif covers 124 hectare (307 acres) with more than half the trails categorized as black diamond or expert. The six lifts and one gondola can handle 11,220 riders per hour. Snowfall is greatest, on average, in December and February, with a typical annual base of 659 cm (21.6 ft). There's a terrain park and the national alpine downhill training centre, boasting one of the three toughest trails on the women's downhill World Cup circuit.

Another option is **rodeling** with sleds on wooden rails. Packages include transport from the summit chalet to a dedicated trail, sled and helmet rentals, a 7.5km guided descent, and a return gondola ride to the summit. Lessons in skiing, snowboarding, and telemark are also available on-site.

Those interested in more downhill fun will also want to be aware of **Parc du Mont Ste-Anne** (www.mont-sainte-anne.com; **© 888/827-4579**), which is closer to Québec City: 42km (26 miles) northeast. In winter, it's the area's busiest ski mountain, with an 800m-high (2,625-ft.) peak.

Where to Eat

Activities are limited to what's offered at Le Massif's base and the summit chalet. Each has a cafeteria and pub. For sweet and savory crêpes, soups, sandwiches, and salads, hit the **Camp-Boule-Crêperie** located in the timber lodge at the top of the Camp-Boule Express lift. There's also fine dining at **Mer et Monts,** in the summit chalet, where the staff promises to serve three courses of *haute cuisine* in less than an hour (if you wish). Pork filet in Maudite beer with sharp cheddar or Muscovy duck supreme does not sound like ski food, though, which is why some people make Le Massif and a trip to Mer et Monts a destination without any plans to hit the slopes.

PLANNING YOUR TRIP TO MONTRÉAL & QUÉBEC CITY

18

The province of Québec is immense: It's physically the largest province in the second-largest country in the world (after Russia); covers an area more than three times the size of France; and stretches from the northern borders of New York, Vermont, and New Hampshire up almost to the Arctic Circle. That said, most of the region's population lives in the stretch just immediately north of the U.S. border.

Québec's major cities and towns, including Montréal and Québec City, are in this band of land along the U.S., with the greater Montréal metropolitan area home to nearly half of the province's population. Québec City lies just 263km (163 miles) northeast of Montréal, commanding a stunning location on the rim of a promontory overlooking the St. Lawrence River, which is at its narrowest here. Most of the province's developed resort and scenic areas lie within a 3-hour drive of either city.

[FastFACTS] MONTRÉAL & QUÉBEC CITY

American Automobile Association (AAA) Members of **AAA** are covered by the **Canadian Automobile Association (CAA)** while traveling in Canada. Bring your membership card and proof of insurance. The 24-hour hot line for emergency road service is ✆ **800/222-4357.** The AAA card also provides discounts at a wide variety of hotels and restaurants in the province of Québec. Visit **www.caaquebec.com** for more information.

Area Codes The Montréal area codes are **514** and **438,** and the Québec City code is **418.** Outside of Montréal, the area codes are **450, 579,** and **819.** You always need to dial the three-digit area code in addition to the seven-digit number. Numbers that begin with **800, 866, 877, 888,** or **855** are free to call from both Canada and the U.S.

Business Hours Most stores in the province are open from 9 or 10am until 5 or 6pm Monday through Wednesday, 9 or 10am to 9pm on Thursday and Friday, 9 or 10am to 5 or 6pm on Saturday, and Sunday from noon to 5pm. **Banks** are usually open Monday through Friday from 8 or 9am to 4pm and usually closed for the entire weekend (although some are open Sat and even Sun). **Post office** hours vary wildly by location, but are generally open from 9:30am to 5:30pm on weekdays. Some are open 9:30am to 5pm on Saturdays, and most are closed on Sundays. While many **restaurants** are open all day between meals, some shut down between lunch and dinner. Most restaurants serve until 9:30 or 10pm. **Bars** normally stay open until 3am, while some "after-hours" clubs open when other clubs are closing and keep people dancing until noon.

Car Rental Terms, cars, and prices for car rentals are similar to those in the rest of North America and Europe, and all the major companies operate in the province. At the Montréal-Trudeau Airport, for instance, car rental agencies include Avis, Budget, and Hertz. Major car rental companies also have offices in the central tourist areas of downtown Montréal and Québec City.

Québec province mandates that residents have radial snow tires on their cars in winter, from mid-December until March 15. Rental-car agencies are required to provide snow tires on car rentals during that period, and many charge an extra, nonnegotiable fee. The minimum driving age is 16 in Québec, but some car-rental companies will not rent to people under 25. Others charge higher rates for drivers under the age of 21.

Cellphones See "Mobile Phones," later in this section.

Crime See "Safety," later in this section.

Customs International visitors can expect at least a probing question or two at the border or airport. Normal baggage and personal possessions should be no problem, but plants, animals, fireworks, and weapons are among the items that may be prohibited or require additional documents before they're allowed in. For specific information about Canadian rules, check with the **Canada Border Services Agency** (www.cbsa-asfc.gc.ca; ✆ **506/636-5064** from outside the country or 800/461-9999 within Canada). Search for "bsf5082" to get a full list of visitor information.

Tobacco and alcoholic beverages face strict import restrictions: Individuals 18 years or older are allowed to bring in 200 cigarettes, 50 cigars, or 200 grams of tobacco; and only one of the following amounts of alcohol: 1.14 liters of liquor, 1.5 liters of wine, or 8.5 liters of beer (24 12-ounce cans or bottles). Additional amounts face hefty taxes. Possession of a car radar detector is prohibited, whether or not it is connected. Police officers can confiscate it and fines may run as high as C$1,000. Visitors can temporarily bring recreational vehicles, such as snowmobiles, boats, and trailers, as well as outboard motors, for personal use.

If you're traveling with expensive items, such as laptops or musical equipment, consider registering them before you leave your country to avoid challenges at the border on your return.

For information on what you're allowed to bring home, contact one of the following agencies:

U.S. Citizens: U.S. Customs & Border Protection (CBP), 1300 Pennsylvania Ave., NW, Washington, DC 20229 (www.cbp.gov; ✆ **877/227-5511**).

U.K. Citizens: www.hmrc.gov.uk or ✆ **0800/595-000.**

Australian Citizens: Australian Customs Service, Customs House, 5 Constitution Avenue, Canberra City, ACT 2601 (www.customs.gov.au; ✆ **1300/363-263** or 612/9313-3010 from outside Australia).

New Zealand Citizens: New Zealand Customs, the Customhouse, 1 Hinemoa Street, Harbour Quays, P.O. Box 2218, Wellington, 6140 (www.customs.govt.nz; ✆ **0800/428-786** or 649/927-8036 from outside New Zealand).

Disabled Travelers Québec regulations regarding wheelchair accessibility are similar to those in the U.S. and the rest of Canada, including requirements for curb cuts, entrance ramps, designated parking spaces, and specially equipped bathrooms. While the more modern parts of the cities are fully wheelchair accessible, access to the restaurants and inns housed in 18th- and 19th-century buildings, especially in Québec City, is often difficult or impossible.

Information on accessibility of specific accommodations and tourists sites is online at **www.bonjour quebec.com**, the official website of the Québec government. Search for "Kéroul," the organization that Tourisme Québec collaborates with to update the database. Kéroul also provides information at its own website The Accessible Road, www.larouteaccessible.com.

Doctors See "Hospitals," later in this section.

Drinking Laws The legal drinking age in the province is 18. All hard liquor and spirits in Québec are sold through official government stores operated by the Québec Société des Alcools (look for maroon signs with the acronym SAQ). Wine and beer are available in grocery stores and convenience stores, called *dépanneurs*. Bars can pour drinks as late as 3am, but often stay open later.

Penalties for drunk driving in Canada are heavy. Provisions instituted in 2008 include higher mandatory penalties, such as a minimum fine of C$1,000 and 1 to 3 years driving prohibition for a convicted first offense, and for a second offense, a minimum of 30 days in jail and 3 to 5 years probation. Drivers caught under the influence face a maximum life sentence if they cause death, and a maximum 10-year sentence and possible lifetime ban on driving if they cause bodily harm. Learn more at **www.saaq.gouv.qc.ca/en**.

Driving Rules See "Montréal by Car," on p. 31, for some driving basics in the province.

Electricity Like the U.S., Canada uses 110 to 120 volts AC (60 cycles), compared to the 220 to 240 volts AC (50 cycles) used in most of Europe, Australia, and New Zealand. If your small appliances use 220 to 240 volts, you'll need a 110-volt transformer and a plug adapter with two flat parallel pins to operate them in Canada. They can be difficult to find in Canada, so bring one with you.

Embassies & Consulates Embassies are located in Ottawa, Canada's capital. There are consulate offices throughout the Canadian provinces, including Québec. The U.S. Embassy information line ✆ **613/688-5335** or 613/238-5335 for after-hours emergencies. The U.S. consulate in Montréal is at 315 Place d'Youville Ste. 500 (✆ **514/398-9695**); nonemergency American citizen services are provided here by appointment only. There is also a U.S. consulate in Québec City on Jardin des Gouverneurs at 2 rue de la Terrasse-Dufferin (✆ **418/692-2095**).

The U.K. consulate in Montréal is at 2000 McGill College Ave., Ste. 1940 (✆ **514/866-5863**). The U.K. consulate in Québec City is in the St-Amable Complex, 1150 Claire-Fontaine, Ste. 700 (✆ **418/521-3000**). For contact information for other embassies and consulates, search for "foreign representatives in Canada" at www.international.gc.ca.

Emergencies Dial ✆ **911** for police, firefighters, or an ambulance.

Family Travel Montréal and Québec City offer an abundance of family-oriented activities. Many of them are outdoors, even in winter. Watersports, river cruises, fort climbing, and fireworks displays are among summer's many attractions, with dog sledding and skiing the top choices in snowy months. Québec City's walls and fortifications are fodder for imagining the days of knights and princesses. In both cities, many museums make special efforts to address children's interests and enthusiasms.

We try to include kid-friendly accommodations, restaurants, and attractions throughout this guide, but also, see "Especially for Kids" in chapter 7 on p. 97 and in chapter 14 on p. 183.

Children who speak French or are learning French might like a guidebook of their own. The fun "Mon Premier Guide de Voyage au Québec" (Ulysse) has 96 pages of photos, miniessays, and activities for kids age 6 to 12. You can find it in provincial bookshops.

Gasoline Gasoline in Canada is sold by the liter; 3.78 liters equals 1 gallon. At press time, a liter cost approximately C$1.40, the equivalent of about US$5.15 per gallon.

Health Canada has a state-run health system, and Québec hospitals are modern and decently equipped, with well-trained staffs. You are unlikely to get sick from Canada's food or water.

In general, Canadians who reside outside the province of Québec are covered by an interprovincial agreement, which allows them to present their own province's health card (for example, OHIP card in Ontario) and have their health services covered by direct billing. In some cases, however, services must be paid for upfront and patients must seek reimbursement from their home province.

Medical treatment in Canada isn't free for foreigners, and doctors and hospitals will make you pay at the time of service. See "Insurance" below for suggestions about medical insurance.

Familiar over-the-counter medicines are widely available in Canada. If there is a possibility that you will run out of prescribed medicines during your visit, take along a prescription from your doctor. Have the generic name of prescription medicines in case a local pharmacist is unfamiliar with the brand name. Pack medications in your carry-on luggage and have them in their original containers with pharmacy labels—otherwise, they may not make it through airport security. If you're entering Canada with syringes used for medical reasons, bring a medical certificate that shows they are for medical use and be sure to declare them to Canadian Customs officials.

If you suffer from a chronic illness, consult your doctor before departure.

Hospitals In Montréal, hospitals with emergency rooms include **Hôpital Général de Montréal,** 1650 rue Cedar (✆ **514/934-1934**), and **Hôpital Royal Victoria,** 687 av. des Pins ouest (✆ **514/934-1934**). **Hôpital de Montréal pour Enfants,** 2300 rue Tupper (✆ **514/412-4400**), is a children's hospital. All three are associated with McGill University.

In Québec City, go to the **Centre Hospitalier Hôtel-Dieu de Québec,** 11 Côte du Palais (✆ **418/525-4444**). The hospital is in Upper Town inside the city walls.

Insurance U.S. health plans (including Medicare and Medicaid) do not generally provide coverage in Canada, and the ones that do often require you to pay for services upfront and reimburse you only after you return home. As a safety net, you may want to buy travel medical insurance. Travelers from the U.K. should carry their European Health Insurance Card (EHIC) as proof of entitlement to free/reduced cost medical treatment abroad (go to www.nhs.uk and search for EHIC; ✆ **0845/606-2030**). For repatriation costs, lost money, baggage, or cancellation, travel insurance from a reputable company should always be sought (www.travelinsuranceweb.com).

Internet & Wi-Fi Most hotels and *auberges*, as well as many cafes, now offer Wi-Fi. Some hotels still offer high-speed Internet access through cable connections. Except at the larger hotels, Wi-Fi is usually free. For travelers in Montréal, Ile Sans Fil (www.ilesansfil.org) lists free Wi-Fi spots in the city. The listing is available as a free iPhone app, too. For travelers in Québec City, ZAP Québec (www.zapquebec.org) lists free Wi-Fi spots.

Most hotels maintain business centers with computers for use by guests or outsiders, or at least have one computer available for guest use. Again, except at the larger hotels, this access is often free. This is your best bet for internet access if you're traveling without a laptop or mobile device with WiFi.

Language Canada is officially bilingual, but the province of Québec has laws that make French mandatory in signage. About 65 percent of Montréal's population has French as its first language (and about 95 percent of Québec City's population does). An estimated four out of five Francophones (French speakers) speak at least some English. Hotel desk staff, sales clerks, and telephone operators nearly always greet people initially in French, but usually switch to English quickly, if necessary. Outside of Montréal, visitors are more likely to encounter residents who don't speak English. If smiles and sign language don't work, look around for a young person—most of them study English in school.

Legal Aid If you are arrested, your country's embassy or consulate can provide the names of lawyers who speak English. See "Embassies & Consulates" above for more information.

LGBT Travelers The province of Québec is a destination for international gay travelers. Gay life here is generally open and accepted (gay marriage is legal throughout the province), and gay travelers are heavily marketed to. Travelers will often find the rainbow flag prominently displayed on the doors and websites of hotels and restaurants.

The **Tourisme Montréal** website, www.tourisme-montreal.org, has a "Gay and Lesbian" link under "Tourist" that lists gay-friendly accommodations, events, websites for LGBT meet-ups, and more. Of several local publications, the most thorough is "**Fugues**" (www.fugues.com), which lists events and gay-friendly lodgings, clubs, saunas, and other resources. Free copies are available at tourist offices and in racks around the city.

In Montréal, many gay and lesbian travelers head straight to the **Gay Village** (also known simply as "the Village"), a neighborhood east of downtown located primarily along rue Ste-Catherine est between rue St-Hubert and rue Papineau. See p. 36 for more about this neighborhood. As the Tourisme Montréal website says, "Rainbow columns on a subway station entrance? I've got a feeling we're not in Kansas anymore!" The Village is action central on any night, but it especially picks up during the weeklong celebration of sexual diversity known as **Divers/Cité** (www.diverscite.org) in late July and early August and the **Black & Blue Festival** (www.bbcm.org) in October, which is one of the world's largest circuit parties, with a week of entertainment and club dancing.

When you're visiting the neighborhood, stop in at the **Village Tourism Information Centre** at 1307 rue Ste-Catherine est (✆ **888/647-2247**), open June to August from noon to 6pm (days vary; call in advance). There's information about everything from wine bars to yoga classes. It's operated by the **Québec Gay Chamber of Commerce** (www.ccgq.ca).

In Québec City, the gay community is much smaller. Geographically, it's centered in Upper Town just outside the city walls, on rue St-Jean and the parallel rue d'Aiguillon, starting from where they cross rue St-Augustin and heading west. **Le Drague Cabaret Club** at 815 rue St-Augustin (www.ledrague.com; ✆ **418/649-7212**), or "the Drag," is a central gathering place with a cabaret and two dance rooms. Over Labour Day weekend, Québec City hosts a 5-day gay-pride fest, **Fête Arc-en-Ciel** (www.glbtquebec.org), which attracts thousands of people.

Mail All mail sent through **Canada Post** (www.canadapost.ca; ✆ **866/607-6301** or 416/979-8822) must bear Canadian stamps. That might seem obvious, but apparently a large number of U.S. visitors use U.S. stamps. A letter or postcard to the U.S. costs C$1.10. A letter or postcard to anywhere else outside of Canada costs C$1.85. A letter to a Canadian address costs C63¢. **FedEx** (www.fedex.com/ca; ✆ **800/463-3339**) offers service from Canada and lists locations at its website.

Medical Requirements Also, see "Health." Unless you're arriving from an area known to be suffering from an epidemic (particularly cholera or yellow fever), inoculations or vaccinations are not required for entry into Canada.

Mobile Phones Cellphone service is good in Québec cities and sometimes spotty in areas beyond city borders. Cellphone service is widely available throughout the regions mentioned in this book.

Visitors from the U.S. should be able to get roaming service that allows them to use their cellphones in Canada. Some wireless companies let customers adjust their plans to get cheaper rates while traveling. Ask your provider for options. Europeans and most Australians are on the GSM (Global System for Mobile Communications) network with removable plastic SIM cards in their phones. Call your wireless provider for information about traveling. You may be able to purchase pay-as-you-go SIM cards in Canada with local providers such as Rogers (www.rogers.com). Since Canadian mobile service carriers use the same formats as in the United States, American travelers can simply contact their mobile carrier to adjust their plan for service in Canada. It will cost a bit more, but it's simple and easy.

If you end up traveling with a phone that doesn't get reception, **prepaid phone services** are an option. With **OneSuite.com** (www.onesuite.com; ✆ **866/417-8483**), for instance, you prepay an online account for as little as US$10. You can then dial a toll-free or local access number from a hotel phone, enter your PIN, and then dial the number you're calling. Calls from Canada to mainland U.S. cost just US2.5¢ to US3.5¢ per minute. Some hotels charge for local and even toll-free calls, so check before dialing.

Cheaper still are calls conducted over the Web. **Skype** (www.skype.com) allows you to make international calls from your laptop or an app on your smartphone. Calls to people who also have the program on their computers are free. You can call people who don't have the service, although modest fees apply.

Money & Costs Frommer's lists exact prices in the local currency. The currency conversions provided were correct at press time. However, rates fluctuate, so before departing consult a currency exchange website such as **www.oanda.com/currency/converter** to check up-to-the-minute rates.

Travel in Montréal is noticeably less expensive than in other major world cities such as New York, London, and Tokyo.

ATMs *(guichet automatique)* are practically everywhere, including bank lobbies, shopping centers, bars, and gas stations. Machines in banks don't typically charge user fees if they are affiliated with your banking institution back home, but ask your bank to make sure. Elsewhere, ATMs are notorious for charging extremely high flat rates to withdraw cash; C$5 on a minimum withdrawal of C$20 is not uncommon. Many institutions (and some taxis) now also accept payment by bank card. Most machines in Canada only allow a four-digit PIN, so check with your bank beforehand and change your PIN if it has five- or six-digits.

Beware of hidden credit card fees while traveling. Check with your credit or debit card issuer to see what fees, if any, will be charged for overseas transactions.

THE VALUE OF CANADIAN DOLLAR VS. OTHER POPULAR CURRENCIES

Can$	Aus$	Euro (€)	NZ$	UK£	US$
C$1	A$1.06	€ 0.73	NZ$1.21	£0.63	$0.97

WHAT THINGS COST IN MONTRÉAL & QUÉBEC CITY	C$
Taxi from the airport to downtown Montréal	40.00
Taxi from the airport to downtown Québec City	34.25
Double room, moderate	from 160.00
Double room, inexpensive	from 100.00
Three-course dinner for one without wine, moderate	25.00
Bottle of beer	2.00–4.00
Cup of coffee	2.00
1 liter of premium gas	1.40
Admission to most museums	10.00–17.00
Admission to most national parks	Free

Newspapers & Magazines The "Globe and Mail" (www.theglobeandmail.com) is the national English-language paper. "La Presse" (www.cyberpresse.ca/actualites/regional/montreal) is the leading French-language newspaper. A sister publication, "Le Soleil" (www.cyberpresse.ca/le-soleil), is published in Québec City. Montréal's primary English-language newspaper is the "Montréal Gazette" (www.montrealgazette.com). Most large newsstands and shops in larger hotels carry the "New York Times," "Wall Street Journal," and "International Herald Tribune."

Packing Montréal and Québec City have four distinct seasons: winter, from November to April; spring, from April to June; summer, from June to September; and autumn, from September to November. Pack light, breathable fabrics in warmer months, and warm layers in colder ones. For more, see the box, "Bracing for Montreal's Winter Chill," on p. 29.

Passports For country-specific passport information, contact the following agencies:

For Residents of Australia Contact the Australian **Passport Information Service.** Visit www.passports.gov.au or call ✆ **131-232.**

For Residents of Canada Contact the central **Passport Office,** Department of Foreign Affairs and International Trade, Ottawa, ON K1A 0G3 (www.ppt.gc.ca; ✆ **800/567-6868**).

For Residents of Ireland Contact the **Passport Office,** Setanta Centre, Molesworth Street, Dublin 2 (www.foreignaffairs.gov.ie; ✆ **01/671-1633**).

For Residents of New Zealand Contact the **Passports Office,** Department of Internal Affairs, Level 3, 109 Featherston Street, P.O. Box 1568, Wellington 6011 (www.passports.govt.nz; ✆ **0800/225-050** in New Zealand or 04/463-9360).

For Residents of the United Kingdom Visit your nearest passport office, major post office, or travel agency, or contact the **Identity and Passport Service (IPS),** 4th Floor, Peel Building, 2 Marsham Street, London, SW1P 4DF (www.ips.gov.uk; ✆ **0300/222-0000**).

For Residents of the United States To find your regional passport office, check the **U.S. State Department website** (http://travel.state.gov/passport) or call the **National Passport Information Center** (✆ **877/487-2778**) for automated information.

Petrol Please see "Gasoline," earlier in this chapter.

Police Dial ✆ **911** for police, firefighters, or an ambulance.

Safety Montréal and Québec City are extremely safe cities, and far safer than their U.S. or European counterparts of similar size. Still, common sense insists that visitors stay alert and observe the usual urban precautions. It's best to stay out of parks at night and to take a taxi when returning from a late dinner or nightclub.

Québec is one of Canada's more liberal provinces. Mass demonstrations are rare and political violence is unusual. Tolerance of others is a Canadian characteristic, and it's highly unlikely that visitors of ethnic, religious, or racial minorities will encounter even mild forms of discrimination. That applies to sexual orientation, as well, especially in Montréal, which has one of the largest and most visible gay communities in North America.

Senior Travel Mention the fact that you're a senior citizen when you make your travel reservations. Many Québec hotels offer discounts for older travelers.

Throughout the province, theaters, museums, and other attractions offer reduced admission to people as young as 60.

Many reliable agencies and organizations target the 50-plus market. **Road Scholar,** run by Elderhostel, Inc. (www.roadscholar.org; ✆ **800/454-5768**) arranges worldwide study programs for those aged 55 and older, and offers a variety of trips to Québec City and Montréal.

Smoking Smoking was banned in the province's bars, restaurants, clubs, casinos, and some other public spaces in 2006. Most inns and hotels are now entirely smoke-free as well. Check before you book if you're looking for a room in which you can smoke.

Taxes Most goods and services in Canada are taxed 5 percent by the federal government (the GST/TPS) and 9.975 percent by the province of Québec (the TVQ). In Montréal, hotel bills have an additional 3.5 percent accommodations tax. A Foreign Convention and Tour Incentive Program provides limited rebates on the GST for services used during foreign conventions held in Canada, for nonresident exhibitors, and for the short-term accommodations portion of tour packages for nonresident individuals and tour operators. Details are at **www.cra-arc.gc.ca/visitors**.

Telephones The Canadian telephone system, operated by Bell Canada, closely resembles the U.S. model. All **operators speak English and French,** and they respond in the appropriate language as soon as callers speak to them. In Canada, dial ✆ **0** to reach an operator. When making a **local call** within the province of Québec, you must dial the area code before the seven-digit number.

Phone numbers that begin with 800, 888, 877, and 866 are **toll-free.** That means they're free to call within Canada and from the U.S. You need to dial 1 first.

Remember that both local and long-distance calls usually cost more from hotels—sometimes a lot more, so check before dialing. Some hotels charge for all calls, including toll-free ones.

To call the province of Québec from the U.S.: Simply dial 1, then the three-digit area code, then the seven-digit number. *Example:* To call the Infotouriste Centre in Montréal, dial 1-514-873-2015.

To call Québec from the U.K./Ireland/Australia/New Zealand: Dial the international access code 00 (from Australia, 0011), then the Canadian country code 1, then the area code, and then the seven-digit number. *Example:* To call the Infotouriste Centre in Montréal, dial 00-1-514-873-2015.

To call the U.S. from Québec: Simply dial 1, then the three-digit area code and seven-digit number.

To call the U.K./Ireland/Australia/New Zealand from Québec: Dial 011, then the country code (U.K. 44, Ireland 353, Australia 61, New Zealand 64), then the number.

For **directory information,** dial ✆ **411**.

Time Montréal and Québec City are in the Eastern Standard Time (EST) zone, that is, 5 hours behind Greenwich Mean Time (GMT). Canada has six primary time zones: For example, when it's 9am in Vancouver, British Columbia (Pacific Time), it's 10am in Calgary, Alberta (Mountain Time), 11am in Winnipeg, Manitoba (Central Time), noon in Montréal and Québec City, Québec (Eastern Time), 1pm in Halifax, Nova Scotia (Atlantic Time), 1:30pm in St. John's, Newfoundland (Newfoundland Time), 5pm in London, U.K. (GMT), and 2am the next day in Sydney, Australia.

Daylight saving time (summer time) is in effect from the second Sunday in March to the first Sunday in November. Daylight saving time moves the clock 1 hour ahead of standard time.

Tipping Tipping practices in the province are similar to those in large Western cities. In hotels, tip bellhops C$1 per bag and tip the chamber staff C$3 to C$5 per day. Tip the doorman or concierge a few dollars only if he or she has provided you with some specific service (for example, calling a cab for you or obtaining difficult-to-get theater tickets). Tip the valet-parking attendant C$2 to C$3 every time you get your car. In restaurants, bars, and nightclubs, tip waiters 15 percent to 20 percent of the check, tip checkroom attendants C$1 per garment, and tip valet-parking attendants C$1 per vehicle. Other service personnel: Tip taxi drivers 15 percent of the fare, tip skycaps at airports C$1 per bag, and tip hairdressers, barbers, and estheticans 15 percent to 20 percent.

Toilets You won't find public toilets on the streets in Montréal or Québec City, but they can be found in tourist offices, museums, railway and bus stations, service stations, and large shopping complexes. Restaurants and bars in heavily visited areas often reserve their restrooms for patrons.

Visas For citizens of many countries, including the U.S., U.K., Ireland, Australia, and New Zealand, only a passport is required to visit Canada for up to 90 days; no visas or proof of vaccinations are necessary. For the most up-to-date list of visitor visa exemptions, visit **Citizenship and Immigration Canada** at **www.cic.gc.ca**.

Visitor Information The terrific website **www.tourisme-montreal.org** offers a broad range of information for Montréal visitors, while **www.quebecregion.com** serves Québec City travelers. The equally good **www.bonjourquebec.com** is run by the province of Québec's tourism department and covers the entire province.

In Montréal, the main tourist center in downtown is the large **Infotouriste Centre,** 1255 rue Peel (✆ **877/266-5687** or 514/873-2015; Métro: Peel). It's open daily throughout the year, and the bilingual staff can provide suggestions for accommodations, dining, car rentals, and attractions. In Vieux-Montréal, there's a small **Tourist Information Office** at 174 rue Notre-Dame est, at the corner of Place Jacques-Cartier (Métro: Champ-de-Mars). It's open April to May 10am to 6pm daily, June to September 9am to 7pm, and October 10am to 6pm; it's closed in winter, but open during Montréal High Lights Festival in February.

In Québec City, there's a tourist office in Upper Town, across from the Château Frontenac and directly on Place d'Armes. It's full French name is **Centre Infotouriste de Québec,** 12 rue Ste-Anne (www.bonjourquebec.com; ✆ **877/266-5687**), and it's open daily from mid-June to August 8:30am to 7pm, and from 9am to 5pm the rest of the year. It has brochures, a lodging reservation service, a currency-exchange office, and information about tours by foot, bus, or boat.

Water Tap water is safe to drink. See "Health," earlier in this section.

Wi-Fi See "Internet & Wi-Fi," earlier in this section.

Women Travelers Montréal and Québec City are generally safe cities for female adults. Do exercise caution, however, especially when walking alone at night.